This City Belongs to You

This City Belongs to You

A HISTORY OF STUDENT ACTIVISM
IN GUATEMALA, 1944–1996

Heather Vrana

UNIVERSITY OF CALIFORNIA PRESS

University of California Press, one of the most distinguished university presses in the United States, enriches lives around the world by advancing scholarship in the humanities, social sciences, and natural sciences. Its activities are supported by the UC Press Foundation and by philanthropic contributions from individuals and institutions. For more information, visit www.ucpress.edu.

University of California Press
Oakland, California

Library of Congress Cataloging-in-Publication Data

Names: Vrana, Heather A., author.
Title: This city belongs to you : a history of student activism
   in Guatemala, 1944–1996 / Heather Vrana.
Description: Oakland, California : University of California Press, [2017]
   | Includes bibliographical references and index.
Identifiers: LCCN 2017004051 (print) | LCCN 2017006970 (ebook)
   | ISBN 9780520292215 (cloth : alk. paper) | ISBN 9780520292222
   (pbk. : alk. paper) | ISBN 9780520965720 (ebook)
Subjects: LCSH: Student movements—Guatemala—History—20th century.
Classification: LCC LA453 .V73 2017 (print) | LCC LA453 (ebook)
   | DDC 378.1/981097281—dc23
LC record available at https://lccn.loc.gov/2017004051

Manufactured in the United States of America

26 25 24 23 22 21 20 19 18 17
10 9 8 7 6 5 4 3 2 1

To every student who dreams of changing the world.

CONTENTS

List of Illustrations ix
Preface xi
Acknowledgments xiii
List of Abbreviations xvii

Introduction: "Do Not Mess with Us!" 1

1 · The Republic of Students, 1942–1952 27

2 · Showcase for Democracy, 1953–1957 62

3 · A Manner of Feeling, 1958–1962 98

4 · Go Forth and Teach All, 1963–1977 128

5 · Combatants for the Common Cause, 1976–1978 164

6 · Student Nationalism without a
Government, 1977–1980 195

Coda: "Ahí van los estudiantes!" 1980–Present 229

Notes 241
Bibliography 297
Index 315

ILLUSTRATIONS

MAPS

1. Political Map of Guatemala *xix*
2. New Transit Plan for Downtown Guatemala City, 1952 *xx*

FIGURES

1. Citizens gathered in front of the National Palace, October 20, 1944 *43*
2. President Arévalo depicted as a woman before a stereotypical indigenous peasant on a float for the *desfile bufo*, 1945 *50*
3. Lionel Sisniega Otero and Mario López Villatoro broadcasting for Radio de la Liberación, Chiquimula, 1954 *67*
4. Cover of the *Boletín del CEUAGE*, May 22, 1954 *70*
5. Carlos Castillo Armas visiting the new University City in September 1954 *75*
6. Front page of the *No Nos Tientes*, 1966 *129*
7. Juan Tecú comic depicting the development of a military officer. *No Nos Tientes*, 1969 *149*
8. "Go forth and learn from all . . ." Mural by Arnoldo Ramírez Amaya, 1973 *153*
9. The bloody symbol of the National Liberation Movement. Mural by Arnoldo Ramírez Amaya, 1973 *153*

10. Youth spray painting a wall with the slogan, "Student Who Listens, Organize and Fight" *176*

11. "Guatemala '78: Home of the World Championships of Assassinations" *187*

12. Protestors confront National Police on La Sexta, August 3, 1978 *192*

13. National Police detain unknown people on La Sexta in Zone 1, Guatemala City, January 31, 1980 *198*

14. A scene of political violence in Zone 1, Guatemala City, ca. 1980 *199*

15. Mourners carry red carnations and process down La Sexta at the funeral for Oliverio Castañeda de León *208*

16. Iduvina Hernández walks with a comrade at the funeral for a union leader from CAVISA, 1978 *212*

17. Funeral for the victims of the Spanish Embassy Fire, Guatemala City, February 1980 *220*

18. Memorial for victims of the Spanish Embassy Fire with Gregorio Yujá's casket, Guatemala City, February 1980 *221*

19. Banner of the Asociación de Estudiantes de Humanidades (AEH) at a protest on International Workers' Day, May 1, 1980 *224*

20. Flyer advertising a protest in front of the Guatemalan Embassy in Mexico City, 1982 *231*

21. Popular organizations protest while under surveillance, ca. 1980 *233*

22. Murals and sculpture commemorating university martyrs in the USAC School of History, July 2016 *235*

23. H.I.J.OS. posters and graffiti on La Sexta, July 2016 *237*

PREFACE

Universitario, this city belongs to you. Construct your talent within her, so that future generations can quench their thirst for knowledge here. May your academic life be sacred, fecund, and beautiful. Enter not into this city of the spirit, without a well-proven love of truth.

DR. CARLOS MARTÍNEZ DURÁN

This precept marks the entrance to the Universidad de San Carlos's main campus in Zone 12, at the southern edge of Guatemala City. It was delivered by renowned Guatemalan physician, professor, and historian Carlos Martínez Durán during his first tenure as rector of the autonomous university after the 1944 revolution, and has been remembered and repeated since. Perhaps it is so enduring because it delimits both the campus and the surrounding capital city as the domain of *universitarios*. But it also demands an undefined love of truth as a precondition of entrance into this community and reminds all students, faculty, and visitors of their duty to learn and serve.

Martínez Durán's words give this book its title, for they poignantly augur its fundamental interventions. They signal the history of a city, one that illuminates urban life in a place usually imagined as rural. They also foreshadow the struggles and missteps that will challenge urban students as they attempt to reach out to the countryside. They suggest a history that will extend across generations to defy the chronological frames that usually shape modern Guatemalan history. Too, they recall a student movement that both precedes and survives the eruption of student politics in 1968. They center students, not rural peasants, foreign officials, or military strongmen, as the protagonists of modern Guatemalan history. Spoken in the present indicative mood, these words—"This city belongs to you"—command *universitarios* to accept their responsibility to future generations.

This City Belongs to You tells one history of students' thirst, not just for knowledge, but also for justice, and the city of the spirit where they sought to quench it.

ACKNOWLEDGMENTS

I began this book my first semester of graduate school. I wanted to find a moment when students changed the world. I wound up writing about nationalism, loss, social class, and—yes—many moments when students changed the world. Countless people have nurtured this work and me across a decade. I would like to express my gratitude to the many individuals, institutions, and associations that made this book possible, for this kind of work cannot be done alone.

Thank you—

To Jeff Gould, who has always asked the toughest questions. His insistence on precision and politically engaged scholarship fundamentally shapes my work and raises my expectations of myself and others. Peter Guardino continues to demonstrate the kind of intellectual generosity to which I aspire. His class on nationalisms became foundational to this book.

To Lessie Jo Frazier and Shane Green for their comments on the book's earlier form. I am also grateful to Judith A. Allen, Wendy Gamber, and Michael McGerr for their support and sense of humor. The estimable Danny James, Jason McGraw, Patrick Dove, and Micol Seigel nurtured this project in different moments, asking formative questions that advanced my thinking on histories of social class, oral history, memory, Marxism, race, and liberalism. Additional thanks go to John French and Patrick Barr-Melej with whom I shared discussions of middle class formation and social movements. Thanks to Greg Grandin for a gesture of generosity and enthusiasm for this project in its very early stages.

To Jo Marie Burt for turning me toward E. P. Thompson many years ago and Matt Karush for early lessons in cultural history. Thank you both for planting the seed.

To the Indiana University Departments of History and Gender Studies, and the Center for Caribbean and Latin American Studies, which generously supported my research for many years through the Susan O'Kell Memorial Award, the Frederick W. & Mildred C. Stoler Research Fellowship, the Mendel Research Fellowship, Tinker Field Research Grant, and finally, a Foreign Language Area Study grant to study K'iche' Maya. I am also grateful to the Doris G. Quinn Foundation for its support.

To the Connecticut State University Board of Regents whose generous support funded this research with a Faculty Research Grant from 2014 to 2016. Additional support from the Southern Connecticut State University's Faculty Creative Activity Grant (2013, 2015) and Faculty Development Grant (Fall 2016) aided in manuscript revision and follow-up research that shaped the Coda.

A Iduvina Hernández, una tremenda ejemplar de una San Carlista comprometida de siempre. Y a lxs jóvenes de H.I.J.O.S.: gracias por su trabajo y ejemplo de lucha y resistencia.

A Thelma Porres Morfín por su apoyo y bondad. Gracias también a Lucrecia Paniagua, Blanca Velásquez, Reyna Pérez, Mónica Márquez, Lucía Pellecer, Anaís García y los demás trabajadores del Centro de Investigaciones Regionales de Mesoamérica en Guatemala a lo largo de los años. Y a Amanda López, Anna Carla Ericastilla, Alejandra González Godoy y todas las archivistas del Archivo General de USAC, Archivo Histórico de la Policía Nacional, y la Hemeroteca Nacional.

To the many friends who opened their hearts and homes to me during fieldwork, especially Jared Bibler, Anna Blume, Caroline Elson, Brie Gettleson, Julie Gibbings, Mélanie Issid, Calvin Knutzen, Lauren Lederman, Este Migoya, John Rexer, Chris Siekmann, Chris Sullivan, Mike Tallon, Ashley Todd, and Allyson Vinci. A Álvaro León, gracias, *huelguero*, for years of friendship. Y a Paulo Estrada, Javier Pancho Figueroa, Iván Guas, Diego Leiva y Allan Reyes Muñoz por su sentido de humor.

To Abigail E. Adams, David Carey, Ricardo Fagoaga, Martha Few, Julie Gibbings, Jim Handy, Michael Kirkpatrick, Deborah Levenson, Carlota McAllister, Diane M. Nelson, Liz Oglesby, Victoria Sanford, Arturo Taracena, J. T. Way, and Kirsten Weld, who graciously welcomed me into a community of Guatemalanists. I am humbled by your kindness and generosity. I could not imagine a better group of co-conspirators.

To engaged audiences at several conferences and workshops for questions from which this book benefitted, especially the Yale University Latin

American History Speaker Series, the University of Texas Lozano Long Conference on Latin American Studies, the Yale University Latin American Studies Working Group, the "A Conflict? Genocide and Resistance in Guatemala" Conference at the University of Southern California Shoah Foundation, and the "Intellectual Cultures of Revolution in Latin America" Conference co-hosted by the London School of Economics and Instituto Mora. Daniel J. Walkowitz offered very helpful comments on some of the material discussed in Chapter 6 when it appeared in an earlier version in the *Radical History Review*. Additionally, writing groups at Indiana University helped me formulate early drafts of these chapters, so my thanks go out to Katie Schweighofer, Nick Clarkson, Sarah Rowley, Laura Harrison, E. Cram, Susan Eckelmann, and Bryan Walsh.

To the Tepoztlán Institute for the Transnational History of the Americas, which has become my intellectual home. At Tepoz, David Sartorius, Elliott Young, Bethany Moreton, Pamela Voekel, Marisa Belausteguigoitia, A. Shane Dillingham, Abel Sierra Madero, and Paolo Vignolo gave especially helpful comments on Chapters 4 and 6. Thank you, too, to the Mazunte-Malaguas Writing Group for sharing the hemisphere's loveliest and most terrifying terrain.

To Siobhan Carter-David, Joel Dodson, Mary Koch, Cassi Meyerhoffer, Yi-Chun Tricia Lin, and Troy Paddock who have been tremendous colleagues at Southern Connecticut State University. I am grateful for Byron Nakamura and Tom Radice for their collegiality and the Yerba Mate Club. And thank you, always, to my students. A special thanks goes out to the students in my "History of Childhood and Youth" graduate course in Spring 2017.

To Kate Marshall at the University of California Press, who has nurtured this project with a sense of humor and sharp intellect. Only once did I call her under duress, and she was perfect then and at every other moment. Thank you to Bradley Depew for his work in the project's final stages. My thanks must also go out to J. T. Way, Diane M. Nelson, Jaime Pensado, and an anonymous reader who read drafts of the manuscript at various stages. Thank you to C. Libby for indexing. Thank you, too, to the Editorial Board at University of California Press.

I am humbly indebted to my friends, family, and kin. Without them there would be no book, and nothing worth thinking or writing, in any case. So, thank you—

To Anne Eller, Dixa Ramírez, Greta LaFleur, Joe Fischel, Megan Fountain, Fabian Menges, Aliyya Swaby, Bench Ansfield, Bruce Braginsky,

Siobhan Carter-David, Cassi Meyerhoffer, Owen Meyerhoffer, Aron Meyer, and everyone at Unidad Latina en Acción who made New Haven a place to call home.

To Jennifer Boles, Devi Mays, Tess Hannah, Laura Grover, Chris Sloan, Ponce and Growler Grover-Sloan, Dan Stevenson, Rachel Dotson, David Díaz Arias, Kevin Coleman, Kalani Craig, Erin Corber, Club Kirkwood, Microcosm Publishing, the Midwest Pages to Prisoners Project, and the Bleeding Heartland Rollergirls who provided moral support during the long years of graduate school.

To the best letter writers, my grandparents Tony and Elaine Vrana, and to Dr. John and Jimmie Miller, whom I miss very much. I must thank my mother and father, Mary and Jon Vrana, for setting formidable examples of hard work, commitment, and love. Thank you for your unremitting encouragement. To my sister, Anna Vrana, thank you for you. Thank you, too, to Samantha Vrana, whom we lost during the book's final revisions.

To Riedell and Dolly Vrana, who make long days bearable.

To David Kazanjian whose rigorous thinking and fierce commitment to a better world are watermarks on every single page of this book. No expression of gratitude is adequate to the debt I owe him for patiently showing me the meaning of a forgotten umbrella.

To E. Cram and Taylor Dean, who are my home no matter the distance.

Of course, always, already, alongside, and ongoingly, to kidd.

ABBREVIATIONS

AED	Association of Law Students
AEU	Association of University Students
CACIF	Coordinating Committee of Agricultural, Commercial, Industrial, and Financial Associations
CEEM	Coordinating Committee of Secondary School Students
CEH	Commission for Historical Clarification
CEUA	Committee of Anticommunist University Students
CEUAGE	Committee of Guatemalan Anticommunist University Students in Exile
CNT	National Workers' Central
CNUS	National Committee on Trade Union Unity
COSEC	Coordinating Secretariat of the International Student Conference
CRN	National Reconstruction Committee
CSE	Students' High Council
CSU	University High Council
CSUCA	Central American Universities' High Council
CUC	Campesino Unity Committee
EGP	Guerrilla Army of the Poor
ESA	Secret Anticommunist Army
FAR	Rebel Armed Forces

FASGUA	Autonomous Federation of Guatemalan Unions
FERG	Student Front–Robin García
FUD	Democratic University Front
FUR	United Revolutionary Front
IGSS	Guatemalan Social Security Institute
INCA	Normal Institute of Central America for Girls
INCV	National Central Institute for Boys
ISC	International Student Conference
IUS	International Union of Students
JPT	Patriotic Workers' Youth
JUCA	Catholic Anticommunist University Youth
MDN	National Democratic Movement
MLN	National Liberation Movement
MR-13	Revolutionary Movement–13 November
ORPA	Revolutionary Organization of People in Arms
PAR	Revolutionary Action Party
PGT	Guatemalan Labor Party
PID	Democratic Institutional Party
PNR	National Renovation Party
PR	Revolutionary Party
PRDN	National Democratic Reconciliation Party
UFCO	United Fruit Company
USAC	Universidad de San Carlos

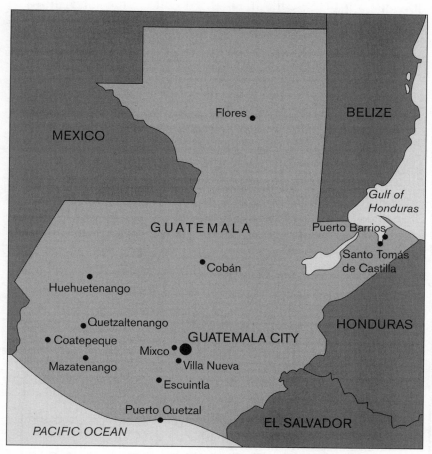

MAP I. Political Map of Guatemala. Based on a map prepared by the U.S. Central Intelligence Agency.

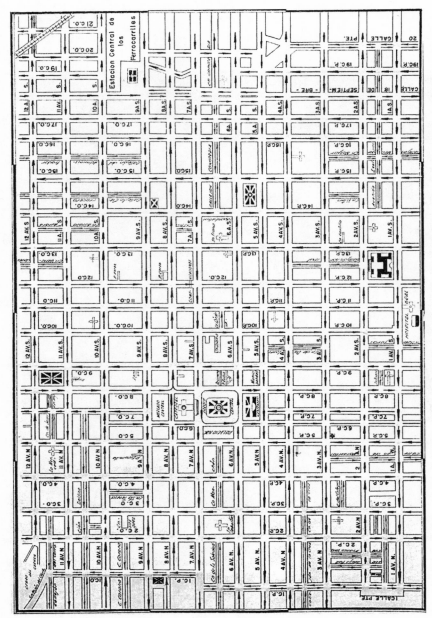

MAP 2. New Transit Plan for Downtown Guatemala City, 1952. Archive of *El Imparcial*. Fototeca Guatemala, Centro de Investigaciones Regionales de Mesoamérica (CIRMA).

Introduction

"DO NOT MESS WITH US!"

TEN O'CLOCK IN THE MORNING seemed to be a fine time to start drinking for university students in 1955, at least on Good Friday, about ten months into military rule. A group of two thousand young revelers gathered in front of Lux Theatre on Sixth Avenue in downtown Guatemala City. They passed bottles of Quetzalteca-brand *aguardiente*. The event was called the *Huelga de Dolores*, or Strike of Sorrows, though it was neither solemn nor a strike. In fact, it was an annual tradition dating to at least 1898. Year after year at the *desfile bufo*, students in extravagant costumes paraded alongside decorative floats that portrayed political controversies and pop culture icons. In 1955, one sign read "Adiós, Patria y Libertad" (Goodbye, Fatherland and Freedom). It was a play on the slogan of the National Liberation Movement (MLN), which vowed "Dios, Patria y Libertad" (God, Fatherland, and Freedom). Students mercilessly lampooned the MLN's leader, president and colonel Carlos Castillo Armas, who had overthrown democratically elected president Jacobo Arbenz the year before. Students' signs called him "CACA" (a slang term for feces and, conveniently, the president's initials) and made fun of his large nose. Armas brought a definitive end to the democratic period known as the Ten Years' Spring (1944–1954), but some students were not easily cowed.

By the beginning of Arbenz's presidency, San Carlistas, as Universidad de San Carlos (USAC) students, alumni, and faculty came to be known, had both collaborated with and opposed the government for decades. USAC was the only institution of higher learning in Guatemala until 1961, so nearly everyone with a university degree had attended the school. Many of its students became national and international luminaries. Friendships—and enmities—formed there shaped the course of the nation's history. Sheer impact and influence is one reason to study the history of San Carlistas.

Another is how the students of San Carlos require historians to develop more complex understandings of the power of intellectual elites. While drinking and chatting, the crowd of young revelers described above read from a peculiar newspaper, the *No Nos Tientes*. The *No Nos Tientes* exemplifies San Carlistas' relationship to Guatemalan state power and protest. Published every year since 1898, even through some of the worst years of civil war violence, this satirical paper was written and edited by San Carlistas (anonymously or using playful nicknames) for San Carlistas. Its pages were filled with comics, fictional interviews, inside jokes, crossword puzzles, and scathing editorials that spared no one. Even its title conveys this tone. *Tentar*, the infinitive of the verb *tientes*, is difficult to translate into English, but it means, roughly, "to mess with," "excite," "agitate," or "disturb." *No Nos Tientes—Do Not Mess with Us*—is more challenge than plea. It implies putting someone to the test, as in "Do not try us," and "Do not tempt us." That this warning was uttered with a wry smile confounds the images that predominate scholarship on student politics and protest: rows of students carrying banners and shaking their fists or student leaders delivering speeches to assembled masses. So, too, does the fact that San Carlistas were both architects of government and key figures in the opposition across the second half of the twentieth century. These contradictions reveal complicated negotiations of identity and belief that can teach us more about class and the university than a romantic story of student activism.

This City Belongs to You: A History of Student Activism in Guatemala, 1944–1996 follows several generations of university students at Guatemala's only public university. Each chapter explores how these students engaged with the university as an institution and Guatemalan and (to a lesser extent) U.S. state apparatuses in the years between 1944 and 1996, a period marked by revolution, counterrevolution, and civil war. Through these encounters, USAC students forged a loose consensus around faith in the principles of liberalism, especially belief in equal liberty, the constitutional republic, political rights, and the responsibility of university students to lead the nation. I call this consensus *student nationalism*.

Student nationalism was a shared project for identity making, premised on the inclusions and exclusions of citizenship.[1] As later chapters demonstrate, student nationalism did not depend on the successful formation of a nation-state or even necessarily a national territory. Nor was ideological or cultural agreement necessary. Instead, student nationalism included many competing discourses that nevertheless provided a more or less coherent way of speaking about power relations. Here, nationalism was less something one *had* or *believed* than a way of making political claims. Rhetorics of responsibility, freedom, and dignity brought San Carlistas into an enduring fraternal bond with their classmates. As the civil war progressed and the military and police declared war on the university, San Carlistas used student nationalism to wage culture wars over historical memory.

By the late 1970s, the reactionary forces of the military and police became ever more brutal and student nationalism began to fray at the edges. Some students turned away from oppositional politics and focused on their studies, work, or family life. Some left USAC for one of the newer private universities, which had reputations for apoliticism and were therefore much safer. Others remained involved in USAC-based politics, often seeking support from international human rights organizations. A small number left the university to join the guerrillas, and some of these young people were killed. While San Carlista student nationalism remained a defining feature of urban, middle-class ladino life, in periods of repression it became a nationalism without a legitimate government. What endured in student nationalism across all of its many variations was the premise of citizenship and equality before the law and, most of all, an unwavering belief in the responsibility of San Carlistas to lead the Guatemalan people.

Most histories of student movements focus on the United States and Europe, and less often on Latin America. But *This City Belongs to You* centers a different place, one overlooked by student movement scholarship until now. It also demonstrates the necessity of a broader chronological frame to fully comprehend the meaning of student movements. When hundreds of students, workers, and military men opposed dictator Jorge Ubico (1931–1944), for example, they sought, in the words of President Juan José Arévalo (1945–1951), to create a "democracy . . . just order, constructive peace, internal discipline, [and] happy and productive work."[2] For the participants in this movement, however, the meanings of terms like "democracy" and "just order" were not obvious, and they evolved considerably over time. Contests over the meaning of democracy would characterize the entire revolutionary era and subsequent counterrevolution. The Committee of Anticommunist University Students (Comité de Estudiantes Universitarios Anticomunistas [CEUA]), which met with the U.S. Central Intelligence Agency to orchestrate the overthrow of Arévalo's successor, Jacobo Arbenz, in its pursuit of democracy and justice, comes into focus here.

In short, this is a history of many generations of young people: their hopes, their actions, their role in social change; attempts to control them; their struggles against the government; and their encounters with the school as a state apparatus and a crucial site for resistance and celebration. In what follows, I draw out these complex histories across multiple generations and consider how San Carlistas debated the terms of democracy and intellectual life and, over time, the political culture of Guatemala's middle class itself.

Taken to its conclusion with the signing of the Peace Accords in 1996 that ended thirty-six years of civil war, this history bears witness to the poignancy of young people's willingness to die for an idea at the hands of the government. Although numbers are inadequate to this form of ultimate sacrifice, it is important to note that between 1954 and 1996, around 492 USAC students, faculty, and administrators were killed or disappeared by government, military, police, and parapolice forces. Of those killed, 363 were students and 104 were professors. Perhaps some gave their lives because they felt real efficacy in their sacrifice. The historical memory of other San Carlistas who had gone before them was powerful and reassuring. For others, there seemed to be little choice. The growing desperation of the pueblo made such sacrifice necessary. Ultimately, this is a tragic and inspiring history that does not quite escape the mythology and martyrology of the San Carlistas. Nor should it.

THE STATE'S UNIVERSITY

The modern USAC is built on a distinguished history of which San Carlistas are very proud. It was founded on January 31, 1676 after nearly a century of petitions to the Spanish crown, when Charles II issued a royal order establishing the Universidad de San Carlos de Borromeo. Seven faculty chairs corresponded to distinct areas of study: moral theology, scholastic theology, canon law, Roman or civil law, medicine, and, significantly, two chairs of indigenous languages.[3] Most students came from the region's elite families—often descendants of the first Iberians to come to the Kingdom of Guatemala—and ranged in age from twelve to twenty-eight.[4] A few poor and indigenous students of exceptional ability were admitted, but matriculation was formally forbidden for African-descended people. Prohibition also extended to individuals who had been sentenced by the Inquisition, or whose fathers or grandfathers had been so sentenced, though these policies were not always enforced.[5]

During the eighteenth century, the university developed a lively intellectual culture, despite frequent complaints about the teaching faculty's erratic attendance. Renowned physician José Felipe Flores, the Kingdom of Guatemala's first *protomédico* and an innovator of dissection techniques and anatomical modeling, studied at the university and later became one of its principal teaching physicians.[6] Between its foundation and independence in 1821, the university awarded 2,000 bachelor's degrees, 256 licentiate degrees, and 216 doctorates, 135 of which were in theology. All of this challenges the long-held presumption that intellectual culture in the Spanish colonies was stagnant, in contrast to Europe. In fact, the number of Guatemalan university graduates grew steadily until independence.[7] In the *Gazeta de Guatemala*, published from 1797, intellectuals collected new knowledge in science, medicine, politics, and economics. The *Gazeta* then circulated, like its authors, throughout Central America, Mexico, and Europe.[8]

The university was undistinguished in the struggles for independence from Spanish rule and did not transform significantly after Spanish defeat. Students and professors in Law and Medicine had played key roles in governance for centuries and may have been uneager to see their privileges challenged.[9] Nor were there many changes at the university in the first decades of federal and later republican rule. In 1821, university rectors instituted a modest reform that scarcely challenged its colonial structure.[10] Three years later, a new national constitution charged Congress with organizing basic education, but the power of the Catholic Church actually expanded at the university. Only after USAC alumnus and Liberal Mariano Gálvez was appointed chief of state in 1831 did the university secularize in earnest. Gálvez's "Rules for the general establishment of Public Instruction" argued that the government ought to oversee the training of professionals and set guidelines for higher education. A system of examinations and titles replaced patronage and cronyism. Like his peers throughout Mexico and Central and South America, Gálvez inaugurated a single academy under the authority of the state, based on the Napoleonic university: centralized, secular, and national.[11] Soon thereafter, however, a series of Conservative Party heads of state who governed from 1844 to 1871 reversed these reforms and returned the university to ecclesiastical oversight.

The university itself became a place where ideas about governance were up for discussion. The university's curriculum, leadership, and even name changed amid the bitter rivalry between Conservatives and Liberals. Even programs of study could signify shifts in this epistemological battle: fewer students enrolled in theology while programs in medicine and chemistry grew. On several infamous occasions, students led plots to overthrow Conservative president Rafael Carrera (1844–1848 and 1851–1865). In 1871, students' support was instrumental to Liberal Miguel García Granados's victory over the last of the Conservatives, the party that had dominated political life since independence. Education reform was a priority for García Granados and his successor, Justo Rufino Barrios, a USAC law graduate. García Granados and Barrios envisioned a plan to modernize education that would purge the university of all markers of its colonial and ecclesiastical past, even changing its name from the Universidad de San Carlos to the Universidad de Guatemala. Barrios's advisor, Marco A. Soto, instituted a sweeping reform informed by French positivism. He reorganized curricula around sciences, letters, and the professions. This new education system would bolster the economic development anticipated from a set of land reform laws that encouraged privatization of coffee-producing lands, prioritized infrastructure construction, pursued foreign loans, seized indigenous communities' communal lands, and, ultimately, depended on a ready supply of indigenous labor.[12] In no small way, the contradictions of contemporary positivism, which at once proclaimed individual equality before the law and presented scientific distinctions between individuals, set the terms for San Carlistas' reckonings with Guatemala's racial codes, a topic that I address at greater length below.

Barrios's other priority, the formation of a single Central American state with himself at the helm, led him to his death at the hand of Salvadoran troops in Chalchuapa, El Salvador, in 1885. Barrios's vice-president served for just two days before another Liberal, Manuel Barillas, deposed him in turn. Barillas was himself overthrown by a Liberal rival, José María Reyna Barrios (nephew of Justo Rufino Barrios). Despite this instability at the highest levels of the state, consistent rule by the Liberal party after the 1870s meant that each successive administration promoted secular education as the means by which Guatemala would progress. Educational reforms and the closely related national hygiene plans devised by these governments reflected the Lamarckian and Mendelian understandings of human progress that Guatemalan lawyers, educators, scientists, and physicians, like their peers elsewhere in Latin America, studied in French, the second language of elites.[13]

While the university was a significant site of state making in these decades, the first of what could be called student movements took shape at the end of the nineteenth century, when students formed university- and *facultad*-based organizations in order to influence extramural politics. In 1898, Reyna Barrios was assassinated and another national university–educated lawyer, Manuel Estrada Cabrera, asserted himself as successor. A group of students from the School of Medicine formed a group called the Guatemalan Youth (Juventud Guatemalteca) to express their support for Cabrera's candidacy. Other students and professors denounced this action on the grounds that the group could not claim to represent all Guatemalan youth and that these types of political expressions were inappropriate for a house of learning. In a time when a small number of the capital city's residents (most of whom had ties to the university) were literate, two newspapers *La República* and *Diario de Centro América* published numerous open letters on the question of the students' and university's role in national political life. This debate would rage in one form or another for the next century, and beyond.[14]

Ultimately, Cabrera was elected president and went on to become one of the most controversial leaders in Guatemalan history, surviving many assassination attempts to serve four terms and usher in the ascendancy of the North American–owned United Fruit Company (UFCO) in Guatemala. Two new student organizations, the Juventud Médica and the Law Society, formed in the first months of Cabrera's presidency. Despite ongoing clashes with these groups, Cabrera presented himself as a great champion of learning and marked his esteem for the university by bestowing upon it his own name, inaugurating the Estrada Cabrera National University.[15] Cabrera's megalomaniacal campaign for education also included the construction of enormous temples to Minerva, the goddess of wisdom, poetry, and medicine, and the mandatory celebration of exorbitant *Fiestas Minervalias* every October. Then, a series of earthquakes wracked Guatemala between November 1917 and January 1918, destroying homes, government buildings, schools, and churches. Thousands of people were left without housing and several hundred were killed. After decades of rule, it was the failure to provide effective relief and related allegations of corruption that were Cabrera's undoing.

A tide of opposition rose rapidly after the earthquake. While some professors, mostly those Cabrera himself appointed, continued to support the president, other faculty and students opposed his arrogant goodwill. The Central American Unionist Party (PUCA) responded by recruiting students to its alliance of urban workers, Catholics, and professionals. The group's first objective was to overthrow Cabrera, but they also sought to revive the dream of a united Central America.[16] One group of young men from PUCA had opposed Cabrera and the traditional Liberal and Conservative parties since their high school days at the elite National Central Institute for Boys (Instituto Nacional Central para Varones [INCV]). The group's most famous member, Nobel laureate Miguel Angel Asturias, dubbed them the "Generation of 1920." Among his fellows were David Vela, Horacio Espinosa Altamirano, Carlos Wyld Ospina, César Brañas, Jorge García Granados, Carlos Samayoa Chinchilla, and Ramón Aceña Durán, some of Guatemala's most famous writers, poets, essayists, and jurists.[17] Cabrera surrendered in April 1920. PUCA's success signaled the emergence of a new intellectual class in the modern Republic of Guatemala, one that viewed itself as the nation's standard-bearer.

The young men of the Generation of 1920 championed the redemptive power of ideas. They came to see their role in national politics as an extension of their educational pedigree.[18] Two years earlier, a group of young Argentine students at the Universidad de Córdoba had successfully demanded co-governance and autonomy and called on their peers across the Americas to join their struggle.[19] Cabrera's overthrow further energized student political life. Inspired by events at home and abroad, several smaller *facultad*-based groups came together to form the Association of University Students (AEU) in May 1920. From this generation of students, and the leadership role they imagined for themselves, sprang the roots of student nationalism.

Though USAC counted around just four hundred students by the 1920s, students' preoccupations with their own class, cultural, and national identity provoked a series of new debates. For instance, one of the principal concerns of the intellectual class that was consolidating by the 1920s was national unity, especially after the Mexican Revolution illustrated the dangers of disunion. Guatemala's indigenous majority represented a significant challenge to ladino students' dream of a national culture.[20] Yet there was little consensus about how to solve what was then referred to as "the Indian problem." Lamarckism was no longer in vogue, having been replaced by the more deterministic writings of Herbert Spencer and Gustave Le Bon, but students also read work by proponents of *mestizaje*, including the Mexican theosophist José Vasconcelos.[21] Much like the debate over the proper role of the university in society, the debate over "the Indian problem" would occupy students for many decades.

The debated and contentious elitism of ladino *universitarios* vis-à-vis the indigenous majority was a defining dynamic of the university and its students. The meaning of "ladino," like that of the middle class, was made and remade through quotidian encounters and flashpoints of violence. But in the most general sense, ladinos are usually people of mixed Spanish, indigenous, and African descent, akin to *mestizos* in Mexico. As is always the case with racial difference, however, attributes like language, dress, career, and location play a decisive role in determining how labels are assigned or identities convincingly performed.[22] Generally, ladinos are defined by speaking Spanish, wearing "Western clothes" rather than traditional hand-woven *huipil*, owning farms or working professional or industrial jobs, and living in certain regions of the country or cities. But apart from national censuses, San Carlistas did not use the word *ladino* to describe themselves. Instead, they signaled their racial difference from indigenous people in debates over culture and literacy, educational plans, and even cartoons, which I discuss at greater length in the chapters to come.

By their own estimation superior to Guatemala's indigenous population and the rest of Central America in terms of arts and learning, Guatemalan intellectuals were also self-conscious of how they compared to Mexico and the rest of the world. In 1921 as representatives of the AEU, Vela, Marroquín Rojas, and Orantes attended a meeting of the International Federation of Students in Mexico City. There they joined Vasconcelos and fellow students in celebration of a new hemispheric student culture and *"ser universitario"* (university identity or even student being).[23] This was just one of many instances when the recent Mexican and Russian Revolutions, and the new state formations that they proposed, informed Guatemalan intellectuals' understandings of political culture, the nation-state, and revolution.[24]

Inaugurating an effort to build national unity, USAC changed its motto from "University of Guatemala—Among the World's Great Universities" to "Go Forth and Teach All" in 1922 and developed its first extension programs the following year.[25] These programs varied widely, but they promoted the same vision: the creation of a more literate Guatemalan pueblo, united by a national culture, and prepared for the future. *Universitarios* would direct expertise from the university out into a deprived pueblo, and this would help the nation unite and move forward into modern life. This way of thinking reflected broader intellectual trends. In 1931, Chilean writer and educator Gabriela Mistral visited Guatemala and delivered a speech on the importance of education for Latin America. She said, "The University, for me, would be the moral double of a territory and would have a direct influence, from agriculture and mining to night school for adults, including under its purview schools of fine arts and music."[26] Mistral affirmed that the goals of the nation-state and the university were linked. As the state attended to the citizenry's social needs, the university attended to its moral needs.[27] Her words also captured the basic premises of emergent student nationalism: the belief that formal education was intimately linked to human progress, and by extension, the responsibility of students to lead the people. Her words connected San Carlistas to larger claims about a Latin American modernity built on private prosperity and public virtue.[28]

Less than eleven years after Cabrera's fall, another dictator challenged the university, once more transforming its political culture. Jorge Ubico y Castañeda (1931–1944) outlawed all student organizations. Like Cabrera, he appointed cronies to high positions within the university and personally supervised its functions. Under this rigid structure the university became known as a "factory of professionals," churning out credentialed graduates with little of the sense of *universitario* duty that had motivated the Generation of 1920. Occasionally, Ubico simply closed the university. When he did permit the university to operate, his control was far-reaching. Early in his presidency, Ubico granted himself authority over the University High Council (CSU) and appointed the university's highest official, the rector, who controlled faculty hiring. Leaving little room for mischief, Ubico even supervised the behavior of students and faculty who were required to conform to certain standards of comportment. The university had become a school of "good manners," chiefly occupied by the reproduction of credentials for the benefit of a small elite.[29]

Civil society was divided. Ubico's dictatorship offered stability that encouraged foreign investment and brought economic prosperity to some. But political parties and most civic organizations were outlawed. Only Ubico's followers could have successful careers in the professions and the Army. In 1942, a small group of friends from the Faculty of Law set out to change all of that. They took up the banner of the Generation of 1920. They agitated for change and soon, demanded Ubico's resignation.

EDUCATION, YOUTH, AND THE CITY

San Carlistas would draw on and expand this celebrated history across the next five decades, sometimes as state-makers and in other moments as targets of government repression.[30] If being a student was a call to lead the nation at midcentury, by century's end, it represented the sacrifice of youth in the struggle for justice. But before we move into that history, a brief overview of Guatemala's education system and students' backgrounds will help to situate San Carlistas.

For most of the twentieth century, Guatemalan education has been separated into three levels: preprimary and primary education, *educación básica* (also called *educación media*), and university. A series of laws passed in the mid-nineteenth century made primary education secular, free, and obligatory for children aged 7–14. As I mentioned above, Mariano Gálvez worked to standardize primary education during his presidency. The liberal reforms of Justo Rufino Barrios provided for the construction of normal schools—one for boys and one for girls—in more than three hundred of the nation's largest towns. The literacy statistics discussed below suggest that these efforts were largely unsuccessful, but education consistently appeared as a priority of the Liberal presidents. At the turn of the twentieth century, the kindergarten movement helped expand formal preprimary education. However, these programs ranged from expensive multiyear programs to inexpensive accelerated programs of a few weeks' length. From their first encounters with the school system, children with scant economic resources received limited instruction. Around the mid-twentieth century, primary education was divided into two sections, basic education (*educación fundamental*) and complementary education (*educación complementaria*). Each of these sections involved three years of study, and a student progressed from one to the next by passing exams. The complementary education curriculum included classes in social studies, math, grammar and literature, music, physical education, natural history, and the physical sciences.

The next level was *educación básica*, more or less the equivalent of a U.S. high school. Education at this level was revised significantly during the 1944–1954 revolution. Under the new program, oral exams in front of a panel of teachers were replaced by written tests and three general education grades (called the *ciclo de cultura general*) were added to the more specialized sequence called the *ciclo diversificado*, which guided students into careers. The revolution also expanded literacy and prevocational programs in the countryside. After the counterrevolution in 1954, these rural education programs continued, but became contested sites of surveillance, developmentalism, and resistance. I address some of them in the chapters that follow. Students received diplomas in teaching, accounting, secretarial work, or the humanities-focused baccalaureate (*bachillerato*) in Sciences and Letters. Hundreds of secondary schools or *colegios* opened during the revolution, but most students were prepared for university study at the more elite schools, like the INCV, the Normal Central Institute for Girls Belén (referred to simply as Belén), and the Liceo Americano. The religious Liceo Javier and Liceo Guatemala, both founded after the counterrevolution overturned the prohibition on religious education, also prepared students for university. Students from all of these secondary schools were involved in the protests outlined in the pages below. Other secondary schools fed into USAC, too, including Rafael Aqueche Institute, the National School of Commercial Sciences, and the Instituto Normal para Señoritas de Centro América (Normal Institute of Central America for Girls [INCA]). Most USAC students came from the capital or had moved there when they were younger to attend one of these *colegios*. Fewer students came from the countryside and from secondary cities like Quetzaltenango (usually after attending the Instituto Normal para Varones de Occidente [INVO]), Huehuetenango, and Escuintla.

The social category of student included a wide range of ages, from the late teens to the early or midthirties. Often San Carlistas took more than four or five years to graduate. Degree programs routinely required six, nine, or twelve semesters of coursework before exams or a practicum, and many students had work or family responsibilities that prevented them from advancing steadily. Also, it was not uncommon for students to take classes intermittently or to complete coursework, but not the thesis or exams required to be awarded a degree. In few *facultades* were the majority of students able to forego work and family responsibilities and study as "full-time students." Programs in medicine and engineering required many semesters of inflexible class schedules, clinicals, service work, and practicums, which made it difficult for students to work while completing a degree. Predictably, these two *facultades* had reputations for being among the most elite and conservative for much of the twentieth century. Quite the opposite was the *Facultad* of Law and Juridical Sciences, by far the largest, most flexible, and most vocal in its opposition to the government. In other words, within the already elite sphere of the university, social status affected one's choice of career. Until a controversial curriculum reform in the 1960s that added general education requirements, USAC students followed specialized programs of study where they attended classes only with others in the same career. This is why the formation of the university-wide AEU in 1920 was so impactful—it united students across *facultades*. The opening of regional campuses in Quetzaltenango, Cobán, Jalapa, and Chiquimula in the late 1970s and in the Petén in 1987 diversified the upbringing of students who would call themselves San

Carlistas. But for most, capital city life, attendance at the main campus, and close friendships with classmates pursuing the same career were fundamental to the *universitario* experience.

There were other options for young Guatemalans. The Instituto Adolfo V. Hall, founded in 1955 by Carlos Castillo Armas, began instruction after primary education and prepared students for careers in the military. Adolfo V. Hall graduates could attend officers' school at the Escuela Politécnica. This was the education received by the military presidents who ruled throughout the civil war. Many of them were, in fact, teachers at the Politécnica. The Constitution of 1956 permitted the foundation of private universities, which gave university-bound students still more options. By 1971, there were four additional universities in Guatemala City, each with a particular emphasis or ideological orientation: the Universidad Rafael Landívar (a Jesuit university opened in 1961 and focused on business and science), the Universidad Francisco Marroquín (founded in 1971, known for North American patronage, championing free market capitalism, and even granting an honorary degree to Milton Friedman), the Universidad del Valle (focused on scientific and pedagogical research and opened in 1966), and the Universidad Mariano Gálvez (also opened in 1966 and guided by a school motto from the Gospel of John).

As they navigated these various educational systems, individual students, faculty, journalists, parents, and even government officials contested the meaning of youth. In Guatemala, the words *joven* or *jóvenes*, *estudiante*, and *San Carlista* were used to denote age, but also institutional and political affiliations.[31] I distinguish between these terms throughout. Like the archival sources I draw on, I use the term "youth" (*joven*) or "youths" (*jóvenes*) to refer to individuals or groups of young people, especially when the group under discussion comprised students from different universities and secondary schools or when the group's makeup was unclear. In later chapters of the book, I use the term *youth* most often when referring to culture or counterculture, as this mirrors contemporary usage. In fact, by 1960, the terms *joven* and *jóvenes* gave way to *estudiante* or more specific descriptors like *San Carlista*, *Normalista*, and *Belenista* when referring to protests or other political actions. Student (*estudiante*) remained the most general and common term, employed as adjective and noun in daily newspapers and university-based publications. Sometimes journalists did not specify or could not know whether students were actually enrolled in classes at the secondary or university level. When this was the case, they often still used the word *estudiante*.

In this way, the term *estudiante* came to signify an oppositional group of young people. I use it when the text I am reading does and, too, to delimit social sectors and organizing strategies. Similarly, I use *San Carlista* when a source does, and also when discussing student, faculty, staff, administrative or alumni bodies at USAC. Interestingly, USAC alumni continue to use the term, even years after graduation. I discuss this attachment throughout the book and revisit it in the Coda. The term *intellectual* is even more general, but I generally use it to link students and faculty to their peers around the world and to position their labor within global networks of production and consumption. That the meanings associated with each of these groups—*jóvenes*, San Carlistas, *estudiantes*, and intellectuals—changed over time is a basic assumption guiding this book. Indeed, part of the work of my research has been to trace these meanings and to discuss the implications of these changes for social class and nation making in Guatemala and the region. All of these shifting identities informed the meaning and remaking of the middle class in Guatemala City.

The city, too, shaped the meaning of being a San Carlista. Profits from exports and banking had turned the capital into a bustling commercial center by the late nineteenth century. New boulevards, theatres, and public gardens and a wave of European immigrants lent the city a cosmopolitan air.[32] North American capital investment soon followed, then a railway that linked Guatemala City to the Pacific and Atlantic coasts and the Western highlands, built by African American and West Indian laborers.[33] The city swelled with migrants from the countryside, its population doubling between 1880 and 1921 (from 55,728 to 112,086).[34] But it was during the presidency of Ubico that urbanization took off. Ubico oversaw the construction of the city's grand National Palace, police headquarters, and Post Office building. Because UFCO and other North American export businesses often financed infrastructural improvement, roads, rail lines, electricity, and water services were developed in some areas and abandoned in others. Elite *capitalinos* countered the reality that the majority of their nation was rural and indigenous with their self-styled cosmopolitanism. Guatemala City's only rival was Quetzaltenango, urban, technologically advanced, and connected to global capital flows, but much smaller and located in the distant Western highlands. By comparison, other cities like Chimaltenango, Huehuetenango, and ports like Puerto Barrios populated by UFCO workers were very small.[35] In material terms, then, an emerging middle class was created through the urbanization, industrialization, and population growth that characterized the Ubico era.[36]

The city's population rose steadily from the 1940s to the end of the civil war, but it doubled during the most intense years of the armed conflict as war refugees fled violence in the countryside.[37] New suburbs and peripheral neighborhoods expanded where they could, though deep ravines at the northern and western edges of the city limited its horizontal expansion. The ever-present threat of earthquakes limited its vertical rise. Some of the city's first elite neighborhoods, like the estates along Simeón Cañas Avenue in Zone 2, and its first slums, like Gallito, Abril, and Recolección, have remained home to the same families since the 1880s.[38] Wealthy businessmen, bureaucrats, and professionals lived in Zones 1 and 2, near their offices and USAC in the city center until gated communities were built in the 1980s and 1990s.[39] Class mixing was common in these central neighborhoods, which proved to be extraordinarily important during protests and natural disasters in the 1960s and 1970s.

Another innovation in urban space shaped student activism and the meaning of being a San Carlista: the University City. For decades, rectors and planners proposed the construction of a separate space for study that would unify the student body and create a studious atmosphere for intellectual exchange far from the hectic city center. The results were mixed. The University City in Zone 12 was built several kilometers from the city center, surrounded by a ring road with just two entrances and one major access road, Petapa Avenue. This became an asset and a liability for student protestors: an asset because they could claim territorial sovereignty, which made any police or military incursion an extreme and illegitimate act; and a liability because the delimited campus made protestors somewhat easier to contain. The relocation also removed students from the mixed-class downtown where they regularly crossed paths with workers, teachers, and others. It reinforced the sense that *estudiantes* were cloistered elites, distant from the pueblo. Yet it also meant that the guerrilla could potentially recruit and even train students within university buildings without being detected. San Carlistas were savvy about spatial politics and knew their city well. The chapters below demonstrate how they skillfully manipulated urban public spaces like the Central Plaza, commercial enclaves like Sixth Avenue (called "La Sexta"), and transportation hubs like the Anillo Periférico, Guatemala City's Beltway.

Until recently, Guatemala City was little more than a dangerous inconvenience for Guatemalanists on their way to more popular locales, like colonial Antigua, pastoral Lake Atitlán, the Western Highlands, or even the remote Petén. The city can feel polluted, chaotic, and perilous.[40] The U.S.

State Department perpetuates fear among foreign researchers with its warning that the threat of violent crime is consistently "critical."[41] For this reason, and because of the imperative to document the government's repression of indigenous peoples in rural regions during and after the war, few researchers conducted long-term research while based in the capital city, and fewer still took the city itself as an object of study, until the end of the war. In something of a reversal of the usual metropole-centric scholarship of nearly every other national context, the city has been almost invisible. Fortunately, this is beginning to change.

Simply put, this difficult city is central to Guatemala's history, politics, and national imaginaries. In this book, I underscore the exceptional and quotidian histories of everyday *capitalinos* and how they reflected on, responded to, and impacted events taking place elsewhere in the nation.[42]

THE MIDDLE CLASS

This brief account of social space in the city reinforces how class is not only an economic attribute determined by occupation or income but is constituted through, and most significant in terms of, interactions *among* social groups and *among* individuals.[43] By midcentury, Guatemalans, like other Latin Americans, saw the middle class as defined by a number of factors, including professionalization, meritocratic and egalitarian values, consumer culture, labor roles, and market mentalities. USAC was the ultimate institutional expression of middle-class values as a public status-granting institution with an illustrious place in national history. It was free from aristocratic and religious ties, nationalist, relatively inexpensive, and located (at least initially) in the heart of the capital city.

Nevertheless, the middle class was scarcely understood by contemporaries. University students who read Karl Marx in study groups were troubled by the unclear role of university students in social transformation and attempted to locate themselves in a revolutionary project. Less revolutionary sectors also worried over the nation's middle class. In 1949, the U.S. State Department's Office of Intelligence Research wrote, "the economic development of [Central American] countries, adapted to the shifting market of the industrial countries of the northern hemisphere and handicapped by a system of landed estates, was so unbalanced as to prevent the emergence of an economically strong and politically conscious middle class."[44] A student survey conducted in February 1950 suggests how mistaken the U.S. State Department officials had been: the survey assumed that students might speak German, French, or English in addition to Spanish and play sports or participate in artistic or literary associations, markers of time for recreation and leisure. It also asked whether the student worked and if they did not, how much money their parents gave them each month in allowance.[45] San Carlistas were intellectual elites, but they lived in the periphery of mid-twentieth-century global capitalism. Many parents of USAC students were businessmen, shopkeepers, plantation owners, doctors, teachers, and government officials from the capital city or urban centers in the provinces. They usually were not members of Guatemala's traditional military and oligarchic elite.

Scholars perpetuate this incomprehension of Guatemala's middle class because national historiography is most focused on studies of indigeneity, poverty, and rural life. The urban ladino middle class is left largely unexamined, in spite of a seemingly unanimous insistence on its importance. As a result, we know very little about a group that wielded great social, political, and cultural power: the professors who trained scholars and professionals, the state makers who crafted policy and drafted constitutions, the doctors who treated illness and promoted certain visions of health, and the educators who guided young people through adolescence and into adulthood. This is an extraordinary omission. Though doubted, ignored, or overlooked, Guatemala's middle class did exist.

Unlike other scholars of the middle class, I do not emphasize mass culture, or the purchasing patterns and cultural tastes of an a priori middle class.[46] Venues other than the university and the busy streets around the city center—like the throbbing nightclubs where rock 'n' roll, jazz, hard rock, and disco filled middle-class ears and the incandescent movie theatres where vibrant images of North American, German, Mexican, and French films and television programs delighted their eyes—are mentioned only in passing.[47] Nor will I limit my argument to observing that attending university and participating in student activism were what the middle class *did*.[48] Both of these approaches use the middle class an a priori analytical category in order to explain a cultural or political phenomenon, like blue jeans, rock 'n' roll, radio, or the election of certain political figures. *This City Belongs to You* does something different. Here, class is discussed as it was formed and reformed through what San Carlistas did, and where and how they did it: their profession, education, interaction with state bodies and institutions, intimate life, ideological explorations, and everyday preoccupations, in a fluid balance of materiality and cultural performance.[49] Thus, the middle class is "a working social concept, a material experience, a political project, and a cultural practice—all of which acquire meaning only within specific historical experiences and discursive conditions."[50]

It is my hope that explaining this historical and analytical context clarifies the stakes of studying the Latin American middle classes.[51] The first historians of the middle class studied Britain and published their work in the very years under examination by this book; for these scholars, the presence of a middle class was a sign of economic and social modernity. Their work informed modernization theory and its derivatives, popular among intellectuals worldwide by midcentury.[52] From the perspective of modernization theory, Latin America's political instability, social backwardness, and lack of a middle class formed a tight tautological knot that condemned the region to premodernity.[53] Quite a burden was placed on the middle sectors that thus became barometers of modernity.[54] San Carlistas made this shared burden— or duty, as they put it—into a way for the middle classes to identify themselves and explain their political actions.[55] Of course for other Guatemalans and their U.S. counterparts, Guatemala's premodernity justified neocolonial projects of resource extraction, anticommunism, and military governance. Bearing all of this in mind, *This City Belongs to You* remaps the very question usually asked by scholars of the middle class by proposing that we pursue how these actions *made* the meaning of the middle class.[56] I hope this will stimulate new ways of writing histories of the middle class.[57]

Student nationalism provided a set of claims for collective identity that revealed contestations and struggles between groups, based on the premises and exclusions of citizenship, ultimately shaping some of what it meant to be middle class in Guatemala.[58] Through student nationalism, San Carlistas made an argument for their antagonistic relationship to other classes and articulated a mode of life that was distinct from that of the commercial and military oligarchy *and* that of the rural indigenous majority.[59] The very terms *estudiante* and *San Carlista* came to represent an already racialized class. Enrollments statistics can begin to illustrate this point. In 1943, the university counted just 711 students. Between 1943 and 1954, the number of enrollments increased more than 450 percent.[60] In just one year between 1950 and 1951, university enrollments grew from 2,373 to 2,824 students.[61] According to the 1950 census, 6,048 individuals had attended any university-level schooling in their lifetime; of this number, 6,031 were recorded as ladino and only 17 as indigenous. Just 845 of 6,048 individuals of the entire university-educated population were women. In the same census, 2,148,560 Guatemalan citizens reported that they had no formal schooling whatsoever.[62]

Even as the university enrolled greater numbers of people, it remained a place for a small number of ladino men. University enrollments increased more than 450 percent during the revolution and they decreased very little after the counterrevolution to 3,245 from 3,368 between 1954 and 1955. The following year, enrollments rose again to 3,809 students in 1956, and up to 4,336 in 1957.[63] To put these numbers in perspective, Honduras counted only 1,107 university students in 1954. The total university enrollment in Nicaragua in 1951 was 897 students, increased to 948 students in 1954, and increased dramatically to 1,718 students by 1961. In El Salvador, the national university had an enrollment of 1,704 students in 1953 and 2,257 in 1960. The University of Costa Rica, which would quickly become an academic leader in the region, still had a relatively low university enrollment of 2,029 students in 1954.[64] Meanwhile Mexico's National Autonomous University (UNAM) reported enrollments of 23,000 in 1949 and nearly 80,000 by 1968.[65]

As I mentioned above, San Carlistas rarely referred to themselves as any particular race or ethnicity, but they expressed racialized identifications in other ways.[66] The students of the 1920s's concern about the so-called Indian problem endured into the revolution and reemerged in debates over whether indigenous people could be granted the right to vote. As participants in the Constitutional Assembly, some San Carlistas expressed their distance from the rural indigenous majority by asserting that illiterate indigenous people needed to be taught the "ABC of civilization" before being granted the right to vote.[67] They also expressed racial difference in their plans for literacy campaigns and extension programming in the 1970s and their drawings of Juan Tecú, a fictional rural indigenous man who was popular in student newspapers from the 1950s through the late 1980s. With an exaggerated nose and ripped clothing, Tecú offered pithy jokes or asked impolite questions in phonetic Spanish. His indigeneity was figured through a lack education and urbanity and communicated to readers by his mannerisms and failure to master grammatical Spanish. During the civil war, guerrilla groups and the popular movement struggled to unite people across racial divides, and so San Carlistas were forced to reckon with their indigenous compatriots in new ways. But only in the 1980s did large numbers of self-identifying indigenous people begin to attend USAC, and only much later did Pan-Mayanism begin to challenge the assumed ladinization of being a San Carlista.

University censuses in the mid-1960s recorded that only between 25 percent and 35 percent of San Carlistas came from families who earned less than a "modest income" and just 6.3 percent of enrolled students' families earned less than the income bracket labeled "of humble origins." National census data confirm that university attendance remained elusive for all but the elite. Just 14,060 out of 3,174,900 Guatemalans (0.44%) had attended any university-level classes in 1964. Only forty indigenous men had attended some university-level study while more than 1 million indigenous people had not attended any schooling at any level. Meanwhile, illiteracy was about 63.3 percent nationwide and higher in rural areas. When enrollment at the Guatemala City and Quetzaltenango campuses ballooned from 8,171 to 22,861 between 1966 and 1975, less than 4 percent of San Carlistas were "of humble origins."[68]

The growing enrollments were probably more noticeable on campus than they were impactful nationwide, but more people had gained access to the tuition, prerequisites, and time necessary for a university-level education. In just four years between 1976 and 1980, university enrollments increased nearly 50 percent from 25,925 to 38,843 students.[69] These numbers reflected a large group of students who took a few classes per term at night and worked during the day, taking advantage of new, more flexible programs of study and the opening of regional campuses. By this time, the Universidad Nacional Autónoma de Nicaragua-León counted 24,000 students (in 1978). In El Salvador, national figures for university enrollment counted about 35,000 students between two universities (the public University of El Salvador and the private Jesuit Central American University José Simeon Cañas). Honduras had a single national university and, later in the 1980s, three smaller private universities, but enrollments did not exceed 30,000 students between all campuses.[70] By comparison, USAC was massive. The multicampus university continued to expand throughout the civil war, and by 1994 counted 77,051 students. In 1999, USAC matriculated 98,594 students, including 19,403 students at the regional campuses and 79,191 at the main campus in the capital city.[71]

The great majority of San Carlistas were men. Throughout the book, I highlight the reciprocal relationship between San Carlistas' rhetorics of gender and political authority. Women began to attend USAC in greater numbers throughout the 1960s, but represented only 21 percent of the student body as late as 1976.[72] USAC women exercised some limited power in intra- and extramural politics. For instance, an AEU women's auxiliary group met with Carlos Castillo Armas's wife after the counterrevolution and Astrid Morales formed the AEU's women's commission around 1962. But the first women's studies course was not offered until 1989 and as late as 2005, only 28 percent of all USAC professors at all ranks and campuses were women.[73] Triumphant narratives of fraternity and sacrifice reinforced this imbalance in enrollment, curriculum, and hiring. Women were key to articulations of student nationalism, but usually as figures or objects that reinforced gendered understandings of valor and responsibility and, ultimately, political authority—and rarely as actors or agents. One recurrent image in student-authored texts was the figure of the feminized Guatemalan nation that was acquiescent to the desires of masculine global superpowers and susceptible to North American penetration. The fraternity of San Carlistas was bound to intervene and protect her.

So too did mourning prescribe different roles for men and women. The pan-generational narrative of masculine heroics occasioned the virtual forgetting of women who were killed by the state, with two notable exceptions, María Chinchilla and Rogelia Cruz. These two examples reinforced traditional women's roles: Chinchilla's death was remembered for its audaciousness (she was a respectable schoolteacher killed in broad daylight) and Cruz's for its sexual nature (the rumored rape and torture of the former Miss Guatemala was widely reported in the press). Only infrequently did San Carlista men acknowledge the productive and reproductive labor of their female comrades. As countless moments in the pages below illustrate, San Carlistas' claims to leadership, responsibility, dignity, valor, and freedom were built on and reinforced strict gendered, classed, and raced understandings of political authority.[74]

This City Belongs to You expands the frame of student movement scholarship by looking beyond familiar places and chronologies. The political lives of San Carlistas complicate a few commonly held assumptions about student activism. They were not electrified by the "Global 1968," nor did they mirror or follow those movements. Additionally, San Carlistas were far from the metropoles even as they connected to students from around the world at regional and international meetings and through multilingual publications as early as the mid-1940s. Furthermore, San Carlistas were not only leftist, nor were they necessarily antigovernment.[75] Most of all, this is not a book about why or how privileged students came to confront a powerful state, although answers to those questions can certainly be found herein.[76] Put differently, this book is not only about what students *did*, but also what their actions *did for* urban life and memory cultures in late twentieth-century Guatemala. Yet it looks at just one important locus of middle class formation, the public university. USAC was the cardinal point for middle class formation in the twentieth century and no book-length English-language study has been published about it, so I have started here.[77] Subsequent histories will have to examine the political and cultural lives and formulations of working-class and indigenous youth, secondary school students, and students at private universities.[78]

Student nationalism required resistance, accommodation, and a diversity of ideological positions and expressions, which ultimately shaped life outside of the university. There was no single meaning for *estudiante*; rather, it became a way for young people, USAC administrators and faculty, national and international politicians, and documents of governance to exert political authority. Over time, the project of student nationalism expanded to accommodate tremendous political change, from promoting statecraft during the Ten Years' Spring to awakening a kind of nationalism without a state at the most violent moments of the civil war when the government had proven its cruelty. For generations of students, it was an exhilarating institutional connection, an identity, and a mantle of responsibility, all at once.

. . .

The six chapters below follow the lives and deaths of San Carlistas from 1942 through the civil war. They outline students' political cultures and strategies of resistance in a captivating interplay between the everyday and the extraordinary. While these young people ate and drank and debated everything from political right to sports teams, they built friendships and an enduring class ideology. The archive of San Carlistas includes pamphlets, manifestos, meeting minutes, police reports, photographs, daily newspapers, memos, memoirs, theses and dissertations, and long *Boletines* written for the Huelga de Dolores, which were meant to be read aloud. Each chapter opens with the *No Nos Tientes*, a newspaper printed for the Huelga de Dolores.

Chapter 1 begins as law students publicly questioned dictator Jorge Ubico's rule, and then expands to assess the political, social, and economic changes that occurred between 1942 and 1952 from the perspective of USAC students and professors. The close relationship between USAC and the revolutionary governments and the political philosophy of the university as a "Republic of Students" enabled the emergence of the San Carlista as a social and cultural identifier. I discuss debates over the meaning and practice of democracy, including voting rights, literacy, and social welfare programs, as well as research into national concerns such as indigenous communities and poverty that contributed to the rise of a certain idea of the Guatemalan nation and its citizenry. The Constitution of 1945 called on teachers and students to become caretakers of the pueblo. They were to protect and expand culture, promote ethnic improvement (*promover el mejoramiento étnico*), and supervise civic and moral formation; in effect, they were to make the people fit for self-government.[79] By the administration of Jacobo Arbenz, this democratic awakening and the invigoration of terms like "democracy" (*democracia*), "fatherland" (*patria*), and "freedom" (*libertad*) enabled the rise of anticommunism within some university sectors.

Chapter 2 tracks the rise of anticommunism at the university and the concomitant fragmentation of student nationalism. I consider a lengthy anticommunist text, *The Plan of Tegucigalpa*, a proposal for government written by Catholic anticommunist students in exile in late 1953. After the 1954 coup, *The Plan* became the founding document of the counterrevolutionary state. Many of the principles of the Revolution endured in the brief period between the counterrevolution and the first rumblings of civil war. Some, like free market capitalism, personal property rights, and political freedoms, guided Catholic pro-Castillo Armas anticommunists and anti-Castillo Armas Arbencistas (supporters of Arbenz) alike. Civil freedoms and electoral democracy, on the other hand, bolstered the Arbencistas alone. Most histories of the period emphasize the determinant role of foreign economic and diplomatic intervention, but this chapter underscores the complex interplay of *internal and external* factors prior to and after the counterrevolution. To this end, I follow negotiations between university staff and faculty, students, and the Castillo Armas regime and their impact on civic life in Guatemala City. Initially, Castillo Armas tried to win over the university by meeting with students and promoting professors sympathetic with the counterrevolution. Only with the May Day and June 1956 protests did relations between the government and USAC become intractably antagonistic.

Chapter 3 focuses on just five years of university life to show how this antagonism became a defining feature of San Carlista student nationalism. Some students and student groups reworked historic values, like service to one's community and a belief in the university's special role in society, into a new political language built around fraternity, mistrust of the government, anti-imperialist nationalism, and renewed pride in the *universitarios'* duty to lead the nation. This political affect undergirded the sense that the university—as arbiter of justice and defender of freedom—was under attack. Popular histories, events, and whole commemorative calendars drew on these historic values to give meaning to the experience of teaching or studying at USAC. Idioms of fraternity, mistrust, and valor began to define student nationalism explicitly against the government while they strengthened an individual's relationship to the university. This was especially important when steeply rising enrollments might have weakened *universitario* unity. San Carlistas no longer derived legitimacy from the government or the Constitution. Instead, they argued for *their* duty to lead the people and the nation toward progress.

Chapter 4 addresses some of the ways that San Carlistas attempted to put these ideals into practice through the 1970s. Students and faculty set out on the march against underdevelopment in the city and the countryside. Yet the political context of the 1970s transformed the rhetorics of freedom, responsibility, dignity, and duty that had formed the base of student nationalism since the Revolution. For instance, anti-imperialist nationalism inspired new university extension programs, but personal encounters with indigenous, rural, and poor citizens in the practice of these programs compelled San Carlistas to reevaluate the university's orientation vis-à-vis the pueblo. Academic debates about development and dependency theory also challenged these attitudes. Development theory, especially dependency theory, helped USAC social scientists to understand why underdevelopment seemed endemic in Latin America even after foreign businesses expanded their investments in the region. Development praxis became the crux of class making for urban ladino intellectuals. For the most part, San Carlistas continued to position themselves as advocates for the periphery and ambassadors of progress, yet their knowledge of the periphery became more intimate. As the civil war deepened, San Carlistas had to reexamine their relationship to the pueblo in order to simply survive the government's vicious, bloody counterinsurgency efforts.

Chapters 5 and 6 discuss these difficult years, but from distinct perspectives. Chapter 5 outlines the creation of a broader popular movement through the late 1970s and early 1980s. Chapter 6, in turn, focuses on how the popular movement developed a new politics of death and urban space in response to a series of violent acts. These acts included the spectacular 1976 earthquake, the massacre at Panzós, and the Spanish Embassy fire, alongside more subtle repression like surveillance at the university. I have separated these two chapters in order to resist the tendency to see resistance and repression as an almost hydraulic system, which obscures the real gains made by the popular left. I argue that as the state expanded its use of violence against San Carlistas, so did San Carlistas expand their resistance, drawing on funereal practices, political feelings, and basic ethical assumptions. Key to this change was a critical reevaluation of the politics of advocacy and representation that had characterized San Carlistas' relations to nonstudents in previous decades. No longer mere acolytes of knowledge as in the 1940s and 1950s, or advocates for periphery as in the 1960s, San Carlistas increasingly understood their political freedom to be intimately bound up with that of the urban and rural poor. In part, students had learned this through their participation in protest campaigns led by these groups. Certain student and faculty leaders like Oliverio Castañeda de León and Mario López Larrave made popular coalition their cause and, ultimately, died for it.

The gradual foreclosure of peaceful opposition invigorated the power of spectacular mourning as a protest strategy. Political funerals changed the space of downtown Guatemala City. When well-known San Carlistas like Castañeda de León and López Larrave were killed, students organized grand funeral processions that led from the university campus through downtown to the General Cemetery. As students staged political funerals and other ritual protests, they created a many-layered space of mourning and memory. Using claims to kinship, fear, trauma, and responsibility, students and professors exhorted the citizenry to take political action. Some Guatemalans questioned the legitimacy of liberalism and its social contract in the midst of such loss and uncertainty. Discarding the reformist possibility that characterized student nationalism since the 1954 coup, some San Carlistas turned to millenarian futures. Political funerals were only the most visible of these acts whereby young people and their teachers dreamed of a future beyond the struggle where young people could live and study freely. Because this politics of death also appealed to human rights law, it helped San Carlistas build new relationships with international organizations. By 1980, student nationalism extended beyond justice, rights, and fraternity, which had characterized previous decades. It became a nationalism without a state.

Young people were left to imagine new futures in its wake. In some sense, political violence against the university was a return to a previous pattern. The incomplete project of national Liberal reform in the late nineteenth century and the failed Central American union in 1920 were both punctuated by violent executive incursions into university life. But what had changed was the magnitude of violence and the students' willingness to resist. The book closes with a Coda that revisits student nationalism through Guatemala City's palimpsestic memoryscape where the past interrupts the present on street corners and school buildings covered with commemorative placards, graffiti, and memorials. In this final section, I turn to the young people involved in ongoing movements for memory in the 2000s and 2010s, who draw on the legacies of San Carlista student activism in order to imagine new political futures for Guatemala.

· · ·

What idea was worth dying for, for a twenty-year-old? In students' writings, it would seem that ideas like democracy, justice, nation, freedom, honor, conscience, duty, independence, and progress were enough. But how could these abstract ideals inspire the ultimate sacrifice? Student nationalism connected these principles to San Carlistas' daily struggles, hopes, and dreams. For some students, democracy meant voting rights, literacy, and social welfare programs; for them, student nationalism was a social contract. For others like the Catholic CEUA, democracy meant the eradication of communist threat in the Americas and so student nationalism was an almost ecclesiastical law. As the civil war drew on, student nationalism became inflected with Marxism and anti-Americanism. To be a San Carlista came to signify opposition to the government, giving new meaning to the old cry: "Do Not Mess with Us!" Regardless of their political beliefs and whether they survived intact, fled to exile, were kidnapped, tortured, and killed or disappeared, all San Carlistas were indelibly marked by the legacy of student nationalism. *This City Belongs to You* seeks to clarify the interrelation of university political culture and social class. While this is a history of youth and ideals, it is also a history of how these young people shaped a university, a city, and a nation.

ONE

The Republic of Students, 1942–1952

We have weapons that our forebears did not want, or were unable
or were unwilling to wield . . . Three weapons that, well-used, can
transform a group of guys . . . into a formidable force, capable of
opposing and overthrowing those with the bayonets. These three
weapons are our youth, our intelligence, and our unity.

" *The* Escuilach *Manifesto*" [1]

BANANAS—ON THE STALK, by the bunch, peeled, held aloft, all of them
long Cavendish bananas grown for export by the United Fruit Company
(UFCO)—formed the masthead of the *No Nos Tientes* in 1949. The anonymous artist was probably Mario López Larrave, a law student who drew most
of the newspaper's cheeky cartoons for many decades. The letters offered a
visual complement to the pages of tongue-in-cheek text that appeared below
them. After an "N" made of Guatemalan bananas destined for North
American stomachs, a portrait of Francisco Javier Arana formed the "O" of
Nos and two interlocking sickles formed the "S." In April 1949, the young
illustrator could not have known the prescience of his figures; rather, he drew
from the anti-imperial spirit of the 1944 revolution that had been so crucial
to his own academic and political formation. Within months, however, one
member of the revolutionary junta would be assassinated and anticommunist
hysteria would begin to ferment and, ultimately, alter the course of the
nation.

López Larrave was just fifteen years old when M41 bulldog tanks closed
in on the National Palace and finally deposed dictator Jorge Ubico y
Castañeda (1931–1944).[2] If school had not been cancelled, López Larrave and
his classmates might have watched the action from the window of their classroom at the National Central Institute for Boys (INCV), just a few blocks
away. Months earlier, a broad movement of university students, young military officers, teachers, workers, and women's organizations had forced Ubico
to end his thirteen-year dictatorship. For as long as many could remember,
the pleasures of daily life, like intellectual exchange, art, music, politics, and

even social gatherings, had been strictly regulated. Ubico, an alumnus, even influenced the boys' INCV curriculum through his friendship with the school's principal. Protests continued while Ubico's handpicked successor, Juan Federico Ponce Vaides, remained in power. The city was seized by democratic fervor, inspired by Rooseveltian democracy and Central America's unique historical moment.

Seen from the windows of INCV, the National Palace was a symbol of Ubico's absolute power and utter decadence: an imposing baroque structure with a grand entryway, dozens of porticos, 350 rooms, numerous patios, and expansive hallways. Nearby, Guatemala's urban poor suffered under laws that demanded their labor for export production and infrastructure construction. The 1934 vagrancy law required all men who lacked an "adequate profession" or proof of landownership to work between 100 and 150 days on massive rural plantations. Another law required all men—except those who could pay a fee—to work for two weeks per year building and maintaining roads. In business and politics, Ubico promoted his friends and family while he limited the opportunities available to others. A growing number of professionals and military officers were unable to advance in the careers for which they had trained.

Outgoing, earnest, and generous, López Larrave was a leader among his peers at INCV. The political opening that came with Ubico's overthrow gave López Larrave's enthusiasm a certain direction. At INCV, he met an outspoken university student leader named Manuel Galich who replaced Ubico's crony as school principal. For the boys, Galich was larger than life. López Larrave's classmate Roberto Díaz Castillo remembered, "the first time I heard him ... the first time that his words—the Word of the revolution—shook that patio filled with adolescents who did not wear the military uniform, we saw in Galich our archetype of a popular hero."[3] For López Larrave, Díaz Castillo, and others of their generation, the revolution offered opportunities that had been foreclosed for many decades.

This chapter begins with Galich, and then expands to examine the political, social, and economic changes brought by the Revolution and their impact on university students and faculty. Throughout, I emphasize how San Carlistas' debates over the meaning and practice of democracy reveal a particular understanding of cultural fitness as the engine of national progress. These conversations helped to define urban ladino intellectuals as they limited the civic participation of Guatemala's indigenous majority. Constitutional reforms extending the franchise, education and social welfare reforms, and university research on indigenous communities and poverty were notable moments when these discussions came to the fore. Simply put, *universitarios* saw themselves as the Guatemalans most fit to determine the direction of the nation even as they fiercely debated the role that the university ought to play in society. Both on campus and off, terms like *patria* and *libertad* came to signify society's most important qualities. Over time, this attitude became a signature of the Guatemalan middle class, as much as discretionary spending, leisure time, and social prestige in the community. For Guatemalans, as for other Latin Americans in the twentieth century, the middle class was celebrated as the key to a redemptive future, as it was critical to modern prosperity and a model of public virtue.[4] During the revolutionary decade, discussions about the meaning and practice of democracy set the stage for the emergence of fierce anticommunist opposition and, soon, counterrevolution.

This chapter also captures some of the texture of daily student life in the 1940s. Student newspapers that printed satire, silly jokes, song lyrics, and comics remind us that in addition to adeptly discussing matters of state, San Carlistas were also pretty funny. Memoirs also fill in some detail—the elation of boyhood, teenage levity, and the self-consciousness of one's later adult years—in a period that has left relatively little to the archival record.[5] Much of this chapter draws on *Del pánico al ataque* by Manuel Galich. Galich published his memoir in 1949, five years after the success of the revolution and five years before counterrevolutionary forces would depose Jacobo Arbenz, who had not yet been elected. Like so many memoirs, it is uncritically inflected with triumphal hindsight.[6] Galich presents himself and his friends as unified underdogs chasing fate, even as their diverse paths after the revolution are enough to call this unity into question. Nevertheless, the text offers insight into the hopes, dreams, and flaws of Galich's generation. His nostalgic playfulness evokes the spirit of student nationalism.

In the first years of the Revolution, *universitarios* built a sense of fraternity, a political kinship, defined by affinities and exclusions. Women were important to the young men as wives, sisters, cleaners, cooks, and secretaries, but they were rarely classmates. Although women had attended the university since the 1920s, they were denied the fellowship and opportunities of male students.[7] Likewise, indigenous students had never been excluded from the university, but they usually appeared in student papers as objects of ridicule or patronizing care because of their presumed lack of education. The impact of these exclusions expanded as the university's influence over urban life extended. The reformed Constitution of 1945 bestowed new rights and responsibilities upon the whole education system. Teachers and students were to protect and expand culture, promote ethnic improvement (*"promover el mejoramiento étnico"*), and supervise civic and moral formation; in effect, to make the people fit for self-government.[8]

UBICO'S DECADENT FACTORY OF *PROFESIONALISTAS*

President Ubico lived and ruled in the manner of his idol, Napoleon Bonaparte. He dressed exclusively in military regalia, enjoyed motorcycle tours of the countryside and city, and hosted opulent dinners. Famously unpredictable, Ubico threw vicious tantrums as regularly as he threw galas.[9] Politics at all levels operated under his control. Ministerial appointments reflected the interests of wealthy landowners, foreign investors, and Ubico's friends and allies. At the local and regional level, Ubico eliminated challenges to his authority by hand-selecting *intendentes* to replace elected mayors in towns nationwide. Lest these *intendentes* become loyal to their communities, Ubico regularly moved them from place to place.[10] Even Ubico's nominally beneficent labor reform, which replaced debt peonage with vagrancy laws, empowered *intendentes*.[11] The extraction of labor from poor men and women was crucial in years when global economic depression drove coffee prices so low that the commodity was scarcely profitable to produce and difficult to sell abroad. At the same time, Ubico deftly allied poor ladino and indigenous citizens to his government through powerful discourses of nation making and progress.[12] Within the Army, Ubico based promotions on loyalty rather than competence. Over time, the officer class grew to resent these appointments and their incompetent superiors. Those who offended Ubico were punished and those who praised him lived well. These limitations paired with economic and infrastructural growth created the conditions for growing antipathy toward Ubico's rule, especially among a small group of educated urban professionals and Army officers.[13]

The only sector that escaped Ubico's punishing hand was Guatemala's agricultural elite, especially UFCO, a Boston-based company formed in the last decades of the nineteenth century by the merger of banana production, distribution, and communication networks. UFCO agreed to build infrastructure in exchange for enormous land grants and preferential treatment: the company that would control one-third of the world's banana trade by the 1950s paid very little in taxes to the Guatemalan government and was permitted to manage its workers with impunity. Of course, growth in export production and distribution networks required a large and skillful middle class.[14] Huge companies required managers to organize workers, accountants to administer finances, lawyers to provide legal counsel and oversee contracts, and engineers to implement technical innovations. Dangerous plantations needed doctors and nurses to staff their hospitals and clinics. Supply shops required more accountants and managers. Children required schoolteachers.

Ubico adapted the National University to fulfill these needs. Like rural banana plantations, the urban university that churned out credentialed graduates was called "the decadent factory of *profesionalistas*."[15] This description of the university as factory is especially grim given Guatemala's bleak labor landscape. Yet if the university was a decadent factory, it was so only for those who went along with the boss. Early in his presidency, Ubico granted himself control over the highest governing body at the university, the University High Council (CSU). From this position, he personally supervised all aspects of university life, including the very comportment of students and professors. Behavior and character became important parts of the curriculum. The institution was transformed from a center for scientific investigation and professional formation to a school of good manners. Galich, then a student, wrote that Ubico "wanted to form the minds of all Guatemalans . . . from philosophy to saddlery, and including science, law, ethics, economy, [and] motorcycling." He joked that Ubico saw himself as "a walking encyclopedia with epaulets."[16]

The belief that the university ought to stay out of national politics governed university affairs. As in other areas of government, Ubico hand-selected the university's rector, deans, and secretaries for their allegiance rather than their proficiency. Deans were rarely experts in the fields that they advised, even though they made hiring and curriculum decisions. The rector retained final say over any faculty hires, but that position was also a presidential appointment. Faculty who opposed Ubico stood little chance of success. Ubico isolated the National University from other Latin American universities, despite interest in international student federations since the 1920s and more recent initiatives by students and faculty to unify Central American courses of study. Outside influence was suspect.[17] In his memoir, Galich evoked the "suspicious grunt of the police chiefs when one asked permission to organize a conference, to receive an illustrious houseguest, [or] to form an indigenous institute," even, he added, "to play chess ... to coordinate an athletic tournament, to go to a library to read silently."[18]

In early 1942, students from the Faculty of Law began to circulate critiques of the government in newspapers and pamphlets.[19] Many of these statements were loosely transcribed in Galich's memoir. The group criticized how the intellectual sector "has frequently been in the service of the dictator, of the autocracy" and "other times it has been rashly divided by differences in caste, religious convictions, by conflicting personal interests."[20] The young men warned of the danger of this disunity that left academics vulnerable to the power of despots. The group itself included brothers Mario and Julio Cesar Méndez Montenegro, Hiram Ordóñez, Manuel María Ávila Ayala, Heriberto Robles, Antonio Reyes Cardona, José Luis Bocaletti, José Manuel Fortuny, Alfonso Bauer Paíz, and Arturo Yaquian Otero. Most of these young men came from similar backgrounds: they were born or had spent most of their lives in the capital city and lived with parents who could afford expensive preparatory schooling for their sons. Ávila Ayala was different. He was about ten years older than his colleagues and was from Jalapa. Despite being a distinguished student, he never achieved the title of *Licenciado*, so valued in Guatemalan society. His *bachillerato* degree only certified him to teach handwriting and calligraphy. Like Ávila Ayala, Fortuny was also from the periphery and never graduated with a law degree. Instead, he quit school and worked for a North American business, Sterling Company. By contrast, Bauer Paíz, one of the youngest of the group, graduated from university by the end of 1942. He had attended the especially elite Colegio Preparatorio, unlike his fellows who had mostly attended the INCV. Mario Méndez Montenegro and Ordóñez had studied abroad. None of these young men were indigenous and most claimed some European ancestry. Most had been friends before university, like Bauer Paíz and Yaquian Otero who ran and lifted weights together because they wanted to lose weight before starting college.[21]

These young men who studied, ate, drank, and worked out together began to expand their conversations beyond the classroom by 1942. They called themselves the *escuilaches*, a term that lacks a singular history. It may be a reference to Spanish anti-French riots in 1766 or a pun on *esquilar* (to shear) and *esquilador* (sheep-shearer). The *escuilaches* were young men who wanted to shear the wool that Ubico had pulled over the eyes of the Guatemalan people.[22] In any case, the *escuilaches* and their classmates were heirs to the political culture that celebrated the university's role in Guatemalan political life that I outlined in the Introduction.

However, this history was discordant with their lives in Ubico's Guatemala. At first, the *escuilaches* limited their critiques to the university administration. They denounced the appointment of ignorant deans and the dismissal of skilled faculty. They decried the lack of intellectual freedom. Soon they linked these grievances to national political and economic circumstances. They equated the university's reigning principle of apoliticism to global fascism and blamed apolitical intellectuals for both world wars, arguing that a just society depended on an active university.[23]

In the middle of the night on May 15, 1942, the *escuilaches* snuck into the offices of the Third Court of the First Instance, the former home of President José María Reyna Barrios (1892–1898). They gathered to read what Galich calls in his memoir, "The *Escuilach* Manifesto." In a romantic passage, Galich recounts the "dim azure light" of the moon where the young men realized their potential: "We have weapons that our forebears did not want, or were unable or were unwilling to wield ... Three weapons that, well-used, can transform a group of guys ... into a formidable force, capable of opposing and overthrowing those with bayonets. These three weapons are our youth, our intelligence, and our unity."[24] Galich's reverence and hindsight intensifies the intoxicating promise of the moment.

His transcription of the manifesto includes an emotional account of the spiritual suffering Guatemala's youth as a result of persistent despotism and greed. He writes that "the youth of Guatemala has never had teachers, ideologues, leaders who spoke to them of the destiny of the nation with a true heart, as Sarmiento and Alberdi spoke to the youth of South America, or Martí and Hostos, to the Caribbean youth, or, finally, Ingenieros to those of America." Galich continues, "We have never known an apostle who did not appear later as a puppet, of a thinker who was not an imposter; ... And what lessons do these teachers of pillage and assassination leave us? They are too bloody to mention." The manifesto reflected the students' transnational intellectual formation by Caribbean and South American positivist forefathers Domingo Faustino Sarmiento, Juan Bautista Alberdi, José Martí, Eugenio María de Hostos, and José Ingenieros, even as it also asserted their isolation. Galich's recounting of the manifesto continues, "If we think about this [we will] understand the eagerness with which the young Guatemalan impatiently awaits someone who will tell him the words that he is wanting to hear, the words of inspiration, of truth, of practical science, of legitimate patriotism, backed up by facts and not by lies."[25] In Galich's retelling, the "young Guatemalan" becomes the figure for the whole of the nation, awaiting someone who can refine him with inspiration, truth, science, and patriotism. Galich writes that the group tiptoed out of the building with "the sensation of new breath in our souls."[26]

Despite their enthusiasm, the young men were patient. While they aimed to prepare students to lead "a large popular movement that [would] destroy from the roots the old institutions and bring about a radical transformation," they estimated that revolution was around ten years away. In the months after the scene described above, the *escuilaches* began by building support within the Faculty of Law. In October 1943, they revived the defunct Association of Law Students (Asociación de Estudiantes El Derecho [AED]).[27] Following the AED's example, a number of other *facultades* founded or revived student associations before the 1943 Christmas recess. Soon, several of these groups banded together into university-wide federation. The group took the name of the Association of University Students (Asociación de Estudiantes Universitarios [AEU]), the student federation formed in 1920, an earlier moment of groundswell in student organizing across Latin America, including Mexico, Argentina, Chile, Peru, Colombia, Uruguay, and Cuba. The formation of a university-wide student group with its own bylaws and juridical norms changed the shape of inter- and intra-*facultad* relationships. The AEU of the 1920s imagined that university reform would follow after broader national reform, and so focused its energies outside of the university on the Central American Unionist movement. The revitalized AEU of the 1940s, by contrast, focused first on internal concerns.[28]

Nevertheless, it was the AEU of the 1940s that would most change Guatemalan society. Their first demand was to replace Ubico-appointed administrators with more prepared candidates. In the Faculty of Medicine, students succeeded in replacing Dean Ramiro Gálvez and his secretary Oscar Espada with Antonio Valdeavellano and Alfredo Gil.[29] Students in Pharmacy followed suit, demanding new administrators and permission to participate in curriculum reform. Amid these early successes, the AEU struggled with a question that would divide the student body for the next six decades: what was the role of the university in politics? One block of medical students refused to join the AEU because they rejected the group's involvement in national concerns, limited as it was. Even AEU president Alfonso Marroquín Orellana advocated a limited role for the university in national and citywide affairs. The *escuilaches* could not disagree more. By September, the avowedly political *escuilaches* had expanded their influence in the AEU and replaced the apolitical Marroquín Orellana with fellow *escuilach*, Gerardo Gordillo Barrios.[30]

As historian Virgilio Álvarez Aragón has noted, joining students across *facultades* enabled the group to exert political power and influence outside the university.[31] For his part, Galich wrote that students found in the new organizations "the democratic exercise that [they] were denied as citizens"— political expression, assembly, and representation.[32] Before long, opposition to Ubico became major point of cohesion among groups that had begun with more disparate and modest aims. The AEU had come to represent "the recapture of student rebellion" or, as Galich's title suggests, "the end of panic and the beginning of the attack."[33]

In May 1944, two events encouraged the AEU to go on the offensive. The first was the overthrow of Salvadoran dictator and Ubico crony Maximiliano Hernández Martínez. University students had been instrumental in the dictator's overthrow, and their Guatemalan counterparts saw this as a victory of the student spirit. The AEU sent a letter of support signed by nearly two hundred students who professed their "faith in the dignified future of our Central American pueblos."[34] We can assume that this was a sizeable percentage of the student body, as enrollment was just 711 students in 1943.[35] The second event that catalyzed university students was the incarceration of their classmate, Ramón Cadena. Arrested on charges only vaguely recorded as "political," Cadena was held in the Central Penitentiary for weeks without due process. Galich and other law students wrote a letter of protest to Ubico on June 12. The letter accused the military tribunal of conducting a false trial and prosecuting Cadena's personal views rather than the facts of the case. Like the letter of support for Salvadoran students, this letter circulated through the university and gathered dozens of signatures. But before it could reach the hot-tempered dictator, the National Police intercepted the petition. Cadena was released. Students celebrated this as a victory and the student body gained, according to Galich, new "confidence in itself and in its unity."[36]

Ubico's desperation also grew. Repression had been the order of the day for more than a decade, but the detention of visiting scholars, repression of student meetings, interrogation of student leaders, and dismissal of professionals who spoke out of place were committed with greater boldness. Ubico fired Ávila Ayala from his post at INCV. Galich wrote that Ávila Ayala was fired because he asked students to apply knowledge from inside the classroom to question the world outside, precisely the kind of teaching that Ubico despised. Of course he was also an *escuilach*.[37] Reflecting on their audacity,

Galich wrote, "we did not know even remotely then, but we already sensed [it]."[38] Opposition to Ubico swelled. Students would no longer simply endure.

FROM STRIKE TO REVOLUTION

On the afternoon of June 19, 1944, the AED assembled for a business meeting. The group counted about a hundred students, just under half of the *facultad*'s total enrollment, though even fewer usually attended meetings.[39] But this afternoon, the assembly hall filled with hundreds of students and professors from other *facultades*, and teachers and other professionals. The crowd presaged an extraordinary turn of events. Perhaps people came to hear the results of the AED elections, which pitted an *escuilach* against an apolitical candidate. More likely, they anticipated something more. As the meeting began, copies of a letter circulated through the crowd. The letter demanded the dismissal of the new Law *facultad* dean and secretary, both recent Ubico appointments. This was an aggressive, but not unprecedented, challenge to Ubico's authority. After all, students in the *facultades* of Medicine and Pharmacy had made similar demands earlier in the year. But this letter went one step further and proposed two suitable replacements. The letter effectively asserted that the students, not Ubico or his hand-selected faculty, should choose administrators. The letter circulated and the meeting continued.

Then, just as the announcement of the results of the AED elections began, two students proposed a general strike. A roar of excitement filled the room. "Of the passive students of the previous fourteen years, there remained not a whit," remembered Galich.[40] The AED leadership resumed the meeting and announced the election results: *escuilach* Mario Méndez Montenegro was elected AED president, Hector Zachrisson as vice president, Manuel Galich and Carlos González Landford as secretaries, and Oscar de León Aragón as treasurer. After a round of applause for the newly elected leaders, the crowd again erupted with a motion to strike. Galich remembered, "A 'hurrah!' sprang from more than two hundred young but virile throats, and applause rang out through our 'first minute of the liberation.'"[41] They planned a meeting for the following day to give the whole university an opportunity to consider the strike declaration and the AED student leaders time to work out the details. For many decades, San Carlistas would define themselves and their social class through a contentious relationship between the student body, the university, and the state. These early assemblies were the first shouts—hardly whispers—of the struggles to come.

The next day, an even larger group gathered. It was one of the first times in decades that large numbers of students of medicine, law, economics, and engineering had gathered as a group. Representatives from the various *facultades* took the dais and expressed their support for the strike. The group also voted to unconditionally support the capital city schoolteachers' strike against Ubico's education minister. The alliance was practical, as many students like Galich and Ávila Ayala taught at capital city secondary schools while finishing their degrees at university.[42] Galich remembers that he and Ávila Ayala left the meeting together and walked from downtown to their homes in the southern neighborhood of Campo Marte in Zone 5, about a three-kilometer walk. They discussed the rising protest as they walked. Anticipating that Ubico would seek retribution, they decided to write two documents: a public declaration of unity between schoolteachers and *universitarios* and a clear statement of the ideology of the group, an *Ideario*. The declaration of unity would protect both groups and improve the students' reputation. The *Ideario* would clearly articulate the group's ideals, in case Ubico judged them to be seditious.

First, the *Ideario* affirmed that administrators and teachers should not be bureaucratic appointments, but rather selected for their academic background and commitment to the university. Second, it argued for the removal of administrators who did not conform to this standard. Third, it prioritized the development of scientific and technical knowledge at the university. It also called for the foundation of a Faculty of Humanities and a research institute on indigenous history and language. It acknowledged students' desire to participate in policy making at the university. Finally, it called for the government to work closely with students to improve the international reputation of the university through scientific and cultural publications and by reinstating the foreign exchange program. The demands sought to recover the National University's historic prestige and reorient its activities toward national improvement. Inspired by classical liberalism with a rights-bearing student at the vanguard, the *Ideario* closed with a declaration that the students' only interest was the "creation of the ideal university."[43] In sum, it articulated professionalism, study, and encounters with state bodies and institutions as the first expression of student nationalism, which would become the most enduring feature of Guatemala's middle class.[44]

Galich's memoir recounts a remarkable meeting that was held the following morning. Galich, Mario Méndez Montenegro, and Zachrisson were summoned to Ubico's chambers. His personal secretary, Ernesto Rivas, received the young men and began the meeting with an offer: Ubico would dismiss his recent Law School dean and secretary appointments if they promised to call off the strike. Galich remembered that the young men responded, "*We could comply with this agreement, but we cannot speak to whether our colleagues would approve a decision that is personally ours*" and Méndez Montenegro confirmed, "In no way can we decide something for the entire University."[45] The students' collective-minded response may have been surprising to Rivas, who was accustomed to Ubico's autocratic style. Negotiations continued, though the young students did not budge. At one point, the telephone rang. It was Ubico. After he hung up, Rivas offered even further concessions to the students. In fact as the morning wore on, he offered concessions to all of the students' demands: the replacement of the recent appointments, the formation of a Faculty of Humanities, and even Ávila Ayala's reinstatement at the INCV. At the nearby Paraninfo, students, professors, and teachers waited for news from the meeting. Five hours later, Galich, Méndez Montenegro, and Zachrisson left the National Palace for lunch.[46]

The three men, all in their early 30s, had been invested with tremendous authority as liaisons between the emergent student movement and the dictator. Now, they had to decide whether to present the assembled crowd with the *Ideario*, the president's concessions, or both. Galich remembered that they met with friends at the cafeteria of the judicial office buildings to discuss the situation. They ordered lunch from Miss Chaíto, a woman Galich remembered as the "guardian angel of the students who worked at the courts in those years," who served the students "not only with efficiency, but also with affection."[47] While fighting for a more just future, Galich and his peers relied upon the manual labor of others, especially the affective labor of women in service positions. We cannot precisely know Miss Chaíto's motives, but we do know that women whose histories have not become iconic also opposed Ubico. Perhaps Miss Chaíto's labor was a political act in itself—providing support for the overthrow of Ubico—rather than the act of personal affection that Galich recounted.

Over beef stew, avocado, tortillas, coffee, and bread, the young men argued. Galich advocated for a more restrained approach. He was concerned that the embryonic movement might be unable to sustain a struggle against the dictator. Further, if Ubico had agreed to their demands, why should they continue to fight? Méndez Montenegro disagreed. As long as Ubico remained in power and the university was not autonomous, their demands remained unfulfilled. The movement could only gain momentum. Finally, he lost patience and, according to Galich's memoir, "stood up and leaned across the table, pointing his finger at me, saying in a decisive tone: 'If you back out now, *escuilach*, I am going to punch you!'" Galich, it seems, found new resolve. They would not accept Ubico's concessions. The young men returned to the National Palace. In Galich's words, "impulse triumphed over caution; intuition overcame reason."[48]

The three students returned to the Paraninfo, which by that time overflowed with "students, teachers, people of all social classes, of all professions, of all of the neighborhoods of the city, who came to witness a accomplishment without precedent in Jorge Ubico's Guatemala."[49] Applause and cheers erupted as Galich reported how Ubico acceded to all of the group's demands. Another student stood to read the *Ideario*. Cries of "Viva!" filled the room and it was unanimously approved. Celso Cerezo Dardón suggested a general strike. Others urged the group to wait and see whether the president would issue a formal response to the *Ideario*. The meeting dissolved into muddled debates and disagreements. Then, in Galich's cinematic retelling, a young student, barely out of secondary school, stepped forward and yelled, "If you don't declare the strike, I will declare my own strike!"[50]

The strike was on. Over the next few hours, representatives from each *facultad* made speeches and listed demands. Students in laboratory sciences demanded better equipment, other *facultades* demanded technical schools for workers and a School of Pedagogy.[51] That their demands hardly differed from those pursued by students in the early 1920s confirmed the university's stasis during the dictatorship. After some debate, the group agreed to give Ubico twenty-four hours to comply. Before the meeting adjourned, a group of young lawyers joined the strike. Now the striking students had support from two important professional sectors, education and law.

After the meeting, the *escuilaches* assembled at Ávila Ayala's house to prepare the long list of demands to be delivered to the president. The young men talked, smoked, typed, and copyedited. On breaks, Galich remembers how they retired to a different room to consult a fortune-telling toy. Regrettably, these fortunes are lost to history.[52] The following morning of June 22, Cerezo Dardón delivered the demands and the *Ideario* to Ubico. Galich remembers that he tried to sleep late, but his daughter's cries woke him. Unable to rest,

Galich went to meet with friends in the offices of the Third Court. His sleeplessness was a stroke of luck, as policemen came searching for him soon after he left. Ubico had ordered the arrest of the student leaders. He had also suspended the constitution. Friends smuggled Galich, Ávila Ayala, and Méndez Montenegro into the Mexican Embassy, where they joined nearly all of the students, teachers, and lawyers who had signed the strike declaration.[53] The group anticipated arrest, exile, or worse. They waited to see how the rest of the nation would respond. An answer came later that afternoon in a treatise entitled "The Document of the 311." Named for its three hundred-eleven signatories, including many professionals and high-profile academics, the document called for an end the state of exception and the reinstatement of the Constitution.[54]

Hand to hand and by word of mouth, the demands, the *Ideario,* and other declarations, slogans, and plans circulated throughout the capital. Small protests punctuated daily life over the next three days. The Ubico regime responded by sending parapolice forces into neighborhoods to loot and attack residents. The protestors were blamed for damages and injuries.[55] On the afternoon of June 25, a group of schoolteachers organized a protest at the Church of St. Francis, located five blocks from the National Palace. Their chants and signs demanded freedom, democracy, and Ubico's dismissal. Memoirs and journalistic accounts of the protest emphasize that the women were well-dressed, professional, and orderly. This was important to the opposition's claim that the imminent attack was unjustified. Ubico ordered the military and police to enclose the protestors. Officers fired shots into the crowd and one young teacher, Maria Chinchilla Recinos, was struck and died in the street. For many, this attack against a teacher—a professional woman who nurtured the nation's children—was unforgiveable. Emboldened, workers' groups came forward to join the strike and Ubico's regime lost what little support it had from small business owners who depended on him to curb worker unrest. According to the Foreign Broadcast Information Service, by the end of June, Guatemala seemed to be "on the verge of a revolution."[56]

Like others who had openly opposed Ubico, Galich, Ávila Ayala, Méndez Montenegro, and Cerezo decided to go into exile in Mexico as the situation deteriorated.[57] In fact, they were on a train to Mexico City when the conductor announced Ubico's resignation.[58] Only eight days had passed since the young men had met with Ubico's secretary. Galich wrote, "It was as if a frenzy overtook us. We hugged. We squeezed one another for a long time. We drank every beer on the train. Some *mariachis* accompanied our celebration with songs from the Aztec land."[59] The young men's Mexican exile became a sightseeing holiday. The group went to the Museo de Bellas Artes, visited a secret *aguardiente* factory, and met with Mexican university students. To Ávila Ayala's dismay, they even saw a bullfight. He despised the *fiesta brava* and spoke, Galich wrote, "in the name of some hypothetical society for the protection of animals—'I don't know how you can applaud such savagery.'"[60] The young men returned to a hero's welcome. Apparently, Galich was embraced so enthusiastically that his trousers fell off.[61]

Two weeks later, Ubico's handpicked successor, Federico Ponce Vaides, was sworn in as interim president. Elections were scheduled for mid-December, but Ponce's dictatorial intentions were clear from the outset. Opposition continued to grow. The AEU sent more demands and petitions to the National Palace. To their earlier demands, they added the reinstatement of all public employees who had been fired for participating in the anti-Ubico strikes, the removal of police from all university buildings, the retraction of threats made against teachers, and respect for "democratic rights."[62] They also demanded university autonomy. In short, Ubico's resignation did not bring order, but instead emboldened the opposition.[63] Ponce maneuvered between the protestors' and his predecessor's expectations, but had little success in satisfying either. For instance, when students convened an all-university congress to assemble a list of acceptable candidates to replace the university's Ubico-appointed rector, Ponce was all but forced to accept one of their suggestions, Carlos Federico Mora.

Ponce also faced competition in upcoming presidential elections. Two new political parties emerged out of the anti-Ubico strikes. Schoolteachers and professionals formed the National Renovation Party (Partido Nacional Renovador [PNR]) on the day after Ubico stepped down. They selected their candidate for president that same afternoon: distinguished professor and doctor of education Juan José Arévalo Bermejo. Arévalo, like many other capital-city-born intellectual elites, had spent many years abroad at university or in exile, and sometimes both. He had attended the National University for a short time before going to Paris. From Paris, he went to Argentina on a scholarship to study education, where he finished a PhD. In 1934, he returned to Guatemala to serve in the Ministry of Education but returned to Argentina two years later after conflicts with Ubico. Students formed another party, the Frente Popular Libertador (FPL).[64] The FPL nominated AED president Julio César Méndez Montenegro as their candidate and National University alumni filled his cabinet. In August, however, the group joined the PNR to form the Revolutionary Action Party (Partido de Acción Revolucionaria [PAR]) and back Arévalo. Méndez Montenegro would have to wait until 1966 for his turn as president. Many things would change by that time.

Meanwhile, Ponce's regime showed more signs of stress. Public protest continued in the capital city. Critics of Ubico, like Luis Cardoza y Aragón, began to return from the exiles in places like Paris and Mexico.[65] On September 15, Guatemala's Independence Day, columns of machete-wielding campesinos paraded through the city center, proclaiming their loyalty to Ponce. The press speculated that the president had bribed the poor rural citizens in an attempt to aggravate urban ladino fears of the rural indigenous masses.[66] The suspicious assassination of the founder of the popular opposition newspaper *El Imparcial* (founded in 1922 by members of the celebrated Generation of 1920) also seemed linked to Ponce's attempt to maintain control. Citizens doubted whether the December elections would take place and if so, that they would be fair. Some students, teachers, and other citizens began to collect weapons for an armed insurrection.

A clearer plan had developed within the armed forces. At around 2:00 A.M. on October 20, young officers in the prestigious National Guard seized the Matamoros Barracks and laid siege to San José Castle, the Army's most important storehouse for powder, munitions, and arms at the southern edge of Guatemala City. The young National Guard officers resented the cronyism that had limited high-ranking positions to loyal officers from elite families and the mistreatment that had characterized their years of service.[67] They distributed arms to between two and three thousand troops and civilians, including some students and alumni, like José Rölz-Bennett and the Méndez Montenegro brothers.[68]

This chapter began with a scene from the following morning, when National Guard tanks rolled toward the National Palace and Ponce and Ubico were perhaps in hiding or had fled the country. Two military men, Jacobo Arbenz and Francisco Javier Arana, and one civilian, National University alumnus Jorge Toriello, assumed executive power. A grand celebration of the revolution was delayed until October 26, when about 100,000 civilians marched through the city center. Students joined campesinos, workers, teachers, and the poor below the balcony of the grand Post Office to greet the new ruling junta. The junta suspended the Constitution, dissolved the Legislative Assembly, and expelled a handful of generals and police chiefs. Ubico's capricious rule was over. Just two years had passed since the *escuilaches* had dreamed of "teachers, ideologues, leaders" who would speak "to

FIGURE 1. Citizens gathered in front of the National Palace, October 20, 1944. Photograph by J. Francisco Muñoz. Enrique Muñoz Meany Collection, Fototeca Guatemala, Centro de Investigaciones Regionales de Mesoamérica (CIRMA).

them of the destiny of the nation with a true heart." Maybe Arbenz, Arana, and Toriello could be just such a trio.

MAKING A REPUBLIC FROM THE UNIVERSITY

For their role in the revolution and elite academic preparation, many student leaders were rewarded with high-level appointments or elected positions in the new revolutionary government. Recent graduates of the university's Law Faculty became architects of the nation-state as ministers in the executive branch, representatives in the Legislative Assembly, and delegates in the Constitutional Assembly. Two years after dreaming up their ten-year plan to create revolution, Galich and the gadfly *escuilaches* began to rebuild the government from the very seats of power they had opposed. This made for a very young government. Alfonso Bauer Paíz, who served as Minister of Economy and Labor, was 26 years old. Galich, the recently elected president of the Legislature, was an elder among the students at 31 in 1944. The average age of a member of Congress by 1951 was 35, but some congressmen were as young as 22. These student-statesmen balanced homework with the legislative agenda, running from Assembly to class on any given day.[69]

Fittingly, education was one of the first issues confronted by the new government. Two weeks after Ponce's defeat, the junta presented Decree 12 to the Congressional Education Commission (CEC). In addition to honoring students for their bravery in the revolution, the decree acknowledged how the university had suffered during the dictatorship. Under Ubico, the decree read, the university was made into a "factory of professionals where investigation was hollow and thinking lost all relevance."[70] A gesture of good will, Decree 12 granted the university autonomy in "intellectual, cultural, and administrative questions." But to the CEC's student-statesmen, it was useless to grant autonomy to the existing institution, formed as it was during the "asphyxiating" dictatorship.[71] They rejected even the implicit limitation of the university's autonomy to "intellectual, cultural, and administrative questions." For the junta, Decree 12 was a symbolic recognition while the CEC balked at abstractions that might be empty in practice. The junta suggested reform while student–statesmen demanded total regeneration. The CEC reasoned that a new nation needed a new university.

The CEC made significant changes to the junta's decree. They began with the university's name. The National University would again be called the University of San Carlos (USAC), a gesture to its prestige in the colonial era. Next, the CEC pledged to extend the university's reach beyond the capital city through extension programs and branch campuses. Additionally, they reserved the right for the university alone to alter, form, or dissolve any programs of study in accordance with society's changing needs. Most importantly, the CEC limited executive power over the university by eliminating an article in the initial draft of the decree that permitted the executive to intervene in the university in certain circumstances. Individuals chosen by the USAC electorate were solely responsible for its operation. National well-being and scientific, technological, and cultural development would be in the hands of the autonomous university.

The CEC also formed two new programs in Mathematics and Humanities, which demonstrated the university's new attitude toward knowledge production.[72] Instead of engineering, an applied science that created technicians, the new USAC emphasized theoretical mathematics. In turn, the Humanities *facultad* would serve as the university's ethical compass.[73] As the keynote speaker at its inauguration, President Arévalo declared, "Our university is indebted to the youth of Guatemala," but "mediocrity, sensationalism, and mercantilism . . . have impoverished us and we are going mad." He continued, "We need teachers for the youth: we need something like priests, charged with telling us in which direction the nation ought to go." The Humanities program was designed to produce just these types of thinkers who would through their word and their conduct inspire "faith, courage, and self-sacrifice" in the youth.[74] Arévalo called on students to lead the people of Guatemala as secular priests.

In these first months of the Revolution, students, faculty, and alumni worked to restructure both the university and the nation in the image of an ideal republic. Their efforts not only revised the laws that governed the university, but also confirmed the presence of a coherent civic block at USAC. The ruling junta, CEC, and daily newspapers consistently referred to students, professors, and administrators as "San Carlistas."

San Carlistas also joined the Constitutional Assembly, which hurried to write a Constitution before Arévalo's inauguration on March 15. The Constitutional Assembly united two generations of San Carlistas: elders of the Generation of 1920, who as members of the Unionist Party had aided the overthrow of Estrada Cabrera, and neophytes who had entered national-level politics with the Revolution. The elders included luminaries David Vela, Francisco Villagrán de Leon, José Rölz-Bennett, Clemente Marroquín Rojas, and José Falla. Some *esculaches* were among the younger generation. Of the Commission of Fifteen that initially drafted the Constitution, fourteen members were lawyers or law students; one was a medical doctor.[75] Unsurprisingly, their chief concerns were universal suffrage, literacy, and federal social reforms, including university extension programs, and the foundation of the National Indigenista Institute (IIN), which sought—in certain terms—to improve government relations with rural indigenous citizens.[76]

While student-statesmen discussed these concerns within the immediate context of Guatemala, they also engaged with larger ideological debates that circulated throughout much of the world after World War II. The Constitutional Assembly employed the new human rights–based language of organizations like the United Nations. San Carlistas were also early members of the International Union of Students (IUS) in 1946, an organization with consultative status in the United Nations Educational, Scientific, and Cultural Organization (UNESCO).[77] Contemporary internationalist ideals were reflected in the Assembly's invocation of the "democratic spirit" that divided the world into two antagonistic blocs: fascist and democratic. In

Guatemala, however, this sweeping call for democracy elided liberal and popular political concerns. This elision enabled a strong governing coalition, albeit one with deep internal divisions.[78] Within a decade, conflicts over the precise meanings and practices of democracy would destabilize the revolutionary governments, a topic taken up at length in Chapter 2.

But even in the Revolution's first months, the tension between liberal political philosophy and popular concerns put intellectual elites at odds with urban workers, rural farmers, and the jobless. Some of these divisions were exposed in the debate over universal suffrage. The ruling junta opposed extending the right to vote to illiterate men and women because they were seen as remnants of feudalism, not modern citizens, and therefore ineligible for the rights and responsibilities of citizenship. The junta insisted that restricting the vote to literate citizens would secure the nation for democracy and protect it against fascism because illiterate people were likely to be exploited by politicians, an argument supported by the historical memory of the presidency of Rafael Carrera and other nineteenth-century caudillos. Initially, the AEU and the AED agreed. Contradictory as this may seem, it serves as a reminder that San Carlistas were literate, ladino, mostly urban—in a word, urbane.

The junta, student leaders, ministers, advisors, and members of the Assembly came from the only ethnic, class, and regional background where the ability to read and write in Castilian Spanish was common. In 1950 (the first post-revolutionary census), 73.8 percent of Guatemala City residents were literate, while national figures including the majority-indigenous periphery recorded only 27.8 percent literacy. Many urban intellectuals accepted this evidence of the link between indigeneity and illiteracy. In summary comments in the national census, unnamed statisticians reiterated the implications of these numbers: "Literacy, taken to mean the ability to read and write, has always been considered one of the best means to judge the cultural level of a population ... while nearly a half of the ladino population (49.1%) is literate, only 10 percent (9.7%) of the indigenous population is [literate]."[79] The elite status of professionals is even clearer in terms of national employment statistics. In 1940, Guatemala's economically active population counted 1,846,977 individuals; of this group of nearly 2 million workers, only 2,145 worked in what were called the "liberal professions" (*profesiones liberales*) as lawyers, notaries, doctors, surgeons, dental surgeons, pharmacists, midwives, and topographical and civil engineers. That is, less than 0.12 percent of economically active Guatemalans had careers in professional fields.

By contrast, 45.8 percent (846,103) of economically active individuals did domestic service work and 42.1 percent (777,509) did agricultural work. Together this nearly 88 percent of the population performed labor that did not require schooling or literacy.[80]

Moreover, professionals were concentrated in the capital city. In 1940, more than half of Guatemala's 413 lawyers lived in the capital. A decade later, around 62 percent of Guatemala's lawyers, doctors, surgeons, dental surgeons, and topographical and civil engineers lived in the Department of Guatemala, where Guatemala City is located. The remaining 38 percent were scattered unevenly throughout the other twenty-one departments. When the 1950 census noted an illiteracy rate (72.2%) that exceeded the recorded indigenous population (53.5%) by nearly 20 percentage points, these data were taken to indicate that there was also a "regular quantity of illiterate ladinos," which led some social scientists to understand rurality as a factor in illiteracy. The same census recorded that only 22 percent of individuals over the age of seven in Guatemala City had attended "any school or classes whatsoever." Plainly, to attend university was extremely rare, and to graduate was even rarer. Most San Carlistas had attended the same preparatory schools and known one another for decades by the time they reached university. Professionals and students formed a small, tight-knit, mostly urban, ladino community.[81]

All of these factors—race, region, and fraternity—weighed heavily on the Constitutional Assembly's discussion of granting full suffrage to illiterate Guatemalans.[82] USAC alumnus and conservative editor of the newspaper *La Hora* Clemente Marroquín Rojas observed that the debate divided civil society into two sectors: on one side "industrial workers, laborers, and some youths and students," and the other "pure gentlemen: many students, but all 'respectable people [*gente decente*].'"[83] North American anthropologist Richard N. Adams looked on and dismissed the revolutionary yearnings of the *escuilaches* because of their apparent hypocrisy. He wrote, "the Faculty of Law, the locus of such radical student protests, [produced] a population of professionals that is apparently incapable of altering the system and is, instead, deeply involved in its continuity."[84] Adams's observation certainly echoed the contemporary belief that the middle class ought to exemplify the "ideal of private prosperity and public virtue thought to be crucial to the smooth functioning of modern societies."[85] Actually, as I mentioned above, there was tremendous ideological difference among the *escuilaches*. Nevertheless, while the ruling junta, the AEU, the AED, and some members of the public opposed the vote for illiterate citizens, the majority of the Constitutional Assembly, many political parties (including president-elect Arévalo's PAR), and most of the general public favored at least an open ballot for illiterate citizens.

Before long, the AEU changed its position. In their statement about the shift, the AEU leadership declared with confidence that it could not "stand against the interests and ideals of the pueblo."[86] In order to achieve political and social equality, the nation needed all of its citizens to participate. Further, they wrote, the restriction of illiterate citizens' right to vote "forecloses and annuls the human character of our laborers, most of all of our industrial workers who have given sufficient proof of their patriotism and civility."[87] Still, they favored an open ballot for a short period while illiterate citizens were taught civic literacy, reading, and writing. As the foremost student group, the AEU represented San Carlistas as custodians of the knowledge and skills that were prerequisites to the franchise.

Not everyone was so easily persuaded. One important event must have loomed large in the newspaper debates over universal suffrage: the violent conflict between ladinos and Kaqchikels in Patzicía on October 22, 1944. Capital city newspapers described the aggression of the Kaqchikels and used the events to demonstrate how rural indigenous Guatemalans were unprepared for full citizenship.[88] They did not report the fatal mismatch of machetes versus guns that placed indigenous combatants at a deadly disadvantage. Flashpoints such as these provided opportunities for middle-class professionals and students to demonstrate their own cultural and political difference, to celebrate their urbanity, and articulate a "dialectical brew of optimism, anxiety, and contradiction" that promoted certain manners as requisite for citizenship.[89]

In *El Imparcial*, just a few months later, illustrious journalist Rufino Guerra Cortave echoed this view when he wrote, "the rural man, the illiterate, the laborer, Indian or ladino, continues in his ignorance and, consequently, continues to be a danger, to be manipulated by the perverse maneuvering of the enemy."[90] For Cortave, the indigenous citizen was not to be faulted for his ignorance, but rather "four centuries of oppression, cruelty, and systematic brutalization of the native" had "made him so indolent and apathetic," and "resigned to his lot."[91] Ongoing oppression rendered the indigenous community (and illiterate ladinos) incapable of participating in the social contract. Cortave continued, "To beings whose lack of consciousness is a cloud in our sky of democratic liberties . . . we must take reason . . .

we must infuse the ABC of civilization." After all, if one had not learned more than the most rudimentary reading, he "is not guilty if he cannot discern good from evil and it is the duty of the rest of the Guatemalans of conscience to show them the path of their own best interest if they are to be part of this society." This task could be achieved "with reason and patriotic honesty as guides."[92] Cortave's quasi-expert discourse declared that only with literacy could one have reason, discern good from evil, and be counted upon to act in their own best interest. The process of coming to consciousness by those blameless for their lack of it required a certain submission to a course of treatment by the more wise.

In *La Hora*, Jorge Schlesinger argued that the "Indian" was an "irresponsible subject" because of "his lack of education and inadaptability." Like Cortave, he encouraged the incorporation of the indigenous as citizens in the national community. But for Schlesinger, inclusion was owed because "he is the pillar of the national economy which is based mainly on agriculture" not because inclusion was "necessary to unify the national conscience," as Cortave had written.[93] In fact, the government was duty-bound to look after the indigenous, if only so "that he may be useful to the fatherland."[94] Cortave, Schlesinger, and the AEU agreed on the conclusion if not on the rationale: illiterate rural indigenous laborers and their ladino counterparts must be enfranchised.

Suffrage became "obligatory and secret" for literate men; "optional and secret" for literate women; and "optional and public" for illiterate men. Illiterate women were not mentioned at all in the Constitution.[95] A woman thusly located in the assemblymen's understanding of political authority could not possibly properly exercise citizenship. The question was settled in the Constitutional Assembly, but it revealed a rift that was not easily mended. Civil society was the precondition of democracy, but education was the precondition of civil society. San Carlistas were charged to infuse the "ABCs of civilization," and in so doing enact the most enduring feature of the new student nationalism: the responsibility of the students to lead the nation.

The new constitution was completed in time for Arévalo's inauguration. On March 15, 1945, President Arévalo stood before a crowd in the congressional chambers. He declared, "We are going to equip humanity with humanity. We are going to rid ourselves of guilt-ridden fear through unselfish ideas. We are going to add justice and happiness to order, because order does not serve us if it is based on injustice and humiliation." He continued,

FIGURE 2. President Arévalo depicted as a woman before a stereotypical indigenous peasant on a float for the *desfile bufo*, 1945. Anonymous Photograph. Collection of Juan José Arévalo Bermejo. Fototeca Guatemala, Centro de Investigaciones Regionales de Mesoamérica (CIRMA).

"We are going to revalorize, civically and legally, all of the men of the Republic . . . Democracy means just order, constructive peace, internal discipline, [and] happy and productive work . . . a democratic government supposes and demands the dignity of everyone."[96] Dictatorship, or order "based on injustice and humiliation," was abolished. Yet real democracy required "internal discipline, happy and productive work," and men who had been "revalorized." Later in the address Arévalo confirmed, "we are [working] directly for a transformation of the spiritual, cultural, and economic life of the republic." The speech was a vow to teach civic values to all citizens who had lost or not yet acquired them. Arévalo added that Guatemalan democracy would become "a permanent, dynamic system of projections into society [by] tireless vigilance."[97] Some of Arévalo's populist contemporaries, like Victor Haya de la Torre in Peru and Juan Perón in Argentina, had made similar claims, occasionally inspiring the support and at other times the ire of the middle class.[98]

Once in office, Arévalo called on San Carlistas to design the tax reform and new social security program, and to lead teams of doctors, lawyers, and engineers into the countryside to organize free clinics. Arévalo and his advisors also promoted national culture through fiction, poetry, music composition, and fine art contests.[99] His democratic vision fused Rooseveltian social liberalism with Lockeian liberalism, the legacy of late nineteenth-century Central American Liberalism, and the populist political style that was *en vogue* across Latin America.[100] His populism empowered intellectuals, experts, and policymakers through interwoven projects of economic development, human welfare, and political tutelage. Before long, advisors and funders from the United States would utilize these networks to implement a kind of soft imperialism in the context of the Cold War.[101]

The Arévalo government designed comprehensive reforms for every level of the educational system. The reforms ushered in a new period of openness. Professors and students returned from exile and brought with them experiences gained in Mexico and further afield.[102] Schoolteachers were encouraged to restructure professional credentialing and rethink their teaching methods. Hundreds of new primary and secondary schools were built with government subsidies. The new Instituto Normal Nocturno, a night school, enabled workers to have access to the nationalist positivist curriculum of the highly regarded *"cultura normalista."*[103] At USAC, administrative reform crafted a republican government for the university: a legislature, the University High Council (CSU); an electoral college, the University Electoral Body; and an executive, the rector. The rector presided over the CSU, but its membership included the deans of all academic units, a professional delegate from every *colegio*, and a student delegate from each academic unit.[104] Elections by secret ballot in the University Electoral Body replaced the personal appointment of the rector. Colegios, like guilds, regulated professionals' training, examinations, and licensure; they served as a political bloc and social organization for members. The inclusion of *colegios* in university governance meant that although San Carlistas changed phases, from student to professional, and frequently, from professional to professor, their obligation to USAC endured.[105]

Education reforms progressed quickly, but Arévalo had more difficulty launching reforms in other areas. His economic policy based on a system of capitalist growth through agricultural export of coffee, cotton, and petroleum and moderate labor and finance reforms suggests he was cautious about impacting export production. The 1947 Labor Code restored the right to unionize to urban unions, but placed limitations on agricultural unions.[106]

Two of Arévalo's most lasting reforms were the formation of the National Institute for the Promotion of Production (INFOP) and the Guatemalan Social Security Institute (IGSS) in 1948. These institutes sought to expand and diversify industry and agriculture, and focused on industrialization, credit, home construction, the indigenous economy, and cooperatives.[107] San Carlistas advised both institutes.

But Arévalo was an educator, and not an economist or agronomist.[108] His uneven policies and their consequences fueled debate over the meaning of the revolution. Historian Piero Gleijeses has argued that Arévalo's economic reforms failed because they did not transform Guatemalan economic structure; the reforms actually reinforced the inequalities that his educational and cultural programming attempted to mitigate.[109] For his part, Arévalo himself wrote in 1939 that any education reform would fail in Guatemala without structural reform.[110] Nevertheless, as president, he pursued precisely the opposite policy. School attendance removed children from the household where they could have learned useful skills and contributed to the family's economic activities. Making matters worse, the government could only afford to send *empíricos* to rural schools. *Empíricos* were a category of teacher who lacked regular credentials. They had not attended a Normal School and were scarcely more educated than their pupils. Worse, they were usually ladino and tackled a difficult job for which they were unprepared: teaching indigenous rural students with scant support and supplies.[111]

Yet the authors of these new plans and programs lived in the capital city where only 7.8 percent of the population was indigenous in 1950. The indigenous citizen-to-be was a stranger, someone known through literature and legend. Despite victorious assertions of national unity that affirmed indigenous Guatemalans' full citizenship in the revolutionary government, chauvinism and misunderstanding endured. Take the words of Antonio Goubaud Carrera, an USAC professor of anthropology and the first director of the IIN: "*Indigenismo*, a word that seems as if it were of recent use, meant 'the protection of the indigenous' at the beginning of the colonial period ... [Now] *indigenismo* denotes a consciousness of social problems that ethnic aspects of indigeneity present, relative to western civilization ... the manifestation, the symptom, of a particular social unease." The gravest problem was how indigenous people lacked a national perspective, and spoke "strange languages," wore "fantastical costumes that set them apart from the rest of the population," were "tormented by beliefs that a simple drawing would eliminate" and "bound by technologies that date to thousands of years before."[112] The IIN's objectives were research and data collection. Its experts began by defining who was "an Indian."[113] Writer and San Carlista Luis Cardoza y Aragón observed in 1945, "The nation is Indian. This is the truth that first manifests itself with its enormous, subjugating, presence." "Yet we know," he continued, "that in Guatemala, as in the rest of America, it is the mestizo who possesses leadership throughout society. The mestizo: the middle class. The revolution of Guatemala is a revolution of the middle class . . . What an inferiority complex the Guatemalan suffers for his indian [*sic*] blood, for the indigenous character of his nation!"[114] In other words, to deliver the middle class—here a synonym for mestizo or ladino—revolution, urban professionals had to venture into the countryside to study the exalted past and teach the retrograde.

There was no bigger advocate of this type of university extension than President Arévalo's good friend, respected surgeon Dr. Carlos Martínez Durán. In August 1945, Martínez Durán was elected as the first rector of the autonomous university. He was a great admirer of John Locke, Max Scheler, Miguel de Unamuno, and José Martí, and when he could, he implemented their ideals at USAC. At his inauguration, he proudly proclaimed, "The student is the pueblo in the classroom!"[115] He famously said, "*Universitario*, this city belongs to you. Construct within her your talent, so that future generations can quench their thirst for knowledge here. May your academic life be sacred, fecund, and beautiful. Enter not into this city of the spirit without a well-proven love of truth."[116] Thus charged, AEU students went out into their city with their "sacred, fecund, and beautiful" intellects. Although these efforts were complex and mediated by regional and ethnic prejudices, to say nothing of students' inflated sense of duty, the university's gaze outward toward the pueblo outlasted the Ten Years' Spring. It became a treasured aspect of San Carlista student nationalism, sometimes referred to as "nation building" or "*hacer patria*."

Building the nation was, curiously, the theme of an homage to Francisca Fernández Hall, USAC's first female civil engineer, celebrated in July 1947. The event began with a speech from president of the Engineering Students' Union (AEI) Héctor David Torres about the role of women in Guatemalan society. He spoke, "women also build the nation, because *hacer patria* does not only mean to defend the nation on the field of battle, nor to attain the highest governmental appointments. *Hacer patria* is to educate the people . . . to acculturate oneself . . . to work loyally and honestly." Torres acknowledged that women did not currently have a place in national-level leadership, but "if they were capable of facing domestic life as a mother, wife, or sister, then they were capable of successfully confronting the intricate problems of science." Importantly, only two women were mentioned in the newspaper's reportage of the event: the woman elected beauty queen of the Engineering *facultad* and Fernández Hall herself. While the university's official *Boletín Universitario* detailed speeches delivered by men in honor of her, of Fernández Hall it reported only that she "expressed her gratitude" on behalf of all Guatemalan women.[117] Women remained marginal to the rising chorus of San Carlistas student nationalism, invoked as figures or objects who helped reinforce gendered understandings of valor and responsibility and, ultimately, political authority.

In the same issue of the *Boletín Universitario*, editors reminded their large readership that university extension was an integral part of national social reform.[118] They promoted the Faculty of Humanities' weekly radio show on TGW, which offered programs on topics as varied as government policy (income tax and agrarian reform), social concerns (consumerism, Guatemala's leading cause of death, and alcoholism), political rights (rights and responsibilities of the press and the Declaration of the Rights of Man in Guatemalan jurisprudence), and narrower topics like citizens' satisfaction with USAC and listeners' favorite Guatemalan writers. One program asked listeners whether they considered Guatemala one unified or many individual nations. Another contemplated the claim that man cannot live without philosophy.[119] The program projected the university as far into the pueblo as the Spanish language and radio signal could reach.

At this time, USAC also became involved in transnational academic exchanges. Free from Ubico's restrictions, the university soon relaunched its lively foreign exchange program and hosted scholars from across the Americas and Europe.[120] In 1950, USAC participated in the World Conference of Universities in Nice, France. The following year, AEU students attended the International Conference of Students in Sri Lanka (then Ceylon), where they met other students from around the world, including Liberia, Cuba, Morocco, Algeria, French West Africa, British East Africa, and England. It is not clear what came out of these travels. Certainly students had adventures and gained new pen pals and a sense of a global student experience. They also began to read a popular international student newspaper entitled *The Student* (not to be confused with the USAC newspaper of the same title). Notably, through the 1950s, San Carlistas traveled to socialist bloc countries, Western democracies, and colonial African nations. Certainly these travels expanded

San Carlistas' perception of the world, especially regarding the effects of U.S. and European imperialism. The imprint of these connections is evident in some anticolonial writings by San Carlistas, addressed in later chapters.

Martínez Durán also traveled widely. Surprisingly, since the Arévalo and Arbenz governments would soon become their sworn enemies, the U.S. State Department and UFCO hosted Martínez Durán for six weeks in 1948. After the visit, Martínez Durán published a multi-part essay about his travels in the *Boletín Unversitario*. The entourage toured Tulane University, the University of North Carolina, Duke University, American University, and Georgetown. According to the rector, they avoided political discussions. For Martínez Durán, the tour underscored two crucial differences between Guatemala and the United States: the large indigenous population and rural poverty. Upon his return, he reiterated the importance of national pride and asked San Carlistas to pay special attention to these unique problems. He planned to offer extension programs in the sciences, technology, philosophy, and art to elevate all Guatemalans. He lamented secondary schools students' poor preparation in the humanities as compared to the United States.[121]

Martínez Durán also emphasized the proper physical environment for learning. In an essay written for the *Boletín Universitario*, he imagined a University City where "the finest of honeys will be distilled from the nectar of the youth ... where life finds fulfillment, and the universal and the national, in a close embrace, will decide the destiny of Guatemala."[122] He envisioned faculty and students living together in a model city where they would be inspired by nearby mountain ranges and could forge new knowledge through neighborliness and sports rivalries.[123] In fact, the construction of a model University City was a regular theme in the *Boletín Universitario* for much of the mid-1940s, as USAC and other Latin American universities began to plan new campuses to promote students' mental and emotional development.[124] The first modest step, a residence hall, was completed in February 1951. According to a special feature story in the *Boletín Universitario*, the residence hall was intended to eliminate the "great enemies of San Carlistas": "malnourishment, dangerous living, and isolation."[125] Residents were treated to films, a lecture series, Saturday luncheons with prominent scholars, and a music library filled with Wagner and Chopin records. The residence hall also fostered USAC's first athletic teams. As advocates of "a sound mind in a healthy body," Congress heartily approved.[126]

The new Republic of Guatemala and USAC came of age together. From exile years later, Arévalo referred to these years as a period of "creole nationalist revolution," invoking nineteenth-century revolutions for independence from Spain and underscoring the revolution's racial character. Martínez Durán's plans for the university complemented Arévalo's efforts to make Guatemala a more fecund environment for the development of national culture.

A REPUBLIC OF SAN CARLISTAS

President Arévalo and Rector Martínez Durán envisioned reciprocal paths toward progress for the nation and the university. A close friendship paralleled their shared professional goals. But their terms ended in 1950, Arévalo's with the election of Colonel Jacobo Arbenz, and Martínez Durán's with the election of engineer Dr. Miguel Asturias Quiñonez.[127] From this moment, the paths of USAC and the Republic of Guatemala diverged. Asturias Quiñonez represented the many conservatives who were not enthusiastic about the Revolution's reforms and had continued to exercise influence through daily newspapers, businesses interests, and the Catholic Church during Arévalo's presidency. Arévalo had prioritized the university, but Arbenz focused elsewhere. Arbenz was a military man, not an educator. Arbenz was inspired by friendships with young Guatemalan communists, including *escuilach* Fortuny (who served as his speechwriter), Alfredo Guerra Borges, Victor Manuel Gutiérrez, Enrique Muñoz Meany, and Augusto Charnaud MacDonald. With them Arbenz read Marx, Lenin, and Stalin; national history; and agronomy in order to understand Guatemala's colonial past and structural inequality.[128] Some of these young men were San Carlistas, but their focus was on land reform and labor, not education.

The new president's study of agricultural history and contemporary agronomy helped him to draft a dramatic agrarian reform and significant public works projects. His agrarian reform expropriated and nationalized idle lands so that *campesinos* could plant and harvest food for sustenance. In turn, his public works projects focused on three large infrastructural developments: a major highway from the capital to Puerto Barrios to rival the North American–owned IRCA train line; the construction of a second port to solve the transport bottleneck caused by inadequate facilities at Puerto Barrios; and the construction of a hydroelectric plant to supplement the expensive and inadequate service provided by the U.S.-owned monopoly Empresa Eléctrica.[129] Arbenz's immediate aim was to promote industrialization while continuing to provide much-needed jobs for Guatemalans in agricultural and manufacturing sectors. He sought to connect Guatemalans to the world through investment in domestic communication and transportation networks. This was also practical, as the United States and the World Bank declined to invest in Guatemala's structural development after hearing of Arbenz's ties to communists. Taken together, the agrarian reform and public works projects undermined the longstanding economic power of North American businesses.

Unlike Arévalo, Arbenz was confrontational toward large landowners, especially UFCO. His programs reoriented Guatemala's rich natural resources to national improvement rather than foreign export by reforming domestic capital and investment. At the same time, his combined offering of land, credit, and literacy drew on a network of contacts between the city and the periphery that had not existed at the outset of Arévalo's presidency. As a result, while Arbenz's literacy program was characterized by less lofty rhetoric than Arévalo's, it may have reached more effectively into the lives of rural peasants.[130] USAC students had little to do with these programs for national development and structural change; instead, a diverse group of foreign intellectuals, Guatemalan intellectuals educated abroad, the International Bank for Reconstruction and Development (later the World Bank), and advisors from foreign businesses including Westinghouse advised Arbenz.[131]

For his part, Asturias Quiñonez did not mind being left out. He did not share Martínez Durán's commitment to civic humanism.[132] Nor did he imagine an active role for the university in the lives of its students, much less in the direction of the nation. Instead, he prioritized the return of lost prestige to USAC and focused on the classroom rather than the world outside. To do so, he courted the support of professionals who had earned degrees from the National University in the Ubico era. Like Asturias Quiñonez, they argued that politics were a distraction to the true academic. Many of them were worried about their alma mater's declining prestige as more and more Guatemalans had attained the prerequisites to attend USAC.[133]

As I have mentioned already, daily newspapers had long debated the appropriate role for USAC and respected academics of diverse political orientations argued for an apolitical university. But by the time Asturias Quiñonez was elected, apoliticism had become a keyword in anticommunist and other conservative students' political vocabularies. They argued that social transformation was simply not their responsibility; worse, it was a communist ruse. Around the same time, the Revolution's most ardent supporters within the university had turned to national politics rather than university administration. Most of the *escuilaches* and their peers had graduated or left USAC to work. This allowed more conservative San Carlistas to shape university governance and student organizations in the early 1950s. A small group of anti-Arbenz, anticommunist students whose influence far exceeded their small numbers stepped into the void. More and more, they denounced the Arbenz government and called for another revolution to wrest Guatemala from the communists' grip. They were called the Committee of Anticommunist University Students (CEUA).

What explains this rising antagonism toward the revolutionary governments, if students were filling the ranks of the nation's growing bureaucracy and enjoying greater responsibility, reputation, and intellectual freedom than they had enjoyed in many decades? For one, the U.S. foreign policy shift from containment to intervention against communism profoundly divided the globe and contributed to a sense of looming danger that was unmistakable in students' publications across the political spectrum. Second, Guatemala's national political scene grew increasingly fractured. In the middle of the Cold War, Arbenz publicly cultivated close friendships with known communists. Meanwhile, the military held on to significant power. Aside from the sixty or so commanders who were dismissed after the October 20 uprising, Ubico's military survived the revolution intact. In fact, fearing another revolt, the 1945 Constitutional Assembly had voted to protect the military as an autonomous entity alongside the executive, judicial, and legislative branches. Finally, Arbenz's 1952 Agrarian Reform presented a real challenge to the interests of coffee barons and *latifundio* landlords. Even though it stopped short of remaking the nation's agrarian structure, it threatened powerful economic interests at home in Guatemala and abroad.

In response to these threats to their influence, military and economic elites, and even influential lawyers, bankers, and journalists, began to look for a political opening.[134] As Greg Grandin has argued, local concerns and global ideologies transformed "an institutional defense of hierarchical privilege into a more contrived ideology confected from component parts of radical Catholicism, martial nationalism, and patriarchal allegiance."[135] The fullest expression of this contrived ideology would take decades to develop, but its roots lay in the anticommunist rumblings of the early 1950s. Possible only in a particular economic conjuncture of prosperity and the invigoration of democratic ideals offered by the revolution, anticommunism imagined Guatemala poised on the edge of a long fall into Soviet hands. As early as

1950, internal factors fused with external factors to mobilize anti-Arbenz sentiment on campus.

San Carlista unity was aggravated by an additional factor. As I wrote in the introduction, in the eleven years between 1943 and 1954, the number of enrollments increased more than 450 percent. In a single year between 1950 and 1951, university enrollments grew 19 percent, from 2,373 to 2,824 students.[136] This rapid growth taxed the university infrastructure and created overcrowded classrooms and registration bottlenecks. Greater enrollment reflected the presence of some less elite students at the university. Of course, this was Arévalo's objective when he expanded the public school system, but in practice the widened enrollments challenged some San Carlistas' egalitarian idealizations. Suddenly, San Carlistas found themselves sharing classrooms with strangers, not just familiar *compañeros* from the capital city's few elite high schools.

These changes created a charged atmosphere for social debate and disagreement. The student-authored editorials, memoirs, and reportage discussed in this chapter and the next suggest that political fracture at the university was precisely the product of the atmosphere of free thinking that the revolution had affirmed was so important to the democratic project. At the same time, San Carlistas' involvement in statecraft during the Ten Years' Spring demanded a certain investment in democratic fitness that upheld students and faculty as democracy's defenders as it excluded people who were uneducated—an exclusion that, as I have shown above, especially affected indigenous people. Student nationalism championed individual rights, civil freedoms, and electoral democracy for the educated elite while the indigenous majority awaited democratic tutelage. Surely not all students and faculty shared these beliefs, but they were common enough to make the San Carlista a coherent political and social subject. In other words, the identities of these urban intellectuals were far from self-evident or a priori; instead, they were formed in dialogue with national debates about the meaning of the nation and of democracy. As Victoria Langland has noted in Brazil, university students negotiated difficult and conflicting identities as intellectual elites in peripheral places.[137] The identifier San Carlista became a palimpsest of the institution's celebrated colonial past, the glory of the revolution, and ongoing debates over the meaning of democracy. It reflected a social consciousness built on a raced and classed definition of citizenship.

Clearly, the revolution's consequences at the university were manifold. During the Ten Years' Spring, university enrollments soared and the ranks of the urban bureaucracy expanded. Professors were no longer anonymous workers and students were no longer mass-manufactured products of Ubico's factory of professionals, lacking collegiality and responsibility. As one student journalist wrote in an essay published in the *Boletín Universitario* in observance of the anniversary of the revolution, "For many years, the word *'universitario'* was used exclusively to denote students and teachers. The graduate was the *'egresado,'* the professional who was submerged in the hustle and bustle of his career and who more or less lost his connection to the Alma Mater."[138] The revolution required more of San Carlistas. The journalist continued, "the word *'egresado'* has been banished from the lexicon of the university . . . the professional does not 'graduate' from the university but instead enters . . . the Professional *Colegio.*"[139] As part of the *colegio*, the San Carlista remained tied to USAC by service commitments and licensure requirements.

The revolution also obliged San Carlistas to build new relationships with the pueblo. No longer mindless products of a "decadent factory of professionals," San Carlistas were to be conscientious leaders who would make the pueblo (understood to be mostly rural, indigenous, and illiterate) fit for self-government. In 1945, Congress considered that "one of the most legitimate longings of the nation's intellectuals has been the organization of a National University" framed by the "nation's own authentic culture" and the community's expectations.[140] Their efforts had mixed results for recipients—remember the stagnant national literacy rates between 1940 and 1950 and the shortcomings of the *empíricos*—but they were generative for San Carlistas.

This chapter has encountered students in a singularly transformative moment when they had come to call themselves San Carlistas and articulate a social consciousness that relied upon raced and gendered difference as conditions of possibility for the formation of a republic. This history is significant, for we know little about the historical processes by which powerful urban, middle-class ladino identities were recognized, resisted, or welcomed.[141] *This City Belongs to You* argues that the contested relationship between students, the university, and the Guatemalan and U.S. governments shaped what it meant to be an urban middle-class ladino, largely through the loose consensus around principles of liberalism and the responsibility of students to lead the nation. Students became state makers, and student nationalism was the spirit of the law.

By the early 1950s, the student had become a coherent and powerful political, social, and economic identity. It was so coherent, and so powerful, that it buttressed one of the U.S. government's most successful campaigns in its war on communism in the Western Hemisphere, the overthrow of Arbenz. When San Carlista cohesion did begin to fracture, it did so precisely along the fault lines of individual rights and free market capitalism, which articulated with status anxiety and racial ambivalence as Guatemalan urban middle-class sectors revitalized conservative social and political thought in the context of the global Cold War. In the early 1950s, anticommunist students emerged from this growing dissensus and took up the mantle of democracy's true defenders, using the language of liberal democracy.

In fact, the revolutionary Ten Years' Spring gave the young anticommunists their most convincing rallying cry: "Dios, Patria y Libertad." Under the Ubico dictatorship, "patria" and "libertad" were weak calls to action. But populist nationalism and the cultural and economic reforms of the Arévalo and Arbenz governments breathed life into Fatherland and freedom. Of course, when young anticommunists of the CEUA cheered "Dios, Patria y Libertad," they had a different national project in mind.

TWO

_____

Showcase for Democracy, 1953–1957

Dios—Patria—Libertad

God, Fatherland, and Freedom

> *Slogan of anticommunist students*
> *and the Armas regime*

Adiós—Patria—Libertad

Goodbye, Fatherland and Freedom

> *Banners at the Huelga de Dolores, 1955*

WHILE MEMBERS OF THE COMMITTEE of Anticommunist University Students (CEUA) cheered "Dios, Patria y Libertad," students at the 1955 Huelga de Dolores waved a different banner: "Adiós, Patria y Libertad." The students bade a scathing farewell to the free and democratic nation constructed during the Ten Years' Spring (1944–1954). In fact, this turn of events had been foretold in the previous year's celebration. The 1954 *No Nos Tientes* featured a playful editorial entitled "An Open Letter to Close-Minded Readers." It read, "We Guatemalans have had frankly wretched luck throughout history: for many decades a group of patriots . . . have handed us over to the gringos so that they could steal banana[s]." But the other agents of imperial expansion, the Soviets, were equally problematic. The editorial continued, "now what is happening is that we want to throw away the sickle even if it's with the hammer, thanks to our sorry luck to be the chosen victims of such foreign-looking, always purgative, leaders." In such a situation, they wrote, "the only one who is not gripped by this idiocy is the student."[1]

In the early years of the revolutionary governments, San Carlistas had been bureaucrats-in-training who worked with the government to build a better nation. But the university, its students, and the meaning of the middle class had begun to change. By the mid-1950s, only San Carlistas could be trusted to resist advances made by Yankee and Soviet imperialists who sought to exploit Guatemala's vulnerability and value. An elaborate float in the satirical parade (*desfile bufo*) also reflected this belief. It depicted Guatemala as an indigenous woman in traditional *huipil*. Two suitors, "Soviet Paradise" and "North American gold," flirted while Guatemala moved listlessly between them.[2] While the float explicitly critiqued the exploitative politics of neocolonialism, it implicitly disdained women's subservience. Perhaps unintentionally, it revealed how gender, race, and class shaped San Carlistas' understandings of political authority. Feminized and indigenous Guatemala was acquiescent to the desires of masculine global superpowers. Again, only San Carlistas could see the risk.

A few months after this float appeared, the anticommunist Liberation Forces of Colonel Carlos Castillo Armas invaded from Tegucigalpa, Honduras, and quickly defeated the Guatemalan military.[3] President Jacobo Arbenz resigned on June 27, 1954, and with that, the Ten Years' Spring abruptly ended. Castillo Armas became interim president. Many Arbenz supporters fled to Mexico City; some returned to the same communities they had left after Ubico was overthrown.[4]

This chapter addresses the changing relationship between university students and the Castillo Armas regime. It traces the impact of these changes on political culture in Guatemala City, especially highlighting the emergence of Catholic anticommunist students as an important political force. Though their numbers were relatively small, anticommunist students were disproportionately influential. They are important, too, for how they challenge our assumptions about student militants and provide an ampler perspective on the issues and anxieties that propelled student activism.[5]

Though only a fraction of San Carlistas supported him, early in his presidency, Castillo Armas and his advisors met with students and professors of all political inclinations in an attempt to preserve a warm relationship with the *universitarios*. To fight the specter of communism, much feared and lingering just on the edges of the Guatemalan nation-state, peeking through the pages of university students' books, and hiding in workers' hearts, the Castillo Armas regime combined firm anticommunist policies with friendly gestures toward the university and workers' groups. Only with the May Day and June 1956 protests did the relationship between the government and USAC become intractably antagonistic.

USAC remained the only institution of higher education in Guatemala until 1961. This meant that San Carlistas were not merely a portion of the middle class; rather, the route to the exercise of the professions necessarily passed through USAC. University study also generated some social meaning for that preparation and labor, and created opportunities for certain friend-ships and rivalries.[6] In the revolutionary decade, to be a San Carlista meant to be a valued expert and proto-bureaucrat. Commitment to Central American unity, sovereignty, democracy over fascism, the secularization of the state, liberalization of social life, and social welfare programs became the *universitarios'* legacy. During the Castillo Armas regime, democratic guardianship justified growing antagonism toward the government. San Carlistas expressed this in terms of freedoms, rights, and responsibilities. Free market capitalism, personal property rights, and political freedoms, guided both pro–Castillo Armas anticommunist students and pro-Arbenz students. Other principles, like civil freedoms, constitutionality, and electoral democracy bolstered groups who opposed Castillo Armas's regime. These growing ideological fis-sures were aggravated by Cold War internationalism and the political and cultural influence of the United States.

The university splintered in the years between the counterrevolution and the beginning of the civil war. Some San Carlistas argued that it was their duty as *universitarios* to protect the 1945 Constitution; others asserted that the fight for justice required the defeat of communism; still others sought a return to apoliticism and the elimination of the role of the university in national political life and, in return, politics in university life. The social role and meaning of "San Carlista" shifted from proto-bureaucrat to state antago-nist in these years. This chapter follows a series of events that provoked this shift. It emphasizes internal factors that enabled the rise of anticommunism and, later, the cohesion of the political left and right.

In fact, the period defies our understandings of the left and the right, in part because these terms attained their contemporary meaning in these years. This brief but complex moment between the counterrevolution and the beginning of the civil war usually appears as either the tragic postscript to the revolution or the telling prequel to the civil war. Furthermore, most of the scholarship about the end of the revolution was written in the midst of the civil war. At that moment, it was difficult to see Castillo Armas's coup as anything but the beginning of many decades of military rule. Historians paid a preponderance of attention to U.S. economic and political intervention, implicating the United States in the Central American civil wars and their aftermaths.[7] But this focus also permitted an erroneous view of Guatemalans as passive, disorganized, capricious, or even self-interested dupes.

The rich counterrevolutionary archive quickly belies these depictions. Complex internal and external factors, especially region, race, land ownership, and education enabled the success of Castillo Armas's disorganized motley crew of Cold Warriors.[8] In order to explain this change, this chapter begins with a discussion of the *Plan de Tegucigalpa*, a student-authored anticommunist plan for government written by the CEUA in late 1953 that would become the foundation of Castillo Armas's 1956 Constitution. For around nine months, CEUA students carried out counterinsurgency propaganda plans devised for them by agents in a CIA field office, spreading leaflets and painting graffiti in an effort to win over the hearts and minds of the pueblo. These middle-class anticommunist students "functioned as a broker between the upper echelons, both domestic and foreign, of reaction and the street thugs and paramilitary forces responsible for some of the worst acts of counterrevolutionary terror."[9] Some, like Lionel Sisniega Otero, transmitted the anticommunism of the upper echelons as a broadcaster for Radio Liberación. Many later joined the military, business leaders, and the Catholic Church to form the National Democratic Movement (Movimiento Democrático Nacional [MDN]) Party. Importantly, even this agonistic brokerage reinforced the social role of the middle class as thought leaders.

In 1955, the U.S. State Department observed, "Guatemala's middle and 'intellectual' classes from the beginning have been deeply and emotionally committed to maintaining the political freedoms, social reforms, and feeling of nationality for which they fought in the 1944 Revolution."[10] This emotional commitment was apparent among the editors of USAC's most widely read student newspaper, *El Estudiante*. An editorial entitled "University and Pueblo" from the June 9, 1955, edition pledged, "Today's struggle was yesterday's struggle and will be the struggle forever, if [the University] is to act with the decency and honesty that the Nation desires." It continued, "The nobility of spirit and the moral respectability that were constant in the youth of the past should be the same virtues that inspire the actions of the students of today. The sacrifices made in a not-distant moment will be lost if the youth of today do not raise the pristine flags bequeathed to them by the students of the past."[11] Less than a year after the counterrevolution, student journalists reminded their classmates of their revolutionary duty to the pueblo.

A year later, protests in May and June 1956 sowed the seeds of the popular movement. I discuss the effects of these protests, weighing newspaper coverage, government decrees, and student-authored press releases.[12] Growing numbers of San Carlistas viewed the Castillo Armas regime as morally bankrupt and asserted that they were duty-bound to fight for the pueblo. After Castillo Armas prohibited trade unions and political parties, the university became one of the few remaining spaces for opposition. The regime came to see USAC and its students as a threat. The chapter concludes by revisiting the ongoing public debate over the appropriate role of the university in national political life. By the time Castillo Armas was assassinated in 1957, Guatemala's "showcase for democracy" had dissolved into States of Alarm and Emergency and political violence.[13] Student nationalism was marked by its oppositional relationship to the state.

ANTICOMMUNIST STUDENTS AS STATE MAKERS

Ever vigilant against communism in the Western Hemisphere, U.S. intelligence officers quickly identified the small ranks of the CEUA as an asset.[14] An intelligence officer from the CIA field office (codenamed "LINCOLN") approached a CEUA member in Guatemala City shortly after the group's formation. At the time, the group counted around just fifty members, but their anticommunist spirit was exuberant, unlike "the cynical politics of [General Miguel] Ydígoras and Castillo Armas."[15] The plan was to intimidate government officials and create the impression of a broad antigovernment movement. For months, CIA staffers spent hours imagining projects for the students to carry out. The CEUA's first action took place on September 15, 1953, when they pasted 106,000 anticommunist stickers on buses and trains. Later CEUA students marked government officials' homes with signs reading "A Communist Lives Here" and sent fake funeral notices to President Jacobo Arbenz and José Manuel Fortuny. One poster that appeared in the capital city read, "*Guatemalteco*: On the day of the Liberation, those who aid Arbenz WILL DIE! Those who support the Patriotic Resistance will fight and WILL LIVE for a better Guatemala! The great day is coming! Choose!"[16] The CIA transmitted publications for the students to distribute and students interrupted public meetings to do so.

With the help of an organization of anticommunist market women, the CEUA distributed thousands of copies of Archbishop Mariano Rossell y Arellano's anticommunist pastoral letter. They sponsored a radio program until April 1954, when armed men invaded the station mid-program and beat the student broadcasters.[17] The infamous "32 Marking Campaign" had students paint the number 32 in public places throughout the capital, and on buses and trains bound for the city. This was in reference to Article 32 of the Constitution, which outlawed foreign political parties. According to CIA

FIGURE 3. Lionel Sisniega Otero and Mario López Villatoro broadcasting for Radio de la Liberación, Chiquimula, 1954. Photograph by Alejandro Guzmán. Fototeca Guatemala, Centro de Investigaciones Regionales de Mesoamérica (CIRMA).

operative Jerome C. Dunbar, "The aim is to create suspense and interest among those who do not know the meaning, and to induce conversation about the symbol."[18] The students' success can be deduced from the reaction they elicited from the Arbenz government (growing numbers of arrests and exiles) and from the support they received from prominent Catholics (the archbishop and the market women's organization).

Many of these covert missions required students to take great risks. By May 1954, the CEUA's membership dwindled. Many militant students had been arrested and some even exiled.[19] There was a debate, too, within the CIA field office as to the efficacy of the projects that engaged in philosophical debates with communism. They were better off, some agents argued, "[creating] dissension, confusion, and FEAR in the enemy camp."[20] For their part, the CEUA students began to critique the propaganda they were asked to distribute. They purportedly found it too divisive and began to suspect that they were being used to bait the Arbenz government into using repressive tactics. By May 26, 1954, ten CEUA students were in jail, no new students had been recruited, and others refused to work.

In fact, the growing counterrevolution no longer relied on covert propaganda operations. A plan for military invasion was underway, led by Castillo Armas and troops of exiled anticommunists. Since Arbenz's election, student exiles gathered in Tegucigalpa, Honduras, and San Salvador, El Salvador where they joined two groups, the Committee of Guatemalan Anticommunist University Students in Exile (CEUAGE) and the Anticommunist Front of Guatemalans in Exile (FAGE). In June 1953, a few months before the CEUA's first public action, the CEUAGE began to publish its *Bulletin of the Committee of Guatemalan Anticommunist University Students in Exile* in order to connect exiled anticommunists throughout the hemisphere. The paper was printed at a shop in Tegucigalpa called Talleres La República and edited by Cosme Viscovich Palomo, Mario López Villatoro (secretary of relations), and Lionel Sisniega Otero (CEUA general secretary).[21] In the pages of the *Bulletin,* Catholic anticommunists shared their conviction that Arbenz had imperiled the nation and its citizens' natural rights. They charged that he had violated the Constitution by forcing them into exile and censuring their political meetings. They called the students, faculty, and administrators who supported Arbenz communist dupes and wrote that the Association of University Students (AEU) was filled with liars. From exile, the CEUAGE pledged to be "a strong nucleus of men imbued with the feelings of Nation, Home, Religion, and Liberty, who [would] try to win for their pueblo the conquest of real democracy."[22] This conquest would demand "great sacrifices, painful work, enormous doses of civic will, a lot of patriotism and honor and more honor."[23] In no uncertain terms, the CEUA's promise evoked the responsibilities of student nationalism.

The group debuted its *Plan de Tegucigalpa* in the Christmas Eve edition of the *Bulletin.* It circulated quickly in a pamphlet. The U.S. Library of Congress catalogued one copy before the end of the year. In March 1954, some students traveled to Caracas to present the plan at the Tenth Inter-American Conference.[24] The *Plan's* focus on education reflected the interests of its authors, who were all students and young professionals. In many ways, its educational ideals were not so different from those of the Revolution. Echoing the neo-Lamarckism that informed *indigenismo* in previous decades, the CEUA prioritized building strength of character. Guatemalan youth "marched blindly" because of a defective educational system. Their personalities were undeveloped, demonstrated by "the skittishness, the fickle spirit, the instability of purpose, the inconsistency of moral values, [and] the lack of constancy in the achievement of the highest ideals."[25] The *Plan* remedied this by providing an education that attended to the growth of the personality as much as the intellect. It included free and mandatory primary education, a literacy campaign, art schools, and centers for rural instruction. Under the *Plan*, the purpose of the university was to "enlighten" and "restore" the pueblo of Guatemala, complementing the government's role as moral guide.[26] Again, this was quite like the role of the university in the revolutionary governments.

There were some marked departures from the Revolution's educational philosophy. A long section entitled "University Autonomy" proposed a budget that eliminated university fundraising from the manufacture and sale of liquor (a significant source of income, especially during the Huelga de Dolores). For the moral compass of anticommunist San Carlistas, it was "a great contradiction that, to a large extent, our greatest cultural institution lives on death." They added that a basic function of the university ought to be to "combat, by all means at its disposal, the destruction of the alcoholic scourge . . . a prelude to crime and prostitution, determinant factor in vagrancy and misery and an imponderable burden on society."[27] Under the *Plan*, the government of Guatemala would become a representative democracy led by the Social Doctrine of the Catholic Church. This resonated with the platform of the Movimiento Estudiantil Profesional (MEP) nearby in Mexico, established by the Episcopate and Mexican Catholic Action between 1945 and 1947.[28] CEUA students likely met the MEP at one of the many anticommunist congresses held throughout the region, perhaps at the Congreso Contra la Intervención Soviética en América Latina, held in Mexico City at the end of May 1954 and advertised on the cover of the *Boletín*.

Like their peers who had helped to draft the 1945 Constitution, CEUA students were concerned about Guatemala's large indigenous population. The *Plan* called for a "government of the pueblo, by the pueblo, for the pueblo" and "attendant to the idiosyncrasies of Guatemala."[29] Like newspaper editors a decade earlier, the CEUA explained how centuries of repression had left indigenous communities "isolated, fearful, distrustful, and suspicious of the ladinos." As a result, the nation formed into two distinct societies, preventing the construction of a "healthy and organically capable pueblo."[30] The CEUA students explained:

> For centuries, for the entire History of Guatemala, there has been a foolish zeal among the men of the government to undervalue the autochthonous, the

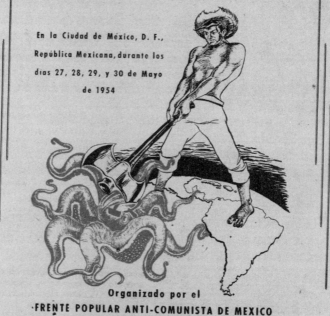

FIGURE 4. Cover of the *Boletín del CEUAGE*, May 22, 1954. Collection of Lionel Sisniega Otero. Archivo Histórico, Centro de Investigaciones Regionales de Mesoamérica (CIRMA).

traditional [*típico*], that which is our essence—the very soul of the Nation—in exchange for ideas and systems that are hardly compatible with the peculiarities of the environment, obliging Guatemala's people to take erroneous routes that, disfiguring the physiognomy of the pueblo, have prevented her from standing up in front before the world and proclaiming aloud: "This is Guatemala."[31]

Instead of celebrating Guatemala's indigenous culture, most statesmen had championed foreign ideas at the pueblo's expense. The toll was exacted upon the very physical body of the nation, disfiguring the body politic by forsaking its indigenous essence. In other words, national unity was necessary for progress and the fight against communism. Only once foreign ideologies had been expunged could Guatemala be herself. The CEUA wrote, "now is the time for us to stop being vessels for imported thoughts, for strange forms and exotic ideologies ... we remember that we are Guatemalans, and that, with mighty national sentiment, founded in the true presence of the fusing [of] *indios* and ladinos, Guatemala stands tall [and] will follow its path." Whether a sincere or strategic appeal, the students sought an authentic nationalism that was "[n]either the extreme right nor the extreme left [but rather] the heart of Guatemala."[32]

Guatemala, a nation figured as female, was the progeny of the indigenous and the ladino. In kaleidoscopic language reminiscent of Mexican pedagogue José Vasconcelos's cosmic race, the CEUA students went on to predict, "like the sexes, the two halves of one destiny will come together to generate the future, and then, the genius of the Guatemalan people will shine." Then, the students added, "Guatemala will be herself."[33] The *Plan* detailed specialized institutions for guidance in "cultural, social, and economic improvement" in order to develop "what [the *indios*] have that is useful."[34] It offered an education system with curriculum taught by indigenous teachers, attentive to the needs and customs of each region.[35] Educational centers (*colonias escolares*) would be built to increase access to education for indigenous communities.[36] The autonomous university was protected under the *Plan*, for without it, "scientific speculation stagnates, spiritual disquiet goes up in smoke, and the founts of knowledge and desire for knowledge run dry." Only USAC could confer degrees and the doors to the university would be open to anyone who could fulfill the prerequisites of enrollment, "regardless of sex, color, nationality, citizenship, political or religious creed, and economic or social position."[37] Whether ladino or indigenous, the *Plan* affirmed each citizen's right to education alongside their responsibility to seek self-improvement. In sum, its education reforms were moderate.

The *Plan*'s land reforms were also moderate. The *Plan* rejected the land expropriations of Arbenz's Agrarian Reform and proposed that the seized property be returned to its previous owners. But it also advocated what the CEUA called a "humanized" version of the modern trade system with fixed minimum export prices, greater domestic investment in industrialized agriculture, and the provision of low-interest loans for campesinos. This would increase the number of landowners while avoiding "the *minifundio* trap," because, the CEUA claimed, maximizing private property was the most effective way to generate wealth as well as "the most just way to achieve the primary aims of life."[38] For the CEUA, the primary aims of life were national economic productivity and individual material advancement. Finally, the *Plan* returned property rights to the Catholic Church and permitted religious instruction in public schools.[39]

As I mentioned above, a small Army of the Liberation invaded from Honduras under the command of Castillo Armas in June 1954, dealing the final blow to the Arbenz government after months of covert propaganda campaigns and diplomatic and economic isolation. On June 27, Arbenz announced his resignation on the national radio station TGW. He began: "We all know how they have bombed and bombarded cities, sacrificing women, children, the elderly, and defenseless citizens. We all know the viciousness with which they have assassinated representatives of the workers and campesinos in the communities that they have occupied." After reinforcing gendered, raced, and aged ideas of victimhood, he identified the vicious assailant as "North American mercenaries." He explicitly denounced how the opposition used communism as a pretext to avenge "the financial interests of the *frutera* [United Fruit Company] and . . . other North American monopolies" that were threatened by the Agrarian Reform. Arbenz went on to outline the role of the United States in the invasion and the treason of Castillo Armas, and then he ceded his presidential powers to Colonel Carlos Enrique Díaz of the armed forces. The counterrevolution had won. Supporters of the revolutionary government, including many students, labor organizers, and, famously, Che Guevara, sought refuge in the embassies of Argentina and Mexico until the governments of Juan Perón and Adolfo Ruiz Cortines assured their safe passage. Many San Carlistas, including Luis Cardoza y Aragón, Manuel Colom Argueta, Adolfo Mijangos López, and Francisco Villagrán Kramer, went into exile.[40]

Like the revolutionaries in 1944, the counterrevolutionaries rewarded their university-based supporters with positions in the government. Some older CEUA students held positions in the presidential secretariat, including the offices of secretary general of the president (Ricardo Quiñonez), private secretary (Carlos Recinos), and secretary of publicity and propaganda (Luis Coronado Lira). Young CEUA leaders Mario Sandoval Alarcón and Lionel Sisniega Otero served in junior positions in the president's cabinet. Other CEUA students worked in ministries of the Interior, Public Health, and Public Education, and the Foreign Ministry. Jorge Skinner Klee led the Constituent Assembly and José Torón Barrios directed TGW, the national radio station.[41]

For some time, Castillo Armas ruled with this close coterie of advisors and without a constitution. He planned to delay the constitutional assembly until he ridded the nation of communists, but by June 1955, the public demanded constitutional rule. Capital city newspapers reported unrest, a petition from the professional lawyers' association, and even a campaign launched by the newspapers themselves. The delayed constitution suggested to some that the democratic tide was changing and that the rights won during the revolution were at risk. The Guatemalan people had become used to constitutional rule after a decade of democratic governance. On the anniversary of the victory of the counterrevolution, Castillo Armas announced that a new constitution would go into effect the following March.[42]

The 1956 Constitution formalized the ideological influence of the CEUA on the counterrevolution, as it adopted many of the principles of the *Plan de Tegucigalpa*: the promotion of the nation's economic activity through the citizen's obligation to contribute "to the progress and social well-being of the nation through work," the state's responsibility to maintain "harmony between capital and labor," and the promotion of credit for small-scale farmers. It differed from the *Plan* on education and foreign capital. Where the *Plan* argued that national progress would come through access to education with expanded private land ownership, the Constitution deemphasized education and invited foreign capital. The 1956 Constitution also broke the monopoly that USAC held on higher education by permitting the creation of private universities.[43]

On campus, pro-Arbenz and pro-Castillo Armas students continued the long-running debate over the role of the university in national politics. In this iteration, the debate centered on three key issues: the new Constitution, the return of exiled professors and students, and Archbishop Rossell y

Arellano's annual denunciation of the Huelga de Dolores (he spoke out against the Huelga nearly every year of his long tenure from 1938–1962). Pro-Castillo Armas students claimed that partisan or sectarian commitments would inhibit objective study and investigation. They equated apoliticism with university autonomy because politics were not the purpose of the university. Arbencistas, on the other hand, drew on the language of the 1945 Constitution and insisted that their education entailed a responsibility to participate in politics.

The Faculty of Law's newspaper *El Estudiante* quickly became identified with the Arbencista position. On the day that the new Constitution went into effect, *El Estudiante* editors dismissed it as an attempt by "the usurping government of the Liberation" to legalize "the most revolting betrayal and the most violent insult that it has inflicted on Guatemala." Editor Jorge Mario García and his colleagues affirmed, "It is on this date when, with the most absolute responsibility to which we are obliged, from our triple condition as journalists, students, and young people, [we] raise the following concerns to the people of the nation . . . constitutional order . . . the invasion of national territory . . . and de facto government."[44] The social responsibility demanded by student nationalism justified their opposition. The editors emphasized their responsibility to speak out in defense of national sovereignty, a duty to which they were bound because of their profession, their status as San Carlistas, and their youth. Other students opposed the new Constitution for its parsimonious funding of the university. The Constitution of 1945 had explicitly stated that the percentage of the national budget allotted for the university would be evaluated each year and adjusted according to the university's needs. The new Constitution fixed the amount at 2 percent regardless of the institution's growth.[45] To some, this seemed to be another maneuver intended to limit the university's impact on national life.[46]

The moderate *Boletín Universitario* also opposed the budget, on the grounds that it compromised the purpose of the university. Its editors wrote, "Over time and contrary to whatever is said about her, it has remained open to the people and its activities have washed over the pueblo that sustains it . . . [USAC] does not only impart knowledge to groups of students, but surpasses its walls and extends into the collectivity . . . within the University of San Carlos of Guatemala, there is an elevated social sense, which translates into action and teaching . . . But with economic limitations, we can only aspire to be yet another campus of higher learning."[47] The editorial made a case for greater funding for the university on the grounds that it inspired the com-

FIGURE 5. Carlos Castillo Armas visiting the new University City in September 1954. Archive of *El Imparcial*. Fototeca Guatemala, Centro de Investigaciones Regionales de Mesoamérica (CIRMA).

munity to self-improvement. It concluded by stating, "A University with a big budget will be every day more a University of the people." Ironically, this argument seems the least likely to win over those who wished to limit the university's influence.

Increasingly, to insist on a role for the university in national political life was to challenge the regime. Even U.S. intelligence understood this. According to U.S. State Department reports in 1955, "exaggerated nationalism with anti-U.S. overtones" was the most significant threat to the regime.[48] The same reports identified the Democratic University Front (Frente Universitario Democrático [FUD]) and *El Estudiante* as antigovernment and alleged that they aimed to promote strikes against Castillo Armas.[49] The U.S. State Department cautioned that students' petitions and protests might be the first intimations of a coming revolution. Agents warned that citizens might revolt once they learned that "we [the State Department] called the plays on domestic political matters."[50] Of course, many San Carlistas already knew that the United States played a decisive role in domestic politics. For the moment, though, they were focused on the new Constitution and the return of their classmates and professors from exile. A wave of expulsions after the counterrevolution had gutted the university of many prominent scholars, including student leaders from the FUD and professors who had been officials or advisors in the Arévalo and Arbenz governments.[51] In his effort to win over university sectors, Castillo Armas met with the AEU and AED in early 1956 to discuss the exiles' status. Perhaps advised by the United States to calm dissent, the president permitted their return.

But in April, two incidents surrounding the annual Huelga de Dolores put students on the defensive once more. First, Archbishop Rossell y Arellano led yet another vigorous campaign among capital city Catholics to excommunicate all Huelga participants and observers. He railed against the licentiousness that seized the capital during the Huelga, especially the abundant alcohol consumption and cross-dressing among parade participants. He wrote, "In a democracy . . . a fundamental mission of all institutions and preferably the whole public is to fight for the cultural and ethical improvement of everyone . . . cultural festivals are worthless when public manifestations of vulgarity are tolerated."[52] Students' licentiousness outweighed the value of their tradition. Still attempting court *universitarios*, Castillo Armas actually defended the students' parade. He offered to personally mend the relationship between the Church and USAC, despite his dependence on capital city Catholics and his friendship with the archbishop. The second incident proved harder to repair. In the middle of the Friday afternoon *desfile bufo*, a bomb exploded in the crowd. General Director of the National Police José Bernabé Linares reported that the police were unable to track down the perpetrators because of a personnel shortage. The case went unsolved.[53] Most student groups, with the exception of the AED, had been in support of reconciliation with the president. But the bombing set people on edge as International Workers' Day approached.[54]

INTERNATIONAL WORKERS' DAY, 1956

Trade unions were outlawed by the new Constitution, leaving student organizations among the few popular groups that could legally demonstrate on International Workers' Day. But thousands of people attended the protests anyway. A handful of unions boldly created floats and banners. The most audacious float belonged to the National Workers' Union of the Guatemalan Social Security Institute (Sindicato Nacional de Trabajadores del Instituto Guatemalteco de Seguridad Social [STIGSS]). The float depicted a worker in chains, under which was painted a series of figures about the egregious condition of workers in Guatemala, including the phrase: "We are regressing to 1935." Another side of the float read: "We demand the repeal of 570 and 584 as deleterious to the right to unionize."[55] Decree 570 was the most comprehensive overhaul of the revolutionary governments' Labor Code. Decree 584 eliminated public workers' right to strike and unionize. Together they reduced the legal recourse available to workers in arbitration against domestic- and foreign-owned businesses.[56]

One group who identified themselves as campesinos from the farm "El Tesoro" in Santa Elena Barrillas carried progovernment signs in the parade. Observers quickly noted how their signs contained none of the orthographic errors that one would expect from rural workers with limited literacy. It seemed likely that they had not written the signs at all; perhaps they were even misinformed about what the signs said. When the group passed Cine Lux on Sexta Avenida, some observers heckled them, calling them dupes. A few blocks later, a mob attacked the campesinos and destroyed their signs. The police responded with force.[57] In another incident, three students, Edmundo Guerra Thelheimer (of the *Facultad* of Law), Fernando Arias Blois (of Engineering), and a Humanities student and well-known painter, Dagoberto Vasquez, were arrested for shouting antigovernment slogans and making slanderous remarks against Castillo Armas. They had apparently yelled "Death to the Liberation!" during the march. Around midnight, agents in civilian clothes and one uniformed lieutenant forcibly entered Arias Blois's house. The young men were taken to a nearby police station without explanation and interrogated the following morning. In an irony so common in Guatemala's small and tight-knit professional class, the students' interrogator was Edmundo Sagastume, one of Thelheimer's law professors and legal advisor to the general director of national security. The three students were charged with possessing communist literature and released later in the afternoon.[58]

Despite the arrests, some students were buoyed by the International Workers' Day demonstrations. *El Estudiante* reported optimistically, "The work stoppages, the signs that the protestors carried, and the expressive floats, as well as the expression of solidarity on the part of the observers . . . [demonstrated] clearly that the workers of Guatemala can never cooperate with this compulsory, sellout, and antinational government."[59] A single-panel cartoon of an indigenous ingénue called Juan Tecú, a feature of every front page, showed Tecú wagging his finger, accompanied by the caption, "This was the first of many . . ."[60] The cartoon captured the unrest that permeated students and workers in the capital city. *El Estudiante* editors boasted that the regime's permissiveness signaled its weakness. They noted how the protests had united workers, campesinos, and university and secondary school students and determined that "the moment [had] arrived to begin the true fight in defense of sovereignty . . . and national dignity." Dignity would, in fact, become a key figure for Arbencistas and anticommunists alike in the coming years. Emboldened, the editors urged the popular sectors to seize the moment. They also predicted a new wave of persecution and imprisonment.[61]

The student body was split. On one side were former members of the CEUA, which had recently disbanded in order to join the MDN.[62] On the other were the editors of *El Estudiante*, the AED, and less vocally, the large AEU. A few anticommunist student newspapers still circulated on campus, but none compared in circulation, scope, or impact to *El Estudiante*. Every edition featured anti-Castillo Armas salvos, each angrier than the last. Outside the university, conservative outlets reported that an international communist conspiracy was headquartered in the USAC Faculty of Law. The centrist daily newspaper *Prensa Libre* hoped for reconciliation. Its influential "Cacto" opinion column printed multiple pleas for resolution and reminded citizens of the national unity they had enjoyed under Arévalo.[63] The Director of *El Estudiante* was repeatedly threatened.[64] Meanwhile, the Castillo Armas regime continued to vacillate between intimidation and conciliatory meetings with student leaders.

The most outspoken San Carlistas anticipated trouble and ridiculed the government's attacks. A late May edition of *El Estudiante* exemplified the ambivalence of the moment. A comic strip entitled "Castillitos en el Aire" depicted an encounter between the President and Tecú, who was caught painting the number 32 on a wall.[65] Castillo Armas asked Tecú, "Does this refer to Article 32 of the Constitution of 1945?" Tecú replied, "No! It means that there are 32 campesinos from San Martin Jilotepeque who are imprisoned for reading Marx, only they are illiterate!"[66] The two-panel cartoon is extraordinarily clever. In the president's question, the artist embedded an accusation against Castillo Armas as a tool of North American capital as Article 32 of the 1945 Constitution prohibited religious, foreign, and international political organizations. He also indicted the president's indiscriminate charges of communism—illiterate peasants could not have *read* Marx. The comic's invocation of San Martin Jilotepeque was deliberate, too. It was a municipality where one of the nation's wealthiest families, the Herreras, owned large fincas and employed hundreds of poor laborers. During Arbenz's Agrarian Reform this land was selected for expropriation, but the oligarchic family resisted. In a few short lines, the comic poked fun at the Herreras, the failed land reform, and the anticommunist students who had participated in the CIA's "32 Marking Campaign."[67] In the final panel, Castillo Armas ran away from Tecú, covering his ears. He feared what Tecú, and by extension, his San Carlista creators, had to say.

Of course he did. His position was anything but stable. The headlines of daily newspapers bellowed in bold and italic fonts about communist successes and defeats in Iran and Algeria, and student strikes in Mexico, Cuba, Argentina, and Paraguay.[68] Nearly every day, newspapers reported arrests for possession of communist materials. Making matters worse, the anniversary of the 1944 Revolution approached and the AEU and AED continued to profess their commitment to its principles. A week before the revolution's anniversary, one of the most influential posts in USAC student leadership was up for election: the presidency of the AED. The elections were so important that the MDN party even backed a candidate, Mario Quiñonez Amézquita, a member of the Catholic Anticommunist University Youth (Juventud Universitaria Católica Anticomunista [JUCA]). All sides seemed certain that the outcome of the election would have some bearing on the national political climate.

National newspapers covered the elections in detail. Quiñonez ran against José Luis Balcárcel Ordóñez of the FUD (a group the newspapers called the "extreme left") and Carlos H. Rosales of the "revolutionary moderates."[69] One poll conducted by students of the JUCA and FUD suggested that Rosales was poised to win. They concluded that the student body was tired of extremist politics and favored a more centrist candidate. For its part, *La Hora* reported that some students suspected that the conservative Quiñonez would triumph in a fixed election. He was, after all, the government's candidate. The election was so important that around five hundred journalists, interested citizens, professors, students, and alumni gathered to hear the results. One journalist listed many famous lawyers in attendance, including Federico Herrera (a student leader in the Faculty of Law in 1900), Mario Sandoval Alarcón (a comrade of Castillo Armas and MDN partisan), and Ricardo Lara and Gabriel Martínez de Rosal (prominent international anticommunists), as well as several justices of the peace.[70] All of these illustrious jurists were San Carlistas and remained invested in the legacy of their alma mater.

The day after the election, *La Hora* carried an alarming headline: "Marxists won the elections."[71] The outcome was a surprise, given the results of the pre-election polls. A closer look at the election reveals an even more unexpected turn of events: in the first round, moderate Rosales won 138 votes, leftist Balcárcel Ordóñez won 112 votes, and MDN-backed Quiñonez won 100 votes. Because no candidate won a clear majority, there was a run-off between the two top candidates, Rosales and Balcárcel Ordóñez. At around 10 P.M., the second round of votes was counted: Rosales secured 103 votes, but Balcárcel Ordóñez had won with 138 votes. The results, apparently, "left many people with their mouths gaping."[72] Some speculated that the outcome was a maneuver by the JUCA and MDN to smooth the way for the radical left to take leadership of the high-profile student group. The student left, which had already attracted the government's disapproval, might be more easily discredited if it could be drawn into the national spotlight. A related rumor asserted that student leaders on the right endorsed Balcárcel Ordóñez and had even encouraged their constituents to vote for him. While their ultimate aim was to hold power in the student group, in the short term the MDN could "mark as marred by 'communism' any civic pronouncement by the AED, from the moment that Balcárcel . . . takes office."[73] On the other hand, *La Hora* reported, "This contest and the intense campaigns in the secondary schools demonstrate that communism has unleashed its battery among the educated youth."[74] Speculation aside, the 1956 AED elections revealed the relevance of student leadership for national politics and a general belief in the government's readiness to intervene in the affairs of the purportedly autonomous university.

A TEST OF CONSCIENCE

One day after Balcárcel Ordóñez's victory, Interior Minister Eduardo Rodriguez Genis announced that public celebrations of the anniversary of the 1944 revolution would be restricted. He went on to say that on previous occasions, some groups "misunderstood their freedom for the state's weakness."[75] Genis's statement may have been a response to the editorial published in *El Estudiante* after the International Workers' Day protests, discussed above. It also represented the regime's new and devastating approach to dissent. As the revolutionary anniversary approached, a secondary school student, teacher, *universitario*, or professor would be arrested every few days.

Police patrolled cafés, secondary schools, classroom buildings, and other places where students and faculty gathered downtown. Expanding its campaign to discredit USAC, the government published lengthy statements in daily newspapers that asserted that communist agitators often posed as students.[76]

Still, San Carlistas were open and unguarded as they planned for the occasion. On June 15, the AED issued a public invitation to all of the people of Guatemala to form a national committee to help organize the commemoration. The AED proposed a schedule of events beginning on June 22 with a juried art exhibition, followed by a talk by Dagoberto Vasquez (who had been arrested for shouting "Death to the Liberation!") on the importance of the fine arts in the 1944 Revolution. The following evening, members of the organizing committee would present a plaque to honor students who participated in the revolution. Julio César Méndez Montenegro would speak as a representative of his generation. A roundtable at the Faculty of Law on the question of the ongoing impact of the revolution would be the focus of the evening of the 24th. The next day would begin with a pilgrimage to the tomb of revolutionary martyr Maria Chinchilla, the schoolteacher who had been shot on June 25, 1944. Literary contests on themes related to the revolution and its resonance among young people and a theatrical presentation by the Faculty of Humanities were scheduled for later in the day.[77] While the organizing committee cordially declined to work with a progovernment group, none of the events were explicitly anti–Castillo Armas. Nevertheless, less than a week before the anniversary, Genis again declared that no observance of the date would be permitted. He also falsely reported that there were no events planned, perhaps in an attempt to suppress public interest.[78]

While the regime redoubled its campaign against the university, the AED escalated its campaign against the regime. This time, the AED targeted U.S. sociologist Frank Tannenbaum, who was scheduled to give a guest lecture in the Faculty of Law. Tannenbaum had been a comrade of Emma Goldman and arrested with Elizabeth Gurley Flynn and Alexander Berkman, and then became a scholar of Latin American labor movements, but he had more recently advised U.S. president Dwight D. Eisenhower and John Foster Dulles and had awarded Castillo Armas an honorary doctorate from Columbia University. For the AED, he was a symbol of intellectual imperialism and leftist betrayal. Students blocked Tannenbaum's entrance into the Law building and used the occasion to circulate statements that connected the Castillo Armas regime to the use of torture of political dissidents. They also demanded that the Secretary General of the United Nations denounce the regime's repeal of labor rights.[79] The protest caused only a minor international scandal, but within Guatemala, it again dramatized the division between the government and one of the university's most powerful sectors. It also marked an early invocation of international human rights by the student opposition, a tactic that would become commonplace in decades to come.

National newspapers considered the meaning of the revolutionary commemoration. The editor of the *Prensa Libre* urged people to quiet their imaginations. After all, he wrote, "It was the pueblo, without flags and without labels, who took to the streets, sick of oppression and the farce made of the rights of citizens [under Ubico]." The objective of the holiday was to serve as a "test of conscience, in order to know whether the subsequent state of things is or is not at the height of that which is commemorated and to have [this judgment] as the basis for improvement or rectification."[80] A truly democratic regime had nothing to fear. For their part, the AEU was careful to celebrate "with highest patriotism and *universitario* dignity." But they cautioned, "dark sectarian forces are moving in the student body," attempting to compromise the dignity of "the upright [moral] position of the *universitario*," according to an article in *El Imparcial*.[81]

Emphasizing the civic nature of the commemoration, the statement continued: "The inspiring call for university autonomy emerged from this valiant youth who steadfastly challenged the government of that era . . . without the heroic aid of the Guatemalan citizen, its dream would not have been achieved so swiftly . . . it was this pueblo who knew how to write one of the most brilliant pages in the precious story of the nation."[82] The statement reiterated the AEU's connection to the pueblo and reframed the revolution in terms of national unity. It upheld the notion that the *universitario* was the intellectual author of the revolution while the regular Guatemalan citizen provided the muscle and firepower. The AEU, unlike the AED, insisted that the commemoration was patriotic rather than partisan. Perhaps this was earnest, but it was certainly strategic. AEU President José T. Uclés was hesitant to rile the president. For its part, the Students' High Council (Consejo Superior Estudiantil [CSE]) declared that June 25 would always be a day of student celebration whose purpose was to rouse the spirit and preserve USAC traditions.[83]

Events began on schedule on June 23, but the dedication in the Faculty of Juridical and Social Sciences was disrupted when attendees learned that plainclothes policemen had raided the nearby Faculty of Humanities. Police photographed various administrative memos, AEU bulletins, and announcements about upcoming protests. Humanities Dean Hugo Cerezo Dardón was in the building at the time and noticed the strangers. When he confronted them, the policemen responded that they were investigators for the newspaper *Nuestro Diario*, so Cerezo Dardón left them alone and returned to his work.[84] In spite of the intrusion, students and citizens gathered the next morning at Plaza Barrios for the procession to Maria Chinchilla's gravesite. Her death was remembered every year as National Teacher's Day. The procession was meant to be somber and reflective and participants brought floral offerings A few luminaries planned to speak.[85]

Instead, a combined squadron of the National Police and Army confronted the crowd at Plaza Barrios and forced them to disperse. The AED called a meeting to discuss the situation. A few hours later, about five hundred people assembled in the Faculty of Law. The meeting was just underway when another combined squadron surrounded the building and demanded that the group disband. They did.[86] Later that evening, the National Police again entered the university, this time interrupting the roundtable discussion on the impact of the revolution that featured some of the brightest legal minds of the revolutionary generation. The police arrested many of the students, professors, and journalists in attendance, including AED president-elect Balcárcel Ordóñez and the other editors of *El Estudiante*.[87]

Guatemalans awoke on the morning of the 25th to a nationwide State of Alarm, in effect for thirty days. It permitted the imprisonment of individuals involved in "suspicious activities" without questioning, and limited travel on public roads after 9 P.M.[88] Constitutional guarantees were limited. For instance, police and military authorities were permitted to use force if an individual failed to stop when questioned. Public gatherings were restricted, though Castillo Armas made an exception for revolutionary commemorations that were held indoors. Government officials warned student organizers that they would be held responsible for any damages or injuries that occurred and explicitly cautioned them against participating in any event organized by "communists."[89] The State of Alarm allowed police agents to detain anyone in violation of the decree.

The AEU called a General Assembly in the afternoon to coordinate a response to the State of Alarm. AEU President Uclés began the meeting with a detailed report on the celebrations in honor of the revolution and multiple police invasions, harassment, and arrests in and around the buildings of the autonomous university. The General Assembly drafted a letter to Castillo Armas that demanded the return to constitutional rule and denounced Sunday's police raids as a violation of university sovereignty. The group also drafted a writ of habeas corpus on behalf of the imprisoned students. They agreed to give the president twenty-four hours to respond, then vowed to begin a progressive strike and to present their case to the United Nations. When the meeting ended at 2 P.M., most of the group had agreed on this course of action, but some uncertainty remained as to when and how the statement and demands would be delivered.[90]

Some students proposed to deliver the letter to the National Palace in person later that evening. Others wanted to read it aloud in Central Park in front of the National Palace that night. Both plans deliberately violated the curfew stipulated in the State of Alarm. Ultimately, a group of students decided to take to the streets right away, and to do so in an orderly fashion. The AEU leadership told the group who planned to march that they had been warned that repression and arrest were likely. Even so, the group counted around five hundred students when it gathered at the Paraninfo around 8:30 P.M. They walked very slowly, tranquilly, tensely, led by some of the very AEU leaders who had urged caution. They sang the national hymn, walked down 12th Street, and then turned onto the famous Sexta Avenida.

There the first gunshots were fired.[91] Students sought cover in doorways and shop windows. Some continued marching forward until the attack was too intense. Newspapers reported that some youths continued to sing the hymn while under fire. Many fell, injured or killed; still others fell to the ground for safety. Alvaro Castillo, president of the CSE and the Economics Student Association (AEE) died at the scene. Julio Juárez, a sixth-year medical student from Quetzaltenango died at the General Hospital, as did Julio Arturo Acevedo (of Humanities) and Ricardo Carrillo Luna (Law). Many others were seriously injured.[92] Police arrested 186 protestors and took them to police stations throughout the city where they were imprisoned for two days before their hearings. Others escaped and hid throughout downtown.

Headlines the following morning reported: "Protest Dissolved: Numerous Killed and Wounded," "Dramatic Outcome of Last Night's Events on La Sexta," and "Additional Emergency Measures to Prevent Student Riots Owe to Presence of Movement from Abroad."[93] Newspapers also announced that a State of Siege had been declared overnight. In a sort of dialectic call and response, the government created and responded to threats to public safety. The state was obliged to protect the nation from the student's riotous advance against the police, especially if it was instigated by outside agitators.[94] In the official account, the police had no choice but to open fire after protestors continued to advance on them despite verbal warnings and sirens. They had acted in accordance with the State of Alarm. The defense minister's statement read: "The cost of victims that [the pueblo] has to grieve is the direct responsibility of the instigators and student leaders who planned the protest for which they must bear the consequences and the weight of law."[95] The government urged citizens not to fear state repression but to give up some civic rights until stability returned.[96] The government may have sought to distance the pueblo from the students by framing the protests as the work of outsiders.

All constitutional guarantees were suspended during the State of Siege. Political activities, party meetings, and private and public gatherings of more than four people were prohibited. A curfew was in place from 9 P.M. to 6 A.M. Military patrols circulated in the capital city and in the countryside. Possession of firearms and explosives was forbidden. National Police and other security personnel, even bodyguards and municipal judicial authorities, were placed under the Army's command. The Army's Public Relations Department reviewed all press, radio, and television news. Military authorities could detain anyone who seemed suspicious and transport them directly to a military tribunal. The minister of defense became the nation's highest judge.[97]

The military also attempted to limit the politicization of the deaths of the assassinated students by providing funeral arrangements, including *nogal*-colored military coffins and an official military hearse. Colonel Antonio Soto presided over the funerals and supervised the families' final visit before burial. The two students of economics (Castillo Urrutia and Carrillo Luna) were buried side-by-side and Acevedo was buried alone. The fourth student was returned to Quetzaltenango.[98] Despite the colonel's efforts to control the funerals, about one hundred university and secondary school students attended. Over the next three decades, martyred students and funeral processions would become a central strategy in students' opposition. But in 1956, few could have anticipated how often they would be called upon to mourn their classmates.

The incident was not easily forgotten. The city grew ever more polarized.[99] Support for the regime grew among the armed forces and business elites; workers, university and secondary school students publicly denounced the government. Some international audiences critiqued the regime's strong-armed response to unrest.[100] The U.S. Embassy predicted that the confrontation would leave "some scar tissue which can never be fully repaired."[101] In the days after the attacks, law students submitted hundreds of writs of habeas corpus on behalf of their imprisoned classmates.[102] Castillo Armas, still bound to the appearance of legitimacy, remained silent for days while the police and military spoke to the press.

On June 28, the AEU convened another General Assembly and decided to present another statement to the president. They demanded that Castillo Armas condemn "the police intrusion" into campus and return the nation to constitutional rule. They also demanded that the imprisoned students and professionals be freed immediately.[103] Finally, they declared a strike. Secondary school students at the influential National Central Institute for Boys (INCV) and Rafael Aqueche joined the AEU strike and submitted still more writs of habeas corpus on behalf of their classmates and teachers.[104] Only forty of Rafael Aqueche's three hundred students attended class during the strike.[105] This certainly caught peoples' attention. Rashly, the Minister of Education discounted the strike as a minority action and chided the young students, saying, "politics is for grown-ups."[106] He recommended that teachers revoke the diplomas of students who had participated.

The crumbling national situation placed Castillo Armas in the middle of the global war against communism. The *New York Times* ran a story that speculated whether the forces of democracy were sufficient to abolish communism in the Western Hemisphere and used Guatemala as an example of the persistence of communist infiltration. Castillo Armas responded at a press conference in Mexico City on June 29, 1956. He retorted, "When communism has been entrenched in the government, up to the president of the republic, like in Guatemala, and where the fight for liberation has not been so bloody as to physically finish all of the communists, the campaign to end this dogma will require a labor of time." He defended the recent escalation of violence in the capital city by stating that students were preparing an attack on the National Palace. At the same time, like his minister of education, he minimized the students' threat by attributing the protests to a small minority.[107] When a reporter asked him whether these problems would prevent him from traveling to Panama for the upcoming gathering of American presidents, he confidently replied: "Of course I am going."[108] Order was restored.

On the contrary, a new order was established. Castillo Armas concluded the press conference with an assurance that the government had no intention of violating the university's autonomy. He denied that the police had raided the Faculties of Medicine, Humanities, and Juridical Science, but he added, "the concept of autonomy does not imply sovereignty ... authorities can enter any center or campus in order to prevent a crime or criminal activities."[109] A U.S. State Department telegram acknowledged that the government's violent reaction marked a decisive turn away from its previous "middle-of-the-road" approach.[110] In the course of just one week, the regime had issued a State of Alarm, State of Siege, and two executive bulletins that held university students responsible for communist infiltration.

Amid the growing uncertainty, a new student nationalism was rising, constituted in opposition to the regime and articulated—as ever—in terms of freedoms, rights, and responsibilities.

TO SIT FACE TO FACE WITH FREEDOM

Political repression in late June raised the stakes of the ongoing debate over the role of the university. Lengthy editorials treated the question. Guatemala's literati chimed in. It seemed as if everyone had an opinion and everyone was a loyal San Carlista. For instance, when *La Hora* editor Clemente Marroquín Rojas asked students to be more moderate in their dissent, he addressed them as fellow *universitarios*: "We have been *universitarios*; we have been defenders of the students' pressure-releasing strikes, at odds with our fellows. Few people have had the student spirit like we have." But in contrast to this pure and universal "student spirit," Marroquín Rojas saw the June protests as foolhardy. He charged that they had allowed "a small group with Marxist tendencies [to] contaminate a huge percentage of students of Law; this percentage has galvanized the school nearly in its entirety." He recounted how two young women delivered speeches before the violent protests on the night of the 25th, saying, "it is natural that faced with a feminine threat, the hearts of all men of the age of twenty will rise, will be aroused, and will take the street in defiance."[111] Marroquín Rojas blamed the young women for provoking their male counterparts, who were truly out of their depth.

For their part, the directors of *El Imparcial* and the *Prensa Libre* urged Guatemalans to settle down, faulting both police and students for their extremism. In *El Imparcial*, David Vela, San Carlista of the Generation of 1920, wrote that the nation struggled to overcome its political and civic immaturity. Secondary school students went on strike because they could not participate in formal politics and were inclined to imitate the older university-age students. This was unfortunate, but their youthfulness was precious and should be protected. Vela agreed that the protest on the night of the 25th was illegal, but he admonished the use of force by the police. On the whole, he urged stability, since Guatemala could progress only once it had ceased to "oscillate between dictatorship and anarchy . . . internal conflict and moral and material backwardness."[112] Similarly, in *Prensa Libre*, Pedro Julio García wrote that the people of Guatemala needed to "build a civic conscience that regulates the actions of governors and the governed."[113] García called on *universitarios* to be humble and strive for solutions rather than spectacles.[114]

Students responded by once more insisting on their constitutional duty to represent, defend, and lead the pueblo beyond strictly academic concerns. San Carlistas derived renewed authority from these claims, especially now that their lives were at risk. The editorial staff of the AEU's newspaper, *Informador Estudiantil*, wrote: "Some people believe archaically that the youth should not raise their voices to condemn the methods of the government as the arbitrary actions that they are, but they forget that our philosophy, our art, our literature, and our politics, just emerging, place before us the inescapable need to make clear to them just who we are and that it is our duty to sit face to face with freedom, with social justice, and with democracy."[115] The student journalists counterposed the government's arbitrary actions to the students' drive for knowledge, freedom, social justice, and democracy.

Key to San Carlistas' defense was the figure of the honorable *universitario*. This was crucial, for instance, when Marroquín Rojas wrote that Marxist agitators (especially the editors of *El Estudiante*) were taking advantage of students' good reputation and "student spirit."[116] Or when one vivid Defense Ministry bulletin, "The University of San Carlos and Low Politics," declared that civic freedoms did not "authorize [students] to convert the student body as an entity, nor any of its student associations, into political parties . . . an excrescence of impenitent Marxists who are trying to tarnish the name of the University of San Carlos." The Defense bulletin continued, "A small group of university students have taken precisely their status as *universitarios* and used one of the traditional student associations in order to establish within it a procommunist and subversive nucleus."[117] The Ministry called for "true *universitarios*" to defend the university's legacy. The rhetoric of the regime linked nationalist zeal to university autonomy-*cum*-apoliticism while antigovernment students linked nationalist zeal to university autonomy-*cum*-responsibility.

In June, the police seized 30,000 copies—two entire print runs—of *El Estudiante* on the grounds that it carried inflammatory information. The publication's treasury was also confiscated. The next edition was written on typewriters and assembled on mimeograph machines. The unedited paper was full of spelling errors and stray typewriter strikes, reading more like a manifesto than a student newspaper. It was the newspaper's firmest declaration against the Castillo Armas regime yet. In it, the editors detailed their arrest, detention, and exile to Honduras. They recounted how they had been taken from their homes at night and interrogated, then thrown half-naked on to the floor of a vehicle and driven to the Guatemala-Honduras border where they were abandoned. They named four men—Mariano Sánchez, Benjamin Aldana, Marco Antonio Archila Obregón, and Colonel Ricardo Alberto Pinto Recinos—as the perpetrators and accused them of being Ubico cronies, Ubiquistas.[118] They lambasted the Castillo Armas regime as antidemocratic and in violation of human rights. The final page of the paper was a letter from *El Estudiante* editor Jorge Mario García to Marroquín Rojas, which accused him of betraying San Carlistas and the student spirit. García held Marroquín Rojas and the regime equally responsible for the deaths of students on June 25, because the journalist had blamed students for the escalated policing for several days before the protests in his influential column. Like the interrogation of Edmundo Guerra Thelheimer by his former professor, the conflict between Marroquín Rojas and *El Estudiante* struck a personal chord: when Marroquín Rojas alleged communist sympathies among the staff of *El Estudiante*, he indicted a dear family friend, AED president-elect Balcárcel Ordóñez.[119]

As the political situation at home worsened, San Carlistas remained informed about events happening abroad. AEU president Uclés wrote to the U.S. National Student Association to express his solidarity with Autherine J. Lucy, a young African American woman who had been admitted to the University of Alabama, but had her admittance rescinded. In his letter, Uclés extended to Lucy the opportunity to study at USAC if the University of Alabama could not guarantee her safety and well-being. *Informador Estudiantil* featured the letter with headline: "AEU Against Discrimination."[120] On June 26, 1956, alongside news of the State of Siege and student disturbances, *El Imparcial* reported on the arrest of Fidel Castro and nineteen fellow combatants in Mexico, young men labeled "subversives," "conspirators," and "terrorists."[121] This would have certainly captured the attention of young *universitarios*. Among some cadres, Guevara's time in

Guatemala during the revolutionary decade was a point of pride. San Carlistas also participated in international exchanges with the communist-friendly International Union of Students (IUS) and the anticommunist International Student Conference (ISC). These congresses helped some San Carlistas to link their struggle against Castillo Armas regime to anticolonial nationalist struggles around the world.

A new, transnational youth power was rising and San Carlistas were a part of it. USAC student representatives attended the first Congress of Latin American and Caribbean Students (CLAE, later the Continental Organization of Latin American and Caribbean Students) in Montevideo, Uruguay, in 1955. Two years later in La Plata, Argentina, the group reconvened to discuss political problems confronted by universities (autonomy, participation in university government, free education, adequate teachers, university extension programs, and literacy) and political problems confronted by students (dictatorships, Latin American unity, imperialism, and worker–student solidarity). The student leaders also discussed what they called "the international student situation," powerful indication that international contacts with far-flung places like Indonesia, Pakistan, India, Burma, and Vietnam had begun to create a global student consciousness at least a decade before 1968.[122] Some speculated that these congresses were opportunities for communist indoctrination. In one instance, *El Imparcial* published a false report that USAC students had pledged allegiance to the USSR and received instruction on how to infiltrate Latin American student organizations while abroad. The student representatives wrote back to the newspaper, assuring that they were of "democratic faith and thinking."[123]

Seemingly every major international interest had some soft imperialist project of exchange or study abroad. The United Nations Educational, Scientific, and Cultural Organization (UNESCO) spent a considerable amount of time and resources promoting transcultural exchange within the Americas.[124] Students of medicine were eligible to apply for a scholarship from the United Fruit Company (UFCO) to pay for a year of study at Harvard Medical School in fields related to public health, hygiene, and industrial health.[125] San Carlistas were also the beneficiaries of Rockefeller and Kellogg Foundation grants in 1956, and both foundations donated trucks and lab equipment to the faculties of Agronomy and Medicine, contributions that totaled $18,000.[126] These programs were part of what A. Ricardo López has called "humanist governance," projects that called on national experts and policymakers to legitimate foreign incursion.[127]

While the national press and even some student newspapers framed USAC students as a homogeneous block, the internal documents of student groups suggested quite the opposite. In contrast to his inspired rejection of racial inequality in the United States, AEU president Uclés offered only a tepid response to San Carlistas' repression. In August 1956, the CSE demanded to know why Uclés had denounced emergency statements from the CSE and even blocked CSE members from a meeting of the AEU. They also demanded to know why Uclés did not invite the AEU General Assembly to his private meeting with Castillo Armas after the protests in June. One popular student from the Faculty of Law named Hugo Melgar was even more antagonistic. Melgar had suffered a gunshot wound to his right leg during the June 25 protests. He asked why the AEU's report on the confrontation did not include interviews with witnesses and instead depicted some of the pro-testing students as rash and vanguardist.[128] For Melgar and the CSE, Uclés's reticence amounted to treason. The AEU continued to enjoy public esteem while Castillo Armas denounced the AED and the group's reputation suffered. Perhaps this was the reason why Uclés was hesitant to openly condemn the regime after June 25. The outspoken CSE and AED had many of their members detained or exiled while other academic units, like Engineering, were determinedly uninvolved and devoted their extracurricular energies to sports, beauty pageants, rock 'n' roll on the radio, and films from the United States, Mexico, and Spain, and so avoided repression.[129]

In their sardonic account of the previous year, the anonymous authors of the *No Nos Tientes* in 1957 addressed the people of Guatemala as "the exploited, the illiterate," who fought the meaningless political battle for bicycle lanes along commuting routes, but remained unable to effect real change. Politicians were always "the same booger in a different nose," while Guatemala was "more screwed than ever." The editors used the slang term *pijazo* to describe the attacks suffered by students. The root of *pijazo* is "pija," a contemporary word for penis, making the mortal gunshots suffered by university students in June a form of emasculation by a penetrative police apparatus. As in 1955, the *huelgueros* ridiculed both communists and anticommunists as dupes of foreign influence "while the blood of the university, today as yesterday, continues to spill in a supreme holocaust of its ideals of freedom and democracy." They wrote that the communist spoke words that he did not understand and obeyed people whom he did not know, while the anticommunist schemed with a rosary in his right hand, the U.S. flag in his left, and his brain in his feet. The communist was preoccupied with predicting the future and the anticommunist could not think at all. In turn, the National Police were "society's dregs, nature's abortions" who "sow[ed] terror, violence, and torture in the flesh of the youth." Faced with such deplorable options, the *huelgueros* warned that in their "pure and rebellious fibers the martyred nation sometimes quivers." With no one else to turn to, it was up to the students.[130]

THE HOPE OF GUATEMALA

In Chapter 1, I argued that the revolutionary governments of the Ten Years' Spring enlisted students in state making as politicians, professionals, managers, and technicians, filling the ranks of the rapidly expanding bureaucracy with San Carlistas. By doing this, the revolutionary governments quelled the social disruption of the revolution and invested students with particular civic rights and responsibilities. This chapter has shown how these shared understandings of responsibility inspired a range of political behaviors after the counterrevolution, from the *Plan de Tegucigalpa* to anti–Castillo Armas *El Estudiante* editorials.

But by the end of 1956, San Carlistas were largely defined by their opposition to the Castillo Armas regime. Student papers argued over and over again that Castillo Armas had compromised the well-being of the people to safeguard the support of the United States. They accused the president of maintaining self-serving connections with the UFCO and U.S. State Department and backing dictatorships in Honduras and Nicaragua.[131] While the 1956 Constitution continued to charge San Carlistas with the duty to contribute to the development of scientific and philosophical knowledge and cultural diffusion, the rights and responsibilities that this entailed became increasingly opaque. Castillo Armas and his functionaries increasingly circumscribed San Carlistas' political power through electoral fraud, intimidation, disappearance, and exile. At the same time, the influence of anticommunist students at USAC had declined. Some had graduated and joined the MDN and others were probably chastened by the regime's heavy hand against the university. More and more, capital city political culture was a high stakes tug-of-war between the Castillo Armas regime and all of its functionaries on one side, and USAC students and the university community on the other.

The role of the middle class in national and international politics remained uncertain. It was invigorated by the 1944–1954 revolutionary decade, then challenged by Castillo Armas's allegiance to traditional military and business elites. Just after International Workers' Day in 1956, *El Estudiante* published an article entitled, "The Role of the Middle Class." It argued, "Almost without exception, History reveals that in every revolutionary moment, when the proletariat and the middle class have acted as allies at the moment of triumph and the ascension to power, before long, the persistent schism and division between the two will emerge." Following an argument familiar to readers of Karl Marx, the anonymous author went on to assert that the middle class was always suspicious of the proletariat. Its passion for revolution quickly dissolved into "sterile struggle" and class divisions. The achievement of true revolution depended on the ability of the middle class to abandon this tendency. The editorial admonished that recent events should have been enough to convince the middle class of its shared fate with urban and rural proletariat, even if it remained "inexperienced so far" in the social struggle. It offered a different interpretation of the middle class in the 1944 Revolution than the one widely shared in popular memory that celebrated how teachers, professors, students, urban workers, and rural *campesinos* worked together to overthrow tyranny and build a great democracy. The editorial argued the 1944 revolution had not been a true revolution. The middle class and workers should join together to present a "great united national front for an ongoing battle with the industrial and agrarian oligarchy," for "a middle class that is deeply revolutionary, in close alliance with the rural and urban proletariat, is the hope of Guatemala."[132]

But even San Carlistas without revolutionary designs called for students to relate in new ways to the pueblo. In a welcome address to incoming freshmen, entitled "University Life: Constant Self-Improvement," student journalist Fernando Martínez Bolaños attempted to articulate this new orientation: "To live the university life is to become an intimate of a group, to share its pain, to laugh with its joys, and to collaborate for its improvement. It is to provide the voice of encouragement in crucial moments, to offer a brave shoulder when someone is in need, and to be always ready to defend the dignified tradition of the alma mater. But it is also to have one's eyes set on the nation, on its path, now brilliant, now unpredictable, but for the true *universitario*, always emerging, stimulating, and extraordinary."[133] Bolaños continued, "To live the university life is to be concerned with one's own improvement, but at the same time [the student] is the force that pushes us to achieve the most sacred ideals of the society to which we belong." Bolaños told new students how they were not merely enrolled in a program of study, but had also entered into a social contract with the pueblo. When Bolaños wrote his essay in January 1956, the university community had not yet experienced the invigorating International Workers' Day protests. Nor had they seen the police open fire on dozens of university students on a historic capital city thoroughfare on a warm evening in June. The year to come would teach students and faculty many things about "crucial moments" and "sacred ideals." At all levels of political life, the stakes were higher by the end of the year.

Then, unexpectedly, on July 26, 1957, a security guard named Romeo Vásquez Sánchez assassinated Castillo Armas after a dinner party in the National Palace. The months that followed brought disorganization and infighting to the ruling party; only the military remained a stable arbiter of power.[134] Former Supreme Court member and San Carlista Luis Arturo González López served as interim president for three months, though his term was taken up by a futile attempt to organize elections.[135] It might have been an occasion for opposition groups to seize power, but they were unable to do so. The Castillo Armas regime had effectively defused rival political parties and the student and labor movements were stuck on the defensive. The AEU and AED struggled to hold regular meetings. The AEU did not conduct a General Assembly until early October 1957 and *El Estudiante* was out of print until September 1957.[136]

When it reappeared, however, a new editorial board renewed its promise to provide a source of "independent and incorruptible" news for the people.[137] The first edition was dedicated to the hundreds of students who had been imprisoned, tortured, and disappeared in the three years of the counterrevolution. From exile in Mexico City, the founding editors addressed their heirs: "You have in front of you the responsibility for one of the nation's most important historical situations."[138] Much of the first edition focused on the upcoming national presidential elections, a contest that the newspaper called a "form of medieval alchemy that combines bones and bananas (above all bananas), strengthened by the lack of scruples and by the millions that the pueblo has had to pay with sweat and with blood."[139]

At first, the university sector's vote was split between Miguel Ydígoras Fuentes (who had lost in the 1950 election against Arbenz) and *escuilach* Mario Méndez Montenegro of the Revolutionary Party (Partido Revolucionario [PR]). *El Estudiante* unequivocally backed the PR and printed a list of PR candidates running for offices nationwide in its pages. The editors wrote that PR candidates, who promoted a platform based on the return of the principles of the 1944 Revolution, and their allies in the United

Revolutionary Front (Frente Unido Revolucionario [FUR]), were the only candidates who resisted "North American meddling in the internal issues of our nation" and remained steadfast "against anticommunist dictatorship, and against the surrender of our [natural] riches to Yankee monopolies."[140] Still, Ydígoras's plan for "Literacy, Bread, [and] Health" resonated with San Carlistas sympathetic to social welfare and agricultural development.[141] After all, similar programs had offered excellent employment for USAC graduates in agriculture, engineering, public health, and medicine since the revolution.

Before the elections, the government blocked Méndez Montenegro's candidacy.[142] Students were left to choose between Christian Democrat and USAC alumnus Miguel Asturias Quiñónez, Miguel Ortiz Pasarelli of the MDN, or Ydígoras of the National Democratic Reconciliation Party (Partido Reconciliación Democrática Nacional [PRDN]). In October, *El Estudiante* presented Ydígoras as a pawn of North America and Pasarelli a henchman for oligarchy. Crassly, the editors declared, "the candidate that does not offer exile will bring the people imprisonment and burial."[143]

By graduation in December, San Carlistas had only one legitimate president: AEU president Edgar Alfredo Balshells. In his commencement address, Balshells spoke, "Our people, like every other, need to be shown the way of truth, and for this the people rely on you and on all *universitarios*." He continued, "We have seen in other parts of the world: it is the university youth who is first to rebel against farce and oppression; the first who points out the anguish of lies and the stupidity of deception, who ... orients the pueblo toward the Truth."[144] Balshells celebrated students' ability to lead, but his invocation of a worldwide student body poised to rebel precisely iterated the great fear of the Guatemalan military establishment and its benefactors. The global reach of his entreaty was evidence of a new and growing internationalism among San Carlistas, cultivated by the very conditions of the Cold War: ideological exchange and polarization and advances in travel and communication technologies.[145]

This chapter has demonstrated how, in just a few years, a series of flashpoints transformed the university, its students, and its relationship with the government. Although rarely discussed by historians, these years produced tremendous changes in Guatemalan political culture. Unlike earlier histories that deemphasized Guatemalans' roles in the counterrevolution and focused on economic factors and foreign intervention, this chapter has shown how Guatemalans, broadly, and San Carlistas, in particular, responded to the new political conditions of the Castillo Armas regime and Cold War geopolitics. The *Plan de Tegucigalpa* empowered anticommunist students by giving them a voice in politics at home and throughout Central America and Mexico. Fears of a global communist conspiracy permitted strict policing of student groups, but at the same time, many students enjoyed travel to far-flung places for international student congresses. The May and June protests were reactions to national social and economic transformations, but they were also protests against transnational developments like the rise of the National Security Doctrine and Cold War anticommunism. The protests also marked the birth of what would become the popular movement. They formed part of an increasingly aggressive strategy by some students who favored direct action over judicial and legal appeals once the relationship between the state and the university deteriorated.

All of these changes continued to transform the middle class. Remember, USAC remained the only institution in Guatemala where individuals could become credentialed in a professional occupation. After graduation, mandatory membership in the professional *colegio* system ensured that an individual professional remained linked to the university and its political culture for as long as they practiced their profession. San Carlistas were not merely a small part of a larger middle class. Rather, USAC was the institution in civil society that represented the middle class. But more than that, the meanings of middle-class identity—from personal relationships to ways of thinking, cultural tastes to professional ethics—were learned, crafted, and revised at USAC. On the whole, the antagonistic relationship between students and the state transformed San Carlistas from the proto-bureaucratic sector they had been during the Revolution into a fragmented oppositional sector. The university's influence continued to grow even as the counterrevolution, generally, consolidated its victory.

Though full of contradictions, the counterrevolutionary years are important for historians to understand. The ideologies of the left and the right that would endure for the remainder of the twentieth century began to cohere in these years. Some San Carlistas of the period, like Hugo Melgar and Mario López Larrave, would become well-known figures on the left while others, like Mario Sandoval Alarcón, Lionel Sisniega Otero, and Jorge Skinner Klee, would lead the ever-more-murderous right. It is very hard to imagine these men as young San Carlistas who studied together, but they did.

During the counterrevolution, San Carlistas continually asserted their right to make political claims *as students*. They crafted their assertions and claims in the idioms of university autonomy, duty, and class privilege that the university not only reflected, but also granted. In coming years, students used this feeling of fraternity to temper and even disguise political critique and to compel fellow citizens to action. As the relationship between USAC and the Guatemalan government continually deteriorated, political affect became San Carlistas' best weapon.

THREE

A Manner of Feeling, 1958–1962

Morality is the ultimate and constant struggle for freedom. It is the duty of the *universitarios* of America to join in this fight, to defend the very essence of the University.

USAC *rector* CARLOS MARTÍNEZ DURÁN, *at the inaugural act of the Third Latin American University Congress, September 20, 1959*[1]

ACCORDING TO THE 1958 *NO NOS Tientes* editorial, Guatemala had enjoyed "frankly wretched luck," since the counterrevolution. But where previous Huelga de Dolores celebrations saw students considering the temptations of "Soviet Paradise" and "North American gold," the 1958 editorial was more direct. Its anonymous authors wrote, "The history of Guatemala continues to be written in blood" by men like Clemente Marroquín Rojas, Enrique Trinidad Oliva, Carlos Cifuentes Díaz, Carlos Sosa Barillas, Carlos Alberto Recinos, who as journalists, lawyers, politicians, police chiefs, and military officers disfigured Guatemalan civil society. The editorial went on to implicate others more directly: "This solemn historical and hysterical editorial cannot fail to mention the notorious assassins who, on a dark and calm night, vilely assassinated our university comrades. In a mockery of the people of Guatemala they still move about freely and they are Santos Miguel Lima Bonilla, Aparicio Cahueque, José Bernabé Linares, Mariano Rossell Arellano [*sic*], Oscar Marroquíñ Rojas, Mario Sandoval Alarcón, Rodolfo Martínez Sobral, Roberto Castañeda Feliche, Ernesto Arturo Zamora Centeno," and more. The rest of the editorial ridiculed Miguel Ydígoras Fuentes for his claims to be learned when he had only attended the military Escuela Politécnica, a school that San Carlistas held in very low esteem.

San Carlistas' derision of the leader continued into the Friday night theatrical revue. Students paid one quetzal for admission to the event and received a small paper ticket (a *billete burloso*) with a cartoon drawing of Uncle Sam and an awkward handshake between two grimacing men. The two men were Ydígoras and Colonel José Luis Cruz Salazar, a leader in the National Democratic Movement (MDN). Uncle Sam supervised the agreement with one hand resting on each man. Falling from Cruz Salazar's left hand was a check in the amount of $200,000. With a pointy nose and arched eyebrows, Uncle Sam was drawn as the comic villain and Cruz Salazar and Ydígoras, his flunkies.

The drawing depicted a secret deal that many suspected had enabled Ydígoras to secure the presidency. Early on October 20, 1957, a victory was declared for Miguel Ortiz Pasarelli of the MDN who had served as interior minister under Castillo Armas and as a Supreme Court justice. But Ydígoras's National Democratic Reconciliation Party (Partido Reconciliación Democrática Nacional [PRDN]) disputed the clearly fraudulent results. They rallied people to their side by charging that the government intended to impose its official candidate on the pueblo. That afternoon, many of the young people who supported Ydígoras crisscrossed the city on bicycles, incessantly ringing their handlebar bells to demonstrate their disgust for Pasarelli's *"continuismo"*—status quo, cronyism, and fraud.[2] The election results were nullified three days later. The following day, a military coup led by Colonel Oscar Mendoza Azurdia seized power. Colonel Guillermo Flores Avendaño governed until elections were held in March 1958. This round of elections pitted Cruz Salazar against Ydígoras and *escuilach* Mario Méndez Montenegro.

Ydígoras would win the election, but as president, he could not hold on to his wide appeal nor could he deliver his promise of stability. San Carlistas responded to the growing uncertainty with rhetorics of political feelings—an idiom of political affect—that allowed them to reach across class, regional, and age divides to fuel mass protests by the early 1960s. The editorial and the cartoon described above reflect three of the most important political feelings that defined San Carlistas by the late 1950s: mistrust of the government, anti-imperialist nationalism, and students' duty to guide the pueblo. San Carlistas consciously used these feelings to distinguish the morally righteous students from the rapacious government. The derision and elitism apparent in the 1958 *No Nos Tientes* gave way to more expansive rhetorics that invited broader coalitions.

USAC Rector Carlos Martínez Durán articulated this political affect in an address to students on the anniversary of university autonomy in 1959. He said, "Dedicate yourselves to your own perfection and the perfection of your neighbor. You are the guardians of university culture, and only one passion belongs to you, that of freedom and of justice. You have to learn that truth and scientific certainty are not enough to live on. You have to hunger and thirst for beauty and morality. Full, whole culture is the best laurel wreath for the authentic *universitario*."[3] Martínez Durán's exhortation underlined concepts familiar to his audience, ideas that were foundational to USAC student nationalism and discussed in Chapters 1 and 2, including service to the community and a belief in the extraordinariness of university culture and the university's role in cultivating the highest values of freedom and justice. But the speech took familiar ideas and raised the stakes: skepticism toward the value of knowledge for knowledge's sake, something San Carlistas usually called "objective knowledge," became the demand to "hunger and thirst." The concern that Guatemala was falling behind became the command to perfect one's self and one's neighbor and to single-mindedly pursue freedom and justice. Together, these preoccupations shaped the affective register of class culture at USAC in the first years of the civil war. While San Carlistas employed rhetorics of political affect across the twentieth century, during the Ydígoras presidency, political feelings compelled them and other citizens to action.[4] By the mid-1960s, political affect further delegitimized the government and held up San Carlistas as the pueblo's loyal defenders.

This City Belongs to You tracks changing political cultures and class meanings in and around USAC and this chapter highlights how feelings-based rhetoric in particular changed the way that students understood the nation and citizenship.[5] Rather than define what these terms meant in some fixed way or pretend to discern students' innermost feelings, conscious or unconscious, I explain how San Carlistas used political affect to effect political change. In other words, their utterances about political feelings compelled them and other citizens to action. Political affect is less a descriptor of an interior state than a performative framework for political action. Examining changes in political affect, first in response to Castillo Armas' assassination, then to the promise of Ydígoras, and later to his recourse to violence and the subsequent military coup, can help us to better understand not only the university and its students, but also urban political culture.

Political affect also helped students to form broader alliances within Guatemala. Guatemala in the late 1950s and early 1960s experienced acute underdevelopment and economic neocolonialism. San Carlista political affect in the mid-twentieth century reflected the long history of extraction visited upon Guatemala by imperial nations, engaged Cold War internationalism, and circulated among new transnational student networks. Alliances that spanned generations were crucial to survival of the left in its partisan, guerrilla, and insurgent iterations. So, too, were cross-class and cross-regional appeals. While protests and commemorative events brought university students into closer contact with urban workers and rural and indigenous farmers, shared idioms brought them into coalition through "a language of class action [that] evolved from one of existential positioning."[6] A variety of texts emphasized a few key semantic figures: dignity, duty, freedom, struggle, fraud, loss, and vulnerability. In this chapter, I discuss texts produced in response to violent moments, spectacular protests, and annual events to demonstrate how this language of feelings built on existing narratives to help individuals to identify with state, religious, popular, revolutionary, or reformist politics. One of the most powerful outcomes of the many student and worker protests of this period was the exchange of ideas and political affect that created a shared history of struggle. Dignity was an especially powerful weapon against the increasingly vicious military state, evidenced by student publications and public commemorations, especially the March 1962 Day of National Dignity, discussed below. What was since the 1945 Constitution a San Carlista responsibility to lead the pueblo became a San Carlista duty; for some, duty bred resistance.

Previous chapters have made clear the importance of shared vocabularies, traditions of struggle, and values to both the left and the right throughout the civil war. They formed another battleground for San Carlistas and soon, the guerrilla and the military, in the war for hearts and minds. As Chapter 2 argued, student nationalism became defined by its opposition to most state institutions during the counterrevolution. But it did strengthen an individual's relationship to one institution: the university. Because few professors taught full-time and few students were able to attend classes regularly, political discourses cast in an emotional register may have helped to cohere school spirit and fellow-feeling among students and faculty.[7] Below, I follow the emergence of these rhetorics of political feelings, highlighting how political affect was wielded to compel political change, from Ydígoras's election through the coup led by Colonel Enrique Peralta Azurdia that deposed him in 1963.

DIGNITY AND DEMOCRACY

The 1957–58 presidential race pitted the nation's most powerful social sectors against one another, each candidate backed by a distinct group: Cruz Salazar and the MDN represented the nation's traditional landowning and military elite and called itself "the party of organized violence."[8] Méndez Montenegro had the vote of the Arévalistas, mostly officials who had served during the 1944–1954 period. Ydígoras, an old Ubiquista, appealed to the anti-Arévalo and anti-Arbenz center, as well as the Church, military rank-and-file, and some businessmen and urban professionals. Ydígoras's campaign platform centered on tax reform, industrialization, the Central American Common Market, improvements in public education, and agro-industrial development in the northwestern department of Petén. He also advocated penal reform, a modified agrarian reform law, and a revision of the Armas regime's restrictive labor laws. In the popular vote in March, Ydígoras won 190,972 votes; Cruz Salazar, 138,488; and Méndez Montenegro, 132,824.[9] However, the MDN retained the majority of congressional seats and could unilaterally reject the election results. To ensure the MDN's cooperation, Ydígoras agreed to reserve three cabinet posts for MDN party members and paid the MDN a monthly amount of Q6,000.[10] This was the infamous handshake depicted on the 1958 *billete burloso*. Ydígoras was a master manipulator and, as an early February story in *TIME* magazine recognized, "With the confidence of a winner ... began expertly easing off on campaign slogans against foreign influence in Guatemala. He talked earnestly of the great need for foreign capital, praised the U.S. for its 'generous help.'"[11] The new president's political maneuvers may have earned him some support among party leaders, but more than half of electors had voted against Ydígoras even before his not-so-secret deal with the MDN. The new president would have to build the stability that he had promised while campaigning.[12]

Nevertheless, Ydígoras made frequent, if awkward, attempts to improve his relationship with the university. In April 1958, he did an interview with *El Estudiante*. The student journalists asked the president about the agrarian reform that he had pledged during the campaign. Ydígoras purportedly remarked, "That was the cause of the fall of Arbenz," and added that the beneficiaries of such a program "were irresponsible *indios* and drunks ... no one can simply give them something for free and ... moreover, not everyone in the world has been born to be a land owner." The title of the interview's final section suggests the tone of the encounter: "Negative Answers to Everything Suggested."[13] If he sought to garner support among students, Ydígoras had failed to win over *El Estudiante*, the most widely read student newspaper. His other efforts to gain student favor also floundered. His relaunch of revolutionary-era cultural programs was thwarted by miscalculation. The crisis in international coffee prices (a disastrous 24% decline in revenues from 1957–1958 and another 12% decline as the year passed) made it difficult for Ydígoras to finance his plans.[14] Ydígoras also reopened international student exchange programs shortly after the election, something that San Carlistas had long enjoyed and benefitted from, but by this time, some USAC students increasingly rejected the programs as imperialist and antinationalist. When Ydígoras placed a wreath on the grave of the students killed by Castillo Armas's forces in 1956, some student groups lambasted the empty gesture. He donated Q3,000 to the Huelga de Dolores in 1958 and even became the first president to attend the events, but San Carlistas carried on as usual and Ydígoras was probably more charmed by his own presence than were the students. One wonders what he thought of the *billetes burlosos* that featured his rotting corpse. Around the same time, the president also contended with periodic strikes among secondary school students who opposed Minister of Education Julia Quiñonez and Ydígoras's dismissal of two beloved school principals.[15] The strikers challenged the minister's qualifications and, finding them lacking, her iron hand in the management of their schools. In 1959, the group became the United Front of Organized Guatemalan Students (Frente Unido de Estudiantes Guatemaltecos Organizados [FUEGO]) and expanded its demands to include the restructuring of the secondary education curriculum in its entirety.

First Lady Maria Teresa Lozano de Ydígoras also made lukewarm gestures to USAC students. She agreed to meet with the small Women's Committee of the AEU in anticipation of University Spirit Week in early April 1958. According to an article in *El Estudiante*, Lozano de Ydígoras arrived late, and then left abruptly. She claimed that she was very busy and had been told that she would meet with a single student representative. When asked about the possibility of rescheduling the meeting, the First Lady replied that she was booked until August and then, according to the article, brusquely turned and left. The report ended with a sarcastic observation: "the university students left very impressed because they had never had the opportunity to speak with a 'First Lady' of the Republic." The journalist attributed the First Lady's response to contempt for students in general. After all, she had ample reason to dislike Guatemalan youth. Around the same time as her unsuccessful visit with the Women's Committee, secondary school students at two elite capital city schools, the Belén Institute for Girls and the Normal Institute of Central America for Girls (INCA), held a hunger strike in solidarity with their peers' campaign against Quiñonez. They had also helped circulate a rumor throughout the capital city that a thriving prostitution ring was based out of the First Lady's alma mater.[16]

Remarkably, given Quiñonez's deep connections to Ubico and Ydígoras, the secondary school students' strike was successful. The minister of education resigned. Buoyed by this success, FUEGO publicly supported the strikes of the National Workers' Union of the Guatemalan Social Security Institute (STIGSS) and the teachers' unions in 1960, both of which were also successful.[17] That the Ydígoras administration resolved these conflicts very quickly revealed important changes in Guatemalan political authority and the relationship between the government and students. First, it was clear that students expected their voices to be heard. The firing of two administrators or the suspension of striking students could provoke major political disruption. Related, a growing number of people could be called upon to mobilize quickly in the event of a protest. University and secondary school students were less isolated than they had been in their opposition to Castillo Armas. Third, all conflict seemed to risk the stability of the Ydígoras regime and the regime responded accordingly, as if it were under constant threat.[18] Finally, the fraternity of San Carlista spirit had expanded to include younger students, women, and girls. They turned the president and First Lady's sense of propriety and order on its head: students were the bearers of moral rectitude.

The months to come saw a constant volley of complaints and denunciations exchanged between USAC and the president. When editorials in *El Estudiante* became especially biting, Ydígoras called the university a "nursery of communism." In reply, the university administration reiterated its autonomy from the president's interference. Rector Martínez Durán's speech at the July 1959 commencement ceremony began, "I am here, as always, with my incendiary words in defense of the sovereign rights of the spirit, of the sacred ideals of freedom and university autonomy." He continued, "in the University, there is room for only the highest politics, which is also the politics of the spirit." He also emphasized the importance of applied knowledge: "As the University of the State, [USAC] cannot be outside of or indifferent toward the largest problems of the nation, of whatever type, and so it must shine its scientific and technical light on them, in the most elevated manner and without compromise."[19] He continued:

> In the name of this freedom, I want as a *universitario* to think and to feel, out loud; to think is sometimes a manner of feeling. And feeling, a man-

ner of thinking. The University is the best place for acquiring an authentic political education, understood as civility, as the noble exercise of citizenship. *Polis* in etymology is nothing other than *city*. And the city is constructed upon this base of the shared virtues of the governors and the community . . . Representatives of all social classes are admitted to the University today, and in this way political education is an assurance of the conservation and progress of democracy, [both] traditional and recent.[20]

Again and again, the rector appealed to the high politics of truth and inveighed against the low politics of self-interest. He praised authenticity over duplicity. He raised the national pueblo above political parties, built on a foundation of "the shared virtues of the governors and the community."[21] Most of all, he argued that the student must also receive an affective education at the university so that society could be constructed on shared virtues for the noble exercise of citizenship. Martínez Durán understood this to be crucial to progress and modernization, particularly through the appropriate exercise of freedom of the intellect. He was careful to distinguish between the freedom to be found in authentic truth and the apolitical knowledge praised by anticommunists.

His predecessor, Vicente Díaz Samayoa, had been an advocate of the apolitical university, but Martínez Durán's return to the rectorship signaled the return of the values of the Revolution to university administration. In his campaign speeches, he spoke triumphantly of university autonomy and promised to begin construction of the University City, something he had been planning since his first term in 1945. But this time, Martínez Durán, like Ydígoras, struggled to unite an increasingly divided constituency. To conservatives, he was a communist; but he was too conservative for the university's more revolutionary sectors. After his first year in office, he convened a commission to revise the university's bylaws. He requested the "invaluable participation" of the AEU and a list of invited alumni whom he called "eternal San Carlistas [*San Carlistas de siempre*]."[22] The list included many notable alumni from the revolutionary generation, like Julio Cesar Méndez Montenegro (then dean of the Faculty of Juridical and Social Sciences), Hugo Cerezo Dardón (poet, essayist, and former dean of Humanities), Rafael Cuevas del Cid (Law alumnus, university secretary, and clandestine member of the Guatemalan Labor Party [PGT]), and Carlos Mauricio Guzman (former dean of Medicine).[23] Even decades after graduation, alumni could draw on these school ties to elicit support. "Eternal San Carlistas" were indelibly linked to a fraternal lineage that bound them to key moments in Guatemalan history, including many that were detailed in the two previous chapters, but also more distant events like the overthrow of Estrada Cabrera.

Powerful invocations of historical memory were not limited to sober occasions like commencement or university reform. Immoderate moments like the Huelga de Dolores also provided ample opportunity for San Carlistas to call upon or undermine this legacy. *Billetes burlosos*, like the one described above for admission to the 1958 Friday night theatrical revue, were designed to undercut a dizzying system of official receipts and lampoon commercial regulation and bureaucratization of the university. While it was a lightning rod for conservative and Catholic attacks on the university, most capital city residents simply accepted the annual interruption that the Huelga de Dolores occasioned. Some made sense of the bacchanal as a safety valve for students under pressure, or an explosion of youthful spirit, or simply a university tradition. Through the late 1950s, however, steam, pressure, and explosion became more than metaphors. Bombings on or near the parade route became an increasingly common occurrence.

Each year before the Huelga de Dolores, San Carlistas wrote scores of editorials weighing in on the event's merit. In 1956, San Carlos alumnus and former secretary of Congress Mario Alvarado Rubio issued a passionate defense of the event. He argued that it was essential to the social life of urban students. He wrote, "There is no way that the students are going to stop being happy and wicked; and it would be horrible for us to ask seriousness of them, when we still spend time yearning for those happy years of irresponsibility before economic and familial problems, for those years—a lot of years— during which we were the despair of professors and deans."[24] In Rubio's view, anyone opposed to the Huelga was clearly plotting against the university. The Huelga, Rubio pointed out, held deep meaning for those who had had "the good luck to be students," and especially "for those who knew what it meant to endure an omnipotent and tyrannical president . . . for those of us who suffered the horrible acts of tyranny . . . and who on October 20 attained a stamp of honor on our first heroic deed."[25] Like Martínez Durán, Rubio celebrated youth, free expression, and the triumph of higher truths. He linked the free and open speech of the Huelga to the students' struggle for democracy against President Ubico's tyranny.

Rubio went on to assert, however, that this esteemed past obliged students to behave honorably in the present. His words articulated claims to moral rectitude that strictly proscribed men's and women's behavior. There was no place for "lewd" insults like those students routinely made about politicians.

He also opposed the cross-dressing that was common among students during the Friday parade, a behavior that he derided as "faggoty." Rubio called on students to return the event to its good name, and bring back its cleverness and its joy. To descend into political sectarianism during the Huelga made students "gossips, *chirmol* makers, corruptors or adulterers of the highest sense of the university" not "youth of courage and ingenuity."[26] *Chirmol* is a Guatemalan salsa customarily made by adult women from roasted tomatoes, onion, lime, salt, cilantro, and *chile*. To call young students "*chirmol* makers" was to emasculate and age them. Young men acted like gossipy oldsters not bearers of the nation's future. Other capital city Catholics also supported the Huelga's playful riotousness as the essence of student spirit while lamenting its recent degradation. The Association of Catholic University Students wrote, "as university students, it pains us to see many classmates use the Huelga as a tool to express the sentiments of the lowest culture that is totally incompatible with the dignity that ought to accompany the name of *estudiante universitario*."[27] If the best features of the Huelga were agile word play, ingenuous jokes, and high spirits, the worst were lewdness and public dishonor.

For similar reasons, the editors of the major capital city newspapers, all San Carlos alumni, were often critical of the Huelga. Many expressed the feeling that it was never quite as good as it had been when they were students. One journalist wrote that the event was merely the most visible part of a general and ongoing social decline. "The sin is all of ours," he declared, but "actually, the saddest thing is the loss of respect for human dignity in a youth called to fight precisely for this human dignity."[28] The journalist was not quite clear what he meant by "dignity," but what he hoped to accomplish by publishing such a declaration was transparent. For Catholic anticommunists, the invocation of dignity suggested order, respect, faith, and gentility. For the groups that were becoming an increasingly coherent left, dignity required democracy, the pueblo, and freedom. And for both sides, dignity seemed to draw on commitment and constancy.

Another unique Huelga accessory, the identification cards worn by parade participants, made this point in students' signature style. The cards featured a cartoon drawing of the biblical story of Adam and Eve. But in this version, it was President Ydígoras who tempted a *campesino* dressed in frayed pants and straw hat to eat a guava. An oration accompanied the image, a play on a sixteenth-century Iberian Catholic "Sonnet to Christ Crucified [*Soneto a Cristo crucificado*]." In the *huelgueros'* hands, "I am not moved, my God, to love Thee" became "I am not moved, Miguel, to fear you." The oration continued:

> You move me, Miguel, move me to see you
> Nailed to the guava tree and now rotten
> Your skin eaten away by time,
> And your testicles without strength or luck
> What moves me, finally, is your law and the way
> That even if there were no "flight," you would shoot the hell out of
> people
> And even if there were no informants [*orejas*] you would still screw
> with people

The students' cunning oration declared their faith in Ydígoras's perfidy. By rewriting this famous colonial-era sonnet and retaining its form, students simultaneously indicted Ydígoras's character, poked fun at his religiosity, and linked both to colonialism. The students were "moved" in the third stanza only because they anticipated Ydígoras's disregard for the rule of law. This discussion of flight was a reference to the Fugitive Law, which empowered police to open fire on a potential suspect attempting to flee the scene of a crime. The sonnet also affirmed that Ydígoras's eager embrace of force would not dissuade the students. In time, he would be exposed. Crucified on a distinctly Central American cross—a guava tree—Ydígoras was stretched, prone and rotting. While the oration demonstrated the students' cruel playfulness and literary skill it also revealed their own religious upbringing and political commitments. It counterposed the dignity of Jesus's martyrdom to Ydígoras's decay. Other important figures recurred in the oration: national natural resources as a sort of Garden of Eden, the impotence of certain politicians and military men, and the indigenous campesino as victim. Chapter 4 addresses how student nationalism took up each of these themes.

Capital city Catholics did not overlook the fact that students' orations were no longer addressed to God. Archbishop Rossell y Arellano continued to publicly excommunicate student participants in the Huelga, sometimes encouraging churches to hold mass during the Friday parade and record the names of church members not in attendance. The Catholic press occasionally published Huelga participants' names and circulated rumors about their immoral upbringing. In 1957, a group of more than a hundred women who identified themselves simply as "the Guatemalan Woman [*la Mujer Guatemalteca*]" published a large paid political advertisement that marveled at how people could celebrate the "antisocial" Huelga and then devoutly observe the Passion of Christ a few weeks later. Like Rubio above, they argued that certain political opportunists had stolen the event from "true *universitarios*" and were using AEU publications "to create a situation of destructive and pernicious friction."

Also like Rubio, the mothers were hesitant to blame young people for their misdeeds. They wrote, "We believe that the youth . . . have not sincerely taken into account how to make their constructive contribution to national problems; that their education until now has not brought them closer to or into solidarity with [the nation] because they have not been given the opportunity to take on their social duties."[29] The women urged students to "distinguish and value civic exercise that is primarily manifested in the daily, silent, anonymous struggle that a man continually bears against the obstacles that oppose his whole self-improvement, in contrast to the other, the sporadic exercise that is only manifest in moments of political crisis." They agreed that the Huelga had declined in recent years, but insisted this was not evidence of wickedness. Young men lacked the opportunity to develop mature masculinity, "subtle ingeniousness" and "sharp irony and humorous jokes," and instead relied on "clumsy and disgusting insults" and "filthy language." The women offered up critiques as if they were heard secondhand: "we have heard [*hemos oído*]," they wrote. They had heard that students were unserious, lazy, crazy, and simply disorderly. Their response to these rumors was almost protective as they maintained that students were productive and creative, just misled, members of Guatemalan society. Conjuring specters of fascism, they cautioned that students risked becoming a servile mass without some freedom to express themselves: "We believe in the dignity of man, and in the inalienable right that he has to enjoy his fundamental liberties and that these are incompatible with blind obedience or submissive passivity."[30]

The women portrayed themselves carefully as mothers raising a politically mature pueblo fit for self-rule, yet another articulation of the gendered, classed, and raced dimensions of political authority in mid-twentieth-century Guatemala. They concluded their statement with the plea for San Carlistas to behave in a gentlemanly and patriotic manner. They wrote that although their critique may sound harsh when it scolds "the children," they felt called to implore students to "recover their gallant civic attitude." They also wrote how they were ashamed of the "rancor, slander and disorder that the students' Huelga leaves every year" because they were "united with the students by blood and affective ties, and because they are the interpreters of the intellectualism of the present and future of our pueblo."[31] The women argued that they sought only to maintain national harmony and productive tranquility as the nation's young leaders-to-be matured. They asked students "to be on alert against those who want to use [their] power for the ends of confusion and national disorder." The nation's future depended on the quality of these young people, who they called its "human material."[32]

Speaking two years later at a regional conference of universities, Martínez Durán echoed their concerns, albeit from a different ideological position. He said, "Morality is the ultimate and constant struggle for freedom. It is the duty of the *universitarios* of America to join in this fight, to defend the very essence of the university."[33] For the Guatemalan women and Martínez Durán, there was no doubt that the nation was changing, and not for the better. The expansion of youth consumer culture, especially North American-inspired rock bands, also alarmed adults.[34]

While the mothers defended the Huelga's function as a social steam valve and encouraged students to behave honorably, participants themselves increasingly insisted that the Huelga was revolutionary. This is exemplified in an *Informador Estudiantil* article that reminded readers that the event was first held in 1898 in protest of the tyranny of Estrada Cabrera and listed the years when events or participants were censored. The student author wrote, "Force has always opposed her," but the Huelga "makes them watch their back!"[35] To insist that the students' political affect was a tool that could catalyze reaction to national and international power holders was a radical claim to make. Catholics, too, referred to this legacy. An anonymous letter received by the AEU in early 1958 read, "We write to you ... because we have seen with gratitude how the current directorate of the AEU has tried to resolve civic and national problems with good sense and have seen how you have managed guiding the student body on the path of dignity and decency."[36] The group probably wrote because the new AEU leadership had forbidden *novatadas*, or pre-semester hazing rituals, which often included head shaving and "dips," where students were covered in various liquids. But the group had missed their mark. In fact, the AEU opposed the *novatadas* because they were an import from North American universities and therefore an inauthentic expression of student culture.[37]

San Carlistas focused on the event's history as they fended off the annual attacks. They often insisted that the Huelga had to be permitted for two reasons: it was an authentic university tradition and it offered an indicator of political dignity in a democratic state. One capital city journalist wrote,

"When one has been a *universitario*, it is impossible to put on prejudices and attitudes of false holiness to repudiate and condemn." The Huelga was a symbol of the eternal struggle of the spirit against the excesses of power. Yet he, too, was critical of students' gratuitous provocations. Not from a perspective "of outdated morality," he clarified, but rather "of simple intellectual guidance, like older brothers to rebellious and trouble-making boys of the family." His feeling of fraternal care required him to intervene. Concerning some students' drunkenness, the journalist asked, "How can they present themselves in public, in front of our mothers, girlfriends, or sisters?" He found it hypocritical that students would demand respect for their rights, then make "everything an object of ridicule."[38]

Actually in 1958, parade floats of the *desfile bufo* mostly ignored the Church and instead dealt dark auguries for the nation's future. At the Paraninfo, students hung a large banner with the nation's astrological reading for the year. It read, "Your future, Guatemala: Black . . ." Another banner read, "Authoritarian Huelga 1958." One float featured the diary of Castillo Armas's assassin, published by the Editorial Liberación, the vanity press of Castillo Armas's political movement. Other banners and floats emphasized Ydígoras's ties to Ubico and both regimes' close ties to the United States.

In 1959, the theatrical revue took a different approach to humiliating the president. The evening opened with a single disembodied voice booming through the theatre's huge speakers. The voice praised Fidel Castro's successful liberation movement and his bushy beard, both evidence of his virility. It ridiculed Raúl Lorenzana, an advocate for counterinsurgent violence and future founder of the Mano Blanca death squad (who could not grow a beard). Before the event, rumors circulated that the MDN planned to provoke confrontations between Catholic and non-Catholic students in order to justify strong-armed policing. Indeed, one student stood and interrupted the theatrical revue, shouting, "The Huelga of the students has no meaning; they accuse us of turning the Huelga into a way of making money. But we say: Don't you make money on the bingo and the bazaars? Isn't this commercializing God?" The student added, "We know that this rebellion of our spirit could cost us our jobs and even our lives." The journalist who reported on the outburst did not speculate that the student was an MDN provocateur, but the student's own conjecture of the costs of participation far exceeded anything that even the most outspoken opposition students had publicly articulated. The heckler was made to leave and the event continued. Conservative newspaper *El Espectador* reported that minister of education, who was in attendance, was overheard exclaiming, "The ladies could have come to see this!"[39] Virtuous manhood, honor, and dignity were concerns for all who commented on the event.[40]

For some, the Huelga was a delightful and uniquely Guatemalan spectacle that served as an expression of freedom against absolute executive power. For others, the spectacle marred the dignity of the nation, and offended the honor of women and the glory of Christ.[41] Dignity and freedom, shared idioms of political affect for urban San Carlistas, framed many of the antigovernment struggles to come. Over time, San Carlistas had learned to deploy an alternate understanding of dignity that challenged the Church and the governments of Guatemala and the United States, and in so doing, they reached across generational and class divides to begin to form a broader opposition to the government. The remainder of this chapter tracks how the language of political feelings compelled individuals to act in more serious circumstances; how and when that happened; and to what effect.

THE *JORNADAS* OF MARCH AND APRIL

On November 4, 1960, the CIA, the U.S. Army, and the U.S. Department of Defense began to organize a group of more than 1,500 Cuban exiles and Guatemalan officers at Finca Helvetia in Retalhuleu on Guatemala's Pacific coast. Their mission was to overthrow the revolutionary government led by Fidel Castro. But from the outset, logistical challenges and second-guessing overwhelmed the commanders. They had difficulty recruiting trained soldiers and pilots and attaining the necessary aircraft and landing crafts. Neither Mexico nor Britain (then ruler of Belize) would authorize an airstrip. Making matters worse, a small number of young military officers who opposed their army's involvement in Cuban affairs launched a coup to overthrow Ydígoras on November 13. The coup was unsuccessful and surviving combatants fled to the east where they recuperated and reorganized. Three of them, Luis Augusto Turcios Lima, Marco Antonio Yon Sosa, and Luis Trejo Esquivel, would go on to use their U.S. School of the Americas counterinsurgency training to lead the Revolutionary Movement—13 November (MR-13) and later, the Rebel Armed Forces (Fuerzas Armadas Rebeldes [FAR]) guerrilla organizations. The attempted coup further damaged the U.S. government's esteem for Ydígoras who was deemed too unreliable to support an important mission. The more dependable Nicaraguan president Luis Somoza

Debayle agreed to host the troops and the United Fruit Company (UFCO) donated two enormous supply ships.

The troops deployed to the Bay of Pigs on the night of April 14 and evacuated five days later. The operation was a failure. To the invaders' surprise, the people of Cuba did not rise up against Castro. Worldwide, Cubans earned the admiration of leftists like Central Americans Mario Payeras, Ricardo Ramírez, and Carlos Fonseca; black nationalists Stokely Carmichael and Amiri Baraka; and Todd Gitlin of the Students for a Democratic Society.[42] Actually, rumors of the invasion had circulated throughout the region for months. Its failure demonstrated to anti-Yankee and anticolonial movements worldwide that a great world power could be defeated. Headlines from *El Estudiante* demonstrated this hope: "Invader Crushed," "Cuba Yes...," "ARBENZ: 'Ydígoras speckled with Cuban Blood...'" and "Active Solidarity Against the Brutal Yankee Aggression Against Cuba."[43] One edition of *El Estudiante* even called for the people of Guatemala to rise up and cleanse itself of the "stain of anticommunists and the Ydígoras regime."[44]

On April 19, USAC economics students gathered to protest Guatemalan involvement in the invasion and marched in support of the Cuban Revolution, now a model of anti-imperial victory. At Central Park, they encountered a number of well-armed anticommunists. With little police interference, the anticommunists opened fire on the demonstrators. Three students were killed and many more were injured.[45] Little was done to punish the assailants. Newspaper articles that discussed the event did not name the responsible parties.

This vicious escalation temporarily checked San Carlistas' open opposition. Many turned their focus to the upcoming December midterm elections, only to have their modest hopes disappointed. Together, the allied conservative PRDN, National Liberation Movement (Movimiento de Liberación Nacional [MLN]) (formerly the MDN), and Democratic Union Party (Partido Unión Democrática [PUD]) candidates received 50 of the 66 available congressional seats and more than 75 percent of the available mayoral seats throughout the country. In fact, less than half of the population voted, and widespread fraud had occurred. To curtail protests, Ydígoras declared a State of Siege on February 2, 1962, the day when the new officials assumed power. The consequences for any public protest would be severe. The election results went uncontested for the month-long State of Siege.[46]

But toward the end of the month, some law students met and drafted a list of demands to bring to the Ydígoras government: the annulment of the midterm elections, the end of the State of Siege, and the removal of two electoral judges. Little had changed since 1956 when the AEU had done the same. The new set of demands also called on the handful of elected officials from opposition parties to resign from their posts in a symbolic rejection of the fraudulent election. Ydígoras was in Nicaragua at the time, visiting with Anastasio and Luis Somoza Debayle. On March 1, students dressed in mourning clothes and held a funeral "to signify grief for the death of freedom and democracy."[47] They unfurled black banners in the *facultades* and shamed the USAC alumni who had benefitted from the fraudulent elections. It was particularly provocative that students would call into question alumni integrity from within the space of their alma mater. Even more, the Law *facultad* was just a block and a half from the congressional chambers, so the funeral would have been visible to the elected officials. After a short ceremony, students walked to the congressional chambers and placed a floral funeral wreath with a note that read, "Legality, democracy, and freedom are incompatible with dictatorship. We express our mourning for the disappearance of an independent legislative power, for the de facto authority that will prevail from this day forward, and for the end of the rule of law in our country."[48] The group sent telegrams to student unions at other Latin American universities and to an international summit of Latin American leaders in Chile to call attention to the electoral fraud. Support for the students' protest grew among Guatemalans who were unhappy with postcoup social conditions. It was a propitious moment for oppositional politics. The recent success of the Cuban Revolution inspired some Guatemalans to study *foquismo* and other military strategies. A small number were encouraged by the guerrilla warfare waged by the MR-13, which had gone public just a few months earlier. A combative spirit of anti-Americanism was rising in Central America and the Caribbean.[49]

On March 4, a bomb exploded at the AEU offices. Around the same time, several new and unknown political groups published paid political advertisements that threatened the AEU and alleged that its student leaders had communist ties. In response to the renewed threats, university students, and soon secondary school students organized strikes and demonstrations at several key locations downtown, including the Municipal building, the Guatemalan Social Security Institute (IGSS), the *Facultad* of Law, the professional *colegio* for Law graduates, and three secondary schools, Rafael Aqueche Institute, INCA, and the National Central Institute for Boys (INCV). The groups brought downtown commerce to a halt by placing thumbtacks, rocks, sticks, and burning trash in the street and on sidewalks. The *Prensa Libre* reported that "Castro-communists" orchestrated the unrest and urged young people to be on alert against communist infiltration at their schools.[50]

Nine days later, protests erupted once more with renewed intensity. Well-coordinated university and secondary school student groups seized control of key thoroughfares throughout the capital. The conflict escalated as police rushed to respond. Students fought with rocks. The police fought with guns. Students from the Normal Central Institute for Girls Belén and the National School of Commercial Sciences joined university students from Engineering to confront police at the Trébol, a transportation nexus where Liberación Boulevard met Avenida Bolívar, which linked the secondary schools and the Engineering *facultad*. Students from Economics fought in Zone 4. Students from INCV, next to the Law *facultad* and across the street from the congressional chambers, fought at some distance from their school on Liberación Boulevard. Skirmishes spread to other parts of the city as residents erected barricades to block police access to their neighborhoods. For the first time, the protests were not limited to downtown and they effectively clogged citywide transportation and commercial networks.[51] Victor Manuel Gutiérrez remembered, "Hundreds of students, including many children of fourteen and sixteen years of age, paralyzed traffic."[52] Their militancy surprised many adults. On March 13, students captured a member of the judicial police and held him hostage in the Paraninfo. The dean of the *Facultad* of Medicine (then located at the Paraninfo) intervened and the hostage was freed, but he had been badly beaten while in the students' custody. Police responded by firing tear gas and rock salt shells into groups of gathered protestors.[53] One student, Marco Antonio Gutiérrez Flores, was killed.

The protestors were emboldened rather than cowed by the violence. The strikes were the first public protests since the 1956 student massacre and in spite of limited constitutional guarantees under the State of Siege, the protests grew. One *Prensa Libre* story read, "The entire city in a blink of an eye has become covered in a dense cloud of smoke and the groups were dissolved [only] momentarily because they immediately unified to resist police action."[54] Secondary school students in FUEGO were instrumental in organizing the street protests, drawing on contacts made during their support of the teachers' and IGSS strikes.[55] The government retaliated by closing all of the capital city's secondary schools. Unlike the university, they did not enjoy the protection offered by autonomy. Secondary school buildings could be invaded and occupied at any time and the Ministry of Education controlled teachers' contracts. Police stormed Rafael Aqueche and opened fire on a group of students standing outside of the National School of Commercial Sciences, killing two and injuring others. But once more, this violence catalyzed resistance among some secondary school students. March 14 began with a four-hour exchange of gunfire at the Paraninfo. Remarkably, only a few students were injured. The government then shut down two radio stations, Radio 1000 and Radio Quetzal, which the strikers had been using to communicate after Ydígoras cut phone lines.

Protests were not limited to the capital or to students. Quetzaltenango-based students had been active since the first days of the strike and continued protests on their campus. Railroad workers and students in the departments of Jalapa and Cobán joined the striking students in the capital. The University High Council (CSU), the national teacher's union (FUMN), and the Autonomous Federation of Guatemalan Unions (FASGUA) joined the strike. Strikers blocked bus service and built barricades in Zone 5 and the barrio of El Gallito, on the western and eastern edges of the city. Even business groups upset with the regime's corruption, instability, and the effect of this instability on foreign investments expressed their opposition to Ydígoras during the protests. The president struggled to guarantee support from the military. Around this time, some young Army officers reached out to the striking students in anticipation of Ydígoras's overthrow, actions reminiscent of the 1944 revolution. The Chamber of Commerce, part of the powerful Coordinating Committee of Agricultural, Commercial, Industrial, and Financial Associations (CACIF) continued to support Ydígoras and denounced the strike. But the Ydígoras regime struggled to demonstrate its control over the mass of protestors that had swelled in just two weeks.

The AEU declared March 15 the "National Day of Dignity" and street skirmishes continued. After the Army rank and file refused to support the president, the police transported campesinos from the countryside for reinforcement. By this point, the strikers' demands included the convocation of a National Assembly to rewrite the 1956 Constitution, the reintegration of MR-13 guerrilla leaders into the army, the indictment of some government officials in a court of law, the dissolution of repressive organizations (including the growing number of anonymous parapolice groups), and the freedom of political parties to openly organize.[56] The CSU and professional *colegios* of Medicine and Economics, bank employees, and radio deejays issued more statements in support of the strikers.[57] On Friday, March 16, emboldened by their preliminary talks with some young Army officers, the AEU proposed building an entirely new government. The police responded by laying siege to campus buildings nationwide. They surrounded the few buildings at the new University City in Zone 12 and destroyed lab equipment at the Paraninfo in the city center. Students in Quetzaltenango organized a large protest, but were forcibly dispersed. The CSU persisted and declared Ydígoras persona non grata on March 20. The government retaliated with a nationwide curfew. Unmoved, the AEU declared a total strike. They declared the University City "liberated territory [*territorio libre*]" and filed a protest permit with the government, daring Ydígoras to deny their right to assemble. Some primary school students even joined in.

In the final days of March, the seemingly endless cycle of protest and retribution slowed. Government offices reopened, police began investigations in Zone 5, Radio 1000 and Radio Quetzal were once more permitted to broadcast, university and secondary school students returned to class, and USAC administrative offices reopened. In many respects, the March protests had enabled the Army and the National Police to extend their reach and practice using greater force against dissenters.[58] But this was not their sole effect. The protests also fueled opposition from younger students, including primary and secondary school students, and inspired ever-broader alliances.

Political feelings like dignity and freedom allowed students to depict their struggle as transcendent, and even spiritual. The meaning of dignity expanded. To act with dignity was to exercise one's rights in a democratic state. Counterposed to this democratic dignity was the Ydígoras government's recourse to violence. Faced with state violence, to act with dignity was to fight the state. These rhetorics of political feeling rallied support and damaged Ydígoras's esteem among U.S. officials. U.S. ambassador John O. Bell wrote in a dispatch to the State Department, "It is impossible to conclude anything but that the President personally determined to use full force against the demonstrators (and as an obvious corollary), anyone else in the way, and to take the opportunity to bully his political enemies. I believe this decision was deliberate and I believe it was a basic political mistake."[59] Ydígoras's reaction to protestors permanently damaged his relationship with U.S. officials.

The opposition was emboldened. In early April, students broadcasted an antigovernment message across the city from the booths at Radio 1000 and Radio Nuevo Mundo. A few days later, another group held a public screening of an anti-Ydígoras film. The annual Huelga de Dolores neared, and its organizers discussed ways to adapt it to the current political conjuncture. The press predicted that the year's Huelga would be especially intense. Anticipating trouble, the AEU General Assembly issued a manifesto that held the government responsible for "the fatal consequences that could suddenly arise as a result of repression or threat to the normal development of our civil and peaceful march." They affirmed that the parade would continue along the route that it had always taken, departing from the Faculty of Medicine at the Paraninfo and heading toward the Faculty of Law. The organizers stated publicly that the event would be carried out with solemnity, offering a peaceful "expression of suffering [dolores]," but given the Huelga's tongue-in-cheek tone, it is difficult to know what they meant.[60] To be safe, the organizers erected barricades between the parade participants and the crowd. But at some point during the march, a military patrol car sped through the barricades and struck one student, César Armando Funes Velásquez, whose back was turned to the street. The vehicle sped away toward the Law *facultad* where, moments later, shots were fired into a crowd assembled at the entrance. Two more students were killed and another was gravely injured.[61]

The story spread that the attacks were planned. Ydígoras called a press conference and refuted the rumor. Concurrently, secondary school students organized a demonstration to denounce the government's role in the attack. Again, military police arrived to dissolve the protests, shouldering shotguns and rifles while the students fought back with rocks. In the fighting, security forces killed another student, Felipe Gutierrez Lacán. In the words of one observer, "The afternoon foretold an unjust fight."[62] While the president insisted that the police acted in response to students' attempts to disarm them, some citizens were suspicious that the government had planned the attack. Some began to call the deaths a massacre and recalled when the Army and police used force against students in 1956. Nearly 10,000 mourners attended the four students' funerals. Labor unions, business groups, women's organizations, and even the Association of Guatemalan Journalists (APG) wrote anti-Ydígoras paid political advertisements.

It seemed that the only sectors steadfast in their support for Ydígoras were landowners, the CACIF, and the Catholic Church. The military's support for Ydígoras was conditional. By mid-1962, the Ydígoras regime had only two assets, its repressive capacities and its zealous rhetoric of anticommunism.[63] These two assets proved powerful enough to put an end the protests. In late April, Ydígoras declared another State of Siege and the police began another wave of arrests. Defense Minister Colonel Enrique Peralta Azurdia received an executive order that charged him with the responsibility to maintain stability in the city. The highest-ranking Army officer had carte blanche to quell unrest. According to broadcasts collected by the U.S. Foreign Broadcast Information Service, most students wanted to return to class by April 27, but the AEU urged them to persist.[64] By early May, the AEU agreed to lift the strike—not in defeat, they assured—as part of a change in tactics.[65] By that time, the government had imprisoned around 2,000 people and killed four USAC students and eleven high school students.[66] These six weeks of protests through March and April became known as the *Jornadas* and they marked a turning point in the government's relationship to student protest.

In Guatemalan historical memory, the *Jornadas* are often recalled as either reactionary outbursts or an extensive plot hatched by the AEU and FUEGO. Pronouncements over the meaning of the *Jornadas* began as soon as the protests themselves ended. As in Brazil and Mexico, such events become important flashpoints in the ongoing negotiation between students and state power.[67] Political scientist and later advisor to the URNG guerrilla Miguel Angel Reyes Illescas summarized the students' approach in the following terms: "They began with a denunciation of the deplorable national situation and the electoral fraud; then they moved on to petitions, persuasion, or information directed at public opinion, later to intimidation; gatherings, work stoppages, strikes; and then they came to direct action: rocks, thumbtacks, sticks, pestilent liquids, and pistols."[68] For Illescas, who was then still a student in social and juridical sciences, the student combatants were strategic and idealistic. Contemporary social theorist Adolfo Gilly was more critical. Writing in 1965, he argued that while the AEU was instrumental in organizing clashes in the streets, it lacked any coherent program to ally with peasants and workers. Because of this lack of leadership, the *Jornadas* were unable to become more than antigovernment street fights.[69] It is true that the students were unable to turn the protests into revolution in the course of two months, but they did strengthen new popular coalitions with labor and other groups, marking a turning point in the radicalization of domestic politics.[70] Another account of the protests appeared in *Guatemala: El significado de las jornadas de marzo y abril*, a remarkable commemorative text published by USAC professor and politician Manuel Colom Argueta in 1979. Colom Argueta stressed how the moment "served as an experiment in and reason for the perfection of paramilitary organizations and repressive methodologies with roots in fascism" as well as the inauguration of the use of "preventative-punitive repression in order to avoid the development of popular forces."[71] Yet he also wrote that the government was unable to control the rebellion "and Guatemala City belong[ed] to no one" for two months.[72] Or perhaps, to paraphrase Martínez Durán, the city belonged to the students.

The *Jornadas* also helped to strengthen urban students' connections to the countryside. Members of the Patriotic Workers' Youth (JPT) joined the October 20th Front, a short-lived guerrilla organization under the military leadership of Major Carlos Paz Tejada and the ideological leadership of USAC engineering student and AEU General Secretary (1958–1959), Julio Rodriguez Aldana. The group's impact was profound, even though it only reached Baja Verapaz before it was decimated by a squadron of police officers.[73] One student combatant, Rodrigo Asturias, was briefly captured then released. Asturias was the godson of President Ydígoras and the son of Guatemala's first Nobel laureate, Miguel Angel Asturias. Asturias's story again reminds us of that agonizing feature of the civil war when godsons fought to depose their godfathers and schoolmates from INCV often found themselves at opposite ends of ideologies and shotgun sights. In the 1980s, Asturias became commander in chief of the Revolutionary Organization of People in Arms (ORPA) under the nom de guerre Gaspar Ilom. Other guerrilla leaders also emerged out of the *Jornadas* and early guerrilla combat, including Edgar Ibarra and Julio César Macías (alias César Montes). Many San Carlistas who became politically active in the late 1970s, like Manuel Andrade Roca and Ricardo Martínez Solórzano, remembered the *Jornadas* as their radicalizing experience. Both would be assassinated in early 1979 for their involvement in the struggle.[74]

Writing more than a decade later, the FAR pointed to these urban protests as the moment that made clear the need to take the armed path of revolution. The group itself was formed when the MR-13 joined with clandestine PGT members, secondary and university students in the April 12 Movement, and combatants in the Edgar Ibarra Front just a few months after these urban protests in December 1962. Similarly, the leadership of the Guerrilla Army of the Poor (Ejército Guerrillero de los Pobres [EGP]), which was formed after a division within the FAR in 1972, wrote that the protests were one of the first moments when rich Guatemalans felt fear of losing their wealth, their power, and their life in retaliation for the injustices they had carried out against the people.[75] These texts indicate the importance of the memory of the *Jornadas*, after which some students, workers, and campesinos shared a history of struggle. This did not mean that the proliferating groups on the left agreed on matters of strategy. But writings after the *Jornadas* took previous rhetorics of dignity and honor and expanded them with new martyrs and fresh evidence of the government's viciousness toward its citizens. Shared idioms of political affect crossed generation, region, and occupation, and spread across factories, classrooms, and the countryside.

USAC had gained a national reputation as a university with a political conscience. Guatemala's first private university, the Universidad Rafael Landívar (URL), which opened on October 18, 1961, became the school of choice for those who desired a religious and apolitical education. URL joined the Instituto Politécnica as a place for the sectors of society that rejected student politics. USAC continued to enroll the vast majority of students, especially those who were attracted by its political tradition, but now students had the option to enroll elsewhere without joining the military. Meanwhile, USAC's renown spread worldwide. An article by Amílcar Burgos that appeared in *The Student*, the trilingual magazine published by the Coordinating Secretariat of the International Student Conference (COSEC), denounced Ydígoras in no uncertain terms.[76] Burgos located the immediate cause for students' protest in the president's democratic charade. Several photographs of orderly protestors printed opposite photographs of violent arrests, funerals, and tear gas bombs accompanied the text. The message was clear: students were dignified and peaceful while the government was aggressive.

International connections continued to shape students' anti-Yankee sentiment, a feeling that had also become an important part of calls for national dignity. Students were profoundly impacted by their encounters with different political traditions at international student congresses of the ISC and the IUS in places like Ceylon, Peru, Switzerland, Austria, Quebec, Uganda, and Iraq, and periods of exile in nearby Mexico, El Salvador, and Nicaragua.[77] In the coming decades, many notable and less notable San Carlistas went into exile, including Alfonso Bauer Paíz, Carlos Figueroa Ibarra, Marco Antonio Villamar Contreras, Mario René Matute, Carlos González Orellana, Iduvina Hernández, and Arturo Taracena Arriola.[78] San Carlistas' solidarity with other Central American students deepened. When two exiled students were arrested in Nicaragua in December 1958, the AEU responded by writing to Nicaraguan president Luis Somoza Debayle and to COSEC.[79] The president of the AED wrote to the president of the student union of the Universidad Nacional Autónoma de Nicaragua (UNAN) and requested Nicaraguan students' intervention to ensure their safety. The following year, the AEU announced its solidarity with the people of Nicaragua against the "disgraceful," "tyrannical," and "nepotistic" Somoza regime.[80] As news of their defiance and sacrifice spread, the AEU received letters of support from student unions around the world. Their success showed how political affect that built on local concerns, transnational solidarities, and shared experiences of oppression could be wielded as a weapon.

The student internationalism that enthralled antigovernment and anticolonial movements worldwide became most visible in the summer of 1968. But in Guatemala, as in Mexico and elsewhere in Latin America, 1968 came six years early.[81] At the end of two months of combat, the streets of the capital and many peripheral cities had been transformed into battlegrounds. Tens of thousands of people had been mobilized in demonstrations, two guerrilla groups had launched rebellions, and around fifty civilians had died. Central Park, the Trébol, city buses, popular radio stations, and certain downtown street corners had become spaces of protest, martyrdom, and popular victory. Many factors, including the visibility of the protests, their risk, and the growing multiclass coalition, bolstered the opposition's claims that they were engaged in acts of dignity and duty in the defense of human rights. The historical memory of earlier struggles and even the 1944 Constitutional Assembly also provided powerful fuel.[82]

Meanwhile, the Ydígoras administration struggled to repair its reputation after its eager use of force.[83] For his allies, Ydígoras was an unstable and strong-armed leader who was increasingly difficult to defend. The U.S. State Department needed better intelligence and more professional police, not the impulsive use of force. The Ydígoras regime spent the remainder of 1962 consolidating its control over the capital city and portraying students in the press as psychotic bomb-throwers implicated in a conspiracy to overthrow the government. One article in *Diario de Centro América* with the headline, "Terrorists Captured," is representative of these efforts. It read:

> Bomb in the hands of a Law Student—2 more were taken into custody. Elements of the national police with the object of paralyzing terrorist activities in the capital city have deployed their best detectives to carry out the capture of those responsible for these criminal acts ... the courts reported yesterday that at 8:30am Mr. Salvador Pineda Longo was detained, a student of Law who, it was established after close surveillance to which he was subjected by his arrestors, was an individual addicted to sabotage and who maintains close relations with Gustavo Quiñónez Leiva, known terrorist...[84]

Pineda Longo was damned by his involvement with the infamously antigovernment Law *facultad* and "close relations" with a "known terrorist." The implication was that like his friend, he might even be "addicted to sabotage."

In many national papers of the period, "terrorist" and "terrorism" were used liberally to denote a domestic threat and to inspire fear.[85]

This sense of being under constant threat was an ever-greater part of life for San Carlistas and other Guatemalans. The threat was not only physical violence; it could take other pernicious forms. In August 1962, a group of students wrote that foreign experts and curriculum were attempting to "domesticate the consciousness of our intellectuals and youth." This amounted to nothing less than an intellectual invasion.[86] The group rejected hemispheric Americanism as pro-Yankee, and instead called for the nation's community of scholars to join together and develop nationalist forms of knowledge that reflected the needs, interests, and resources of the people. They reached across generation and into the university's legacy: anticolonialism connected the *próceres* who fought Spanish colonial power to the student combatants against the dictatorships of Estrada Cabrera and Ubico to the protestors of the *Jornadas* to the Huelga's drunken revelers.

By 1963, the Huelga was no fun at all. Instead of wisecracks, the *No Nos Tientes* featured retrospective summaries of the spectacular injustices San Carlistas endured in the previous year. The student authors also struggled to make sense of a coup that had occurred less than a week before the paper was printed. The coup deposed Ydígoras, suspended the Constitution, and positioned Peralta Azurdia as both defense minister and president. The anonymous writers of the year's editorial noted that these events were only part of the ongoing exploitation and deception of the people. The year's editorial was entitled "The Progress of Our Struggle" and it engaged in none of the word play and double entendre that characterized the paper's previous seven decades. Instead, it argued that the free exchange of scholars and ideas was necessary for the progress of scientific and cultural knowledge, but cautioned how direct intervention or interference into the educational and pedagogical plans of another nation had dire consequences for the development of national culture and freedom of thought. It concluded with a call to action: "We will always be the first in defense of the conservation of peace and security for Guatemalans, but we cannot deny the inevitability of violence in a community whose fundamental characteristics are misery and social decay, [and] where those responsible remain in power."

The *No Nos Tientes* also featured a reprinted CSU statement that speculated that the Peralta Azurdia coup was intended to prevent Juan José Arévalo's likely bid for president in the coming elections, as Arévalo had spent several months reconnecting with Guatemala's political and military elite from exile in Mexico and had returned to Guatemala on March 30, the day before the coup. Demonstrating growing concerns around sovereignty and international aid, one feature entitled "Foreign Educational Interference in the Guatemalan University" featured a terrifying cartoon of the Statue of Liberty and a history of the Alliance for Progress in Guatemala and Central America. Lady Liberty held aloft a missile instead of the torch of liberty, an automatic pistol instead of a book of law, and wore combat boots, a mask, and a shoulder-holstered scabbard instead of a robe.[87]

Again, unlike any previous edition, the second page of the *No Nos* was composed entirely of a proclamation issued by the AEU in observance of the first anniversary of the *Jornadas*. The AEU wrote that the struggles had cost Guatemala "the blood of its best sons," but that the sacrifice would serve "as the basis for the construction of a better nation." *Huelgueros* honored the dead as martyrs not just for Guatemala, but for all of Latin America, which was united in the struggle for democracy and against despotism. The student leaders offered themselves to the pueblo of Guatemala as democracy's loyal and true representatives. Once more, they claimed it was their duty to combat the corruption, opportunism, and incapacity of the government. Finally, and importantly, they outlined the lengths they were willing to go to in the fight for freedom: "Although our greatest hope is that the current political situation will be resolved without unnecessary sacrifices, the truth is that we can neither deny nor ignore that this hope could be altered by factors beyond our control ... in excess of the framework of critical thought and civility and citizenship."[88]

These were not romantic thoughts or mere flights of fancy. Remember that by the beginning of 1963, the MR-13 had joined with the April 12 Movement, the PGT, and the Edgar Ibarra Front to form the FAR. As the war developed, each group focused on a particular strategic location: the Edgar Ibarra Front in the mountainous Sierra de las Minas, the MR-13 in the lowland parts of Izabal and Zacapa, and the PGT in Guatemala City.[89] FAR combatants recruited students at USAC and secondary schools, usually through word of mouth. If San Carlistas wanted to fight the escalation of force "in excess of the framework of critical thought and civility and citizenship," as the AEU statement had read, they probably knew whom to ask.

UNITY THROUGH FELLOW FEELING

The university changed dramatically after the Peralta Azurdia coup, yet the ideals and—in Martínez Durán's words—the "manner of feeling" developed during the Ydígoras regime would continue to shape USAC political culture until the end of the civil war. The lessons were impossible to forget: the state could be ferocious and alliances with the pueblo were vital. The San Carlista "manner of feeling" was contestatory and transnational, full of struggle and contradictions. Focusing on a performative political affect helps to make sense of San Carlistas' rhetoric and actions. For instance, at first, university students were willing to work with Ydígoras because they were optimistic that he would follow through on his campaign promises and were committed to the rule of law, leading by example, and being of service to the community. But over time, after many reprisals, electoral fraud, revolutionary Cuba's inspiring success at Playa Girón, and state violence, some *universitarios* definitively changed their position. They built broad alliances with groups outside the university, even some members of the military. They wrote to international student and government bodies. Importantly, as this would be the hallmark of student nationalism in the coming decades, they began to hold the government in low esteem. The university and its students were the real arbiters of truth and justice.

Although some promising early moments ended in disappointment, students subtly invoked dignity, freedom, and duty to elevate their cause and bring more people into their struggle. San Carlistas demonstrated how political claims in the affective register could lead to a call for a politics by a class-for-itself while also providing a rhetorical space for contestation and cross-class alliance. What dignity meant to San Carlistas is, in any case, less clear than what they could accomplish by uttering or addressing these affective claims to an audience. The more interesting historical question is not to define what San Carlistas and others meant when they wrote about "freedom" or "dignity," but to understand what these types of affective appeals achieved. As San Carlistas wrote and read calls for dignity and freedom, and sovereignty and democracy, they shifted the shared idioms of political affect used by the left. This was the case on the right, too, where Catholic citizens' letters, U.S. intelligence briefs, and national newspaper op-eds offered interpretations of duty and dignity. On each side, tales of heroism filled pages. These affective negotiations further distinguished the right from the left in civil war-era Guatemala.

During the Ten Years' Spring, students were civil servants in training. Accordingly, student nationalism emphasized students' role in national progress, especially their obligation to focus on questions of national concern and lead a people that were believed to be unprepared for self-government.

Chapter 2 outlined how this changed under the Castillo Armas regime when *universitarios* defined themselves as nationalists against the North American business elite and, later, against the Guatemalan military and police in the name of nation, liberty, and democracy. But in the mid-1960s, an increasingly enmeshed security apparatus comprising military, paramilitary, and police forces elaborated their counterinsurgency war. In June 1965, Comando Seis of the National Police was formed to respond to "public safety emergencies" and collect intelligence on potential threats, namely in the capital city. Five months later, Colonel Rafael Ariaga Bosque launched "Operation Cleanup [*Limpieza*]" to coordinate the actions and intelligence of the nation's main security agencies. U.S. Public Safety Advisor John Longan was sent from Venezuela to organize the operation.[90] This new program also marked the beginning of targeted abductions.

When their resistance to the military and police began to take an ever-greater toll, San Carlistas staged symbolic funerals for democracy, political funerals for their classmates, and built barricades in the streets. They no longer derived legitimacy from the government or the Constitution; instead, they appealed to abstract principles such as justice, honor, and conscience as they argued for their duty to lead the people and the nation toward progress. It was the rhetoric of feelings of fraternity, dignity, honesty, and valor that permitted San Carlistas to define student nationalism explicitly against the government. To some extent, this had been happening since the *escuilaches* met by candlelight. But this moment was exceptional. Contemporary administrators, journalists, bureaucrats, and even students tried to explain the dramatic shift.[91] The question that had been posed since the beginning of the twentieth century took on more meaning throughout the civil war: what role did the university have in society? And what consequences did this have for national political life?

Even seemingly lackluster events became occasions for an antigovernment salvo. At the inaugural ceremony of the secretariat of the Association of Humanities Students (AEH) in 1961 incoming president Carlos Alberto Figueroa's speech emphasized the importance of the humanities in general, but then turned toward students' responsibility in "the fight against dogmatism and the fight for freedom." Figueroa spoke, "The freedom that we ought to seek, compañeros, is achieved in only one way ... knowledge combined with social practice ... We are free insofar as we can know the real extent of our spiritual and material needs and insofar as we can, on the basis of this [knowledge], effectively transform society and nature ..." To their detriment, Guatemala's intellectuals remained bound "by the circumstance of national underdevelopment (the intellectual in an underdeveloped nation is more a slave than anyone)." Lack of strong traditions in sociology, political science, and history impoverished an intellectual just as economic underdevelopment impoverished a worker or campesino. Figueroa pledged that he would fight to make sure that these advances were made.[92]

His words resonated with those delivered by Rector Martínez Durán two years earlier. Both men spoke of freedom and the desire to think and to feel. Both men claimed the university's special role as leader of the nation's cultural and political development. Martínez Durán emphasized harmony and understood the university as a community "constructed upon [a] base of shared virtues" and celebrated how the admission of all social classes provided an "assurance of the conservation and progress of democracy." But Figueroa saw that unity as something yet to come. He closed his speech with a call for unity: "It will be beautiful when we feel like brothers, all of us, in the search for truth there is something that ought to unify us."[93] Figueroa's confident use of the future indicative tense—"it *will* be beautiful"—and his fraternal inclusiveness rendered the search for truth as essential to the *universitario*. We do not know how many people heard his speech, though he did reprint it in the first AEH bulletin of his term (a publication with a print run of 300 copies). Though the impact of this speech was probably minimal and it was unlikely to have changed the way that San Carlistas understood freedom, it communicated through an idiom of political affect that made sense to his audience of San Carlistas—students, professors, administrators—and probably some parents. His speech itself acknowledged the common ground: "There is something that ought to unite us [and that is] our *Patria Guatemala* with her painful reality, her ineffable misery, reflected today by many writers and also her beauty and our love for her, sung by the poets." In the idioms of political affect, San Carlistas used loss and violence to create unity against foreign threat and promote a shared project of national and nationalist growth.

FOUR

Go Forth and Teach All, 1963–1977

Id y enseñad a todos / Go forth and teach all
Official motto of the Universidad de San Carlos

Id y aprended de todos / Go forth and learn from all
San Carlista muralist Arnoldo Ramírez Amaya, 1973

FLOPPY-HAIRED AND BESPECTACLED LAW STUDENT Mario López Larrave drew the masthead for the *No Nos Tientes* in 1966, as he had in 1949 and so many years since. Two restrained and bloodied prisoners formed the letters N in *No* and *Nos*. A torture manual, a military cap with the words "Dictatorship Made in the USA" in English across the front, two student protestors with big banners, a smoking Molotov cocktail, and Lady Liberty in chains formed the remaining letters. The masthead evoked the tone of the paper, which pitted heroic students against foreign oppressors and a complicit state in a battle for Guatemala. The edition's editorial declared, "On this date of Sorrow, which for every university students carries even fuller meaning with the unhappy memory of our martyrs, there is nothing else to promote in this traditional periodical but the urgent need to once again raise up our declaration, now under the mark of the most profound solemnity, of the right to open and vigorous struggle."[1]

The rest of the editorial was a revision of the classic USAC student polemic, entitled "Somos los mismos," first published in 1922. Updated and reprinted in 1944, 1955, and again in 1966, the text articulated San Carlistas' fraternal lineage in terms of a timeless struggle against tyranny. The students' enemies, the *chafarotes*, had remained the same "from the time when [we] were a Colony of Spain, to the time when [we] became a Colony of the United States." In Central American argot, *chafarote* means something between "cops" and "pigs" and comes from the verb *chafar* (to mash or muss, as one would remove wheat from chaff).[2] After 1944, the *chafarotes* were those who had betrayed Arévalo; later, the *chafarotes* were those who backed

Ａ Ｎ Ｏ Ｓ Ｔ Ｉ Ｅ Ｎ Ｔ Ｅ Ｓ

NO TOLERAMOS CUARTELAZOS · VOTOS ALTERADOS · LIBERTAD, SI CHAFAS, NO

| AÑO...RANZA PRESIDENCIAL | VIERNES DE DOLORES DE 1966 | EPOCA DE SECUESTROS Y ASESINATOS |

Editorial

Torturado, encapuchado, gaseado, a veces fusilado, posiblemente "marineado" y siempre hambreado, Pueblo querido de Guatemala; en este Viernes de todos los Dolores, del año en Desgracia de 1966, la Voz del Estudiante Universitario —de ese estudiante de la Universidad Autónoma de San Carlos, que se debe y se muere por vos—, en esta ocasión además de un puñado de jacarandosa alegría, viene a ofrecerte un RECORDATORIO, que no puedes en momento alguno relegar al olvido:

¡QUE LOS CHAFAROTES DE GUATEMALA, FUERON Y SIGUEN SIENDO LOS MISMOS!

Para demostrar esta afirmación nuestra, hagamos un poco de Historia, mientras ellos se siguen cagando en la idem.

Demostraremos con pocas palabras, que tanto durante el tiempo en que fuimos Colonia de España, como durante el tiempo que venimos siendo Colonia de los Estados Unidos, los chafarotes son los mismos.

(Pasa a la página nueve)

AMOR FILIAL

Con ocasión de celebrar el Día del Padre (y ante la imposibilidad de celebrar el de la madre), fué capeada la elegante figura del constitucional jefe de Gobierno, cuando intercambiaba cariñosos reburnos de felicitación con su hijito mayor, recluído en el hospital Bella Aurora. Al fondillo, presencia la escena, su sobrinito y coronelito Peralta Méndez, próximo paciente de dicho centro hospitalario, pues desde el 6 de marzo se le viene agudizando la aftosa militar.

BUENOS DIAS...

Por
Coco Palmieri Ydígoras Peralta
Méndez Montenegro

He sido, soy y seguiré siendo... amante de... la farándula, la oropén la y la camándula. Y es por eso que hoy me desayuné en el Maya Excélsior con Manuel Zinceña Pliéguez (ninguno de los dos pagó la cuenta, y Meme firmó un vale a nombre de Ramiro Samayoa). Almorcé luego en el Biltmore, con Ramiro Samayoa (ninguno de los dos pagó tampoco la cuenta, y Ramirito firmó un vale a nombre de Manuel Zinceña). Y por la noche, cené en El Emperador con Mini-Mini (esta vez sí pagó... Mini-Mini).

Terminando la cena, se me ocurrió —como estaban próximas las elecciones presidenciales— hacer una entrevista a alguno de los candidatos. Y fué el mismo Mini-Mini, quien me sugirió hiciera esa entrevista al gran estadista, enorme estratega, y sin par guerrero, Coronel y Piloto Aviador, Ganador de la Cruz de Hierro, la Cruz Azul, y la Cruz de Ceniza, MIGUEL ANGEL PONCIANO SANDOVAL ALARCON.

Y fué así como me encaminé al abandonado Hipódromo del Norte, en mi lujoso B.M.W. (el mismo en que recorrí Centro América con Chichí... chichicha). Al llegar a los Arcos, un esbelto y apolíneo soldado (colmilludo, patilludo, bigotudo, como diría Miguel Angel Asturias) me franqueó la entrada y me dijo: "Pase Ud. y vaya adonde pace el coronel Ponciano".

La lujosa fachada del edificio ostentaba la leyenda: Establo nacional. En el mástil ondeaba una bandera tricolor: azul, blanco y rojo, luciendo enmedio una cruz dagada, sangrante y ratolina... te. Traspuse el viejo portón y entré al zaguán empedrado que lucía entre sus adoquines zacate, estiércol y una que otra chenca. Fuí pasando de apartamento en apartamento (allí les llaman cubículos) y buscando el nombre de MI CORONEL, fuí leyendo varios nombres, que en sendas tablitas, estaban en las respectivas entradas.

El primero era "LUCERO" (poético pseudónimo del coronel Zea Carrascosa). Retinto, refogoso y recabreo.

Le seguía "RAYO" (coronel Callejitas). Bailador, trotador y conspirador.

En el siguiente piafaba "MAGO" (Balta Morales), hermosísimo mostrenco, podenco y bien renco.

A su lado y en un oloroso pesebre, se contoneaba una linda y veterana yegüita "COQUETA" (Molly D'Shtal). Fino ejemplar tordillo, fondillo, calientillo.

Desentonaba entre (la pléyade de finos y bellos exponentes de la raza caballar, un sucio y enfermizo jamelgo, "FRANCHUTE", Muleto del Champ, que no era ni retinto, ni tordillo, ni de trote, ni de silla. Al contrario, en un pedazo de lámina y al lado de su afrancesado nombre, ostentaba sus características: asalariado, choteado, taimado, menguado, arrastrado. Nos asomamos a su barda y entonces lo oímos, tratando de pronunciar a puro relincho, el nombre de Julio César... Nos contó después el cuidador de la cuadra, que tenían a Franchute en ese lugar, pues era el caballito que había servido para aprendieran a jinetear todos los presidentes, desde Juan José Arévalo hasta el chocho de don Miguel, pasando por Cara de Hacha y Pollino. Este séptimo, montaba y era montado por Franchute.

Mi emoción llegó al máximo, cuando se me indicó que habíamos llegado a la mansión, no del Pájaro-Serpiente de

(Pasa a la página ocho)

FIGURE 6. Front page of the *No Nos Tientes*, 1966. Satirical Publications Collection. Archivo Histórico, Centro de Investigaciones Regionales de Mesoamérica (CIRMA).

Arbenz's Agrarian Reform (it was too moderate and capitalistic for the editors). Anyone who supported U.S.-imported anticommunism was a *chafarote*. *Chafarotes* supported Castillo Armas. They formed "a caste of the insatiable 'new rich,' yet [were] ancient, ongoing—and for their whole life—sons of bitches" who would "sell out the lower classes of the nation, who would deny their humble origins in order to become the foot soldiers of the creole Oligarchy, allied with the reactionary Clergy . . . marionettes of Imperialism, willing to drown and asphyxiate their Sovereignty." The editorial concluded, "They continue being the same . . . but WE, THE STUDENTS, ALSO CONTINUE BEING THE SAME!"[3] *Chafarotes*, inconstant and disloyal, represented the antithesis of the committed San Carlistas.

Perhaps, too, the cadres of youth more devoted to counterculture than to social transformation were *chafarotes*. By the mid-1960s, young people helped to create a vibrant music industry in radio, television, film, and records that was at first informed by North American styles, but increasingly in tune with a new Latin American rock sound. In 1963, Radio Panamericana studios recorded a compilation of Guatemalan groups (*¡Aquí estamos!*) and a musical film called *Nosotros los jóvenes* brought Mexican bands to Guatemalan movie theatres.[4] Around the same time, daily newspapers like *El Gráfico*, *La Nación*, *La Tarde*, and *La Semana* devoted whole sections of their paper to youth culture. The youth section of *El Gráfico* was called "Puerta abierta a la juventud" and for the entire month of May 1965, it was devoted to interviews with popular rock bands, like Los Electrónicos, Los Reyes del Ritmo, Los Beatniks, Los Yaquis, Los Traviesos, Los Americanos, and Los Marauders. Most of the bands' members attended elite schools like Liceo Guatemala, Liceo Americano, and Liceo Javier or were in the first years at Universidad Rafael Landívar. A smaller number went to USAC. The interviews made no mention of the ongoing protests that were taking place at many of the very schools where these young people studied. Instead, they focused on the musicians' favorite hobbies, bands, aspirations, and ideal girlfriend (in terms of physical appearance and manners).[5] This mediascape of cars, women, guitars, and drugs was out of sync with the other realities of Guatemalan life: state repression, civil war, racism, and inequality.

This chapter discusses how San Carlistas sought to solve underdevelopment and challenge North American imperialism in the 1960s and 1970s. On the attack against underdevelopment, San Carlistas strode confidently into the countryside and urban poor neighborhoods and, following the motto of their alma mater, set out to "Go Forth and Teach All!" While it is not clear whether they improved the lives of others, it is clear that these experiences changed how San Carlistas understood themselves. Like AEH president Carlos Alberto Figueroa in Chapter 3, many San Carlistas promoted a sort of scholarly nationalism characterized by research and social action. USAC social scientists looked to contemporary development and dependency theory to understand why underdevelopment seemed endemic even after foreign businesses expanded their investments in the region. Latin American integrationism, which characterized regional politics after World War II, deepened.[6] The experience of exile among leftist faculty and students also contributed to the theory's appeal, especially for those who went to Paris, Buenos Aires, and Mexico City, where *dependentistas* and *desarrollistas* gathered. Yet in their encounter with dependency theory, USAC social scientists found that Guatemala's semifeudal economy, natural resources, and large indigenous population complicated extant explanations of their nation, even those from the left. This led Guatemalan *dependentistas* to elaborate a theory that took into account these crucial differences. This chapter provides a brief intellectual history of USAC *dependentistas* and then explores how they related to new extension programming and protests against natural resource extraction, particularly mining in rural Guatemala, a place far from San Carlistas' daily life but crucial to their thinking about national development.

Between 1966 and 1975, enrollment at the Guatemala City and Quetzaltenango campuses grew from 8,171 to 22,861 students.[7] Despite this dramatic increase, the university remained a place for the still small percentage of the population that had access to the tuition, prerequisites, and time necessary to attain a university-level education. Remember, the 1964 national census reported that just 14,060 out of 3,174,900 Guatemalans (0.44%) had attended any university-level schooling. Only forty indigenous men had attended some university-level study while more than 1 million indigenous people had not attended any schooling at any level. Moreover, less than 4 percent of San Carlistas were of "humble origins," which for the university-wide census meant that their families earned an income of less than US$100 per month. Meanwhile, illiteracy in 1964 was about 63.3 percent nationwide and 81.6 percent of people who lived in rural regions reported having never attended school at all.[8] Enduring social stratification fueled San Carlistas' long-standing conviction that it was their duty to bring culture and knowledge—in a word, progress—to the pueblo.

In the 1940s and 1950s, university administrators debated "the dreams and needs of the nation" and viewed students as an "intellectual vanguard" tasked with "promoting, conserving, spreading, and transmitting culture."[9] This was especially clear in April 1958, when the AEU outlined its "Cultural and Social Missions" in its newspaper, *Informador Estudiantil*. The group's leadership wrote, "acknowledging the multiple wants that the Guatemalan people suffer as the result of economic, cultural, and social backwardness, it is the imperative ... duty of *universitarios* to spread education and culture, promoting the improvement of the nation." With a missionary zeal, students aspired "to awaken, create, and promote civic spirit," "to promote and invigorate in the Guatemala [a] full national conscience," and "to strengthen the connections between the University and the pueblo." A Central Executive Committee coordinated activities suited to each *facultad*'s expertise. For instance, medical and dental students organized hygiene campaigns, taught preventative medicine and nutrition, and saw patients. Agronomy students gave talks about natural resource management, introduced new crops, and donated seeds. Economics students met with residents to discuss local commerce, bank credit applications, the organization of cooperatives, and "the need for technological advancement in small local industries." Law students planned talks on legal codes, but also provided legal aid, met with local judges to check on trials in progress, and visited jails to become acquainted with their conditions. Humanities students, in turn, met with teachers and parents to discuss their pedagogical challenges, donated books to libraries, and organized recreational activities. In every case, students' plans were guided by the belief that their duty was to transmit education and culture outward from the university to the needy pueblo.[10]

The rhetorics of dignity, freedom, and duty that characterized student nationalism during the presidencies of Ydígoras and Peralta Azurdia, highlighted in the previous chapter, also saturated development plans. When Canadian-owned nickel mining company Exploraciones y Explotaciones Mineras Izabel S.A. (EXMIBAL) proposed a new mine near Lake Izabal, professors of economics asked their students and colleagues, "Are you prepared to defend the national patrimony...? The *Facultad* of Economics at the University of San Carlos of Guatemala will be on the front lines and will lend all of its resources to ensure that the wealth of our subsoil will be used by Guatemala and for the benefit of Guatemalans."[11] This call for defense drew on the language of political affect that obligated San Carlistas to protect and defend the nation from foreign threats. It was, after all, their duty as San Carlistas.

Extension programming, natural resource conservation, and dependency praxis enabled the formation and contestation of social class in ways that often also challenged older positivist mindsets, including ideas about intellect, literacy, preparedness, and civic value that had undergirded university-based development plans for decades.[12] Previously, a sort of colonial "humanist governance" had positioned "democratically capable professionals" in an advisory role over other citizens who were still developing their democratic potential.[13] But by the end of the 1970s, critique of the historical relationship between the university and the pueblo was common. In 1978, law student and journalist José Luis Balcárcel Ordóñez observed that students and professors were "agents of developmental interpellation."[14] His reference to Louis Althusser's 1969 essay "Ideology and Ideological State Apparatuses" was meant to cast doubt on the university's connection to the pueblo. But as the previous three chapters have demonstrated, power, collaboration, and class making at USAC were complex. San Carlistas were not only produced, or "steeped in," ideology by a capitalist bourgeois education system; they were also the agents of its reproduction. And as intellectual elites in a peripheral nation, they were hailed by ideologies of their own making. Several students were self-conscious about this and published articles in student papers where they reckoned with their class status and relationship to the state. I discuss some of these articles below.

The archive for this chapter is especially diverse, including theoretical texts, cartoons, student theses, paid political advertisements, company literature, and student newspapers. Across a variety of texts, San Carlista faculty and students considered the university's relationship with the pueblo. Though this had been a topic of heated discussions for many decades, state violence and new alliances among students, workers, campesinos, and the guerrilla transformed the debate. USAC-based plans for development offered a crucial challenge to the military's entwined missions of surveillance, repression, and development. Development praxis—evident in new plans for extension programming, protests against natural resource exploitation, and even the indigenous comic strip hero Juan Tecú—became the crux of class making.

SAN CARLISTA *DEPENDENTISTAS* AND "A NEW INDUSTRY FOR GUATEMALA!"

Soon after petrol and nickel reserves were discovered in the subsoil, Guatemala's political, military, and educational sectors scrambled to offer plans for their development. On July 19, 1945, Juan José Arévalo met with the Interamerican Development Commission to discuss North American investment. Article 95 of the Constitution, commonly called the Petrol Law, restricted his plans. The Petrol Law protected natural resources as national patrimony and placed limits on extraction by foreign companies.[15] Typical of revolutionary-era nationalism, sovereignty could not be sacrificed for capital. A tense but robust conversation about extraction, environmental protection, and domestic and foreign oversight unfolded across the next three decades in newspapers, policy, and academic publications. Castillo Armas quickly revised the Petrol Law and promoted the generous use of natural resources to generate revenue and stimulate industrialization.[16] He asserted that Guatemala was incapable of transforming its natural resources into profit on its own, so cooperation with foreign companies was necessary in order to provide the people with the foreign products they wanted, enable technical and financial cooperation with international organizations, and generate capital.[17]

Presidents Ydígoras Fuentes and Peralta Azurdia (1963–1966) followed suit. The military consolidated its power over civilian life under both presidents, but the Peralta Azurdia regime—which ruled by fiat rather than election—was particularly fierce. Elsewhere in Latin America, developmentalism occasioned a new kind of democratic neocolonial rule that gave middle-class professionals the opportunity to advance.[18] In Guatemala, however, the economic and military elite quickly scrambled to manage development programs, seeking to limit middle-class San Carlistas' ability to expand their influence through these programs. Meanwhile, legacies of colonialism gained explanatory power over contemporary inequalities. Guatemalan *dependentistas* were less famous than their counterparts, but they too looked to Central America's geography, economics, and history to explain the region's persistent inequality.

During these same years, the National Police formed the professionalized Comando Seis "emergency" intelligence division and organized Operation Limpieza to coordinate the nation's various military, police, and paramilitary organizations. The significance of this new method of counterinsurgency became especially apparent in early March 1966 when over three days, combined forces raided homes nationwide and captured dozens of men and women from prominent labor and guerrilla organizations, primarily the Guatemalan Labor Party (PGT). Many of those arrested were tortured and executed. A few escaped. As they had a decade earlier, the AEU filed numerous writs of habeas corpus on behalf of the arrested leaders. Student publications referenced them as "*los 28*." The brazen act of political violence prompted the AEU to publish public statements about human rights abuses in newspapers like *El Imparcial* where they named the individuals they held responsible. Suggestive of their impact, some of the accused responded to the group's leadership directly, demanding that their names be cleared.[19] On the whole, Peralta Azurdia's presidency inaugurated a policy that "'braided' war, development, and military control of the state together . . . into a pure, military modernism."[20]

In 1966, a rare political opening permitted USAC *escuilach* Julio César Méndez Montenegro (1966–1970) to win a bid for president, backed by the center-right Revolutionary Party (PR). Some optimistically called it "the Third Government of the Revolution." Democratic florescence was circumscribed, however, when the group Mano Blanca appeared in June. Its program included paramilitary intimidation, kidnapping, and torture. Mano Blanca spread its message—anticommunist counterinsurgency at any cost—by leaflets and blacklists distributed throughout the capital city and the interior. At this time, most kidnappings were carried out by plainclothes men armed to the teeth. Groups like Mano Blanca could take credit while the National Police and the Army remained blameless.

Meanwhile in the countryside, the Army's actions were notorious. In Zacapa, for instance, Colonel Carlos Arana Osorio along with 1,000 Green Berets from the United States and about 5,000 Guatemalan troops, targeted the FAR and its civilian supporters. Somewhere between 8,000 and 15,000 people were killed in Zacapa during Arana Osorio's eighteen months of service between October 1966 and March 1968. Just months into San Carlista Méndez Montenegro's administration, the fallacy of the "Third Government of the Revolution" was unmistakable. Guatemala ended 1966 under a State of Siege that suspended all constitutional rights and placed the police, military, and paramilitary groups, and even security guards and local police, under the control of the minister of defense.

Perhaps it is remarkable that in such an atmosphere of political repression, San Carlistas could focus their attention on social inequality and underdevelopment. But because the military had so deftly merged repression with developmental modernism, a fight against one demanded a fight against the other. After Méndez Montenegro assumed the presidency, three exiled law professors—Francisco Villagrán Kramer, Manuel Colom Argueta, and Adolfo Mijangos López—took advantage of the democratic opening to publish a treatise entitled *Foundations for the Economic and Social Development of Guatemala*.[21] This text was to be the platform for their new political party, the Democratic Revolutionary Unity (URD), later the United Revolutionary Front (FUR). Like Peralta Azurdia, they argued for government-managed industrial technical planning, but unlike him, they explicitly opposed military government.[22] In their view, Guatemala's development lag was caused by the *latifundio* system; high birthrate, illiteracy, and unemployment; and massive rural-to-urban emigration that outpaced infrastructural capacity.[23] They were horrified by what they called the "subhuman" conditions of the "enormous and miserable" popular class that "felt as if it had no alternatives," while a small elite enjoyed "high standard of living, enlightenment, and refinement."[24] In effect, the urban elite professors' sympathetic account permitted little choice for the "miserable" masses: rural destitution or integration by industrialization.

In Part VI of the treatise, Villagrán Kramer outlined a "Social Integration Policy" to persuade indigenous communities to participate in national culture. The policy included puppet shows, plays, films, fairs, circuses, and radio and television programs; literacy programs in prisons and in the military; and community-based events organized by unions and civic organizations. Participants could receive economic incentives like land parcels and salary increases for learning to read and write in Spanish. The objective was "integration [that] will bring with it the effect of the formation of a nationality—today practically nonexistent from a social perspective." Integration rather than acculturation meant that indigenous and Western belief systems could synch harmoniously.[25] Drawing on key idioms of San Carlista student nationalism, he asked secondary and university students for their "*buena voluntad*," "revolutionary consciousness," and participation.[26] Social integration would bring "a new stage of progress" and "recuperation of national dignity."[27] Ultimately, the policy was never put into practice.

The same year, beloved economics professor and former AEU president Bernardo Lemus Mendoza published *Various Routes for the Development of Guatemala*. Like the law professors, he argued that Guatemala remained underdeveloped as the result of subsistence farming and feudalism, but he added imperialism to the list of contributing factors.[28] Influenced by Chilean José Medina Echavarría's *Filosofía del Desarrollo*, Lemus Mendoza wrote that only a certain type of development could bring about fundamental change in the structures of production, distribution, and consumption. The basic impediment to development was the contradiction between new and old relations of production.[29] Guatemala remained stuck between semifeudalism and a "backward capitalism."[30] He lamented that by 1966, only 20 percent of agricultural land under cultivation in Guatemala utilized "technologically modern" methods. Development meant "the abandonment of all precapitalist forms of work, the mechanization of all forms of production, the augmentation of productivity and intensive use of available resources."[31] Lemus Mendoza was especially concerned with financing development. He located three possible development routes for Guatemala, which he called dependent capitalist, independent capitalist, and noncapitalist. He warned against the dependent capitalist path, characterized by import substitution industrialization (ISI) and the fetishization of industrialization, noting how foreign businesses had little interest in developing a nation for economic self-sufficiency.[32] In Lemus Mendoza's analysis, this route made Guatemala reliant upon cheap manual labor and the importation of foreign techniques and technicians. This only served *latifundistas*, commercial importers, bankers, foreign businessmen, and the caste of self-enriching military and religious men.[33] He also noted that the independent capitalist route had become impossible. The ability to amass great fortunes through primitive accumulation relied upon "colonial looting, long work seasons, the absence of social services, [and] low salaries."[34] The world-system of the 1960s simply did not permit such a route. Here he drew on Paul A. Baran's *The Political Economy of Growth.*[35] Ultimately, Lemus Mendoza advocated a mixed privately and publicly funded program with incentives for the private sector. He drafted an agrarian reform that would target inefficient production, provide technical help for producers, and support agricultural subsidies and *minifundios* while placing strict limitations on foreign imports and exports. True economic progress depended on finally breaking with colonialism and the "anachronistic yoke of feudal landowners."[36] He also recommended that large landowners, foreign businessmen, and investors be barred from policy making. Their role was to invest in agricultural modernization.[37] Actually, Lemus Mendoza's recommendations differed from those of Peralta Azurdia (who had served as the head of the Department of Agrarian Affairs before his coup against Ydígoras) on this single point. As minister of agriculture, Peralta Azurdia had maintained a traditional zone of sugar, beef, and cotton cultivation along the Pacific Coast under advisement by the three sectors Lemus Mendoza sought to limit.[38]

Academic debates about development and dependency theory informed San Carlistas' views on contemporary issues. One case in particular drew San

Carlista *dependentistas'* attention to the Guatemalan subsoil. In 1965, the Peralta Azurdia government had granted Exploraciones y Explotaciones Mineras de Izabal (EXMIBAL) a 385-acre land concession northwest of Lake Izabal. EXMIBAL was an open pit mining program proposed by the Canadian International Nickel Company (INCO) and Hanna Mining Company of Cleveland, Ohio. Cleveland-based McKee Latin America was contracted to construct the processing facilities. According to the business plan, the government of Guatemala would get around 30 percent of the capital generated by EXMIBAL in its first ten years of operation. This would decrease the tax burden on the company and return profits to Guatemala. Other Central American investors would be invited to buy shares of the company after the first decade, and the International Finance Corporation of the World Bank (IFC) would acquire titles for up to 6 percent of the company's assets. The project was delayed six years by rising costs of operations, but by this time, the Guatemalan government and the World Bank had approved the business plan. Construction on the mine began in earnest in 1974 and 1975, financed by the Guatemalan government with a $15 million loan from the IFC and a $13.5 million loan from the U.S. Export-Import Bank.[39] This was precisely the sort of dependent capitalist development path that many *dependentistas* had opposed.

The initial business plan outlined social programs that would benefit workers and the Kekchí Maya community of El Estor. An electric generator and water treatment plant were necessary for the function of the mine, but they would also benefit the community. The company would build housing, schools, and stores for its workers, and thereby expand infrastructure in the region. As for employment, the company advertised that the construction phase would require about two thousand temporary contractors. The production phase would need only seven hundred trained technical employees. These permanent trained employees would be eligible to buy company housing and could register for more advanced training provided by the company. A June 1969 promotional pamphlet addressed this obvious division of labor. It reassured citizens that although at first the company would have to rely on foreign workers because Guatemalans lacked technical expertise, it would prioritize educating Guatemalans.[40] In fact, there would be scholarships to fund the study of mineral mining abroad for ten students who were required to return to Guatemala and work for a mining company for the length of their study abroad, at minimum. Astutely, the company's public relations materials spoke to a public caught between nationalist ideals and their desire for development. The crux of the problem was this: the minerals and petrol discovered in the subsoil belonged to Guatemalans, but they were not beneficial without the financing and expertise required to extract them. Playing to these concerns, one marketing circular explained how EXMIBAL's logo "brings together diverse images into a symbolic graphic design": "The Maya hieroglyphs that represent 'red' and 'earth' (and thus the lateritic ore) [are] enclosed within a placard and marked with the words EXMIBAL and Guatemala in a type of print that combines, subtly, the Hispanic-colonial past with modern sensibility." The flyer detailed how "the hieroglyphs were taken from Maya Codices" and "part of the image from a rock carving at Quiriguá," a Classic Maya city located on the opposite side of Lake Izabal from El Estor.[41] EXMIBAL's logo put a Mayan face on a foreign project, indicating the importance of the Mayan past to Guatemala's national identity in the present.

While EXMIBAL's long financing and approval process dragged on, Colonel Carlos Arana Osorio, notorious "Butcher of Zacapa," was elected to the presidency. After assuming the presidency in July, his campaign promises of seeking reconciliation and peace were quickly abandoned. He declared a State of Siege on November 13, 1970, that would last for more than a year.[42] An overnight curfew was in place and political activity of any kind was prohibited. Security forces were empowered to arrest and search without warrants and so conducted numerous home raids. Intelligence reports received by the United States confirmed that most members of the paramilitary organizations came from the military; in other words, little, aside from the uniform, distinguished official counterinsurgency forces from death squads.[43] Within the National Police, the Cuerpo de Detectives was formed in November 1970 and became a semiautonomous intelligence command that carried out forced disappearances and executions with impunity.[44] A secret Defense Intelligence Agency bulletin dated January 12, 1971, reported, "During the state of siege . . . security forces quietly eliminated many terrorists and bandits, mainly in the interior of the country. An estimated 200 have been killed in San Marcos department alone. In Guatemala City, police apprehended or killed about 30 suspected terrorists, including the Chief of the Communist Party's terrorist arm. Bolstered by these successes, the army has closed all roads leading from the capital and is making a house-to-house search for subversives in a determined effort to cripple leftist organizations."[45] The report glosses over the 200 deaths of residents of San Marcos and the promise of still more unnamed deaths in other rural departments while emphasizing the thirty capital city terrorists. Again, as before and through-out the war, the lives of rural and largely indigenous people were counted and valued differently to those of urban and often ladino Guatemalans.[46]

In fact, this issue was addressed in two books published by USAC social scientists during the State of Siege. Both texts debated colonialism, development, region, and class. The chief point of disagreement was whether inequality was rooted in class or ethnicity. The first, *Guatemala: An Historico-social Interpretation* by Carlos Guzmán Böckler and his French collaborator Jean-Loup Herbert, argued that internal colonial relations between indigenous and ladino populations were the root of structural inequality and underdevelopment in Guatemala. The modern nation-state was derived from this oppressive and antagonistic relationship, which had changed little since the colonial period. It followed that the only hope for freedom from oppression for the indigenous masses was to throw off the yoke of ladino rule and form an autonomous indigenous state.[47]

Marxist historian Severo Martínez Peláez took a different approach. Under his direction, researchers at the USAC Institute for Social and Economic Research (Instituto de Investigaciones Económicas y Sociales [IIES]) explored how capital investment in industrialization could contribute to underdevelopment in peripheral places like Guatemala. Martínez Peláez and the IIES researchers looked to Andre Gunder Frank's *Capitalism and Underdevelopment in Latin America: Historical Studies of Chile and Brazil* (1966) and *Latin America: Underdevelopment or Revolution* (1969), which historicized relations between a provincial center and subperipheries. In *La patria del criollo*, Martínez Peláez examined enduring class antagonism as inequality's root cause. His analysis emphasized how feudal exploitation through the *repartimiento* system in the colony connected Guatemala to a capitalist metropole, and from there, to the entire European capitalist system. Like Baran and Gunder Frank, Martínez Peláez argued that after independence, political elites prevented a competitive economic structure from evolving in order to maintain their privileged access to the rural economy.[48] As an orthodox Marxist, Martínez Peláez defined colonialism as a state of service to the economic interests of the dominant classes of a foreign society. At the same time, he argued how the "wealth accumulated during the colonial period came from the work of indigenous people subjected to servitude," an exploitative extractive system that persisted to the present.[49] By subsuming indigeneity to class exploitation, his book both reflected and contributed to the ineffability of the indigenous subject to the ladino left in the 1970s.

Read by the leftist guerrilla, as well as the military and police, *La patria del criollo* became a standard text at USAC, where it is still assigned.[50]

Martínez Peláez influenced other dependency theorists. *Dependentistas* Fernando Henrique Cardoso and Enzo Faletto read *La patria del criollo* closely.[51] Cardoso rejected Guzmán Böckler and Herbert's analysis for its focus on trade rather than production in capitalism and, especially, for its ahistorical and essentialized understanding of the "indio." He also distinguished between the colonial and feudal exploitation of indigenous laborers, unlike many USAC *dependentistas*. At the United Nations Economic Commission for Latin America and the Caribbean in Santiago, Chile, Cardoso worked closely with another San Carlista, Edelberto Torres-Rivas.[52] Like his peers, Torres-Rivas became interested in dependency theory in order to explain the contradictions he saw in the society in which he was born and raised. An adolescent and teen during the Ten Years' Spring, Torres-Rivas wrote, "political militancy formed my sensibility, but above all, it stimulated in me the interest and desire to try and understand and explain the reason for … the failures of modernity in Central America."[53] His research highlighted how underdevelopment was caused by the metropole's penetration of the periphery and semiperiphery through investment and technical knowledge and the prevention of self-sustaining economies in the periphery. He echoed his contemporaries' belief that the middle class had a crucial role to play in the formation of modernity, a departure from some groups on the left and a topic to which I will return below.[54]

In 1972, another influential USAC sociologist, Mario Monteforte Toledo, joined the discussion.[55] Monteforte Toledo had served in both the Arévalo and Arbenz governments, then fled to exile in Mexico after the counterrevolution. His book *Centroamérica: Subdesarrollo y dependencia* reiterated how dependency was fundamental to Central American economies. Guided by Baran and Gunder Frank, but also V. I. Lenin, Rosa Luxembourg, and Karl Marx, Monteforte Toledo wrote of the rapacious greed of imperial powers vis-à-vis colonial enclaves.[56] He delimited stages of economic development from Spanish colonialism to independence movements, Liberal reforms to the Good Neighbor Policy, and ended with the Alliance for Progress. His analysis was informed by dialectical materialism insofar as the transition from stage to stage was compelled by a state of crisis, always under the sign of unequal development. Echoing the sentiment of the 1966 *No Nos Tientes* editorial that began this chapter, Monteforte Toledo saw U.S. foreign policy, fiscal policies, cultural penetration, and investment strategies in Guatemala as colonial practices.[57] He argued revolution would come only from "the internal forces of a society, which will determine the nature, the depth, and the end of an eventual revolution." He also wrote that a true Latin American revolution would be very difficult, because "through it one must achieve at once independence, liberal reform, capitalism, and socialism."[58]

Around this time, Arana Osorio inaugurated his own plan of military-led agricultural commercialization financed by a $23 million loan from the U.S. Agency for International Development (USAID). The plan zoned whole territories, most famously the Franja Transversal del Norte (FTN), for the development of agricultural, livestock, timber, hydroelectric energy, and petrol exports.[59] The FTN included the northern reaches of the departments of Huehuetenango, Quiché, Alta Verapaz, and all of Izabal, a region that had been the site of dispossession since the nineteenth-century coffee boom. Then, Kekchí and Achi' peasants were removed from their land in the interest of German émigrés who built massive coffee plantations. Decades later, still more indigenous peasants were dispossessed when President Estrada Cabrera granted a 165,000-acre plantation to UFCO. After the counterrevolution dismantled Arbenz's Agrarian Reform, the Armas government encouraged intrepid farmers to develop the region and, a few decades later, a new wave of ladino peasants arrived, seeking stability and freedom from the seasonal cycle of migrant labor. A different sort of project was developed by the Maryknoll and Sacred Heart orders of the Catholic Church in the 1960s when they brought Mayas from Jakalteko, Mam, Q'anjob'al, Chuj, and K'iche' groups to colonize, farm, and develop transformative Catholic communities in the region without the stain of agrarian reform.[60] Across a century, commercialized agriculture and mining arrived to the northern departments and western highlands by way of subtle and not-so-subtle coercion. While some communities were displaced, others were established and encouraged by incentives provided by industry and government.

In late 1970, a few new programs combined agricultural development and counterrevolutionary objectives. The Agricultural Development Bank (BANDESA) began to distribute loans to small- and medium-scale farmers and the National Institute of Agricultural Commercialization (INDECA) controlled the price and supply of grains. The Institute for Agricultural Science and Technology (ICTA), founded two years later, promoted the use of foreign fertilizers and pesticides and the cultivation of foreign crops.[61] These programs also authorized even more surveillance and military presence in the departments where the FAR and, after 1974, the new Guerrilla Army of the Poor (EGP) were strongest. These sites were geographically distant to San Carlistas in the capital city, yet students and faculty discussed them in their critiques of a government that they viewed as a collaborator in the dispossession of the pueblo's land and natural resources. Volunteers from the Medical Students Association (AEM) reflected on the situation, observing that there was an "increase in internal colonialism with relation to foreign dependency," which was creating a national culture of "dictomania."[62] Guided by dependency theory, San Carlistas could see rural peasants and urban poor as victims of internal colonialism, rather than willful resisters of modernity, as had their precursors.

Lateritic ore began to emerge from the earth in April 1975. USAC faculty and students redoubled their protests against foreign extractive industries. The fight to protect Guatemala's natural resources became a battle over moral authority, as USAC competed with the private universities, foreign business interests, and the military for the ability to determine Guatemala's development. Faculty and students wrote to daily newspapers about natural resources and national patrimony. Administrators issued a statement that affirmed that Guatemalan citizens should receive any wealth that was extracted from the national soil.[63] The AEU denounced EXMIBAL in *El Gráfico* (founded in 1963 by San Carlista Jorge Carpio Nicolle) and *El Imparcial*. They demanded that the government protect rural workers against exploitation by large companies and establish relations with the Organization of Petrol Exporting Countries to keep pace with international laws and price controls as foreign petrol speculation expanded in the Petén.[64] Meanwhile, EXMIBAL continued to attempt to allay public concern. An investors' pamphlet concluded with a section entitled "Benefits for Guatemala," which claimed that EXMIBAL would benefit the region through the influx of capital, the exploration of a new product, stronger training programs in mining and related industries, and revenue generated by taxes and tariffs.[65]

In an attempt to regain oversight over these development programs, USAC administrators and faculty volunteered to form an advisory board or lead community education programs to clarify recent legislation that changed the restrictions placed on foreign companies.[66] Economics students highlighted growing civil unrest and located its cause in the exploitative system of international business, especially the international division of labor. Taking their critique further, they wrote that the middle classes were complicit in Guatemala's civil and economic unrest as their political action was usually limited to participation in political parties and elections, which only served the interests of dominant sectors and enabled "fascistization."[67] Their analyses preceded the Spanish translation of Immanuel Wallerstein's *Modern World System, Volume 1* in 1979, but they shared his critique of nationalist political struggles and the complicity of bureaucratic states in governing the flow of resources from the periphery to the center.[68]

Students and faculty were also increasingly critical of the North American academy's influence over Guatemalan intellectual life, which they related to their critiques of resources flows and neocolonialism. This was a complicated critique to maintain because foreign funds helped administrators to meet the rising demands placed on their institution. USAC received substantial loans and scholarships from the Ford Foundation, the Rockefeller Foundation, the Regional Office of Central American Programs of USAID (ROCAP-USAID), the U.S. National Science Foundation, and the universities of Kansas, Michigan State, Oklahoma, and Puerto Rico.[69] After petrol companies opened a program of study and offered twelve scholarships at Universidad Francisco Marroquín (UFM), the dean of the USAC Faculty of Engineering wrote to national newspapers announcing his willingness to collaborate with the government's Directorate of Mining and Hydrocarbons. He, unlike UFM faculty, was unattached to any private business interest and so could be trusted to uphold national interest. He wrote again in late February with curriculum suggestions, but received a curt reply: the program was already underway. The dean responded with a public letter that argued that it was unfair for foreign companies to train the individuals who would supervise and manage them, as they were likely to be more loyal to the company than to the people of Guatemala.[70] In May 1976, the Engineering *facultad* again proposed a commission of USAC representatives to investigate the benefits of mining programs. They also denounced the government's renewed attempt to gain sovereignty over Belize after petrol deposits were discovered there, a series of events they said revealed the influence of transnational businesses on national foreign policy.[71]

Faculty were more likely to publish their research on dependency and natural resource management, but many students in law, economics, and engineering began to study these topics in their theses.[72] One student, Alfredo Figueroa Mendez, wrote his thesis on the legal foundations of the revised Petrol Laws for the Faculty of Juridical and Social Sciences in 1977.[73] His analysis extended beyond jurisprudence, to conclude that the skillful use of natural resources would improve the national economy. He argued that foreign capital may be necessary to jumpstart exploration and exploitation, but a state-owned company like Pemex or Petrobras should manage extraction and ensure that Guatemalan petrol was reserved for domestic consumers.[74]

The importance of nationalization of petrol and nickel extraction for national development had become common sense among many sectors at USAC, particularly in the social sciences. In 1978, a new newspaper founded under Rector Saúl Osorio Paz, *7 Días en la USAC*, published a long feature story and survey on the construction of an interoceanic petrol pipeline. The paper's editorial staff was unanimously against the pipeline, but their readers' opinions were more divided. Of the students polled, 23.5 percent reported that they believed the pipeline would help national development. Among those who opposed the pipeline, their reasons for opposition included national sovereignty (15%), ecological or national security (21%), and concerns about economic dependence.[75] Later in 1978, student organizations issued long press releases that linked struggles over the pipeline to a recent increase in the cost of fares on urban buses. The fare hike protests united urban Guatemalans across class but also triggered spectacular government repression, events that I discuss in detail in the next two chapters.[76]

This development praxis carried serious risk. Within a few years of forming a USAC-based commission to study the impact of EXMIBAL, Adolfo Mijangos López and Julio Camey Herrera were assassinated; and Alfonso Bauer Paíz was wounded and forced into exile along with Rafael Piedra Santa. Their recommendations had been simple: the company should be taxed as others were, it should be made to compensate for the harm done to natural resources, and it should contract with national companies for the transport of the extracted nickel.[77] Even this moderate critique of the private sector was prohibited.

Regional allies took note. In early 1979, the Central American Universities' High Council (CSUCA) issued a statement that read, "The situation has become so grave because capitalist development plans have become increasingly aggressive, creating an even greater dependency." It continued, "the economic penetration of Guatemala by transnational companies ... has exacerbated social problems, since transnational interests do not care much at all about the interests of the nation."[78] Three decades of tense debate over dependency had produced rich historical explanations for Guatemala's deep inequalities. The military government seemed increasingly willing to employ violence to ensure their continuation.

THE STUDENT, *EL ESTUDIANTE*, AND JUAN TECÚ

The university and the military waged a war of words. USAC recommended its own advisory committees and extension programming while the military recommended state-controlled cooperatives, limited redistribution of wealth, foreign and domestic financing, and limited agrarian reforms that justified greater military presence in guerrilla strongholds. Both sides sought to incorporate rural campesinos in the workings of modern capitalism. In the midst of these competing plans, one ubiquitous figure emerged in the student press: the barefoot indigenous ingénue called Juan Tecú. Tecú was the distinctly urban nationalist fantasy of an uneducated rural indigenous man. Lacking the civic consciousness of the urbane San Carlistas, he alone could speak truth—sarcastic, biting, ironic, and irreverent truth—to power. Like the natural resources at El Estor, Tecú represented the underdeveloped potential of Guatemala.

Tecú appeared on the front page of every edition of *El Estudiante* from June 1955 into the 1980s in a small single-framed comic called "Juan Tecú's Slingshots [*Hondazos de Juan Tecú*]." The comic comprised an image of the boy wielding a slingshot and a pithy joke about a national political event or personage, usually written in student slang, with an indigenous accent, mispronunciation, or double entendre. The joke was usually on some sector that the students opposed, like the president, the military, the Catholic Church, or the U.S. government. Of course, from the pen of urban ladino intellectual elite men, the joke was also on Tecú.[79] The students' physical representation of Tecú (messy-haired, malnourished, dressed in rags) and his mannerisms (ungrammatical Spanish and uncouth questions) constituted San Carlistas' place in the social order.[80]

Other student publications also published Tecú comics. The 1966 *No Nos Tientes* almost did not make it to print, but when it did, it included a half-page image of Tecú chasing President Ydígoras Fuentes and two conservative presidential candidates, Juan de Dios Aguilar de León and Miguel Angel Ponciano, shouting, "Go to hell, *chafarotes*!" The politicians perspired and grimaced as they ran and money fell from the president's pockets. The caption read, "This is the small, medium, and large desire of all of Guatemala!" Tecú held a broken chain in one hand and with the other, he tossed away a ballot marked March 6, 1966. Again, Tecú was a powerful threat to the politicians, but he was also an unflattering caricature: his clothes were patched, his feet were bare, his hair disheveled, and his nose exaggeratedly large. He smiled with enormous teeth through a thin wiry moustache.

That year, the Guatemala City municipal government denied the *huelgueros'* usually pro forma petition to assemble for the Huelga de Dolores. Instead, Colonel Ariel Rivera Siliezar encouraged the students to organize events on campus and indoors.[81] When a defiant group of students read the first *Boletín* over loudspeaker on Sixth Avenue, National Police officers chased them through the Elma office building.[82] Five days later, the AEU announced that the traditional celebration would be held in public when conditions were better and when a government that "permitted the lively expression of humor and critique of public functionaries once again ruled."[83] The government's prohibition simply confirmed its undemocratic essence. The government also forbade the *No Nos Tientes*, but its editors did not comply. On April 1, police entered the AEU offices and arrested a number of student leaders and took them to the headquarters of the Second Corps counterinsurgency unit.[84] They seized about two hundred copies of the paper.[85] In this atmosphere of repression, the editorial that began this chapter was especially prescient as it told of heroic students who always stood up to the *chafarotes* who sold out the pueblo.

Sometimes the distinction between the San Carlistas and the *chafarotes* was less clear. San Carlistas also used Tecú to manage these uncertainties. In an early August 1966 edition of *El Estudiante*, Tecú's slingshot took aim at the winner of the recent presidential elections, Julio César Méndez Montenegro, the *escuilach* who had helped overthrow Ubico and since then served in several governmental posts. Tecú spoke, "What a strange honeymoon, that of poor Mr. Julite, [first] they take him, now they bring him, from one garrison to another." The comic referred to the moment in late 1965 when Méndez Montenegro, then a candidate for USAC rector, was called upon to run for president after his brother Mario Méndez Montenegro was assassinated. His journey from student leader of the revolution stationed at the "garrison" of the university to secret puppet of the military high command, the face of the façade of civilian governance in the National Palace, was indeed strange.[86] A month later, Tecú trained his slingshot on the Méndez Montenegro government once again. The caption read, "They have returned two, now we wait for them to return the twenty-eight." The comic referred to two San Carlistas in exile who were permitted to return by the new government while *los 28*, the *guerrilleros* who had been disappeared in early March, and remained missing.[87] In this comic, Tecú was not a lone jokester.

He spoke for a collectivity that resolved to wait until their friends, class-mates, and family members were returned. By October, Tecú was less patient. From his usual spot on the front page of *El Estudiante*, he spoke, "What rubs me the wrong way, I disturb; what disturbs me, I insult; what insults me, I strike; what strikes me, I kill; and what kills me, I terrify."[88] Tecú captured the sentiment shared by growing numbers of people on campus, in the city, and in the countryside: the time for waiting was over.

Tecú made another cameo in the 1969 *No Nos Tientes* as "Juan Pueblo" in the final frame of a comic that depicted the development of a Guatemalan military officer across his lifetime. The first frame depicted the officer as a child with a distended belly, crawling on hands and knees and fighting off starving dogs and a pig for food; the next portrayed his poor basic education and his even poorer military training at the Politécnica, where a sign read, "75% of each class goes on to become president while the other 25% become [government] ministers." His classmates studied textbooks entitled *Slow Torture* and *The Inquisition*, learned to follow the leader and sing in unison, and practiced sucking up to Uncle Sam. In the comic's final frame, a full-grown and magnanimous colonel posed in front of a box with the Red Cross emblem with a smoking semiautomatic rifle slung over his shoulder. He extended his arms toward Tecú as if to embrace him and exclaimed, "We will rise from underdevelopment!" Tecú replied, "Yes, but . . . whose?"[89]

Tecú was cleverer than the military, but his creators stopped short of rec-ognizing Tecú's intelligence. They inferred an intellectual hierarchy with their fellow formally educated San Carlistas (the anonymous authors of the comic) at the top, followed by Tecú and the pueblo (as students of the school of the street), and finally, the completely ignorant military men of the Politécnica at the abject bottom. After a decade of interwoven war, develop-ment, and military control that extended from Ydígoras through Peralta Azurdia, this cartoon must have been especially satisfying to read.[90]

A few years later, Tecú again appeared in the *No Nos Tientes* as a spokes-man for "the poor [*los pobres*]" in a three-panel comic strip entitled "The Philosophy of the Vulturegovernment." This comic was drawn in the same style as the late 1950s comic strip "Castillitos en el Aire," which had merci-lessly ridiculed Castillo Armas, discussed in Chapter 2. In "The Philosophy of the Vulturegovernment," power shifted subtly from the president to the truth-telling pueblo across three frames. Here, the joke pivoted on President Arana's campaign slogan: "The poor are the reason for my government." Tecú responded to this claim with an unspoken question mark, drawn in a thought

FIGURE 7. Juan Tecú comic depicting the development of a military officer. *No Nos Tientes*, 1969. Satirical Publications Collection. Archivo Histórico, Centro de Investigaciones Regionales de Mesoamérica (CIRMA).

bubble. In the second frame, Arana declared, "Now there will be no poor [people] in my regime" and Tecú replied, "I believe that ..." His response was completed in the third frame: "... it has already destroyed 5,000 campesinos ..."[91] Tecú, the truth-telling ingénue, permitted students to tell the military just how awful they were.

Tecú endured for decades as a sort of *universitario* mascot. At first, he was a youthful jokester. As the national situation deteriorated, the fictional youth became more foreboding. Tecú was uncultured and uncivilized, so he was unable to successfully navigate the social contract, but he also never had the chance to try under the military government. His creators played on this contradiction. He was identifiable by his straw hat, tattered shirts, high-water pants, bare feet, stereotypical Mayan nose, and thin frame; he noted simple truths and scarcely looked directly at his readers. Only after the fraudulent presidential elections in 1974 did Tecú break the fourth wall.[92] In a comic in the *No Nos Tientes*, brawling military commanders, Kjell Eugenio Laugerud García and José Efraín Ríos Montt, loomed over a torn flag of Guatemala and the bones and skulls of the pueblo. Laugerud García emerged the victor with one foot propped up on Ríos Montt's back and one hand holding a blood-soaked dagger, the conservative National Liberation Movement (MLN) party's symbol. Both commanders averted their eyes, but Tecú looked directly at the reader and demanded, "After the fraud, which of you bitches [*putas*] will be able to defend me?" It is unclear whether Tecú's insulting address was directed to the candidates, the military government, or even San Carlista readers. But it was extraordinarily clever in how it raised the question of political representation. Not long before it was published, Laugerud García (1974–1978) had been declared the winner of yet another election characterized by fraud and low voter turnout. INDECA had passed into the hands of Army Colonel Enrique Ruata Asturias, formalizing the military's control over the distribution of donated foodstuffs like corn, beans, rice, dry milk, vegetable oil, and corn flour. Through Tecú, San Carlistas expressed their conviction the military was unable to fulfill the basic premise of good governance: defending the pueblo.

Tecú was an ideal mascot for urbane San Carlista students in the era of extension programming and dependency theory's vogue. In later editions of *El Estudiante*, Tecú appeared as a guest contributor in fictional interviews with public figures. As in the earlier comics, poor grammar and crude manners signaled his ignorance of certain forms of knowledge. Underdeveloped and uncultured, Tecú was a peripheral protocitizen. Over three decades, his slingshot remained unfired but his clear sense of right and wrong revealed latent democratic potential. For his creators, Tecú offered the opportunity to speak openly against the government. Sometimes, through him, San Carlistas were able to rethink some of their presumptions about rural and indigenous citizens. He was just the kind of politically literate subject USAC students and administrators sought to create through extension programming.

"ONLY THE PUEBLO CAN SAVE THE PUEBLO!"

When students returned to school after the Holy Week holiday in 1973, they found that enormous murals covered the walls of three classroom buildings. The murals were painted by Arnoldo "El Tecolote" Ramírez Amaya and some friends as "a gesture of rebellion against the conservative and repressive university system." The Economics, Law, and Humanities buildings formed the Plaza Rogelia Cruz in honor of a San Carlista who was disappeared and tortured in January 1968. A large multistory mural of Cruz's famous headshot covered one wall, declaring: "MUJER EN NUESTRA LUCHA FALTA EL FUSIL."

Cruz was kidnapped for her ties to the FAR amidst the incessant wavelike intensification and diminution of urban violence during the Méndez Montenegro presidency. Relatively little is known about her political opinions.[93] In fact, reflective of the gendered dimensions of revolutionary life and martyrdom, what is most recalled about Cruz is her body.[94] Thin, blue-eyed, brown-haired, and with a distinctly Spanish last name, Cruz won Miss Guatemala in 1959 and represented Guatemala in the Miss Universe contest. When she returned to Guatemala after the competition, she enrolled at USAC to study architecture and probably connected with FAR militants at this time. She may have used her status to operate within the city above suspicion, for despite a handful of arrests, she remained free to move about the city. On January 11, her body appeared under a bridge fifty miles from the capital in Escuintla bearing signs of torture, including cranial trauma and traces of poison in her stomach. Then, as now, representations of Cruz emphasized the likelihood of sexual assault during torture and her relationship with PGT leader Leonardo Castillo Johnson. In fact, there may be no evidence to suggest that she was raped.[95] As the putative representation of the ideal Guatemalan woman, her torture, rape, and abandonment separated her from her male comrades. Other murals denounced what Ramírez Amaya called the "ongoing national situation," picturing the logo of the MLN party as a dagger dripping blood and implicating North American businesses in Guatemala's suffering.

Ramírez Amaya was the artistic director of a new USAC-based magazine called *Alero*. Organized in 1970 by a group of San Carlista artists and writers dedicated to social change and conscious of their revolutionary obligation, *Alero* was the maximum expression of the spirit of student nationalism of the period. Unlike the rising counterculture that refused engagement with the deteriorating political situation, *Alero* spread political art and literature beyond campus and regularly published treatises on human rights, mining and petrol, and urban transportation issues. The group combined what might have been seen as a sort of countercultural aesthetic rejection of tradition (long hair on men, miniskirts on women, marijuana, an avid interest in North American youth culture) with the political commitments associated with San Carlistas. Under the leadership of Lionel Méndez Dávila and Roberto Díaz Castillo, *Alero*'s reputation grew and the editors began to receive submissions from famous writers like Mario Benedetti and Jorge Cortázar.[96]

The project of "muralization" (*muralización*) was part of *Alero*'s broader effort to raise political awareness among students. The murals also drew attention to the presence of the illegal PGT and its youth affiliate, the JPT, which recruited students from the numerous and often short-lived leftist political groups that proliferated on campus.[97] Purportedly, PGT members tried to interrupt the artist's work and even called the police to intervene while the young man and his assistants were painting. *Alero* editors denounced the censure of Ramírez Amaya as part of a broader effort to limit dissenting views within the left. The group felt as if their work had been targeted by the PGT and some of the murals may have expressed that concern.[98]

USAC rector Rafael Cuevas del Cid, himself a clandestine member of the PGT, tried to reframe the situation as the conflict deepened. He spoke of the murals as a "critique of the national system, of a society of consumerism, and, naturally, of some aspects, or positions, correct or not, regarding university life."[99] By this account, they were simply evidence of the freedom of expression at the university. The archive of these murals is ridden with speculation. While an *Alero* article insisted that Ramírez Amaya had been censored, the accounts given by three historians, Ricardo Sáenz de Tejada, Edgar Ruano Najarro, and Juan Carlos Vázquez Medeles, do not discuss any controversy surrounding the murals.[100] On the contrary, Vázquez Medeles writes that the

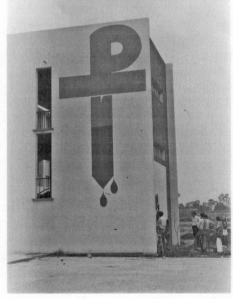

FIGURE 8. "Go forth and learn from all ..." Mural by Arnoldo Ramírez Amaya, 1973. Photograph by Mauro Calanchina.

FIGURE 9. The bloody symbol of the National Liberation Movement. Mural by Arnoldo Ramírez Amaya, 1973. Photograph by Mauro Calanchina.

very day that the classroom buildings were inaugurated, Ramírez Amaya, Edgar Palma Lau, and Marco Antonio Flores decided together to paint the huge murals as a sort of positive expression of student life. Still, the rumors provide a window into emerging partisan conflict among the campus left.

Rumor and controversy aside, the murals were also important visual representations of the changing idioms of political affect at USAC. Ramírez Amaya offered a striking revision of the university motto, simultaneously capturing university's complicated relationship to the pueblo and denouncing U.S. imperialism. One mural read, "Go forth and learn from all / or else / eat shit," painted in the style of the logo of U.S.-based soft drink brand Coca-Cola. Ramírez Amaya's revised university motto demanded that students draw closer to the pueblo. His Coca-Cola logo punch line counterposed the pueblo to excrescent Yankee imperialism. Ramírez Amaya's work inaugurated what would become an ongoing tradition at the University City. Today, countless murals cover the outside walls of almost every classroom building, something I discuss in the Coda. But in 1973, the murals were a bold new statement against imperialism and the government.

In November, San Carlistas elected dental surgeon Dr. Roberto Valdeavellano Pinot as university rector. Known as the "developer" (*desarrollista*), he ran on a platform of university democratization, expanded extension programming, and comprehensive curriculum reform. His election was a victory for leftist groups on campus and, interestingly, a matter of concern for the U.S. State Department. A confidential telegram sent from the U.S. Embassy to the Secretary of State read, "Communist Party (PGT) supported candidate Roberto Valdeavellano Pinot won the race for Rector of San Carlos University last night, beating GOG [Government of Guatemala]-supported candidate Humanities Faculty Dean Guillermo Putzeys Alvarez." The message went on to position the election in terms of national and international politics: "Blunting most serious challenge in recent years to its domination of the national university, PGT allied forces won by making concessions to independent Marxists who had supported two minor candidates in primary rounds." While Valdeavellano was "not a PGT member," the report concluded that he "will enter office committed to [the PGT] party and will certainly leave PGT members in key USC [*sic*] positions." In terms of the broader impact of his election, "his victory will have little short-term effect outside university community and will probably have almost no repercussion on March national elections. In long term, the victory will leave PGT in command of important base of operations in national life."[101] Note how the embassy officer was not confident that the rector's election would have no impact on national presidential elections. A closer look at his proposals for the university make clear why the U.S. government would be concerned.

As rector, Valdeavellano promised the "formation of a new type of *universitario* (student, professor, professional) . . . equipped not only with scientific and technological knowledge, but also with social ethics and an expansive conscience."[102] Of course, San Carlistas had long celebrated their "social ethics" and "expansive conscience." How exactly could Valdeavellano "convert" the student into "an authentic servant of the pueblo" as he declared he would?[103] On December 1, 1975, he presented a Plan of University Development to the public. It was ambitious. It would "renovate [the university] from its foundations," "nourished by great successes achieved in the past, and inspired by the highest principles for the future." In concrete terms, nine regional campuses and around fifty new degree programs would be created.[104]

The only problem was funding. The government was unwilling to increase the percentage of the national budget allocated for USAC. Instead, President Laugerud García encouraged Valdeavellano to accept funding from the Inter-American Development Bank (IDB) like Guatemala's private universities. Valdeavellano demurred on the grounds that this would be harmful for "sovereignty, university autonomy, and the nation's economy."[105] He was wary of IDB plans that prioritized the diversification of the economy and expansion of infrastructure in the areas of energy, transportation, and communication. San Carlistas had been critical of the IDB as North America's "agency of penetration and humiliation" since the 1960s.[106] At any rate, the rector and the IDB did not share scholarly priorities: the IDB emphasized regional unity and mobilization of financial and human resources through communications and transportation, while USAC extension programs under Valdeavellano worked to connect the minds and hearts of the pueblo and the university for a better Guatemala.[107]

Valdeavellano's election prompted a change to the university's general philosophy on extension programs.[108] Under his leadership, extension philosophy transformed from one of unidirectional diffusion of culture and knowledge to a more reciprocal relationship between *universitarios* and the pueblo, a deliberate effort to draw closer to the pueblo.[109] This was the change that Ramírez Amaya called for in his murals. San Carlistas would "go forth and learn from all."

This was the change, too, that seemed to follow from San Carlistas' reckonings with dependency theory. The old debate over the role of the university in national life took on a new dimension. Autocritique of extension programming helped some San Carlistas to rethink their relationship to the rural and urban peripheries. Old missions of teaching, research, and service were reoriented toward collaboration and connection. Faculty correctly recognized that this was a daring change. Director of the University Extension Division Julio Hernández Sifontes affirmed that considering, discussing, and critiquing extension programming were "all forms of militant action."[110]

The change incited mixed responses among the faculty and students. By this point, few San Carlistas would have advocated for an apolitical university, but not everyone was enthusiastic about the risk involved in collaborating with peasant and worker organizations. The specter of "outside agitators" was worrisome for some. Furthermore, while some partisans of the PGT and FAR who remained at the university seemed to think it was possible to transform the relationship between USAC and the pueblo through extension programming, others disagreed. For instance, although San Carlistas filled its ranks at all levels, the FAR leadership doubted the university's revolutionary capacity. They wrote, "Everyone knows (unless you have forgotten your academic studies) that these institutions are part of a social superstructure . . . To change the petty-bourgeois mentality of a caste or social class, we will wage an ideological war."[111] The FAR offered a revisionist history of the 1944 October Revolution that argued the revolution had only secured the bourgeoisie's rise to political and economic power over the landed oligarchy and installed "the dictatorship of the bourgeoisie," which "guaranteed capitalist rights, known as 'human rights.'"[112] The FAR agreed with San Carlista *dependentistas* that economic dependency and lack of self-determination were the roots of dependency. But they challenged the idea that the state could serve as the guarantor of individual interests. They argued that integral social development of the pueblo could occur only after an agrarian, anti-imperialist, and anticapitalist revolution changed the relations of production. So they also sought to destroy the labor system that valued intellectual over manual labor. Despite their critiques of the institution, the FAR continued to recruit at USAC.[113]

The young communists of the JPT also rejected Valdeavellano's promises as more hot air from the university bureaucracy, even though, according to the U.S. Embassy intelligence briefing described above, the rector was backed by the PGT (their parent organization). These cautionary statements against the revolutionary potential of the university were a reminder that the university and the revolution operated by distinct logics. In their newsletter *Juventud*, the JPT claimed that education was stagnant because the national elite's primary interests were oppression, exploitation, and censorship.[114] The group wrote with unreserved disgust for the "Myth of the Student," which beguiled both the student and the university with its presumption that youth became instantaneously revolutionary upon enrollment. On the contrary, they claimed, the university was not the least bit revolutionary. For one, its student body was politically diverse. Also, they argued, bourgeois student political parties diffused revolutionary potential by manipulating the student movement through supposed "student leaders" who were sell-outs, dema-gogues, and opportunists. These false leaders often spouted ultrarevolution-ary slogans that actually undermined the revolution. These "coffee-shop-, cantina-, or discotheque-revolutionaries were traitors of the popular move-ment, easily charmed by the 'agents of imperialism (the CIA),'" according to one JPT newsletter.[115]

The disparagement of discotheque revolutionaries is a reminder of the consumer culture that flourished in the capital city. It also illuminates how countercultural messages of antiwar, free love, and psychedelics alienated some youths as they attracted others.[116] For some, these amusements amounted to neocolonial bread and circuses that compelled Guatemalan youths to emulate Yankee music, buy Yankee clothes, and even sing in English. In fact, some adults tried to cultivate the appeal of popular music in an effort to channel youth rebellion into less revolutionary outlets. The Instituto Guatemalteco Americano (IGA) established a "go-go discotheque" where Radio Sensación hosted parties and Guatemalan bands performed.[117] Of course, the distinction between countercultural aesthetic rebellion and political commitment, articulated by both the guerrilla and the countercul-tural revolutionary youth, oversimplified the politics of culture. Youth cul-ture offered Guatemalans new ways to connect to their peers around the world, akin to the international student congresses favored by other stu-dents.[118] Even the police may not have seen the distinction so clearly. Throughout the Arana Osorio presidency, the National Police carried out drug raids that justified or provided cover for surveillance and kidnapping of political targets.[119]

The JPT maintained its critique of the university, soon targeting "the developer's" purportedly provocative intention to remake the university's relationship to the pueblo. They wrote how Valdeavellano's statements failed to elicit public debate and discussion because no one cared about "the atti-tude and the vision of those who are limited by an institution like the University." Academics could "evaluate things and situate their participation without effectively leaving the three hundred-year old academy" while a plan for *action* was sorely—and tellingly—lacking. Without a plan, the promise to open the university to "the most oppressed classes" was a merely a "meaningless declaration," a "declaration into thin air [*declaración al aire*]."[120]

Neither the stoned nor the stoic youth was of value to the revolution. The bitterness of this critique of the rector and the university is a reminder that the FAR and the PGT had endured about a decade of targeted kidnappings, torture, and executions by 1975. The government's security apparatus responded to the growing mass movement with selective kidnappings that singled out peasant cooperative leaders and trade unionists, and less often, university students and faculty who were identified as collaborators or combatants. Around this time, too, the Catholic Church became a target of the security apparatus's murderous embrace, and religious leaders with ties to Catholic Action were killed. These killings aimed to isolate the guerrilla from their support base and to complicate already difficult relationships between urban, rural, ladino, and indigenous Guatemalans.

Despite the FAR and PGT's critiques and the threat of violent retribution, there was actually a good deal of discussion about how to expand the university's reach. In addition to the statements and essays mentioned above, USAC administrators and faculty gathered at Hotel Aurora in nearby Antigua, Guatemala in August 1977 to evaluate the old system and make plans for a new one. Extension Division Director Sifontes, Valdeavellano, and a number of Guatemala's most distinguished writers, scientists, historians, playwrights, dancers, artists, poets, economists, lawyers, and engineers attended the seminar.[121] The participants proposed a range of programs and publications, but underlying all of the proposals was the conviction that extension programs must be based on "real dialogue within and outside of the university walls."[122] The professors would cultivate a critical conscience regarding the university's responsibilities and commit to fulfilling them. They would foster critical analyses of mass culture and teach this critique. Above all, they would operate by the maxim that "real knowledge produces change." Far from a welfare program, this projection into the community was a labor that would spark social change; the programs would rouse learners into action.[123] Importantly, these USAC-led extension programs represented a civilian alternative to ongoing military-led development.

The assembled professors agreed that the old extension system had serious limitations. It emphasized indigenous education through individual patrons or sponsors, while regional campuses had difficulty building relationships with the communities in which they were located, often because they did not understand the social realities of their neighbors. Making matters worse, faculty employed vocabularies and educational models that were copied from abroad, and then "rigidly, but poorly," executed in the Guatemalan context. Sifontes called this "diffusionism," and wrote that in this system, knowledge "was generally created in the capital, [and] tended to be more injurious than beneficial to the university and its recipients."[124] These problems described the rare situation where facilities, materials, students, and faculty could be arranged. More often, extension services were chaotic and inconsistent. One scholar whose presentation focused on the educational potential of comics said that the old system failed to reach peripheral communities because the university continued to understand them to be "anthropological . . . in opposition to a supposed elevated or superior culture that the university represented."[125] By contrast, new pedagogical methods understood illiteracy as a complex structural condition and acknowledged different forms of literacy and the production of useful knowledge outside of elite circles.

Presenters gave talks on a range of proposals in fields like dance, orchestral and traditional music, fine art, sports, science, and journalism. Each related their area of expertise to new understandings of the relationship between the pueblo and the university, their thinking informed by dependency and development theory, Augusto Boal, Paolo Freire, and the Frankfurt School.[126] Some scholars revisited radio programming as a way to educate indigenous populations in areas where written literacy was rare. The Casa Flavio Herrera, founded in 1973 in a mixed working- and middle-class neighborhood about two kilometers from USAC, hosted cultural programming like film screenings, theatrical performances, roundtables, and seminars led by student groups. The West German film *Tattoo* (1967), Rainer Werner Fassbinder's *Effi Briest* (1974), and several French films were the centerpieces of the 1977 season.[127] The organizers of the USAC film library hosted film screenings that began with an informal chat, followed by the film, and a concluding discussion. The goal was "to develop a critical conscience in spectators and teach ways of seeing and disarm the tricks of mass communication" as an act of self-defense.[128] Critical spectatorship could extend the period of "a student's critical conscience" past the moment when students become "conformist, assimilated, and uncritical" as professionals.[129] Fine arts programs promoted Guatemalan artists who addressed structural transformation and national themes in their work and planned to nurture popular participation by hosting exhibitions at informal arts centers instead of elite galleries. The most ambitious plan sought to create a new set of universal signs and symbols untainted by capitalist exploitation.[130]

For their part, students from Agronomy and Engineering went to rural departments and exchanged farming and construction techniques, intending to "collect knowledge derived from the experiences of the population to submit them to scientific method." They sought out individuals from these peripheral locales who had experience with a scientific problem and tested their solutions.[131] This was a remarkable turn. Uneducated, possibly even illiterate, rural people were asked to become research scientists. In this way, extension programming could "enrich in a reciprocal form the plurality and knowledge and experiences that may explain and render intelligible biophysical and sociocultural phenomenon in our surroundings."[132] Similarly, a philosophy of extension offered by the committee on publications planned to promote "a dialogue [and] the exchange of experiences with the community" in order to help people better understand the experiences of their fellow citizens and create "solidarity with the marginal sectors."[133] This commission, which included Roberto Díaz Castillo. Mario Maldonado, Rene Eduardo Poitevín Dardón, Manuel Andrade Roca, and Francisco Albizúrez Palma, planned a new publication that would be devoted to articles, letters, literary works, and other materials created by the popular sectors "to express their needs, ideas, and sentiments."[134] In addition to contributing content, workers and campesinos would help with layout, printing, and distribution in their unions, campesino leagues, and community groups.[135] Poitevín Dardón in particular had been increasingly disillusioned by the university and had recently published a remarkable denunciation of its failure to overcome what he saw as its bourgeois self-interest in *Quiénes Somos?: La Universidad de San Carlos y las clases sociales.*[136]

This new extension philosophy and the programming that it inspired were intended to forge reciprocal relationships based on mutual aid. In his opening remarks on the first morning of the conference, Valdeavellano spoke, "At the same time as the *universitario* projects himself into the pueblo, by means of the knowledge [he] acquired in the classroom, he will also receive from the same pueblo its wisdom and experiences." The new extension programming would enrich the student's classroom experience, ultimately making him a better professional because he would have not just classroom learning, but the pueblo's "wisdom and experiences." In this way, the new extension programming would "elevate the institution," too.[137] Moving forward, extension programs "must take up the perspective of the exploited, produced by its position within antagonistic social relations of production."[138] USAC public health expert Carlos Gehlert Mata affirmed Valdeavellano's plan: "We have faith in what we set forth. We firmly believe in a university of the people and for the benefit of the people . . . Only the pueblo can save the pueblo!"[139] In other words, Valdeavellano and his colleagues reasoned that the pueblo, the *universitario*, and the university would benefit from the new extension programs.

GO FORTH AND LEARN FROM ALL . . . OR ELSE

Unfortunately, San Carlistas recorded little information about how—or if—their plans worked in practice. Administrators, faculty, and students focused on what they planned to do and the broad changes they hoped these plans would effect. By reading these types of texts, the preceding pages have discussed how some San Carlistas revised presumptions about rural and indigenous citizens that characterized student nationalism in previous decades. I argued that academic debates about development and dependency theory, encounters with indigenous, rural, and poor citizens in print and, presumably, in field sites where extension programs were implemented, and autocritique of the failures of extension programming compelled San Carlistas to reevaluate the university's relationship with the pueblo. From the first extension program in 1922, San Carlistas who were guided by their fantasies and fears of rural indigenous people and cultures determined that the indigenous majority was resistant to progress. In these early decades, extension programs focused on modernization and the integral development of the personality, the body, and the spirit. This philosophy changed somewhat after the Ten Years' Spring, when literacy and technical skills were prioritized, but the programs remained limited by urban San Carlistas' prejudices, as the debate over universal suffrage discussed in Chapter 1 made clear. The first real change in the relationship between the university, the government, and the pueblo occurred after the counterrevolution. For one, the large antigovernment protests discussed in Chapters 2 and 3 brought students and faculty into closer contact with organized workers and campesinos. Also, after anticommunism grouped students, workers, and campesinos into one subversive mass, some San Carlistas began to understand that these disparate groups did, in fact, share some political goals. But where intellectual culture was concerned, San Carlistas continued to believe that knowledge emanated outward from the university and onto a grateful pueblo.

This changed by the late 1970s, however, when student nationalism no longer required San Carlistas to act as acolytes of knowledge or leaders of a backward pueblo. Instead, they were duty-bound to collaborate with workers and rural campesinos, to share experiences, combat alienation, and form a true national culture. University extension came to emphasize collaboration and rejected programs that depended on a helpless and victimized pueblo, an attitude that differentiated San Carlistas from some of their peers elsewhere in the region.[140] Faculty acknowledged that university discourse had previously used "*lo popular*" to support elite culture and ideology.[141] Where earlier programs sought to instill a set of moral reflexes, harmony, faithfulness, and service (as Balcárcel Ordóñez charged when he called students and professors "agents of developmental interpellation"), new programs attempted to rise above social divisions. It remained the San Carlistas' duty to protect the nation's natural resources (its subsoil and its citizens) from rapacious foreign exploitation, so *dependentistas* put theory into practice in extension programming and their opposition to EXMIBAL and petrol extraction. Dependency theory also helped USAC social scientists and students to link Spanish colonialism to North American neocolonialism and as a result, not just the role of the university in the nation, but also the very foundation of the nation-state was up for discussion.

The environment in which extension programs were redesigned continued to be deeply stratified and unequal. Within these limitations, San Carlistas attempted to reconcile fairly radical policy revisions with a number of internal and external factors: the university's broader agenda and its budget; the military governments' own development programs; an escalating counterinsurgency effort; worldwide student and popular decolonial movements; and the decline of Keynesianism and the emergence of neoliberal governments. San Carlistas' reckonings with these global changes through dependency theory and praxis revealed the importance of race and class to San Carlistas' visions of progress. Remember how San Carlistas argued petrol and nickel deposits at El Estor deserved protection because they were part of the nation's wealth. They deployed the same logic to argue that, as part of national patrimony, indigenous people should be protected. But San Carlistas' sole figure for depicting indigenous perspectives (Tecú) was terribly essentialist, even as they worked more closely with campesino organizations and more and more indigenous people moved to the capital city because they were displaced by the civil war. Tecú embodied the uneducated *indio* stereotype who could not yet successfully wield the rights of citizenship on his own, the same stereotype that had informed San Carlistas' restriction of the franchise in 1945. In no comic or interview did students permit Tecú to show concern for this flat depiction.

San Carlistas' racial subjectivities were premised on the legitimacy of a universal liberal disciplinary state society *and* exclusion from it.[142] At times these fantasies seemed to confirm guerrillas' suspicions that the university was inexorably bourgeois. But they also reflected new possibilities for the university and its students in local guerrilla and global intellectual networks. As the previous chapters have made clear, San Carlistas occupied an uncertain position as urban ladino intellectual elites at the public university in a peripheral nation.[143] USAC *dependentista* Torres-Rivas called this "a peculiar feeling"—aspirational and precarious—being at once unable to enjoy the luxury of the capitalists yet spared the miserable conditions of the workers.[144] This indeed was a peculiar set of feelings for San Carlistas who were hard at work trying to imagine a new relationship to the periphery and who had inherited idioms of political affect based on solemn duty, responsibility, and freedom—feelings that left little room for indulgence—and the ludic Huelga de Dolores. The contradictory demands of this political affect help explain the disparagement toward *pesados* and hippies articulated by the JPT, FAR, and some San Carlistas by the mid-1970s.

Sovereignty, universal rights discourse, development, and even foreign threat were the conditions of possibility of USAC student nationalism in the late 1960s and early 1970s. San Carlistas' plans to protect the pueblo and national patrimony from foreign neocolonial threat, even in their new collaborative form, laid bare several strategic questions and contradictions. Similar questions challenged contemporary guerrilla groups: how useful was a nation-state-based political project? Who could be included in the nation? One old question remained unresolved: what was the role of the university? Related, who could lead social change? The university's motto, "Go Forth and Teach All," had long raised the same questions.

USAC extension programming and natural resource development plans failed to solve social inequality, but they succeeded in changing the conversation. Rural and urban poor citizens were no longer easily blamed for national problems. The overwhelming power of North American capital was to blame. USAC muralist Ramírez Amaya's revision of "Id y enseñad a todos" to "Id y aprended de todos, si no comed caca"—reflected the significance of this transformation. As the military escalated its war on the left, it became imperative that the university make good on this motto.

FIVE

_____

Combatants for the Common Cause, 1976–1978

The government of Laugerud has a choice: either continue covering up crimes against the people or dismantle the plan of the
fascist [military and economic] sectors ... Only with a strong
unified front of popular and student organizations can we stop
the criminal hand of fascism and only by creating, developing,
and consolidating these organizations can the community confront crime and fascist terror.

Association of University Students (AEU), The Jornadas of August 1977[1]

IN 1976, THE *NO NOS TIENTES* editorial observed, "In Guatemala, the social
faults [*fallas*] are deeper than the geological faults [*fallas*]." Faults of both
types were very much on the minds of capital city students and their families
during the Huelga that year. Just months had passed since a devastating
earthquake had wracked Guatemala. The capital was among the places hit
the hardest. The city lay in ruins. Its dense population and precarious architecture meant that around 30,000 citizens were killed and a million residents
lost their homes. Citizens quickly realized the man-made dimensions of this
natural disaster. Wealthier neighborhoods were built on more solid ground
and with superior materials and survived the earthquake with little damage
while poor, working-class, and even middle-class neighborhoods were demolished. Social *fallas* also signaled the government's failure to provide much-
needed aid.

It was precisely this situation that concerned Mario López Larrave. Since
drawing the poignant masthead of the *No Nos Tientes* in 1966, he had completed a thesis on procedural law, written a book on the history of Guatemalan
labor law, become a professor at USAC, and founded the university's Labor
Orientation School. His career was focused on "the deplorable and depress-
ing situation that prevails in this beautiful, tragic, ill-fated Guatemala,"
conditions that had "inspired the University of San Carlos, as a whole, and

the *Facultad* of Law to reflect on concrete forms of aid for our brother workers of the city and the country."[2] López Larrave was well known for his commitment to building an alliance between the university and workers that extended beyond pledges of solidarity. Perhaps evidence of the professor's success, the crowd that assembled in mid-1976 to celebrate his new book included workers, students, distinguished faculty, university administrators, and other interested onlookers.

In the introduction to *Breve historia del movimiento sindical guatemalteco*, López Larrave argues for the importance of history in the making of workers' class-consciousness and outlines the long history of industrial worker and rural campesino solidarity. He also expresses the hope that his book might teach students the importance of organized labor in the nation's history. He lists the few available archives for Guatemalan labor history, including the Ministry of Labor, oral history interviews, and the sparse collections of labor unions and federations. He notes how the dearth of labor history is another consequence of the counterrevolution's attack on labor, and positions his book as a first step in fighting this historical erasure. His text was the ideal inaugural volume for the USAC University Press's Popular Library series, part of efforts to counter the "erroneous idea that the university should be only a factory of technicians . . . a path for the improvement of the individual social or economic status of a student," according to the series description. The series was "intended especially for workers" as proof of "an alma mater that identified with its pueblo, that assumed its historical responsibility . . . beyond the closed environs of the classroom."[3]

López Larrave's book reflected how the relationship between *universitarios* and the broader community had been evolving over the previous decade. The professor reminded his readers that the conditions confronting workers were "distant from the situation of privilege in which we as *universitarios* find ourselves," but he insisted that unity was of the most absolute urgency.[4] No longer were *universitarios* making appeals *on behalf of* the pueblo. Instead, they sought to *collaborate with* the pueblo in spite of—even because of—social difference. For its part, the right, led by President Kjell Eugenio Laugerud García (1974–1978), believed that this growing coalition of workers, campesinos, students, and professors foretold another revolution.[5] The military, police, secret police, and paramilitary groups responded with violence.

This and the following chapter focus on how San Carlistas adapted the political culture of the university to this ongoing escalation of violence, following a series of extraordinary events like the 1976 earthquake and the massacre of Kekchí Mayas in Panzós, and everyday incidents like surveillance and arrests. As the state expanded its repressive apparatus against San Carlistas, San Carlistas expanded their resistance strategies within that apparatus. Alongside workers and peasants, in formal and informal workshops, neighborhood organizations, reading groups, unions, political parties, and guerrilla cells, students managed to create a formidable opposition to the military, police, and landed oligarchy in the late 1970s. Chapter 5 highlights transformative moments that brought students, workers, and peasants closer together. Chapter 6 discusses the new politics of death that emerged as more and more members of this popular opposition were disappeared, tortured, or killed. The chapters overlap chronologically in order to avoid obfuscating meaningful loss and significant gains within a reductive narrative of hydraulic action and reaction.

By the mid-1970s, San Carlista students and professors had critically reevaluated the politics of advocacy, representation, and solidarity that characterized their relations to nonstudents in previous decades. No longer acolytes of knowledge and progress as in the 1940s and 1950s or advisors and spokesmen for the periphery as in the 1960s, San Carlistas increasingly understood their political freedom—and survival—to be intimately bound to that of the urban and rural poor in opposition to the military and business oligarchy. As in previous moments of change, the university's shifting student body can explain some of this democratization. Between 1976 and 1980, USAC enrollments increased from 25,925 to 38,843 students, nearly 50 percent in just four years. More than other enrollment swells, these numbers reflected a large group of students who held regular jobs and took just a few classes per term during night classes, a trend enabled by new programs of study. Not only were San Carlistas reimagining their relationship to the pueblo; the pueblo was increasingly enrolling as students.

San Carlistas often challenged, but rarely sought to overthrow, the government even as the relationship between the university, Guatemalan society, and the state changed considerably across the course of the civil war. The republican democratic ideal was imperiled, but it endured, strengthened by an atmosphere of contention, debate, and compromise in the public sphere. As previous chapters detail, student nationalism's loose consensus survived the counterrevolution in part because the counterrevolutionary and military presidents intermittently worked to preserve their relationship to the university. Their periodic meetings with students, concessions to students' demands, public relations campaigns, and reluctance to use physical violence (with a few significant exceptions) meant that students continued to direct petitions and demands to the government. This complex balancing act, or even ambivalence, is difficult to untangle. In fact, some of the best scholarship on the period argues that the 1954 counterrevolution decimated the scholars and statesmen who upheld the republican ideal and therefore extinguished republicanism among the right and the left.[6] On the contrary, Chapters 3 and 4 have shown how student protests, polemics, and political funerals *relied upon* constitutional authority and principles of liberalism, even as these ideals began to seem increasingly imperiled.

When acts of violence did challenge the republican ideal that had been so crucial to student nationalism, some San Carlistas began to shift their view to look beyond the state, questioning liberalism and its social contract. In place of reformist possibilities that had characterized student nationalism since the 1954 coup, these San Carlistas considered more millenarian futures. Like the urban workers studied by Deborah Levenson, students who had been an integral part of state making for decades began to see the government as "alien and dangerous" and individual state functionaries as "murderous psychopaths" or "barbarous," "heartless," and "not human beings."[7] While students' rhetoric strategically referred to the Constitution and even to the university's own foundational documents, student nationalism extended beyond justice, right, and feelings of fraternity, which had characterized it in previous decades.[8] Once a nationalism premised on the ideal of equality before the law, literacy, and urbanity, student nationalism, set against the bloody excesses of the government, became a nationalism without a state. The state had proven incapable of protecting the lives of its citizens. In other words, both the murderous state and insurgents undid the republican ideal, the statist horizon of student nationalism. Living San Carlistas were left to imagine new futures in its wake.

GEOLOGIC FAULT AND SOCIAL FAILURES

Just hours before the 7.5 magnitude earthquake struck, moviegoers in Guatemala City watched Hollywood stars Charlton Heston, Ava Gardner, George Kennedy, Zsa Zsa Gabor, Walter Matthau, and Lorne Green traverse the ruins of quake-wracked Los Angeles in the worldwide box office-hit *Earthquake*.[9] The silver screen city stirred consumer aspirations in

Guatemalan audiences. The film opened with a long sequence of aerial shots of downtown skyscrapers, highways, the Mulholland Dam, and the Hollywood Hills. National and foreign banks aggressively funded a number of towering all-glass buildings in this new international style in Guatemala City.[10] Guatemalans were also drawn into a technological sensory experience by the film's new Sensusurround system that used deep bass sound waves to simulate the sensation of earthquake tremors. Eerily, the film's final frames— a wide shot of emergency vehicles, dazed citizens, and the skeletal remains of burnt buildings—presaged the collapse of the modern city.

At 3:03 A.M. on February 4, the earth's crust cracked open at the intersection of the Motagua and Mixco fault lines just ten kilometers from the capital. The nation shook for interminable seconds while the Caribbean and North American tectonic plates split vertically, then shifted horizontally.[11] Nationally, around 23,000 people were killed and 70,000 wounded; in the city, an estimated 3,370 people were killed and 16,549 wounded. About half a million *capitalinos* were instantly homeless as 99,712 homes in the capital were destroyed.[12] Water, electricity, and telephone services were interrupted and many thousands of people were buried alive. Quickly known as the "earthquake of the poor" (*el terremoto de los pobres*), the disaster revealed the structural inequities of the architecture of daily life. The Motagua and Mixco faults had caused earthquakes for centuries, so wealthier citizens lived in neighborhoods located far from the most dangerous zones. The only land affordable to the city's growing poor population after the migration booms of the 1940s and early 1970s was located in unsafe areas. Making matters worse, earthquake-resistant building materials were expensive, so poorer residents built homes from cheap and salvaged materials, like cardboard, tin, and cement blocks, which were very unsafe in earthquakes.[13]

The disaster revealed the government's inability to respond to crisis. President Laugerud's response became infamous: "Guatemala has been wounded, but not mortally wounded."[14] Some people began to speculate that the government had profited from relief funds donated by foreign nations.[15] As days passed without tangible assistance from the government, citizens were left to manage on their own. Members of the university community, including López Larrave, joined neighborhood and workers' groups and traveled to the countryside and poor peripheral neighborhoods in the capital city. Historian Virgilio Álvarez Aragón described the spontaneous response as an anthill that walked the city streets, looking for ways to be of assistance to those in need.[16] At first extemporaneously, and later within *facultad*-based organizations, San Carlistas who shared the belief that they were obliged to help their neighbors were among the first to rescue the injured. They went to affected neighborhoods where they demolished houses that were at risk of collapse and provided aid to people in need, recovered bodies and personal effects, distributed water and food, and rebuilt homes. As early as February 9, just five days after the earthquake, the AEU had organized a system of student brigades to bring assistance. Around 2,500 San Carlistas joined the relief effort.[17]

It was something that many students later remembered as central to their conscientization.[18] A year later, San Carlista and statesman Manuel Colom Argueta wrote, "The 1976 earthquake stimulated the social conscience ... if [Guatemalan society] could withstand an injury of natural provenance, then it was possible to overcome an injury caused by the inhuman, disrespectful, and antidemocratic exercise of power against massive sectors of those who are exploited, marginal, or limited by the economic and social system."[19] The AEU founded an Emergency Committee to coordinate the various student organizations' relief efforts and prepare for future natural disasters. The *facultades* of Engineering and Medicine dominated the committee. These students had important skills for the rebuilding effort; they also tended to come from wealthier families and would have had more free time and less experience with poverty, with the exception of some who had practiced in free clinics. As I mentioned in the Introduction, these degrees required extensive programs of study, including at least six years of classes and practicums that impeded other employment. Many were shocked by the poverty they saw while involved in the relief effort. The contrast between their own lives and the precarious lives of their fellow citizens put a point on the most enduring feature of student nationalism: students' duty to lead the people through the diffusion of culture and knowledge.[20]

As Chapter 4 detailed, many classes, roundtables, and seminars examined dependency and underdevelopment by the late 1970s, but the earthquake relief was many students' first experience working with the rural and urban poor. In the countryside, young students saw first-hand the social conditions in which the majority of Guatemala's population lived. Carlos Paz Tejada, a San Carlista since the 1940s, wrote from Mexican exile that the relief efforts were a sort of revelation to the students, such that "the coexistence [*convivencia*] and the solidarity that they [students and workers] developed nurtured the spirit of social commitment that prevailed in the university."[21] Francisco Villagrán Kramer recalled, "the major effect of the earthquake, without a doubt, was to expose to the light of day the crude reality of [a] country . . . that operated on the basis of clearly established hierarchies that [up until then] were observed and respected."[22] These and other anecdotal memories of the earthquake's aftermath suggest that the critique of colonialism that many professors and students had developed during the 1960s found a larger audience after the unnatural disaster. A handful of scholarly publications charged that USAC's foreign-based engineering curriculum had cost many thousands of Guatemalan lives. It seemed likely that much of the damage could have been avoided if Guatemalan engineers had learned to work with earthquake-resistant materials.[23]

If some students were compelled to assist the relief efforts for academic and political reasons, others like the Social Christian youths of CRATER were called by their faith. Formed in the late 1960s, CRATER united students from several elite Catholic *colegios* in the capital city who had been instructed in the Social Doctrine of the Catholic Church by Maryknolls and other progressive Catholics. At Social Training Workshops (*Cursillos de Capacitación Social*), young people learned about the "Third Way," eschewing communism and capitalism to live together in a different sort of society. CRATER was unique for how it brought together San Carlistas and students from Universidad Rafael Landívar, the private Jesuit university founded in 1961. *Landivarianos* were mostly children of financial and political elites, raised on Catholic anticommunism and material wealth.[24] But through CRATER they learned to see the earthquake as a display of structural inequality and to critique how state policy undermined simple humanitarian policies such as land reform, health care, and literacy.[25]

Religion also figured into other citizens' explanations of the earthquake. Divine reaction dominated popular understandings of the seismic event. A survey conducted for the Institute of Nutrition of Central America and Panama (INCAP) reported that of the 101 families surveyed regarding the cause of the earthquake, 26 answered "God's command"; 21, "God's punishment"; 17, "Only God knows"; 13, "God's Word"; 2 replied, "God's lesson"; and 10 responded "Because of a volcano." Only one family replied that the earthquake was caused by "a geological fault." For many, spiritual penitence explained the earthquake and its outcomes. Eleven families had no response, but the survey did not detail whether the families replied, "I do not know" or simply remained silent.

Perhaps so many families replied that God caused the earthquake because on the day after the disaster, Archbishop Mario Casariego broadcast a long and punishing speech over national radio. He warned: "God put his finger on Guatemala and luckily not his hand . . . does not the good and wise Father correct the child who loves him?" He continued, "And have we not resisted so much that we have forced God to do so? This tragedy was a punishment from God."[26] In the context of the Archbishopric's tireless campaigns against the university, discussed throughout the book, Catholic Guatemalans could only understand the statement one way: the earthquake was God's *light* punishment for the nation's slide toward communism; they must atone to prevent more severe punishment. In reaction to Casariego's statement, a group of Catholic priests circulated a Pastoral Letter, entitled "United in Hope." The letter—remarkably—blamed "the so-called upper classes, formed by those who retain wealth and power [who] have succumbed gradually to the advance of immorality, to immoderate desire for profit, to the insatiable search for pleasure. The baseness and immoral decadence that one finds in these sectors of our society is incredible." The letter continued, "The grave problem of landownership in agrarian and urban spaces is the basis of our entire unjust situation . . . the dormant National Reconstruction Committee (CRN) has created and maintained a climate of tension. Its task was to centralize relief from insecurity, fear, repression in our nation."[27] CRATER and the priests' defiant letter tell of a growing movement of socially conscious Catholics, led by Jesuits and Maryknolls.[28]

A month after the disaster, President Laugerud's relief effort was finally underway. It focused on places where mutual aid groups had gained appeal and integrated "Army officers, civil functionaries, and civilians from the private sector, the business sector, workers, students, and cooperatives."[29] In Laugerud's CRN, national and international businesses, the far right MLN party, and the military appeared to be the pueblo's saviors. The CRN further undermined spontaneous community-based aid efforts by splitting the nation into recovery zones to be managed by specific business or military interests. For instance, the Castillo brothers (the wealthy owners of Cervecería Centro Americana, S.A., manufacturer of Gallo, Victoria, Sol, Dorada, and Moza beers since 1896), the Salvation Army, Oxfam-World Neighbors, and a California-based church group called Wings of Mercy managed the primarily indigenous department of Chimaltenango. In other departments, the Herrera family organized relief, an unsubtle strategic choice since the family owned large farms in the area and regularly hired laborers at the most meager wages. These workers were called *mozos*, a derogatory term used since the nineteenth century to describe poor agricultural laborers.[30] In each zone, the militarized CRN provided building materials to communities for free or at a subsidized cost, and functioned as a sort of social welfare organization. The CRN ranked recipients of government aid based on their loyalty and patriotism, further extending its structure of surveillance into needy communities. Soon, it began to function more like a mechanism for social control than a relief agency.[31]

The relief effort fed ongoing political tensions. National newspapers with ties to the Castillo and Herrera families reported that some volunteers spread antigovernment propaganda as they rebuilt homes. Students seemed particularly vulnerable to this charge. The press even singled out individuals, like architecture students and members of the USAC political group PODER Dwight Ponce Quezada and Horacio Mendizabal García, for harassment. In their coverage of the earthquake relief, reporters called into question the character of the two young men, even going so far as to imply that they had come from bad families.[32] In another instance, *La Nación* charged that a group of psychology students instigated a land occupation. The editorial claimed that students had advised residents of the neighborhood to occupy a tract of land adjacent to Colonia El Milagro.

Quickly, AEU general secretary Luis Vallejo wrote to the director of *La Nación* to contest some of the editorial's claims.[33] He wrote that a student group had entered El Milagro to offer free grief counseling to community members after the earthquake, but quickly realized that the community needed help to recover the bodies of their family members and to repair sewage systems before any counseling could be effective. To counter the newspaper's claim that there had been "ongoing subversive organizing," Vallejo wrote that individual *facultades* had been providing assistance since February 9, but had not arrived in El Milagro until later. He also emphasized that not all students involved in the earthquake aid were affiliated with the AEU, so the AEU leadership could not be held responsible for their actions. In fact, he said, the AEU had difficulty organizing its student brigades because classes had been suspended after the earthquake. Vallejo confirmed that psychology students had been working in El Milagro, but reiterated that the group's primary concern was to provide grief counseling—only paranoid minds could read sectarian aims into such beneficent acts of community service. While he had the editor's and the readers' attention, Vallejo described the problems confronting the residents of El Milagro, emphasizing their precarious housing and how some had been made to pay rent for homes that collapsed in the earthquake. Counter to the *La Nación* editorial that claimed students had instigated the land occupation, Vallejo detailed how El Milagro residents decided to hold a general assembly where the group reached a consensus to seize and occupy the land of a nearby property owner in protest. Vallejo wrote that professional protocol required the student counselors to meet their clients wherever they lived, and so the counselors had spent time on the occupied property, but had played no role in planning the occupation.

Vallejo concluded his otherwise patient and precise response by denouncing the newspaper's ethics. After all, it was owned by Roberto Girón Lemus, who was also the president's secretary of public relations. If *La Nación* was so repelled by sectarianism, as its editorial had claimed, then it ought to "shed the mask of the pseudodemocracy that it has concealed through constant untrue news reports and reactionary stories that have corrupted the pueblo day after day."[34] Vallejo also wrote that it was absurd to blame students while any number of injustices proliferated in the city: "Is it instigation and agitation . . . to help with relief from endemic social ills, to fight to protect their health by installing a health clinic or trying to establish a little school?"[35] Vallejo reminded the editor how the earthquake and subsequent relief efforts actually inspired some students to study topics that would bring real benefit to the nation.[36] Unfortunately, there is no record of the editor's response and it is hard to say whether Vallejo was able to circulate his rejoinder beyond USAC campus. Nevertheless, the letter remains an important index of the AEU's stance in the aftermath of the earthquake.

The earthquake and escalating government repression limited other aspects of youth popular culture, even among sectors of young people who professed to be apolitical. For weeks after the earthquake, radio stations that usually played popular music were used to convey public messages from the government.[37] More generally, police raids of popular discotheques were more common after Laugerud García's election. Migration and exile further reduced the number of youth consumers and creators. Of course the subculture of rock music did not disappear entirely, but it did change. Instead of songs about women, drugs, and cars inspired by U.S.-based bands, Guatemalans began to listen to and write Nueva Canción and Nueva Trova, genres of protest music from Chile, Nicaragua, and Cuba. In comparison to this distinctly Latin American protest music, North American–inspired rock seemed bourgeois, imperialist, and shamefully (rather than avowedly) apolitical.[38]

As the dust settled, the fate of the approaching Huelga de Dolores was unclear. Some speculated that the event would be canceled, in light of the still dangerous conditions of roads and buildings. But in early March, the publicity committee distributed a press release that declared that the Huelga was more important than ever, as "an opportunity to denounce and protest the misdeeds committed by the government in the recent moment of national emergency as well the constant repression in which the nation has lived for many years."[39] They proposed some adjustments to the traditional Huelga, given the desperate post-earthquake conditions.[40] Instead of planning a single "Grand Soiree" in Guatemala City at the Lux Theatre, as was the custom, the organizers discussed producing a touring event that could be staged many times over the course of a week in the capital and the countryside, since poor and delayed road reconstruction impeded access to the city. They agreed that all funds generated from ticket and beer sales would be donated to the AEU Emergency Committee and earmarked exclusively for the reconstruction of schools and pharmacies in the neediest communities. To safeguard against the likelihood that Laugerud's CRN would embezzle relief funds, the AEU promised to manage the donations itself.[41]

The Huelga's organizers, the Honorable Committee, prepared for potential unrest by limiting the consumption of alcohol and urging students to maintain the moral comportment appropriate to a nation recently overcome by loss. They debated whether the *desfile bufo* parade, with its lewd posters and chants, public drunkenness, and scantily clad, cross-dressing students, should be cancelled. As in other years, some *universitarios* critiqued the event as an attempt to mollify the pueblo's real complaints. Still others advocated for the event and saw the satirical parade as a pedagogical "day of popular teaching and concientization."[42] In the end, the *desfile* was cancelled. But the AEU urged students to participate in other events and emphasized their political importance, arguing, "the present moment is favorable for initiating an intense campaign of denunciation and protest against the injustices committed by the government—the instrument of national and international oligarchies."[43]

Without the *desfile bufo*, the most provocative critiques of the government emerged in print, especially in the *No Nos Tientes*.[44] The year's editorial, with which this chapter began, plainly proclaimed, "in Guatemala, social faults [*fallas*] are deeper than geological faults."[45] Enumerating the many ongoing social injustices endured by capital city and rural citizens, the anonymous editors continued, "Economic and political fraud, the tortures and slaughters, jingoism and idiocy, the corrupt businesses small and large, cynicism and ineffectiveness, in one word, *corruption*, constitutes a backdrop against which the drama of February 4, 1976, developed." The editorial decried the privileges the traditional oligarchy gained when multinational businesses invested in the relief effort while the majority of the population suffered.[46] In a feature entitled, "To the Perpetual Victims," authors positioned San Carlistas as truth tellers against the tripartite vested interests of the Laugerud government, sensationalistic profit-minded daily newspapers, and Archbishop Casariego. They wrote, "The *No Nos Tientes* is standing up, but not on its feet like that bastard [*pizote*] Laugerud says of our nation when everything is actually going to shit."[47]

The editors of the *No Nos Tientes* insisted that their paper was driven by commitment to the people in contrast to the profit motive of *La Nación* and other mainstream papers. The *No Nos Tientes* did not sell an expensive special edition about the catastrophe, "with the only motive to starve you of your money, you, the perpetual victims, as do *El Tiempo*, *La Tarde*, and the toilet paper called *La Nación*."[48] The anonymous student editors referred to the editor in chief of the *Prensa Libre* as the ambassador of the Order of the Dark Beers, linking the paper to the Castillo family.[49] Like the Herrera family, the spectacularly rich Castillos employed thousands of poor Guatemalans in their urban beer manufacturing plant, yet were willing to donate only "a dozen pairs of underwear" to the relief effort. Making matters worse, the *Prensa Libre* had printed multiple photographs of the Castillo family's meager donation. Students also lampooned *El Imparcial* as the proprietor of the large supermarket chain, Supermarket Montúfar, which had donated various cans of Kerns brand juices—but only the dented cans that could not be sold. The Rotary Club, for its part, donated three whole bed sheets and ensured that a photograph of this charitable act was printed in *La Hora*. In reference to Archbishop Casariego's declaration that the earthquake was divine punishment for rampant radicalism, the students joked that it was "divine perhaps for those who are filling their pockets with the sale of bricks, *lámina*, awnings, hoes, pickaxes, and other tools that you, the perpetual victims, buy on credit or at double the price." The editors wrote that most relief efforts were part of a dishonest attempt to rebuild the "imprisoning, dominating, and stifling . . . decadent and agonizing structures that choke us, that make us bleed out, that immobilize us," rather than those that provide shelter for the pueblo. Extending their building metaphor, the editors called on the people to sweep away the old structures and build new ones from "new cement."[50] Their wry wit undermined the sham altruism of the business sector, the press, and the government.[51]

FIGURE 10. Youth spray painting a wall with the slogan, "Student Who Listens, Organize and Fight." Fototeca Guatemala, Centro de Investigaciones Regionales de Mesoamérica (CIRMA).

While USAC fought off external attacks from the archbishop and the press, it also faced challenges from within. Two political parties, PODER and FRENTE, dominated the AEU after the earthquake. Both groups were on the left, but they disagreed on the one key question that had for decades divided the student body: the university's role in national politics. Although it supported candidates for student leadership like Vallejo, mentioned above, PODER primarily focused its attention on concerns outside of the university. The group openly supported the guerrilla and rural communities in resistance, and it distributed information about the military's counterinsurgency actions.[52] PODER's leaders suggested that students practice organizing at USAC in preparation for the real work of revolution: organizing campesinos and workers. Instead of public university-wide electoral politics, PODER members turned to clandestine and collective politics.[53] Many read the writings of *universitario*-turned-guerrilla César Montes (the alias of Julio César Macías). News of counterinsurgency atrocities in the countryside added a sense of urgency to their study. San Carlista historian Virglio Álvarez Aragón recorded the memories of one radicalized student, Pedro Pablo Palma (nom de guerre: Pancho), who said, "the group made the decision that those who joined the organization would break with the miniworld called university, and really dedicate themselves to work, to organizing a struggle of national dimensions." The university itself was no longer a priority.[54]

FRENTE stepped into the void left by PODER's turn away from university politics. Its members represented a wide and uneasy alliance of the university's left and center parties. It prioritized building coalitions between powerful blocs instead of refining policy positions.[55] As a result, FRENTE dominated AEU and *facultad* elections for many years and enjoyed the support of many university administrators.[56] If there was ideological cohesion in FRENTE's coalition, it centered on the political discourse of human rights, legal appeals, historical memory of the 1944 Revolution, and the new National Front Against Violence and Repression.[57] Many members of FRENTE were also affiliated with the communist Guatemalan Labor Party (PGT) and its youth branch, the JPT. Critics of the group, including PODER, claimed that human rights were nothing more than conciliatory, timid, cowardly, and bourgeois politics.[58] They especially saw FRENTE's focus on legal appeals for human rights violations as evidence of the co-optation of their radical potential by *burgueses*. This growing rift paralleled the disunity of the Guatemalan left beyond campus.[59]

In a commemorative publication about the 1944 Revolution, FRENTE students characterized Guatemala's economic structure as neocolonial. They linked the Guatemalan government to other CIA-backed dictatorships in the hemisphere, including Chile, Uruguay, Brazil, Bolivia, El Salvador, Nicaragua, Paraguay, Haiti, and Argentina. They called for the restoration of a state of lawfulness, their rhetoric bolstered by quotations from the Constitution of the Republic, and they berated police, soldiers, and commanders, calling them thieves and anticommunists.[60] Most importantly, they called upon the people to pursue the path of "unity" with "those who are for the defense of the rights of the pueblo [and] for the respect of the democratic liberties and the most elemental human rights."[61] They also warned against reactionaries who would refuse to join in the struggle. Echoing the words of labor lawyer and professor López Larrave, FRENTE called on workers, campesinos, employees, soldiers, police, teachers, housewives, professionals, and secondary school students to join together.[62]

Soon, FRENTE's public strategy would be challenged by extraordinary acts of violence against their members and sympathetic professors. FRENTE would respond by amplifying its appeals to human rights. In so doing, they once more reworked the republican ideals central to student nationalism, again articulated in the terms that defined *universitarios*: rights, duties, responsibilities, and freedoms. What had inspired the *freedom to* build the nation during the revolution now demanded *freedom from* harm by that same state.

MARIO LÓPEZ LARRAVE: "HONEST, REVOLUTIONARY, AND HARDWORKING MAN"

López Larrave was stuck in meeting after meeting on June 8, 1977. At five in the afternoon, he had a free moment to stop by his office in Zone 4 and drop off some papers before teaching his evening classes at USAC. Although he usually parked elsewhere, that day he parked in a convenient public lot. A witness remembered, "When he exited the parking lot with his car, there were shots fired. The car stopped in the middle of the street ... They fired twice. And the folks who did this fled the scene in a red Datsun 120Y."[63] López Larrave was a professor and former dean of the Faculty of Juridical and Social Sciences, director of the Labor Orientation School, an advisor to more than a hundred unions, a member of the advisory board of the university, and a potential candidate for university rector. He had worked tirelessly to bridge campus, the factory floor, and the rural plantations. His death was a priority for the repressive forces, and his visibility made him an easy target. Despite his fame, the accounts that filled city newspapers in the days after the assassination did not explore motives or name suspects.

Dissatisfied with this lack of accountability, students, administrators, and labor leaders worked to shift the tenor of public dialogue about López Larrave's assassination. San Carlistas sent paid political advertisements and denunciations to university and national newspapers. A public political funeral was planned to unite the social groups that López Larrave had mediated in life and to travel to symbolic city spaces like the university, workers' commuting routes, union headquarters, and the General Cemetery. The funeral began with a short ceremony on campus. López Larrave's coffin and the crowd that accompanied it filled the main plaza between the rector's office building and the Main Library. This wide-open space was later named the Plaza of Martyrs. After a short ceremony, the group left campus and processed slowly along Petapa Avenue toward Zone 1. Eight pallbearers and thousands of workers, professionals, students, housewives, and children dressed in their finest clothes accompanied the body of their beloved professor, mentor, lawyer, and advocate. At the General Cemetery, rector Dr. Roberto Valdeavellano delivered the funeral oration. He spoke of López Larrave as an exemplary citizen, a man of dignity, an honorable *universitario*, a labor activist, friend of the pueblo, and someone who was kind to everyone.[64] The eulogy praised López Larrave as a martyr, one who suffered and died instead of renouncing his beliefs.[65] In death, López Larrave triumphed as "the beautiful and dignified exemplar of the path of the student, of the university teacher, and of the democratic professional." Valdeavellano celebrated how López Larrave's "spilled blood" "strengthened and elevated" the San Carlista.[66] The loss was expressed in spiritual terms, making López Larrave into a Christ-like figure whose death saved others.

The edition of *Voz Informativa Universitaria* published just after the assassination provides a glimpse into the university's social and political atmosphere.[67] Beside a story about Valdeavellano's eulogy was an advertisement for the university press that featured books on the history of Guatemala and Guatemala City, critiques of foreign investment and land ownership in Central America, and popular studies of canonical Marxist texts. It also included López Larrave's *Breve historia del movimiento sindical guatemalteco*, which was a bestseller at the time of his death, and Manuel Galich's *Del pánico al ataque* (discussed at length in Chapter 1).[68] If the press' marketing was apt, then critiques of imperialism, primers on dialectical materialism, Guatemalan history and folklore, and Nicaraguan revolutionary hagiography advised San Carlistas' worldviews from the page while López Larrave's funeral and public protests advised them from the street. In Chapter 6, I discuss in greater detail how political funerals mediated social life with so much tragic repetition in the many deaths that would follow.[69] San Carlistas' distinct mode of life, culture, and interests—different and even antagonistic to those of other classes—their class discourse, movements, and later formal structures—were guided by these readings and experiences.[70]

The AEU sent an obituary-communiqué to the press that linked López Larrave's assassination to these larger political and historical concerns and promised a redoubling of opposition. It read: "To us, the popular organizations and the student organizations, falls the work of strengthening ourselves so that we can develop a common front that fights for the rights of the popular masses marginalized by the electoral manipulations of the political parties who [are] interested in maintaining the present state of things." The obituary-communiqué did not specify what form the strengthening might take, what sort of common front was desired, who was invited to join, or where or how the fight for rights would take place. But it did position the popular and student organizations against political parties and their failures. The AEU continued: "Only with a strong unified front of popular organizations and student organizations can we stop the criminal hand of fascism and only by creating, developing, and consolidating these organizations can the community confront crime and fascist terror."[71] The AEU transformed their eulogy into a call to action in a time when the political nature of some deaths was overdetermined.

López Larrave's assassination did not intimidate workers and the pueblo into inaction. In November 1977, seventy workers walked 250 miles from San Ildefonso Ixtahuacán in Huehuetenango to the capital city to protest the illegal closure of the tungsten mine owned by Minas de Guatemala. The previous year, the group had attempted to collectively bargain with little luck, and the company announced that it intended to close the mine immediately. This violated federal regulations that prevented factory and mine closures in response to strikes. USAC agronomy student and National Workers' Central (CNT) organizer Mario Rolando Mujía Córdova had advised the miners to draw attention to the illegal closure. The march seemed to follow his advice.[72] The miners hoped that other indigenous workers from isolated highlands communities, sugar cane workers on the southern coast, and the capital city's industrial workers would join them. They stopped in some of these communities where they shared food, music, and lodging. They also organized general assemblies to discuss local concerns, which were well attended. Detailed national newspaper coverage helped the march to capture the attention of the Guatemalan public. Such a challenge to the government was spectacular and almost unthinkable. Surprisingly, the miners boldly refused external representation by national political figures, including Manuel Colom Argueta. They suspected that Colom Argueta, who was running for president, might use them to his political advantage.[73]

President Laugerud, also conscious of upcoming elections and growing public support for the miners, seemed ready to forestall a general strike. He encouraged the company to reopen the mines, pay back wages, and even negotiate a contract with the CNT. All of this was settled before the miners reached the capital city. Yet the group decided to continue onward in solidarity with the sugar workers from the Pantaleón factory, who had also been fired but had not regained their jobs. At Central Park, 150,000 workers from across the nation gathered to hear the Ixtahuacán miners address the crowd in Spanish, their second language.

Remembered as the "Glorious March of the Miners" and the "March of Dignity," the strike had mixed outcomes. Workers, often divided by industry or location, built and strengthened connections. But while the Ixtahuacán miners' jobs were restored, the Pantaleón workers' jobs were not.[74] After the march, the government showed new resolve to dismantle solidarity between students and workers. Security forces identified Mujía and two other students as individuals responsible for organizing the Ixtahuacán miners. Mujía was assassinated on July 20, 1978, while at work in the Huehuetenango CNT office.[75] Security forces continued to unleash four months of retributive violence against other students at the Huehuetenango branch of USAC where Mujía studied. Not long after his assassination, another agronomy student and Mujía's replacement in the CNT, Julio Vásquez Recinos, was kidnapped.[76] An eyewitness remembered, "They kidnapped comrade Julio Vásquez Recinos, who appeared fifteen days later in the Río Selegua at the El Tapón bridge [in southern Huehuetenango] without testicles, without fingernails, without his right hand, and tied to another comrade who was never identified."[77] In early September 1978, another young student and labor organizer named María Eugenia Mendoza Rivas was kidnapped and raped by the army. Mendoza was released, then kidnapped and raped again, at which point she was tortured and killed. Her body was left on the streets of Huehuetenango.[78] Mendoza's death demonstrated how the military's strategic focus on the countryside affected San Carlistas. Some of the Ixtahuacán miners were also kidnapped, tortured, and killed. Again, the outcome of the march was complicated. On the one hand, the government was unsuccessful in preventing rural and urban workers' unity. This had been the miners' greatest objective. On the other hand, the government's recourse to exceptional violence afterward cost many organizers their lives.[79]

The 1978 elections for university rector reflected just how much the relationship between San Carlistas and the state had changed. University elections continued to be raucous fêtes in a nation that rarely held democratic national elections. Since the late 1960s, candidates had elaborated domestic and sometimes even foreign policy agendas during their campaigns. The elections provided a sort of political theatre. A reporter from *El Imparcial* noted, "All of the electors were preceded by applause, deathly silence, or hissing, which contributed a festive and happy atmosphere."[80] As they had since the revolution, high-profile national figures served as electors. In 1978, ex–vice presidential candidate René de Leon Schlotter and Guatemala City mayoral candidate Carlos Gehlert Mata cast votes. Student political parties like

FRENTE sponsored candidates. In 1978, an economist named Saúl Osorio Paz (backed by FRENTE) ran against Bernardo Lemus Mendoza.

Osorio Paz's wide-reaching platform underscored *universitarios'* duty to lead the pueblo toward a progressive and just future. He vowed to defend university autonomy and national sovereignty at all costs. His plans focused on increasing the percentage of the national budget allotted to the university and advocated research, university exchanges, and the creation of a postgraduate program. He vowed to spread knowledge nationwide, especially in peripheral rural communities and marginal urban communities through newspapers, cultural centers, and recreation facilities.[81] In place of conservative hierarchical teaching models, he proposed renewed attention to research. His social outreach included curriculum reform, publication of affordable textbooks for students and teachers, the invigoration of university extension programs, improvements to facilities at satellite campuses, and salary increases for professors to allow them to teach full time. He promised to "link the university to the people's interests," to "assist in the removal of obstacles to its development," and "channel new techniques of production to the popular sectors."[82] He obliged the university to challenge the government. In sum, Osorio Paz proposed nothing less than to entirely remake the university's orientation—to students, to faculty, to the pueblo, and to the government. All of these plans should sound familiar. To some extent, they were the same reforms that San Carlistas had been attempting to make for three decades.

His opponent, Lemus Mendoza, was less enthusiastic about the university taking an active role in national politics and culture and enjoyed the support of the current rector, Valdeavellano, and the University High Council (CSU).[83] FRENTE students decried Lemus as "the official candidate," using language they usually reserved for undemocratic national elections. They even wrote an open letter to the CSU, complaining that powerful interests backed certain candidates, corrupting the democratic process.[84] When Osorio Paz won, Lemus supporters in the administration denounced the results and demanded a second vote.[85] Osorio Paz remained the winner. In his victory speech, he asked for "the unity of students, professionals, and teachers, in order to exalt our university" and expressed his hope that partisan divides could be overcome.[86] The event closed with shouts of "Viva!" and the recitation of various student chants and songs, including "La Chalana," the student hymn that always accompanied the *desfile bufo* during the Huelga de Dolores.

Despite his calls for unity, Osorio Paz's election was met with a flurry of resignations from administrators and faculty who disagreed with the new mood of university politics. This new mood was exemplified in April when USAC hosted the National Youth and Student Festival.[87] More than three hundred youths from the city and the departments gathered on campus. To simply permit the festival was controversial, but Osorio Paz even helped to plan the event. Bolder still, Osorio Paz invited a special guest from Nicaragua, Enrique Mejía Godoy. Mejía Godoy was a singer-songwriter who had been in exile for more than a decade because of his support of the Sandinista National Liberation Front (FSLN). Mejía Godoy performed his most famous song, "Quincho Barrilete."[88] The lyrics tell the story of a fictional boy named Joaquín Carmelo (nicknamed Quincho Barrilete), who was forced to work as hard as a grown man. In the morning, Quincho worked with team of oxen and in the afternoon he sold small items on buses in order to help his siblings attend school. After an earthquake, Quincho was forced to live outdoors. The chorus declared, "Long live Quincho, Quincho Barrilete, young hero of my city, long live all of the young men of my land, living example of poverty and dignity. Long live Quincho, Quincho Barrilete, whose name will not be forgotten, because in the streets, plazas, parks, and shantytowns, the pueblo will repeat it." Quincho captured the hopes of San Carlistas and the Guatemalan, Nicaraguan, and Salvadoran pueblos. The song ends with the promise that Quincho would return one day soon to face the struggles of his people. After Mejía Godoy's moving performance, Osorio Paz called for a moment of silence in honor of the workers and students killed in recent years.[89] He concluded, "It is beautiful, what we are seeing today," a reference to the mass of young students who had assembled despite "hidden enemies" and "the challenges of work, of learning, of culture, and of art," in the pursuit of democracy.[90] Like Quincho, Osorio Paz celebrated a time when the youth of Central America would be united by possibility rather than cowed by hard labor and fear.

In inviting Mejía Godoy, Osorio Paz also demonstrated adeptness at rec-ognizing the interests of his student body. In mid-February 1977, the AEU issued a manifesto that denounced a rumored intervention of U.S., Nicaraguan, and Guatemalan troops in El Salvador on the grounds that this violated the nation's sovereignty and the interests of the pueblo. But the manifesto also made two other important points: the people of Guatemala, El Salvador, and Nicaragua were united by their histories of dictatorship and were therefore bound to stand together against tyranny "and to fight and to win a future of well-being and democracy that are now nonexistent."[91] In mid-July 1977 alone, San Carlistas received letters from Nicaraguan and

Salvadoran students. One letter came from Sandinista Tomás Borge, and requested solidarity for Sandinista political prisoners who were held in prisons without a charge and without outside contact. Borge had appealed to San Carlistas alongside the United Nations Commission on Human Rights, Amnesty International, International Red Cross, and other "American civic, progressive, and democratic organizations," who also received copies. The USAC Student Movement of Psychology (Movimiento Estudiantil de Psicología [MEPS]) typed and mimeographed copies of the letter to which they appended the news that Borge had been arrested. They added a general statement of solidarity with the people of Nicaragua: "We remember how state repression and the government's clandestine repression and the reactionary right are not exclusive to one nation, but that to maintain a false 'democracy' in our nations is and will be the answer to the pueblo's struggles for its liberation and that [this] is a demonstration of the weakness and impotence of the Central American governments."[92] Also in July, the AEU received a letter from the General Association of Salvadoran University Students (Asociación General de Estudiantes Universitarios [AGEUS]), commemorating the fifth anniversary of Salvadoran president Arturo Armando Molina's armed intervention against the University of El Salvador. The AGEUS appealed to the AEU *as students*, seeking the AEU's support and pledging their own, affirming, "We have not forgotten that we have a common enemy and only by uniting our forces will we achieve a total triumph in the fight for the freedom of our pueblos."[93] Like San Carlistas' idioms of political affect, the AGEUS students framed their struggle as a fight for freedom and wrote to their comrades in the third personal plural "we."

A few weeks later, the AEU invoked revolutionary unity when it vowed to "[stand] in solidarity with the struggle of the pueblo, which confronts fascist, racist, reactionary regimes that are fomented and sustained by imperialism; [salute] the great conquests of the pueblos who propel the struggle against imperialism around the world; [salute] the workers who built a new society." In the same statement, the AEU connected the death of Mario López Larrave, the march of the Ixtahuacán miners, and the numerous recent general strikes as evidence of the dire need to deepen unity between students and workers. They wrote, "in the heat of the struggle, the combative and sympathetic spirit of our pueblo has been fine-tuned."[94]

Just four weeks later, Kaibil special forces carried out one of the most infamous massacres in Guatemalan history, at Panzós, Alta Verapaz. For months, Maya Kekchí residents of communities near Panzós had filed complaints with the municipality over the attrition of communal lands to large agricultural production, a state-sponsored resettlement plan for displaced farmers, the construction of a large hydroelectric project financed by international development funds, and the installation of a military camp near their homes.[95] All of these projects were linked to the government's ongoing Franja Transversal del Norte (FTN) project. On May 29, the group went to the municipal building in Panzós to meet with mayor Walter Overdick to discuss their grievances. The subsequent events have been difficult to verify. Depending on the source, between 30 and 150 troops arrived in the community around three or five days before the massacre. Likewise, it is unclear how many campesinos were in the town square when the gunshots occurred. But while soldiers had guns, campesinos fought back with machetes and sharp sticks, more prepared to go to work than to fight an army. Witnesses agree that for five minutes shots were fired from state-issued handguns in the square and from submachine guns on a nearby hill.[96] After the gunfire ceased, troops blocked all entrances to the square and began removing bodies in large dump trucks. The army kept outsiders away from Panzós after the incident. Patrols occupied the town for weeks after the massacre while citizens hid indoors or fled. Decades later, the Guatemalan Forensic Anthropology Foundation (FAFG) found thirty-four corpses buried in a common grave in the general cemetery of Panzós. A report by the Commission for Historical Clarification (CEH) listed fifty-three dead by name, but noted that the list was incomplete.

One detailed account of San Carlistas' reaction to the massacre can be found in Ricardo Sáenz de Tejada's well-researched biography of Oliverio Castañeda de León. Based on an interview with Indiana Torres Escobar, one of Castañeda de León's comrades, Sáenz reconstructed some students' experiences of the night of the massacre. Recently elected AEU general secretary Castañeda de León and a handful of close friends (many members of FRENTE and the JPT) were gathered at a friend's apartment in Zone 1. It was late and the friends had been listening to the radio and talking about politics for hours. Suddenly, the radio broadcast was interrupted by a report of an armed attack against the military in Panzós, leaving many dead and wounded. The students had known for weeks about escalating tensions in Panzós and feared the worst. The streets of the capital city and other urban areas nationwide were deserted because of rumors of reprisal. Official news of the massacre reached the city the following morning in newspaper headlines that corroborated the radio report that peasants led an armed attack against the military and municipal government. The AEU Secretariat met to discuss their response. Their meeting was interrupted by a phone call from the Autonomous Federation of Guatemalan Unions (FASGUA). The caller told them that indigenous leaders from Alta Verapaz had come for a meeting at the FASGUA offices nearby and the AEU leaders were invited to join them. The caller also confirmed what the students had feared: the *campesinos* were attacked by the military—not the opposite—and hundreds were dead in Panzós.[97]

Castañeda de León had been elected AEU general secretary the week before the massacre. His opponent was Alejandro Cotí of the Student Front–Robin García (Frente Estudiantil–Robin García [FERG]), the name adopted by students within PODER who decided to remain involved in university politics. Unlike FRENTE, the FERG supported an armed path to social change.[98] While it recruited among the student body, it aligned itself more explicitly with the popular movement. In an election with the highest voter turnout in years, Castañeda de León won by a slim margin, just 4,696 votes to Cotí's 3,867, with 501 ballots null or blank.[99] Castañeda de León and Cotí mirrored the divisions of the broader Guatemalan left.[100] The popularity of both candidates suggested that San Carlistas were primed for radical change and even confrontation. There was no viable candidate representing the campus right in the 1978 elections.

On the way to the FASGUA offices, Castañeda de León picked up a friend, Edgar Ruano Najarro. On Saturday mornings, the two delivered copies of *El Estudiante* around the city.[101] Ruano was AEU undersecretary of outreach and an editor at *Inforpress*, a weekly news bulletin of political analysis and a critical source of antigovernment news in Central America. At the FASGUA offices, the two young men met with Panzós community leaders to determine an appropriate response to the massacre. The group agreed that their first priority was to help those who had fled to the capital city, including the many who arrived at Roosevelt Hospital with injuries. They also planned a meeting of the FASGUA, the AEU, and the National Committee on Trade Union Unity (CNUS), a broad coalition of unions formed in 1976. Ultimately, partisan divides undermined the effort: the CNUS disagreed with the JPT and PGT on points of strategy, and since many FRENTE and FASGUA members were affiliated with the JPT and PGT, the CNUS refused to work with them. But FRENTE students organized with FASGUA, and Castañeda de León and Ruano Najarro agreed to write a paid political advertisement to condemn the massacre in the name of the AEU.

FIGURE 11. "Guatemala '78: Home of the World Championships of Assassinations." Protest against the Massacre at Panzós, Guatemala City, 1978. Fototeca Guatemala, Centro de Investigaciones Regionales de Mesoamérica (CIRMA).

The AEU and FASGUA also organized a march to protest the government's failure to protect the people of Panzós.

The march was held on a rainy day and is remembered as the "March of the Umbrellas." Thousands of people attended, including the National Police and undercover intelligence officers, who took photographs. Three days later, secondary students organized another march and called for the defense minister's resignation. Meanwhile, Castañeda de León and the AEU leadership conducted interviews with survivors to construct a report of the events to counter the government's account and misleading newspaper coverage.[102] This was crucial because Panzós remained isolated while the military forbade entry to doctors, the Red Cross, and the national press corps.[103] Aside from *Inforpress* and reports written by the AEU, FASGUA, and CNUS, there were few sources of news to refute the military government's official radio broadcasts.

The CNUS had been planning a separate event to commemorate the death of López Larrave later in the week and quickly transformed the event into a protest of the massacre. Some eighty thousand people attended.[104] An unusually long manifesto written for the event placed López Larrave's assassination alongside unequal land ownership, racism, the power of the banks, corrupt military and political leaders, exploitative economic imperialism, and the massacre at Panzós. The CNUS split the people of Guatemala into two groups: on one side was the government, which was controlled by the financial oligarchy. On the other side were "workers, campesinos, and salaried middle sectors, who possessed nothing more than their labor power." The manifesto declared that state ministries of education, finance, and labor; the courts; and the Army were under the sway of the oligarchy and foreign powers. They estimated that more than 30,000 citizens had been killed in the oligarchy's struggle to maintain its power. For the CNUS, this was an atmosphere of "fascistization . . . the negation of all universally recognized rights, such as the right to free association, the right to petition, the right to protest, and freedom of expression."[105]

Given the close ties between the business sector and the military government, the charge of fascism was not far off. The rising costs of electricity and telephone service, sugar, bread, public transportation, rent, and clothing enriched the wealthy in order to starve the people. It was an "outbreak of repression," they wrote. They continued, "Faced with this growing struggle of the masses, now the oligarchy and imperialism have taken off their mask and have unleashed a new wave of repression, that had its most shameless manifestation in the genocide committed against the peasants of Panzós." They asked the public to unite and "oppose by all means . . . the rising cost of living" and "the voraciousness of imperialism." Every large labor federation, the AEU, the USAC administration and almost every *facultad*, the secondary school students' coordinating body, and teachers' unions signed the manifesto. It was the first text to name the government's mass killings as genocide, and yet it confirmed that Panzós was not the first. On the contrary, it read, "hundreds of cases . . . have simply been forgotten."[106] For San Carlistas, justice had come to mean historical consciousness that demanded the remembrance of deaths and loss. At the same time, this new understanding acknowledged that there could be no singular origin or definitive body count in genocide—it was an infinite violation of humankind.

The manifesto called on the people to demand that the government end its repression and remand "those intellectually and physically responsible for the genocide at Panzós to the appropriate courts." This seems somewhat disingenuous, given the group's condemnation of the government ministries, national businesses, and the Army as tools of the oligarchy. But then again, the manifesto closes with the demand for "exemplary punishment of those responsible for the genocides at Panzós."[107] Just of whom and how that example would be made remained secondary to calls for unity and analyses of ongoing structural repression. The massacre was just a symptom of the new political order. This new political order required that San Carlistas conceive of their relationship to law, justice, and rights in new ways. I discuss some of the new formulations of justice that came out of these difficult years in Chapter 6 and the Coda.

Like so many moments of popular organizing, the legacy of the Panzós massacre is complicated. It led to public outcry and accusations of genocide against the government. It inspired congressional debate on land reform and agrarian policies, although little came from these debates. In the countryside and the city, the massacre further polarized the conflict between those seeking a political solution and those seeking an armed one. The PGT and JPT, FASGUA, AEU, smaller student and teachers' groups, and CNUS united briefly in early July to sign the CNUS-authored document that had linked the assassination, the massacre, and the increasingly high cost of living as slow thefts from the pueblo by the powerful.[108] But the deep rift remained: the PGT, JPT, and FRENTE-led AEU were opposed to armed conflict and argued that the right moment for revolution was not yet at hand. The FERG and some members of CNUS were no longer willing to wait for the right moment. They would create it.[109] The armed struggle *of resistance* became the armed struggle *for revolution*.[110]

In following weeks, it became clear that the massacre was not an isolated event. More campesinos were disappeared and threats against workers, students, and intellectuals multiplied.[111] In broad terms, the Panzós massacre marked a turning point for both the security forces and the guerrilla. Over the next decade, repression would become increasingly generalized and focused on rural communities; the careful selection of individual operatives in the city would give way to a scorched earth approach to counterinsurgency. For their part, the Military Commission of the PGT claimed that the massacre had changed the stakes of the struggle. They backed up this claim with a successful ambush of the military police garrison near Panzós in Polochic where they killed eighteen soldiers. It was the most lethal guerrilla attack since the 1960s. It also profoundly split the PGT.[112] Immediately, the central leadership of the PGT issued an official statement that denounced the attacks. The AEU and Osorio Paz followed suit. In response to this wave of denunciations, the FERG publicly declared its support for the CNUS and announced the creation of a FERG branch for secondary school students.

Despite partisan conflict, the massacre at Panzós sparked spectacular demonstrations of popular unity. A shared idiom of political affect imagined a
moment—not too far off—when this united popular movement would
return justice to Guatemala. This moment of optimism ended with one final
massive protest before unprecedented levels of state violence. In early July, a
group of nonunionized city bus drivers called for an increase in daily wages.[113]
Their wages were impossibly low, they argued, given the high cost of living.
After their initial request was unsuccessful, drivers throughout the city began
progressive strikes. Each day, the drivers shortened their routes. On July 10,
the buses ceased to run altogether.[114] The city was frozen. The drivers were
taking a big risk, as the ongoing reprisals against the Ixtahuacán strikers had
made quite clear that the government would not tolerate dissent. The recent
election of General Romeo Lucas García (1978–1982) on July 1, 1978, served
as a further warning. In an election with less than 40 percent voter turnout
and unprecedented fraud (Lucas García won more votes than there were eligible voters in several municipalities), no candidate won a majority. Congress
was charged with electing a candidate, but only thirty-five congressmen
showed up for the vote. Every single one of them voted for the general. Lucas
García began his presidency by raising the cost of basic goods, reversing all of
the moderate reforms of his predecessor, and empowering the military and a
growing number of death squads.[115]

Given this political climate, the only place where the striking bus drivers
could protect their buses and bodies from harm was the one sovereign space
shielded from military incursion by a constitutional guarantee: the USAC
campus. Whether autonomy implied or included sovereignty was uncertain,
but as I discussed earlier in the book, when the sovereignty of campus was
violated, the public spoke out. There may have been some disagreement
among the students about whether to welcome the bus drivers on campus,
given the risk. Deborah Levenson cites a July 14, 1978, article in *Diario
Impacto* and another from July 15, 1978, in *Nuevo Diario* in which FRENTE
and its JPT/PGT-based leadership opposed the strike out of fear of police or
military action on campus. But to the contrary, Álvarez Aragón has written
that all students welcomed the drivers. He recalled that students from
FRENTE organized marches and distributed flyers about the strike on citywide buses. Students organized openly in large groups, their faces unmasked,
behind the FRENTE banner in support of the bus drivers. For their part,

FERG students worked in smaller groups, wore masks to conceal their identity, and built barricades from car tires and burning buses to protect campus. Still other students organized food, speakers, and music for the strikers. Rector Osorio Paz issued a public statement of support.[116]

As the strike continued and support grew among the general public, Labor Minister Carlos Alarcón Monsanto agreed to convene a group of leaders from three transportation-related labor unions, the CNUS, the bus owners' association, the Catholic Church, Congress, and the ultrapowerful Coordinating Committee of Agricultural, Commercial, Industrial and Financial Associations (CACIF), longtime opponent of the university left. The labor minister's committee narrowly approved a proposal for a wage increase based on a universal 5-cent fare hike. However, the proposal doubled the cost of transportation. In response, the CNUS and National Federation of Transport Workers (FENOT) quit the committee. The decision was clearly intended to create a rift between the striking bus drivers and the pueblo who would be forced to pay the higher fare.

Instead, the pueblo seized the city in waves of strikes and street combat through August and October. Three hundred people were arrested. The government repeatedly shut down meetings of the CNUS and other unions and federations. Secondary school students once more emerged at the forefront of these demonstrations, throwing desks and chairs out of classroom windows and into the streets to build barricades.[117] Many students of this group also organized incredible denunciations against the fearsome police chief German Chupina in massive protests held directly in front of the National Palace throughout the month of August.[118] Security forces attacked university buildings, disrupting classes and upending offices. But by early October, even government employees and members of the press had joined the strike. Offers by an USAC affiliate to supervise and administer a new urban bus system were rebuked.[119] The strikes escalated. The AEU General Assembly declared a university-wide work stoppage for October 9 and decided to organize Student Support Brigades that would leave campus each morning to provide support for people engaged in street combat around the city.[120]

A police report from one day in early October 1978 provides a view of these long days of skirmishes. The report states that at 10 A.M., secondary school students from the INCV secondary school detained a city bus and punctured its tires, leaving it stranded and blocking traffic at the busy intersection of 9th Avenue and 9th Street in Zone 1 directly in front of the school.

FIGURE 12. Protestors confront National Police on La Sexta, August 3, 1978. Photograph by Mauro Calanchina.

The influence of the FERG at INCV primed the students for such direct action. Police arrived ten minutes later, and students attacked the advancing police with rocks and other debris. Additional students climbed onto the roof of the school and showered the police with rocks. By 11 A.M., the students had advanced three blocks to the intersection of 9th Avenue and 12th Street. At 11:30 A.M., the report stated, "The Situation [was] controlled by the National Police with the use of tear gas."[121] Other protestors planned simultaneous attacks throughout the city in order to overwhelm the police. Nearly eight kilometers from where INCV students fought, residents of the Carolignia neighborhood in Zone 19 began attacks at 8 A.M. This group also showered police with rocks and set neighborhood buses ablaze. Still more groups organized meetings at the Plaza Italia around 10 A.M. By 3 P.M., police intelligence estimated that nearly three thousand people had gathered there. Elsewhere around 2 P.M., students blocked traffic on La Reforma in Zone 10 at the busy juncture of two roads under the Aguilar Batres Bridge of Guatemala City's Beltway, the Anillo Periférico. In site after site, protestors quickly erected barricades and launched strategic offensives against small police units until police reinforcements arrived. Then they quickly disbanded and, according to police, fled to the USAC campus.[122]

This time, the USAC administration wrote paid political advertisements that fell short of endorsing the protests, but they also criticized the government's response. The AEU denounced the Lucas García government as a mockery of democracy, claiming that the July presidential elections were as fraudulent as his promises of peace and democratic opening had turned out to be. In turn, the CSU cited legal precedent to demonstrate the unconstitutionality of the government's dissolution of the peaceful assemblies.[123] They wrote that these violations were particularly onerous because Lucas García's vice president, Francisco Villagrán Kramer, had been taught to know better. Not too many years earlier, Villagrán Kramer had coauthored the markedly progressive plan for social and economic development with Manuel Colom Argueta and Adolfo Mijangos López, discussed at length in Chapter 4, and before that he had served as a part of the Constitutional Assembly in 1945. Although Villagrán Kramer claimed to have sought public office within the Lucas García administration in order to effect change from within the system and even resigned before the end of his term, many San Carlistas came to distrust him.[124] As the previous chapters have shown, the belief that it was one's duty as a student to transform society left ample room for interpretation and conflict.

Finally after three months of fighting, the government agreed to a public transportation subsidy. As in the case of the Ixtahuacán miners' strike, the protestors' demands had been met, but at a great cost. The Lucas García government had shown itself willing to use intimidation, disappearance, and assassination in order to destroy the university.[125] Students had railed against the state's failure since the 1976 earthquake, and instead of looking to the state for the protection of their rights, students, workers, and other community members began to turn to one another. The celebrated "Republic of Students" was becoming a "Republic of Students and Workers," at least for groups like the AEU, CNUS, and FASGUA. After the Glorious March of the Miners, the Panzós massacre, and the transportation strikes, a shift in students' language was clear: San Carlistas no longer fulfilled their duty to unify the nation in order for the state to deliver freedom. The government's attacks on individual students and the USAC campus were an assault on the republican ideal that was central to the university's foundational credo and its constitutional legitimacy. But rather than abandoning student nationalism, state repression inspired San Carlistas to revise it. They rejected the authority of the military government and carved out new allies and strategies of resistance.

The relationships that students, campesinos, and workers forged between 1976 and 1978 represented a serious threat to the military government. The guerrilla expanded its recruitment efforts at USAC after the earthquake and the Ixtahuacán strike, two moments when San Carlistas had been especially critical of the government. The government reacted with increasingly vicious forms of violence to quell public support and intimidate would-be guerrillas. At the university, 23 assassinations and kidnappings occurred between 1974 and 1978; 211 occurred between 1978 and 1982.[126] Students responded to these real threats by revising existing forms of protest, especially the Huelga de Dolores and the constitutional guarantee of university autonomy, in order to make more profound critiques of the government. USAC faculty and students changed their idioms of political affect to accommodate a new politics of death when existing forms of protest proved to be too dangerous or ineffectual. This new politics of death appealed to international aid organizations and potential foreign advocates by drawing on the language of human rights. It also demanded mourning work from Guatemalan public. San Carlistas responded to violence by reshaping mourning into a politics of death that gave them life in a time when life was imminently revocable.

SIX

Student Nationalism without a Government, 1977–1980

> If one dies, it is because someone had to die in order to keep hope alive.
>
> *Association of Aqueche Students (AEA) and Coordinating*
> *Committee of Secondary School Students (CEEM),*
> *August 1, 1977*[1]

DESPITE THE PROMISE OF REPRISAL, the Honorable Committee of the Huelga de Dolores printed the *No Nos Tientes* in 1980. Its editorial warned, "We are in the ultimate moment. Our old enemies, the lackey liberationists, the great landowning bourgeoisie, and the clique of reactionary military men (all faithful servants of Yankee imperialism), have decided to play all their cards in the vilest assassination campaign, with the goal of silencing the cries for freedom that resound with greater strength nationwide."[2] Instead of censoring the publication, stealing its treasury, or imprisoning its editors, as they had in the past, the students' enemies took a more extreme approach. On March 22, Julio Cesar del Valle, Marco Tulio Pereira, and Iván Alfonso Bravo Soto gathered to distribute the newspaper. Shortly after they met, they were kidnapped, strangled, shot, and left to die in a yellow Volkswagen in Zone 16. The words, "This is how the PGT will die" were spray painted on the side of the vehicle.[3] A few days later, the Secret Anticommunist Army (Ejército Secreto Anticomunista [ESA]) claimed responsibility.[4] They wrote, "For every anticommunist who is killed in such a cowardly way, we will kill 20 communists ... we have seventeen more communists [to kill]."[5] The ESA claimed the youths' lives to avenge the killing of notorious death squad boss Colonel Máximo Zepeda, who had been assassinated a few days earlier on the highway to Amatitlán. The letters "PGT" were spray painted on the side of the truck where Zepeda's body was found.[6] These parallel killings exemplified the violence that characterized daily life by this point in the civil war.

For nearly a century, the *No Nos Tientes* had offered a place for students to air antipathies under the cover of anonymity and satire. The thinning veil of levity had dropped. Surviving members of the Honorable Committee agreed to reprint and distribute new copies of the *No Nos Tientes*.[7] The *Facultad* of Medical Sciences issued a paid political advertisement that read, "Faced with the new aggression of which the University has been object with the capture, torture, and assassination of the students . . . [the *Facultad* of Medicine] condemns the repression that continues to intensify, more brutally and indiscriminately, against all sectors of the pueblo." The denunciation also "[pointed] out that this path will only provoke the growing popular uproar."[8] The declaration appealed to the idioms of political affect, practices, and ideologies discussed in Chapters 4 and 5. Student nationalism had adapted to new forms of state violence. San Carlistas began to see themselves as part of a collectivity that extended beyond the walls of their classrooms and meeting spaces to the indigenous campesinos in the countryside and the unionized urban factory worker.

Rising violence against the university was justified by President Fernando Romeo Lucas García's (1978–1982) charge that it was a "center [*foco*] of subversion that intends to overthrow the government."[9] Lucas García claimed that a network of radicals had infiltrated USAC and diverted its focus from knowledge production to partisan politics. Speaking at a press conference in Mexico, the president seemed at pains to prove that his administration could crush dissent. Similar student protests in El Salvador and Nicaragua caused some to see an international conspiracy. Certainly San Carlistas were in close contact with their peers in El Salvador and Nicaragua: the letter from Tomás Borge to the AEU, discussed in the previous chapter, suggests as much. But Lucas García's larger point was the same one made by conservatives across the twentieth century: the university had no role in politics. Mexico City newspaper *El Excélsior* reported that Lucas García refused to dialogue with "ill-tempered [*berrinchuda*]" students "who only want to overthrow him."[10] The message was equivocal: on one hand, if students were ill-tempered and childish, their protests could be dismissed as bratty tantrums; on the other, the serious claim that the university was a "center of subversion" invited repression. Quickly, students, faculty, administrators, and alumni sent statements to national and regional newspapers to disavow the charge. They emphasized how USAC was a place for freedom of thought and a diversity of opinions.[11]

As ever, the debate over the university's role in society served as a sort of cipher for the larger issue of democratic and participatory national politics.

USAC alumni in Congress either affirmed or criticized the president's declaration. Partisans of the right in the National Liberation Movement (MLN) and the Democratic Institutional Party (PID) agreed that USAC was subversive and saw the press conference as an opportunity to gain international support for counterinsurgency. Most members of the Revolutionary Party (Partido Revolucionario [PR]), and Christian and Social Democrats were less supportive, but still questioned whether the university had a place in national politics. The student body was also divided. Many students declared that participating in national politics had been their constitutional duty since 1945; others used the moment to denounce their enemies. Former AEU secretary general Leopoldo Urrutia Beltrand told the newspaper *Impacto* that the university had "unconsciously fallen into the web of extremists and [had] posed the solution to national problems in the tenor of the ideals, models, and schemas that operate in totalitarian countries."[12] USAC rector Saúl Osorio Paz and two student leaders responded in *Nuevo Diario*: not only did the university have a constitutional duty to respond to national problems, but this was the very purpose of the public university.[13] As I have argued across the previous five chapters, this was a central tenet of student nationalism and foundational to the cultural, political, economic, and even emotional meaning of the urban middle class. To challenge this was to challenge the fundamental markers of urban ladino middle-class life. Even students at the rival Jesuit-run Universidad Rafael Landívar (URL) agreed that San Carlistas should view the university as catalyst, albeit for reform rather than revolution, and they wrote a letter to the AEU expressing their support.[14]

Lucas García's declaration presaged the deadliest years of the civil war for San Carlistas.[15] In hindsight, the assassination of law professor Mario López Larrave in June 1977 inaugurated a new epoch of fear. San Carlistas adjusted their political practices and beliefs accordingly, forging a new politics of death within student nationalism. They did so through organizations for families of the disappeared, at protests and political funerals, and in paid political advertisements and letters to international human rights organizations. For about a decade, psychology students recorded testimony from survivors of political violence.[16] The AEU began to refer to people who had been kidnapped by the government as *desaparecidos* and worked to locate them, dead or alive. One of the first formal organizations to do this was the AEU's Committee of Family Members of Disappeared People. During the 1975–1976 academic year, the committee printed the names and arrest information of 250 people in a memo entitled "People Disappeared in the Republic

FIGURE 13. National Police detain unknown people on La Sexta in Zone 1, Guatemala City, January 31, 1980. Fototeca Guatemala, Centro de Investigaciones Regionales de Mesoamérica (CIRMA).

of Guatemala." They also distributed Xeroxed handouts that featured an identification card photograph of an individual, their name, and some basic facts including their age, marital status, nationality, and the circumstances of their arrest. The entry on José Ramiro Estrada Guardado noted that he was twenty-one, single, and Guatemalan. He had been arrested on May 15, 1971, by the Cuerpo de Detectives at a capital city playground and was probably held at the prison of the Second Corps. Like most *desaparecidos*, Estrada Guardado did not become a famous martyr and was never found.[17]

San Carlistas' politics of death took shape through a range of formal and informal practices. Below, I discuss eulogies, investigations, paid political advertisements, processions, and even special flowers. San Carlistas' death rites and rituals were political acts. They further united the popular movement and provided it with a way to dispute authority in spite of fearsome repression. Political funerals fused mourning, protest, and fellowship. They processed through the city's commercial downtown, expanding the participatory public of the funeral beyond family and friends and momentarily creating a new public that was compelled to take action. Death rites marked the transference of the individual body to the social world and enabled

FIGURE 14. A scene of political violence in Zone 1, Guatemala City, ca. 1980. Fototeca Guatemala, Centro de Investigaciones Regionales de Mesoamérica (CIRMA).

individuals to "express and enact their social values, to articulate their visions of what it was that bound them together, made individuals among them unique, and separated this group from others."[18] While assassinations were part of a coordinated effort by the military, police, and parapolice organizations to curb the growing popular movement, the political funerals they occasioned made possible a new politics of death. The result was a claim to responsibility, rights, and representation that once more remade the affective terrain of student nationalism and ultimately shaped memory politics through the end of the civil war and into the long peace and reconciliation process.

The field of memory studies has reminded scholars of how loss and mourning can spark rupture as well as reconciliation, a theme taken up in the Coda.[19] But this is different from understanding the political power of death in its contemporary present. In the brutal 1970s and 1980s, San Carlistas required political strategies and rhetorics that could quickly respond to acts of violence. Invocations of martyrdom did not at first interpret loss for a juridical audience, but instead produced an immediate political effect (and affect): the moral authority of San Carlistas and the popular movement vis-à-vis a morally bankrupt state that had stolen a life. Mourners sought redress and acknowledgement from a bankrupt state *and* "[reimagined] the possibility of community on the basis of vulnerability and loss."[20] The bodies of the deceased belonged to the political community, exerting agency—the power to create change in the world—long after an individual life ended. The body enabled the living to "justify actions, claim and dispute authority, or create and use the cultural categories that mediate social life."[21]

Faced with an utterly bankrupt state, San Carlistas integrated secular millennialism and international human rights discourse into student nationalism. They used the social life of death to call into question individual, governmental, and international authorities; justify the actions of the guerrilla and reformist left; reclaim moral authority for the university community and challenge the moral authority of the government; and rearticulate the various and palimpsestic meanings of student nationalism as a marker of ladino middle class life. Across the 1970s and 1980s, USAC was home to a full pantheon of figures—martyred San Carlistas and living *estudiantes comprometidos*—who led the struggle for justice and for freedom. This is the difference between a politics of death and a politics of memory.

A NEW POLITICS OF DEATH AND
SPECTACULAR MOURNING

On July 28, 1977, Robin Mayro García Dávila and Anibal Leonel Caballeros traveled by public bus to Mixco, a hardscrabble town on the fringes of Guatemala City, to attend a clandestine funeral for three classmates, all members of the Guerrilla Army of the Poor (EGP). Dissenting members of the Rebel Armed Forces (FAR) formed the group between 1972 and 1974. From exile in Mexico City, EGP leadership responded to what they saw as the FAR's errors. They moved away from Che Guevara's *foquismo* toward "prolonged popular war" and sought to include indigenous people in the leadership and indigenous demands in the group's basic revolutionary goals.[22] Its membership was comparatively diverse, including ladino and indigenous FAR veterans, ladino university and secondary school students, and radicalized Catholics. In Guatemala, the EGP organized across multiple regional fronts: the mountains, the countryside, and the city.[23] In the highland departments of El Quiché, Huehuetenango, Alta Verapaz, and Chimaltenango, the group maintained close relationships with rural organizations like the Campesino Unity Committee (Comité de Unidad

Campesina [CUC]).[24] In the city, the EGP allied with union leaders and university and secondary school students, like Caballeros and García.

Caballeros was vice president of the Student Association of the Rafael Aqueche Institute. He had also served as president of student organizations at the Simón Bolívar Institute and the National School of Commercial Sciences, where he met García. At just twenty years of age, he had assembled an impressive résumé of student leadership.[25] García, in turn, was enrolled in his first year of an agronomy degree at USAC, but remained close with his former classmates. He served as an intermediary between the EGP and secondary school students.[26] Caballeros's and García's political activities were precisely the kind that alarmed the government. Just six weeks had passed since the assassination of López Larrave when the two young men took the bus to Mixco. General Kjell Eugenio Laugerud García was still president, and the military was very much devoted to its strategy to neutralize solidarities between the popular sectors by interweaving "war, development, and military control of the state together . . . into a pure, military modernism."[27]

Although the trip to Mixco should have been quick, neither young man returned home that evening. In the early hours of Saturday, July 30, Caballeros's body appeared near the university. People gathered on campus throughout the day to denounce his death. A couple of days later, students, parents, EGP members, and concerned citizens accompanied his body to the General Cemetery. There was still no sign of García. Mourners turned Caballeros's funeral into a call for García's appearance. They carried posters and banners that read, "We want Robin alive!"[28] García's parents hoped that public outcry could save their son. The mourners continued to march for days after the funeral, turning a single funeral into a week of protests known as the "*Jornadas* of August 1977." The government's campaign of targeted violence failed to divide the popular sector. Workers' unions, professional organizations, teachers' unions, university students, secondary students, and university authorities came together in opposition to state violence.

Secondary school students organized general assembles and progressive strikes in the first days of August. Protestors blocked city traffic with automobile caravans that encircled the National Palace and La Sexta. Buses painted with the phrase, "Queremos a Robin vivo!" competed with billboards advertising Wrangler jeans, cigarettes, opticians, bars, restaurants, clothing stores, and hotels. La Sexta had been the commercial heart of the city and the key symbolic site of capital accumulation for centuries, but after the 1976 earthquake it had become a crowded, polluted site of delinquency and sex trafficking.[29] La Sexta also cut a path directly through Central Park, past the National Palace, and northward toward the residential zones where many students and faculty lived. For its historical significance and accessibility, it was an exceptional protest site. It was the perfect place to protest the government's—and capitalism's—excesses.

On August 2, García's family wrote a letter to president Laugerud García, declaring a hunger strike in response to the "government's total refusal to concern itself with the clarification of these reprehensible acts." Boldly, the family declared that "military, police forces, paramilitary and parapolice groups" were directly responsible for the imprisonment, torture, and assassination of thousands of Guatemalans. They linked their loss to that of "all of the Guatemalan homes that still suffer the absence of a father, of a child, of a husband, of a brother."[30] San Carlistas worked to spread awareness on campus. On August 3, a group of students ran through university buildings, interrupting classes and imploring students and teachers to join them for a march from campus to the National Palace. Around four thousand people joined them.

García's body appeared the following morning near the highway to the Pacific coast. Like Caballeros, García bore signs of torture and strangulation. The coroner's reports stated that he had probably been dead for five or six days. The assassins left just two things in the pockets of the pants that were found on García's corpse, pants that were not his: his identification card and a piece of paper signed by the ESA.[31] Shortly after it was identified, García's body was taken to the Administration building on the USAC campus. Thousands of people came to pay tribute. García's body lay in state in a building that faced the Plaza of Martyrs, an important gathering place for rallies and protests on campus.

The death energized the university opposition. Faculty and administrators eulogized García in the press. At a special General Assembly, the AEU decided that the burial of García must be transformed into "a powerful demonstration of repudiation and condemnation of the repressive methods of the government and fascist reactionaries."[32] The group carried García's body to the Aqueche Institute (Caballeros's secondary school), located near the National Palace. At Aqueche, speakers from several groups—the AEU, the National Committee on Trade Union Unity (CNUS), the Coordinating Committee of Education Workers of Guatemala (CCTEG), and Coordinating Committee of Secondary School Students (CEEM)—

demanded that the government take responsibility for the killing, echoing the García family's letter to the president. Across the decades of civil war and reconciliation, these types of demands on the state would become increasingly common.

On Friday, August 5, twenty thousand secondary school students accompanied the body from Aqueche to the National School of Commercial Sciences, García's alma mater. Later in the afternoon, about seventy thousand people marched to the National Cemetery. Schoolmates and teachers took turns carrying the casket. Most of the mourners were between sixteen and twenty-five years old.[33] Participants carried a red carnation and raised it silently in the air as they passed the National Palace. The exact origin of the carnation as symbol is hard to trace. It may have even been borrowed from the coup-turned-popular movement against Portugal's Estado Novo in 1974. Perhaps it was a critique of the excesses of the government, its red petals a solemn reminder of blood spilled and florescent life lost. It became a powerful sign of the new revolutionary collective conscience through repetition at student funerals.[34]

While there must have been speeches, weeping, songs, car engines, horns, shouts, shuffling feet, and vendors hawking water and fruit, newspapers and commemorative publications highlighted the mourners' silence. *El Gráfico* reported how "the interminable columns of secondary school and university students, without a single yell, without even one raised voice, occupied twenty blocks of the center of the city . . . At no moment did the burial have the character of a protest."[35] Historian Jay Winter distinguishes between liturgical silences that are compelled by the transcendent and sacred, sacrifice and redemption; political silences, tactical refusals to speak for the sake of letting the past be past; and essentialist silences that reserve aural spaces for others who are authorized to speak.[36] The silence at García's funeral combined several of these meanings, including sacrifice, redemption, and hallowed aural space for certain individuals to choose to speak or remain quiet. But their political, tactical refusal to speak also marked students' refusal to mourn in the usual manner. Loss enabled a broader politics of witness.[37] Mourners deliberately guarded the break between speech and silence and so maintained an invaluable representational space "from which the voice of prophecy might be heard."[38]

Although speaking *out* was deadly, the collectivity shared an unspoken imperative to speak *of* the death. San Carlistas' mourning framed the deceased individual as an intimate, a friend or son, of the people. At the

National Cemetery, one eulogy told of a resurrected García: "Robin's struggle will endure in our mind for centuries and centuries and one day, not long from now, his figure will emerge from the oceans, from the mountains, from the farmlands, from the workers and from the dusty campesinos in a nation of love . . . of dreams, of bread for everyone." The eulogy continued, "And this must be so, because we believe in the resurrection of heroes, who like you, Robin García, 'do not die, but close their eyes and keep soaring.'"[39] García—now Robin—was no longer an unknown student, but a familiar killed for bringing justice to the pueblo. García's resurrection promised justice "not long from now." The casket marked the act of violence. Once it had been lowered, the martyr's name remained imbued with political power.

Like other aspects of student nationalism, gender shaped martyrdom and mourning. Only rarely were women mourned as martyrs. In fact, the only well-known female San Carlista martyr was Rogelia Cruz, discussed in Chapter 4. A transcendent pan-generational narrative of masculine heroics offered homosocial emotional intimacy that extended beyond a funeral rite or commemoration. A paid announcement by the AEU on August 4 read, "Robin García has not died! He is living in the conscience and the united and organized struggle of thousands of young people who are reclaiming their freedom. Robin García lives in every one of us, just as does Leonel Caballeros, Lic. Mario López Larrave, and the tens of thousands of the best sons of our pueblo, who met death for the only crime of dreaming of a life of popular well-being and social progress."[40] Masculine heroics in death and life reinforced gender divides.[41]

As one of Guatemala's "best sons," García lived on in the struggle. The AEU continued, "He has not died. He lives in your ideals. He lives in this huge movement . . . He lives in every one of us who were and are willing to continue fighting for the legitimacy and respect of human rights in Guatemala."[42] The funeral oration of another young student reiterated García's everlasting life. He spoke, "The physical life of a person may disappear from its original form, but [may] never be destroyed fully." He went on, "Robin Mayro García Dávila lives through his ideas and the material work he achieved in life . . . Who has said that Robin García has died? Who is this blind man who cannot see this light, which casts heat and vitality upon workers' and campesinos' thought?"[43] The eulogies asserted that García continued to live through the social body and reflected the categories and relations that mediated social life. But the political power of the funerals—their ability to create change in the *present*—resided in the contrapuntal play of the objective and subjective, past and future, intimate and abstract, individual and familial, partisan and commercial. Eulogies and obituaries were performative utterances that made true the call for collectivity. They were rituals with transformational agency whereby the public itself, without the presence or explicit invocation of a deity or priest, became witness. This is the San Carlistas' unique contribution to the theorization of the political power of death.

The ability to draw on these various modes was crucial to the movement's survival. In late 1977, security forces killed an average of one trade unionist a day and carried out numerous massacres against rural citizens. The politics of death were an important way for students to connect to these groups. Student nationalism, which once drew San Carlistas into the national project as bureaucrats and acolytes for national culture and progress, increasingly appealed to more abstract and even millenarian notions of life, hope, and progress. Heroes lived on in popular memory, on the horizon as hope, to be reborn "in a nation of love . . . of dreams, of bread for everyone," not just for students, workers, or campesinos.[44] Seen in this way, the funerals of López Larrave, Caballeros, and García, and the other funerals to come, were not processions toward a grave, but rather toward new political forms. This was the city that gave rise to the popular saying "Salir de Guate*mala* y entrar en Guate*peor*."

"THERE WILL BE REVOLUTION . . ."

Around the time that García and Caballeros were killed, Oliverio Castañeda de León was elected treasurer of the AEU, the position he held until his election as AEU secretary general in 1978. Castañeda de León had not been radicalized as a secondary school student, unlike Caballeros and García. The Castañeda de León family lived in Colonia San Sebastián, one of the city's oldest neighborhoods just a few blocks from Central Park, where they shared a sizeable library and record collection, large family dinners, horseback rides, sports, and travel. His mother's family came from Guatemala's rural bourgeoisie and owned land and several factories where they employed many laborers. His father was a pediatrician who had personally treated many generations of Guatemala's elite; his family had a successful business in Zacapa.[45] On a trip to London with his sister, who went to study English at King's College, Castañeda de León had a homestay with a family of British trade unionists. In postdinner discussions, the siblings learned the history of English workers, unions, and party politics. Inspired, upon his return to Guatemala, Castañeda de León finished secondary school and enrolled at USAC to study economics.[46]

In his first year at USAC, Castañeda de León took a class on Guatemalan economic history with Severo Martínez Peláez, discussed at length in Chapter 4. Not only was Martínez Peláez one of the nation's most influential intellectuals, he was also a popular teacher. His lectures were standing-room-only. As in his research, Martínez Peláez taught a version of Guatemalan history that emphasized the exploitation of people and the land and the endurance of colonial patterns into the present. Castañeda de León soon joined reading groups with comrades in the Patriotic Workers' Youth (JPT).[47] In 1976, he began writing for the JPT periodical *Juventud*.[48]

Martínez Peláez's influence is clear in the editorial of the 1977 edition of the *No Nos Tientes*, which Castañeda de León coauthored. It began, "Conquistadors and colonizers, creoles and *peninsulares*, landowning coffee planters, businessmen, and industrialists, liberals and conservatives, everyone, each group in their era and grouped in their respective social classes, have [*sic*] utilized violence as a resource to maintain their hegemony and dominion over the popular classes of Guatemala." All of Guatemalan history was the workers' struggle. The editorial continued, "such dependency has meant the exploitation of the workers' pueblo in various forms, from the most terrible of slavery, *encomiendas*, and *repartimientos*, peonage and *mozos colonos*, to the modern form of salaried labor." Revolutionary consciousness could not come from the "interminable discussion of a group of well-meaning men" but from "experience extracted from the daily struggle of the workers' class and their political organization." The writers saw "class war" coming and advised workers to prepare by joining unions (only 5% of Guatemala's workers were unionized in 1977).[49]

The first *boletín* of the following year's Huelga de Dolores focused on the precariousness of the present. In the twelve months since the editorial described above was written, San Carlistas had lost López Larrave, García, Caballeros, and scores more classmates, professors, mentors, and friends. The *boletín* read:

> From the present date, [the Honorable Committee] suspends the following constitutional guarantees: substitutes Habeas Corpus for Corpus Christi; will no longer guarantee life, corporeal integrity, dignity, and integrity of one's person, property, and kin of any public functionary; the death penalty

will not be of extraordinary incidence, but rather will be our daily bread; the home is violable and the women inside it, too; no Guatemalan will be able to expatriate, unless in a Red Cross airplane or one owned by the [elite landowning] Herrera Ibarguen family.[50]

One's corporeal integrity, property, home, and kin were violable in the new Guatemala. Corpus Christi, the rite of the martyr, would replace habeas corpus, the right to have the body.[51] The students' humor fell flat when they addressed the farce of due process. Writs of habeas corpus and other appeals to nation-based juridical rights failed.

Some members of the popular movement adopted human rights rhetoric in order to gain international attention through Amnesty International and the United Nations. Others rejected liberal rational modes of mourning, especially a desire for closure, reconciliation, and restoration paid to the rights-bearing subject. Many also rejected religious modes of mourning that asserted that an individual's reward would come with death. Political violence had triggered ontological, not just political, crises.

In 1978, the thirty-four-year anniversary of the democratic revolution against Ubico coincided with ongoing transportation strikes against a bus fare hike, mentioned in the previous chapter. At 9 A.M. on October 20, a mass of students and workers assembled at the Trébol, a knot of highways, bus stops, pedestrian footbridges, food carts, and shops. This was an ideal meeting place for students coming from the University City in the southwest corner of the city, professors coming from central residential neighborhoods in Zones 1 and 2, and workers coming from the southeast and downtown. The mass marched north to Central Park and La Sexta. At Centenario Park across from the National Palace, Castañeda de León took to the stage and began to speak. He implicated the state and top national leaders in more than a decade of disappearances and assassinations. His speech ended with the prophetic assertion: "They can kill the best sons of the pueblo, but they never have and they never could assassinate the revolution. Because to do that, they ... would have to kill six million Guatemalans. As long as there is a pueblo, there will be revolution!" The crowd dispersed and some students headed toward El Portal, a popular bar located nearby on La Sexta.

All of a sudden, multiple shooters opened fire, issuing a volley of shots that injured five pedestrians. One bullet struck Castañeda de León in the spinal cord. A second bullet entered through his right ear, and a third entered through the left upper side of his face. He died just fifty feet from the bar, inside the doorway of Pasaje Rubio.[52]

FIGURE 15. Mourners carry red carnations and process down La Sexta at the funeral for Oliverio Castañeda de León. Photograph by Mauro Calanchina.

Rector Osorio Paz met with the Castañeda de León family the following morning. He led a funeral procession from the family home south on La Sexta to Central Park. Newspaper and witness reports counted between twenty thousand and fifty thousand people who joined the procession.[53] As with García's funeral, students carried no banners, just wreaths, red carnations, and the casket. Again, headlines reported silent mourners.[54] A few days later, members of the AEU, CEEM, and several workers' organizations organized another march from Plaza Italia to the site of the assassination. Around four thousand people came. National Police intelligence officers of the Second Corps photographed the protest and recorded in their notes that the marchers held President Lucas García, Interior Minister Donaldo Álvarez Ruiz, and National Police Director German Chupina Barahona directly responsible for the assassination.[55] At around 7:30 P.M., the group placed their carnations at the entrance to Pasaje Rubio and sang the national anthem. No confrontations were recorded.[56] In the coming days, young people from the private universities and secondary schools, citizens of all ages, and Guatemalans exiled in Mexico expressed their support for the USAC community in letters and paid political advertisements.[57] The political motives of the death and the impunity with which it was carried out were clear.

The legitimacy of the state was in question and the university at risk. What remained of the student nationalism celebrated since the Ten Years' Spring? San Carlista idioms of political affect reflected new interpretations of the shared values—dignity, duty, integrity, and freedom—that had defined them for decades. It was now the San Carlistas' *duty* to fight the injustice of the state, to face the asymmetry of violence with *dignity* and *integrity*, and to find *freedom* in both the struggle in the present and the imaginary future. Death practices provided evidence of loss to demonstrate how the state had broken the social contract. For instance, professors from the Economics *facultad* declared that Castañeda de León's only crime was "to have followed through with his duty as a conscientious *universitario*, defending the interests of the nation's masses." They went on, "The sacrifice of the student Castañeda de León is the tribute that the honorable youth pays in order to patriotically exercise their rights as citizens."[58] Martyrdom had become a patriotic duty. Students from Architecture wrote, "Beloved *compañero*: you are present and you will live in the struggles of your people, in every child's heart that beats happily as it awakens in the new nation present today."[59] Perhaps Castañeda de León's death did signal a new moment, but for a short time it also shut down public protest. USAC students and administrators reported being followed.[60]

In fact, Guatemala's intelligence apparatus had been compiling data on members of popular organizations since at least the late 1960s. Military commissions, paramilitary groups, the Judicial Police, and the Regional Telecommunications Center (CRT) had lists of the names and addresses of Guatemalan Labor Party (PGT) members, active leftists, ultrarightists, and other individuals involved in protests. The CRT was created in 1964, with financial and advisory support from the U.S. Office of Public Safety, to coordinate information and actions between the growing number of security forces and the Guatemalan Army and Air Force. The CRT shared information with security forces and intelligence networks throughout Central America through the Central American Network of Security Telecommunications and elsewhere through INTERPOL. In the confidential documents of the General Direction of the National Police, there was an entire folder dedicated to the October 1978 transportation strike. Most of the information compiled by the Corps of Detectives tracked the political associations of individuals involved in the strike. In the same folder was an undated and unlabeled list of forty-five names, all people associated with the popular movement, including many of the same names that had appeared in an ESA communiqué circulated on October 18, 1978. By the end of the 1980s, many of the people whose names appeared on the two lists had been assassinated. Castañeda de León's name appeared in red ink.[61] Command Six of the Second Corps of the National Police had collected information on Castañeda de León for at least two years. Police photographers documented him at the march for Panzós in June and a march in solidarity with the people of Nicaragua in September.[62]

Counterinsurgency forces continued to carry out selective kidnappings and assassinations in the city and large-scale massacres in the countryside. Fear became a way of life. As San Carlista guerrillero Mario Payeras remembered, "political assassinations became quotidian."[63] The truth was often unknowable and the rule of law, void. In reply, student politics in extremis disrupted everyday life and undermined the sectors that maintained the status quo: government, business, and the Catholic Church. The Catholic Church had long since declared San Carlistas sworn enemies. San Carlistas parlayed by attacking commerce and the ritual hierarchy of the Catholic Church. San Carlistas and other members of the popular movement asserted that if their bodily integrity could be disrupted at any moment, in any context, then death rites would disrupt political, commercial, and religious life.

San Carlistas held the political funerals of López Larrave, García, and Castañeda de León on La Sexta and nearby cross-streets, challenging traditional spatial practice, undermining the hierarchy of the Catholic Church, and opening the protests to broader sectors of the population.[64] As I mentioned above, La Sexta had become an increasingly crowded and polluted thoroughfare infamous for its informal economy, the underside of the modern consumption, profit, and exchange that it was built to represent. Its proximity to the National Palace and its decline after the earthquake made it an obvious synecdoche of the nation's decay. Once a space of capital investment and modernity, association and civility, San Carlistas added loss and mourning to the urban palimpsest. They wielded the coffins of their comrades and wove itineraries of insurgent spatial practice by funereal flânerie, blocking commerce and transportation en route.

This phrase, *funereal flânerie*, captures the many layers of the political funerals described above: individual mourning, presence and visibility, but also the spontaneity of a pedestrian public. Processions were less formalized than a burial ceremony. Individual mourners might walk in and out of the procession as the mourning mass moved forward. The political community created by funerals was temporary. Further, while students created a political public through participation in the ritual, people named a number of reasons for attending. One San Carlista reported that he went to López Larrave's funeral because he was the best friend of the deceased's nephew and that going to support his friend was the right thing to do. He was actually opposed to López Larrave's politics.[65] Another student went simply because everyone else was going.[66] Funerals also provided a rare opportunity for members of the popular movement to assemble in public with at least some assurance that they would not be killed.

The funerals were an improvisation with the ritual of the Catholic Eucharist that reflected Guatemalan urban ladino society, where traditional Catholicism, Liberation Theology, and newly popular Protestant denominations competed for fallen souls.[67] In Catholic liturgy, transubstantiation is the process undergone by Christ's body in the Eucharist, where wine and bread are transformed into the blood and body of Christ through God's power. In *revolutionary* transubstantiation, student bodies were transformed from bloodied corpses into agents in the body politic. Central Park and La Sexta supplanted the sanctuary as Eucharistic spaces. In the democratized miracle, gathered masses rather than ordained priests gave the blessing. The power of the crowd transformed the body into spirit. In their homage to Castañeda de León, psychology students wrote, "You, Oliverio, are present in this struggle and you will be present forever so long as we see the actions of your blood, the fertile blood that pushes us to conquer more and better victories in the popular struggle to obtain true and final liberation."[68] Christ-like Castañeda de León was transformed by the masses; in turn, his blood sustained the popular movement. Salvation would not come through an intermediary, nor must freedom wait for the hereafter.

Christianity's central image is that of a beautiful young man whose life was cut short by a group of oligarchic rulers because his political convictions challenged their authority.[69] López Larrave, Caballeros, García, and Castañeda de León transformed easily into such a figure. Similar insurgent syncretisms of revolutionary secularism and religious millennialism were influential in El Salvador, Nicaragua, Brazil, and South Africa in the same years.[70] The martyr would bring redemption and liberation to the pueblo on earth: the deceased body, the elemental equivocation of a body in material and spirit forms, offered figurative means by which to reimagine the body politic. In revolutionary transubstantiation, there was no priest or extensive liturgy, only the pueblo. From flesh to spirit, spirit to flesh, the martyred student body delivered salvation through the masses. Memorialization saturated the cement street

FIGURE 16. Iduvina Hernández walks with a comrade at the funeral for a union leader from CAVISA, 1978. Photograph by Mauro Calanchina.

corners of La Sexta with symbolic capital when student-theologians invoked the body and blood of martyrs without the Church's intervention.

In some respects, the Catholic Church and USAC were competing institutions. As I have discussed across the previous chapters, the USAC's relationship to the Catholic Church was complicated. In some respects, the university had been in tension with the Church since the expulsion of religious orders and closing of the Universidad Real y Pontífica de San Carlos Borromeo in 1829. Of course, the damning pastoral letters issued by Archbishop Rossell y Arrellano in the 1940s and 1950s and, later, Casariegos, did little to warm the relationship. When the Universidad Rafael Landívar opened, the break became more pronounced. Students who desired a religious education attended URL, not USAC. Through the 1970s and 1980s, Liberation Theology was much less influential in urban Guatemala than it was in El Salvador and Nicaragua, despite the work of Maryknolls, CRATER, and some Jesuits. Most of the capital city's religious organizations opposed protest as an invitation to violence.[71]

The political economy of death prescribed different roles for men and women. Commemorative publications and funeral eulogies positioned students as sons of the pueblo, not only partisans or San Carlistas. The most famous martyrs—García, López Larrave, and Castañeda de León—were all young ladino men of the city's intellectual class with records of public service and solidarity with urban workers. Castañeda de León attended the elite preparatory school Colegio Americano and traveled throughout Guatemala and England. López Larrave was a well-known lawyer, but also a researcher, professor, and administrator. García had distinguished himself as a leader and scholar at preparatory school. Each of these men could reflect multiple and sometimes contradictory meanings in the "political economy of death."[72]

The gendered division of loss would endure through the end of the civil war and into postwar reconciliation politics. Even as greater numbers of women attended the university than ever before throughout the 1970s and many women played key roles in student organizations and university administration, they were largely ignored as martyrs with the power to fuel San Carlistas' affective and moral appeals to national and international governments, courts, and NGOs. Men, especially young men, were martyrs and public mourners; women were wives, mothers, sisters, and girlfriends of the disappeared, and private mourners. Invoking her deceased student, one of Castañeda de León's teachers wrote, "You did not die, no, because I am living, you did not die, because misery, ignorance, malnourishment, hunger, unemployment and injustice still exist and so long as all of these flaws remain, so will there be thousands of Oliverios, Marios, Robins, Ernestos, Rogelias, Victor Hugos, and more."[73] In fact, thousands of Rogelias were *not* mourned as were Oliverios, Marios, Robins, Ernestos, and Victor Hugos. While San Carlista women were captured, tortured, and disappeared, they infrequently appeared in commemorative texts. Although counterinsurgency forces adopted a different approach to urban San Carlista women than they did to rural indigenous women, it is likely that many instances of violence against San Carlista women went unreported.

The deaths of López Larrave, Caballeros, García, and Castañeda de León made clear that the individual's natural right to live and the political right to peacefully assemble were not protected by the State. San Carlistas responded by creating a broader insurgent community and looking beyond liberal rights. Some responded by refusing to settle accounts or let go. For instance, after his death, the AEU General Assembly declared that Castañeda de León would serve posthumously as the general secretary of the AEU until he completed his elected term on May 22, 1979. An empty chair marked his presence at AEU sessions. A daily minute of silence observed in every classroom marked his perpetual return.[74] The AEU added Castañeda de León's name to its title and became the Association of University Students "Oliverio Castañeda de León." The Student Front–Robin García (FERG) had done something similar. Faced with death, San Carlistas forged a revolution in being, time, and space. They prevented quotidian forgetting, destabilized urban living spaces, made apparent the injustice of the State, and offered a safe—or safer—space for the public to gather. This new politics of death had transformed student nationalism.

THE FORECLOSURE OF DEMOCRACY

On January 25, 1979, Congressman and USAC professor Alberto Fuentes Mohr was assassinated. He was driving in his car on busy Avenida Reforma at midday on his way to a meeting with Vice President Francisco Villagrán Kramer. Never before had such a high-profile and centrist political figure been assassinated. Two months later, his colleague and friend Manuel Colom Argueta shared the honorific. The deaths of Fuentes Mohr and Colom Argueta, two of the few public figures left who continued to advocate an electoral rather than insurgent approach to social change, signaled the foreclosure of democracy. Like López Larrave, Colom Argueta began his political career at USAC in the 1950s. He was a leader in the massive protests of June 1956 and March and April 1962. Through the 1960s, he published on economic development and social democratic politics. His political career forced him into exile in El Salvador and, later, into Guatemala City's mayoral seat. All the while, he worked to establish the United Revolutionary Front (FUR), a social democratic party. His efforts were blocked by bureaucratic maneuvers and, just as often, kidnapping, death threats, and attempted assassination.

After years of rejection, president Lucas García promised that the FUR would eligible to participate in the upoming 1982 presidential elections. In an interview with the London-based weekly newsletter *Latin American Political Report*, Colom Argueta said, "In this moment when they have recognized my party, the challenge is to make sure that they do not kill me."[75] His friends and colleagues urged him to leave the country, but in an interview for the student newspaper *Voz Informativa Universitaria*, he insisted, "There is so much to do in our country that an unproductive minute is a moment lost, and every moment lost will be called upon by History, by the new generations, by the critical world of the future."[76] On Wednesday, March 21, Colom

Argueta gave a talk about the March and April 1962 protests to the USAC *Facultad* of Architecture. He spoke about how these protests and the 1944 revolution were the two defining moments of contemporary Guatemalan history. He emphasized how they offered important lessons to the popular movement in 1979: the power of university and secondary school students, the effectiveness of neighborhood-based resistance, and the government's willingness to use force against the pueblo.[77]

Colom Argueta was killed the morning after this talk. He, with two bodyguards, was driving from his Zone 9 office to the university. Following a common security method, the bodyguards drove behind Colom Argueta in a separate car. They were shot first. Colom Argueta tried to flee, as he had in other assassination attempts. But he was intercepted and killed at the corner of 3rd Avenue and 5th Street in Zone 9.[78] Once more, Rector Osorio Paz carried the casket of a friend and colleague to the Paraninfo Universitaria where the USAC community held yet another wake. Anonymous editors organized a publication of his last talk and concluded their introduction with this affirmation: "Manuel Alberto Colom Argueta is dead. His dreams and hopes, bound to the last drop [of blood] with those of the pueblo of Guatemala, are not vanquished."[79] The Colom Argueta and Fuentes Mohr assassinations became models for other targeted clandestine assassinations for their expedient use of intelligence gained from government informants who had received a cash reward for their assistance.[80]

Both Fuentes Mohr and Colom Argueta had worked to create a democratic opening in Guatemalan politics. They had longstanding friendships with Vice President Villagrán Kramer (who would soon resign) and had worked to repair the relationship between the pueblo and the state through electoral representation. After their deaths, the nonrevolutionary left was devastated. Their assassinations signaled the failure of some of the most basic principles of democracy: political right and responsibility, justice and freedom, electoral dissent, and representation and equality before the law. Some San Carlistas retreated to apoliticism, and some left the country in forced or semivoluntary exile.

Exile had by this time become an important tactic among the left and the right. The right cast out problematic leftists by threatening them until they felt compelled to leave. For the left, exile became a way to survive the war and, sometimes, a place to rebuild community before returning home. Mexico City was a popular destination, but key figures on the left also fled to Havana, Chile, Paris, or elsewhere in Europe. Exiles would often leave, return, and then leave again in a pattern of circular exile. This pattern and the long tradition of Guatemalan exile in Mexico City meant that there was a large network of church and community groups, friends, and family members who welcomed recent arrivals. The Catholic Guatemalan Church in Exile (Iglesia Guatemalteca en Exilio [IGE]) became an important home for the left and organized effective campaigns for public awareness and international solidarity in the early 1980s.[81] In Mexico City, Guatemalans met exiles from Uruguay, Argentina, and Chile. Since the counterrevolution, San Carlistas had reimagined the local and the global through anticolonialism and critiques of Cold War geopolitics, but exile and intimate transnational student networks and international human rights organizing made this even more important. Some San Carlistas returned from exile to leave the university and join the guerrilla.[82]

While Castaneda de Léon, Caballeros, and García were united in death, in life they represented rival political parties at USAC. As I mentioned in Chapter 5, the split between the FERG and FRENTE had a profound effect on San Carlista political culture. Exemplifying this difference is a document from the AEU archive, probably a FERG publication, which detailed a curriculum for "Security Measures." The curriculum included seven workshop discussions including the theory of violence, fascism, physical training (especially long runs), hand-to-hand practice and theories of combat, and military training. The objective of these trainings was to "safeguard our organization from whatever sort of attack to which it may be subject on the part of the [reactionaries]." But even more interestingly, the students sought to "educate [themselves] to correctly interpret all of the manifestations of capitalism, so as not to become confused by bourgeois distractions such as romanticism, adventurism, and spontaneity that try to pervert the *J.* of the *rev.*" The words youth (*juventud*) and revolution (*revolución*) were abbreviated throughout the document. The training sought to create conscientization and military knowledge "to be placed in the service of *P.* [party] whenever this is necessary, to liberate the country."[83]

By contrast, FRENTE was the only party that participated in the 1979 AEU elections. Learning from the death of Castañeda de León, they ran as a full slate and deemphasized individuals' names to protect their lives. The group dominated AEU elections for several years. The Central American news outlet *Inforpress* understood the party's continued success as evidence of San Carlistas' rejection of FERG's more radical platform. But the group's success was also its burden. It failed to adopt effective security culture until the 1980s, an oversight that probably contributed to Castañeda de León's and other student leaders' deaths and kidnappings. By contrast, the FERG, learning from the EGP, had always instituted certain methods, like traveling in groups, remaining as anonymous as possible, and keeping an unpredictable schedule, to ensure safety.[84]

More generally, San Carlistas attempted to secure their safety through international solidarity. Student groups and sports teams openly exchanged letters, telegrams, and invitations with students in Nicaragua and El Salvador. The Continental Organization of Latin American and Caribbean Students (OCLAE) issued a "Declaration of Solidarity with the Pueblo and Students of Guatemala," on October 20, 1979 that denounced the Lucas García government as a dictatorship and noted the date: the thirty-ninth anniversary of the defeat of Ubico and the first anniversary of the death of Castañeda de León. The declaration closed by calling on the people of Latin America and the Caribbean to "unite their struggles against imperialism and oligarchy . . . sure that sooner than later, they will triumph."[85] San Carlistas who joined the guerrilla had even closer, if clandestine, contact with their Central American comrades. Across decades of struggle, Guatemalan, Salvadoran, and Nicaraguan students were united by anti-imperialism and their struggle for a regional Central American interpretation of Marxism.[86] For this reason, the Sandinista victory on July 19, 1979, was a victory for all Central Americans. In fact, the headquarters of the AEU, called the Casa del Estudiantes, was home to a number of Nicaraguan exiles until early October 1979. There is little archival trace of this, except for a very polite letter written from the AEU dated October 2, 1979, asking the last remaining Nicaraguan refugee to leave by the tenth, as the AEU needed to use the space for other things. After all, the revolution had triumphed about three months earlier. The AEU respectfully asked if the individual would take a serious look at their situation and consider returning home.[87]

The AEU also reached out to potential international allies, writing to the Human Rights Commission of the United Nations and Amnesty International in November 1979 to denounce the CIA's role in the assassination of Puerto Rican Angel Rodriguez Cristóbal, a letter they dated "Year of the Victory of the Nicaraguan People." A similar letter was sent to the Puerto Rican University Federation (FUFI) and Puerto Rican Independence Party, with additional wishes for success in their struggle for freedom. U.S. president Jimmy Carter received a version of the letter with an additional paragraph: "The series of atrocities that your government commits on a daily basis against the people who fight for freedom is known around the world, even though you try to control the media, some of those [freedom fighters] still manage to inform the people of their real successes that took place nationally and internationally."[88] Simply put, international solidarity and the Sandinista victory empowered San Carlistas on the left.

At the same time, San Carlistas continued to forge deeper solidarities with other Guatemalans. The government looked upon these solidarities with deep suspicion and, often, with a finger on the trigger. The FERG and CUC joined forces in January 1980 to protest the government's treatment of indigenous campesinos and the militarization of the Quiché communities of Chajul, Nebaj, San Juan Cotzal, and San Miguel Uspantán.[89] Press conferences and meetings had failed, so the group adopted a strategy that had been particularly effective in Nicaragua and El Salvador: the seizure and occupation of public and Church property, called a *toma*.[90] The Spanish Embassy in Guatemala City would be the group's target.

On the morning of January 31, twenty-seven campesinos and students entered the embassy, wearing hats and handkerchiefs to cover their faces. The group announced their presence and declared the embassy occupied. They carried signs, written declarations, and many days' worth of food. They stated that they did not bring weapons because they had come to meet with Ambassador Máximo Cajal López. They read a declaration that began, "All of this injustice, all of this evil, and all of this cowardice from the National Army is what we have come to denounce to the capital, but here we were also persecuted and threatened by the repressive forces. The newspapers and radios did not want to publish anything [we did] because their workers are also threatened with death by the government." They said that this left them no alternative but to occupy the embassy in order to "bring [their] demands to the entire pueblo of Guatemala, and to all of the pueblos of the world." They closed by affirming their commitment to remain inside the embassy until the government agreed to investigate the ongoing violence suffered by their communities.[91]

While the group inside read their statement, other San Carlistas, including theatre and journalism students, stood outside to support them. Police began to gather around the perimeter of the building. Around 11:30 A.M., the protestors unfurled a banner along an outside wall. It read, "WE CONDEMN THE SLAUGHTER OF CHAJUL." As the situation escalated, the ambassador requested that embassy staff be allowed to leave. He offered to stay, along with his secretary. The occupiers agreed to let the workers go, on the condition that they would be permitted to contact the Red Cross. They also permitted the ambassador to call government officials in order to attempt to forestall police intervention. Despite his attempts to deescalate, Cajal failed to persuade the police to leave. He seemed unable to reach many Guatemalan officials by telephone. When president Lucas García received news of the occupation from his interior minister, his response is reported to have been, "Get them out by any means!" Perhaps wary of repeating the recent Sandinista victory, Lucas García felt it was most critical to put an end to the story that was circulating through the city by radio and word of mouth.[92]

Around 1 P.M., government security forces entered the embassy gardens. The ambassador and one protestor reportedly used a megaphone to request that they retreat. The ambassador informed the police that the occupiers had agreed to withdraw. Nevertheless, armed security forces, including uniformed and undercover officers from the National Police and Army Intelligence opened fire on the embassy. The attack violated international law that banned invasion of a foreign embassy without the consent of the ambassador.[93] Security forces began to scale the balconies and break windows in an attempt to enter the building. Cajal seems to have told the police that if they persisted, everyone inside would die. A fire was started by some combination of Molotov cocktails and flamethrower, though accounts differ on when and why they were fired and, importantly, by whom.[94] All reports agree that the fire burned for nearly ten minutes before firefighters and rescue workers could intervene. A photographer for *El Imparcial* captured several images of police and other authorities standing by.[95] One witness recalled the terrible work in the morgue of separating the bodies. Morgue workers spoke of auto-immolation and sacrifice.[96]

The AEU rushed telegrams to news outlets and student unions around the world.[97] They wrote letters to all democratic Latin American heads of state and the United Nations, calling for the diplomatic isolation of Guatemala and support for Spain in its repudiation of the Guatemalan government. They also demanded the immediate dismissal of the three officials linked to the event, Interior Minister Donaldo Álvarez Ruiz, National Police Director Chupina, and Manuel de Jesús Valiente Tellez.[98] Meanwhile, Lucas García referred to the event as a "terrorist massacre."[99] Police records called the group "terrorists," "provocateurs," and "murderers."[100] The national press reported headlines like, "Fearsome Genocide in the Spanish Embassy," "Government Denounces the Guerrilla Massacre," and "Thirty Nine Deaths

FIGURE 17. Funeral for the victims of the Spanish Embassy Fire, Guatemala City, February 1980. Fototeca Guatemala, Centro de Investigaciones Regionales de Mesoamérica (CIRMA).

in the Occupation of the Spanish Embassy: Invaders of the Diplomatic Seat Self-Immolated with Their Prisoners."[101] They failed to report the survival of one campesino, Gregorio Yujá.[102] Yujá had been taken to Roosevelt Hospital and placed under police supervision. The following morning at 8 A.M., he was kidnapped from his hospital bed and disappeared. His body reappeared the following day outside of the rector's office on campus. Yujá had been tortured and badly burned a second time.

A crowd assembled on the morning of February 2 at the Paraninfo, including university students, professors, but also the "simple [*sencillo*], humble [*humilde*], poor." One student remembered the embassy fire as "the sort of thing that not only as a student, but as a citizen in general . . . made you full of anger and want to do something, to want to demonstrate that and to want to speak out."[103] A stream of wooden caskets seemed to wash over the thousands of marchers as they walked to the General Cemetery. Marchers—mourners—covered their faces and wore hats and sunglasses. Some people carried signs. At the end of the procession, several campesino groups, unions,

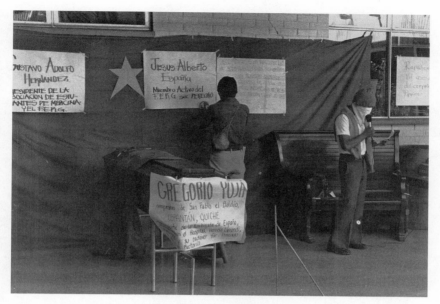

FIGURE 18. Memorial for victims of the Spanish Embassy Fire with Gregorio Yujá's casket. Guatemala City, February 1980. Fototeca Guatemala, Centro de Investigaciones Regionales de Mesoamérica (CIRMA).

and the AEU carried large banners painted with denunciations. At the General Cemetery, a speaker recited the name of every individual killed, to which the people responded, "Present in the struggle! [*presente en la lucha!*]"[104] At a press conference a few days later, Rector Osorio Paz bravely declared, "At the university, they do not teach how to destroy the lives of human beings and they do not teach how to use firearms; they do teach . . . life and so that we may live better."[105] For their part, the CUC issued its seminal "Declaration of Iximché." The declaration linked the Lucas García government to five centuries of indigenous oppression since colonization. It reiterated that in order to triumph, the struggle must bring together "workers, *campesinos*, students, slum dwellers, and other popular and democratic sectors," for "the sacrifice of those lives brings us closer now than ever to a new society, to the Indian dawn."[106]

By contrast, the bodies of ex–vice president Eduardo Cáceres Lenhoff and former foreign affairs minister Adolfo Molina Orantes, who were also killed in the fire, lay in state at the National Palace with highest honors. President Lucas García, the vice president of the Legislature, the president of the

Supreme Court, three ex-presidents (Arévalo, Arana Osorio, and Laugerud García), diplomats, and Catholic Church officials attended the funeral. Their bodies were conveyed to the cemetery by hearse, not the pueblo.[107]

The fire fatally damaged the Lucas García government's international reputation. The government of Spain denounced Guatemala's violation of international law and Cajal voiced his fear of retribution by Guatemalan security forces, ordering additional bodyguards. However, international attention failed to save San Carlistas' lives. After the fire, FERG students were singled out. Gustavo Adolfo Hernández and Jesús España were killed on their way to the embassy martyrs' wake. They were walking with a group of fellow students and union leaders who had been in hiding at the FASGUA headquarters when, one block from the Paraninfo on the corner of 11th Street, they met with officers from the National Police Command Six counterinsurgency squad.[108] A few students were carrying guns, and a shootout ensued. In the fray, USAC student Liliana Negreros was disappeared.[109] This confrontation occurred just a month before the funeral of Archbishop Oscar Romero in San Salvador when government security forces opened fire on a crowd of about two hundred thousand mourners. Even funerals had become unsafe.

WHEN THE NATIONAL ATE THE ACADEMIC

The bloody campaign of the counterinsurgency forces did not divide the popular movement. Instead, solidarities between students, urban workers, and rural peasants proved to be surprisingly resilient. In death, López Larrave once more united the labor, peasant, and university communities as they mourned him together. García's funeral offered unity in an otherwise fractious moment between student groups, including secondary students and center-left and radical-left university parties. Castañeda de León's public assassination shocked the people of Guatemala because it occurred at midday with total impunity and tens of thousands of mourners came to his funeral. And the assassinations of Fuentes Mohr and Colom Argueta sent a clear message: the Lucas García government would not tolerate even centrist electoral dissent. After dying and mourning together at the Spanish Embassy, students' and campesinos' solidarities deepened.[110] Each demonstration, funeral, or protest represented the joint efforts of parties and organizations (student groups FERG and FRENTE, the labor unions

FASGUA and CNUS, as well as the JPT, PGT, EGP, and CUC) and count-less interpersonal alliances and friendships.

By March 1980, San Carlistas were at risk simply for being students or associating with students. The National Police forcibly entered campus twice that month. On March 6, a new Pontiac was driven inside the university, left near the Political Science building, and then set on fire.[111] The day before, FERG leader Alejandro Cotí was kidnapped near the Periférico in Zone 1. He was driving with his wife, who was forced to leave the car before her husband was driven away by six armed men.[112] Two days after his disappear-ance, Cotí was found dead in his car on the side of the road between the capi-tal and Amatitlán.[113] Instead of a large public funeral, Cotí's casket followed a shortened route within the university campus where organizers hoped autonomy could protect the mourners.

This was the context for the 1980 Huelga de Dolores, which began this chapter. The event was nearly canceled. But the Honorable Committee issued a statement that made clear three points: first, the Huelga de Dolores would be observed; second, because the event included important political content, it would be open to nonstudents; and third, no liquor would be sold at the events in order to limit the potential for violence.[114] On the same day that the ESA claimed responsibility for the deaths of the three students who were distributing the *No Nos Tientes*, two other members of the USAC community were assassinated: well-known lawyer, professor, and former student leader Hugo Melgar y Melgar and his chauffeur, Fernando Cruz Juarez. Chillingly, Melgar y Melgar had written a letter to be read in the event of his death.[115] He wrote, "Given the major problems confronting the millions of oppressed and dispossessed, our solidarity is fundamental." He hoped that "without being forced to reach martyrology, it is enough to take a fair and honest attitude toward others and to identify with just causes, which are those of the masses exploited by imperialism and the national bourgeoisie."[116]

Like so many others, the professor lay in state at USAC. Once more, Osorio Paz presided over the funeral. In his eulogy, Osorio Paz asked, "Of what type of society are those who govern? When will this human butcher shop end?"[117] Unexpectedly, the secretary of public relations for the president replied. He lamented how many good Guatemalans—scholars, military offi-cials, troops, students and university professionals, commanders and agents of the National Police, workers, and campesinos—had lost their life to extremists on the left *and* the right. He also reminded the pueblo that the

FIGURE 19. Banner of the Asociación de Estudiantes de Humanidades (AEH) at a protest on International Workers' Day, May 1, 1980. Anonymous photograph. Fototeca Guatemala, Centro de Investigaciones Regionales de Mesoamérica (CIRMA).

government had ample resources to act against any extremist group that chose violence instead of dialogue.[118] At the same time, the secret paramilitary ESA continued to target USAC students and faculty with impunity.[119]

On May Day 1980, combined counterinsurgency forces disappeared thirty-one students and union members.[120] Students involved with labor organizing at López Larrave's Labor Orientation School were kidnapped. In several instances, masked individuals destroyed offices, interrupted meetings, and scrawled graffiti on campus. The identities of the perpetrators of these attacks were never revealed, though popular memory on the left seems to hold that these attacks were attempts to demonstrate the need for greater police intervention and stricter military rule on campus. In this atmosphere, open meetings of student groups were simply too dangerous. Instead of mass protests, masked students did flash literature drops, where they quickly boarded buses, passed out propaganda, and then jumped off before they could be identified.[121] They also held rallies on campus to recruit members to the growing number of leftist organizations and guerrilla groups.

In June, July, and August 1980, the security apparatus kidnapped, tortured, and disappeared nearly all of the capital city's trade union leadership.[122] Using Argentine computer network analysis and an Israeli computer system, military intelligence forces were able to target locales with high electricity or water bills or with peak usage during nighttime hours, which indicated potential clandestine meeting places, printing presses, or large homes with many residents. The addresses of suspicious buildings were sent to troops who conducted sudden searches. Using these methods, the security forces were able to raid at least thirty guerrilla safe houses and arms caches.[123] Violence around USAC peaked in the same months. In the first weeks of June, the CSU wrote a paid political advertisement that listed the USAC dead: two from Psychology (professor Carlos Alberto Figueroa Castro and Edna Ibarra de Figueroa) on June 6 and engineer Eduardo René Ordóñez and two individuals who were mistaken for *universitarios* on June 9. State agents attempted to kidnap student leader Victor Valverth from the parking lot of the Engineering school on June 10.[124] Compared to a list compiled by political scientist Paul Kobrak, the CSU failed to name at least thirty more disappearances or assassinations from those two weeks.[125] Assassinations had become so commonplace that newspapers ran headlines like, "Another University Functionary Killed!"[126] Undeterred, the FAR detonated propaganda bombs (incendiary devices that propel hundreds of small flyers into the air) throughout the capital, including the National School of Commercial Sciences and Aqueche Institute.[127] It was common knowledge that the FAR and EGP recruited at both schools. Secondary school students held nationwide strikes through July and August.[128] In an unsubtle attempt to improve its public image among parents and students, the Army began donating supplies to the capital city's poorest public schools.

By this point, it was hard to imagine an act of violence that could shock the USAC community. Yet that moment came on the morning of July 14, 1980. As students exited a city bus, around twenty-five men hidden in a pickup truck and panel van opened fire. Eight students were killed and sixteen were injured.[129] The government attributed the crime to subversives who wanted to destabilize the government.[130] An hour later in Quetzaltenango, the director of the School of Juridical and Social Sciences and his wife were killed. In a paid political advertisement, university officials declared, "The reactionary sectors are trying to drown the University of San Carlos in a blood bath, so that [we] will be obliged to close the university and [permit] intervention by reactionary sectors."[131] The university administration decided that the university should remain open.

The war against USAC continued. Public statements from the archdiocese exacerbated rumors of guerrilla infiltration within the university by detailing a handful of high-profile recruits like Ricardo Ramírez (nom de guerre: Rolando Morán).[132] Morán was the son of a distinguished Guatemalan family. He had studied in elite preparatory schools in Honduras and Guatemala where he learned English and business from UFCO managers. During the Arbenz presidency, he studied law alongside *escuilaches* like Manuel Galich. It was during these years that he first met Che Guevara in dive bars near the old USAC Law School. With the counterrevolution, he went into exile, but on his return in 1959, he passed through revolutionary Cuba where he met Guevara again. He found a confidant in Fidel Castro and became a member of the JPT, then founded the FAR in 1962, and in 1966 renounced the FAR and founded the EGP.[133] Mario Payeras, a philosophy student and fellow EGP leader, was another high-profile San Carlista combatant. Payeras's early meditation on the indigenous question echoed Guevara, arguing that the experience of guerrilla combat, especially urban ladino combatants' first encounters with indigenous communities and nature, created revolutionary consciousness.[134] On September 3, 1980, architecture dean Gilberto Castañeda Sandoval submitted a letter to the CSU requesting a leave of absence in order to join the guerrilla. Castañeda Sandoval wrote that despite his position in what he referred to as the "petit bourgeoisie," he was called to join the armed revolution with the EGP. He wrote, "considering the . . . the details of the July 14th massacre, I have decided to clearly state my position and to join the people's struggle."[135] The CSU scrambled to distance itself from Castañeda Sandoval.

Rumors of student radicalism multiplied. In November 1981, the police received reports that students had installed equipment to manufacture explosives in the carpentry shop at Aqueche Institute. They also heard that a group of students received arms training in the basement of an USAC academic building and that the same group traveled to various locations in the countryside on the weekends, implying that they trained for combat with the guerrilla. Other reports detailed that students received political indoctrination as core curriculum at the Santiago Institute.[136] Denunciations of the university became a regular feature of daily newspapers.[137] Rector Osorio Paz was especially vulnerable. Most of the people who had elected him were dead, in exile, or neutralized by fear.[138] Before long, he also left Guatemala.[139] One supporter joked how Osorio Paz could absolutely return and resume his work as rector, only he would have to live in a secret bunker buried on campus to do so. Understandably, it was difficult to find a replacement.[140]

As the *No Nos Tientes* editorial foretold, 1980 was a critical year for

Guatemalans. Labor unions went underground, the guerrilla regrouped, and students tried to restrategize and stay alive. At USAC, the death toll for 1980 counted 125 students, administrators, and professors.[141] Organizing within the AEU had become difficult, because the group's effectiveness relied upon visibility and the university's positive reputation. Visibility was too dangerous and the university's reputation had declined. Joining the guerrilla began to make sense to more students. The FERG had given up on electoral student politics and joined the EGP and the CUC to form the FP-31 (Popular Front-31), named for the martyrs of the Spanish Embassy fire.

Tellingly, the most popular float in the 1981 *desfile bufo* featured a group of kidnappers. *El Gráfico* reported, "The public repeatedly applauded the float that depicted a group of 'kidnappers,' various costumed students jumped off the float and, in a very funny parody, captured random spectators."[142] The previous year's parade also included a farcical arrest scene starring some students dressed as "the agents of order" and others as "the detained." To this day, students in the *desfile* often playfully kidnap their friends from the crowd. Parodies of disappearance revealed a growing cynicism.

Amnesty International wrote in 1980 that the government had declared war on the university.[143] The National Police and other counterinsurgency forces also actively recruited at USAC at least as early as 1974. In exchange for information, collaborators could receive a special ID card, training, a monthly salary (around Q400.00), gifts, promotions, and even large homes. San Carlistas in the popular movement knew that informants (*orejas*) swarmed USAC and some were prepared to mete out justice accordingly. One such *oreja*, Adán de Jesús Melgar Solares, was stripped and dragged naked through campus. In front of a large crowd, he was brought to Petapa Avenue, stoned, doused with gasoline, and set on fire. It was a chilling indication of the depths of anger and desperation.[144] Even noncombatant San Carlistas reported receiving threats by telephone, brief arrest and detention, threats from professors regarding course grades, the visible presence of death squads and unmarked cars, indiscriminate shooting, fires and destruction of personal property, and increasingly limited funds for USAC and student groups.[145]

Simply put, the years of repression damaged the university. Student organizations became cliquish, defensive, and closed to new ideas and members. The academic quality of students and professors diminished.[146] Few students participated in university politics. Those who did focused on campus-related demands.[147] Most leftist students and professors were isolated from university life, whether in voluntary exile abroad or hidden in secret locations in the capital.[148] As one San Carlista remembered, in the years between 1977 and 1980, "the national ate the academic."[149] The relationship between the state and the individual was no longer based on political right, but rather on states of exception.

Across a half century, student nationalism had adapted to various political changes. By 1980 it had become nationalism without a government. The previous five chapters demonstrated how San Carlistas became figures for national progress, first as builders of a new "Republic of Students," then as responsible citizens driven by their duty to lead the nation, and then as acolytes of progress. This chapter has demonstrated how San Carlistas suffered and responded to rapacious state violence through political funerals and coalitions with the popular movement and, to a lesser extent, international human rights organizations. When the state's murderous capacity challenged the social contract, calls for millenarian futures replaced demands for representation and rights. Feelings of fraternity among San Carlistas, campesinos, and workers deepened as they bore one another's bones across the city. These corpses were the frames on which the new social body could be constructed. Mourners demanded justice in life. In the words of Aqueche students after Robin García's assassination, "If one dies, it is because someone had to die in order to keep hope alive."[150] By the end of 1980, San Carlistas had seen plenty of death and had little hope. Yet the war would continue for sixteen more years.

The effects of violence had settled. The republican ideal, the statist horizon of student nationalism, was undone both by the murderous state and student radicals. San Carlistas became casualties in the government's Cold War battle against the most enduring sector of civil society, the university. What, now, could it mean to be a San Carlista?

Coda

TODAY NEARLY EVERY WALL ON CAMPUS is filled with multicolored figures of sacrifice and struggle. Iconic identification photographs, revolutionary quotations, and the names of classmates and professors who were disappeared during the war greet students as they go from class to class. Students play basketball in a plaza named for Oliverio Castañeda de León and lean their bikes against a mural of Robin García. The space for memory is also a space for life. Yet at every turn, a testament of the university's past reminds students of their responsibility and of the sacrifice of those who came before.

In the preceding chapters, I have demonstrated how a relatively small group of students, faculty, and alumni—San Carlistas—shaped the meaning of the middle class through their encounters with the university as an institution and Guatemalan state apparatuses in the years between 1944 and 1980. Across decades of cooperation and contention, they forged student nationalism, based on faith in the principles of liberalism and the responsibility of university students to lead the nation. Political affect, especially feelings like dignity, freedom, and duty, deepened their claims. Student nationalism made sense of their shared experience.

Student nationalism changed across the later twentieth century. In the 1940s and 1950s, student nationalism compelled students to reform the nation, but it was aimed at radicalizing the nation through the 1960s and 1970s; by the end of the 1970s, student nationalism became a nationalism without a government after a series of violent flashpoints revealed the military regimes' murderous goals. A new politics of spectacular mourning became especially powerful in this conjuncture. As the reactionary forces of the military and police grew more brutal, student nationalism began to fray at the edges. Some students turned away from protest and focused on their studies, work, or family life. Some left USAC for one of the newer private universities, which had reputations of apoliticism or even outright opposition to the popular movement. Others remained involved in the opposition, but fled to Europe or North America in exile, often seeking support from international human rights organizations. A small number left the university to join the guerrilla. While the legacy of San Carlista student nationalism remained a defining feature of urban middle-class ladino life, by the end of the war, it lacked the ability to cohere the community.

Over nine years of research for this book, I casually asked USAC alumni, "What does it mean to you to be a San Carlista?" They often replied in similar ways: "an opportunity," "a huge responsibility," "sacrifice," "to study to return to the pueblo what belongs to the pueblo," "a commitment to transform reality," "[to have] a historical presence," "to align [myself] with the people," "[to have] a history of blood," "to be critical," "to love my alma mater."[1] One former AEU leader explained to me that he often heard people say things like, "Here come the students! [*Ahí van los estudiantes!*]" in poor rural and urban communities since at least the 1990s. He explained that this statement reflected the pueblo's belief that San Carlistas could bring change by listening to their struggles and advocating on their behalf. I met San Carlistas in bars, restaurants, on the sidewalk, in the park, even on the bus. These brief conversations revealed how the effects of San Carlistas' meaning making linger in post–civil war Guatemala.

The book's chapters end in 1980, just before a wave of terror struck the city and the countryside. Between 1980 and 1983, eighty professors and administrators were assassinated or disappeared. Three rectors abandoned their post after repeated death threats, and the military and police regularly patrolled campus. Student political organizations suffered, some deterred by fear and others having abandoned the university for the armed struggle. At least a whole generation of professors and students was affected.

In 1982, dissent within the military led to a coup against President Fernando Romeo Lucas García (1978–1982) with General Efraín Ríos Montt at the helm. Ríos Montt's "election" seemed an improvement, for a brief moment: he restored university autonomy, pledged federal aid for the university's financial crisis, promised investigations into the thousands of unresolved cases of forced disappearance, and formed special military courts that, although they militarized the juridical process, reinstated some legal procedure. Then, twenty-two San Carlistas were disappeared between July and October. When faculty, students, and staff protested, Ríos Montt struck

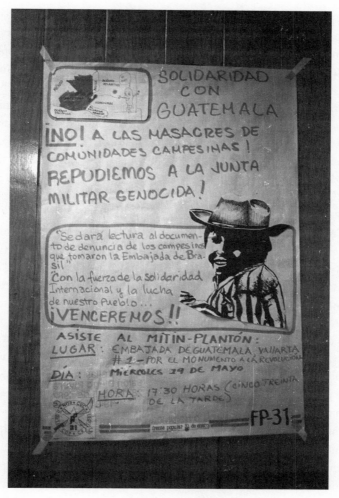

FIGURE 20. Flyer advertising a protest in front of the Guatemalan Embassy in Mexico City, 1982. Fototeca Guatemala, Centro de Investigaciones Regionales de Mesoamérica (CIRMA).

back. To sidestep accusations of violating university autonomy, he employed the strategy of his North American counterpart, Ronald Reagan. Reports of drug trafficking and rampant drug use justified police presence on campus at all hours. But this was merely a trace of the regime's brutal bent: during his fifteen and a half months as president, Ríos Montt is alleged to be responsible for the deaths of 1,771 Ixil Mayans and the displacement of 29,000 people during fifteen massacres in the Ixil region.

Despite repression, enrollment at USAC continued to grow. The four private universities comprised only 8 percent of the nation's university enrollments in 1980.[2] USAC continued to be an important locus of open and clandestine antigovernment organizing. Police, military, and paramilitary groups continued to respond violently. A pattern of protest/repression cohered. Emboldened by another coup (this one against Ríos Montt), San Carlistas on the left organized with urban labor unions, rural campesino groups, and the guerrilla for a few months in 1983. The new president, Óscar Humberto Mejía Victores (1983–1986), turned his attention toward urban counterinsurgency, expanding arrests, interrogations, and raids. He granted amnesty for retired combatants, but continued to pursue the active guerrilla. All the while, scorched earth violence besieged the countryside.

In September 1985, the university hosted a huge protest to demand the president's resignation. A group marched from campus to downtown and rallied in front of the National Palace. In response, the military invaded campus with an armored tank and five hundred troops. They occupied campus for four days. Soldiers vandalized classrooms, offices, and laboratories; stole files; and spray-painted defamatory messages throughout campus. This show of force occurred just as the eyes of the world were trained on Guatemala's democratic transition: the first nominally free election in years was scheduled for November 1985 and pitted three San Carlistas (Jorge Serrano Elías, Jorge Carpio Nicolle, and Marco Vinicio Cerezo Arévalo) against one another. Cerezo won and become the first civilian president in two decades.

A slow democratic transition was unfolding. San Carlistas participated in the Unity of Labor and Popular Action (UASP), a new group that investigated the cases of thousands of *desaparecidos*, aided the return of refugees, and promoted the dissolution of the Civil Defense Patrols. Many were also close to the Guatemalan National Revolutionary Unity (Unidad Revolucionaria Nacional Guatemalteca [URNG]) in this period. Student political parties that openly aligned with the guerrilla routinely won university elections as the government's campaign of violence continued. After a few years, open political organizing at USAC waned. The guerrilla continued to recruit clandestinely.

In August and September 1989, thirteen students (including the AEU leadership) were arrested and assassinated. Enabled by a police infiltrator, this wave of violence again moderated political opposition at USAC. Still more San Carlistas fled into exile. Three years later, policemen opened fire on a group of students leaving the *desfile bufo* of the Huelga de Dolores. Five

FIGURE 21. Popular organizations protest while under surveillance, ca. 1980. Fototeca Guatemala, Centro de Investigaciones Regionales de Mesoamérica (CIRMA).

students were injured and one was killed. USAC administrators rallied behind the students and, unlike 1956, the agents were charged, though the case was never heard in court. Students were emboldened. While the decades-old pattern of protest and retribution continued until the signing of the Peace Accords, students' manifestos, editorials, and paid political advertisements increasingly equated justice with human rights and demanded that the state ensure the safety of its citizens.

On December 29, 1996, the last of eleven agreements comprising the Peace Accords was signed with some San Carlistas at the table (notably Ricardo Ramírez [alias Rolando Morán] and Ricardo Rosales [alias Carlos Gonzales] of the URNG). The war had endured for thirty-six years, two weeks, and a few days. Many Guatemalans hoped for peace, and in peace, the opportunity to rebuild national unity; others dreamed of justice, truth finding, and reconciliation. The guerrilla demobilized. Most of the students who had attended USAC during the final years of the civil war had graduated. Many dedicated their professional lives to the principles that animated their student years, but they did so in archives, law offices, and classrooms. Private universities proliferated after the end of the war, but USAC remained the alma mater of all but 20 percent of the university population into the 2010s.[3]

When the painstaking research of the United Nations-sponsored Commission for Historical Clarification (CEH) began in early 1997, San Carlista Alfredo Balsells Tojo was at the helm. In the years since, the combative spirit of student nationalism in the streets has become archival and historical practice. For many USAC alumni—"San Carlistas de siempre"—fulfilling their social duty has meant working in the state, the archive, and the corrupt judicial system that still occasionally manages to get a guilty verdict for war crimes. In many respects, this is a continuation of the work that San Carlistas had done since the 1970s, when student nationalism began to fuse local understandings of justice with international human rights discourse.

Some San Carlistas had begun this hard work even before the war ended. Frank La Rue cofounded the Center for Human Rights Legal Action (CALDH) in 1994 and has since become a world leader in international human rights advocacy. Iduvina Hernández, journalist and cofounder of the NGO Security in Democracy (Seguridad en Democracia [SEDEM]), was a friend of Castañeda de León and many other AEU members who were disappeared in the late 1970s. Her long career in human rights work began before she returned from exile in Mexico City in 1989. Congresswoman Nineth Montenegro, founder of the Grupo de Apoyo Mutuo (GAM), is also a San Carlista. Thelma Porres, archivist at the Centro de Investigaciones Regionales de Mesoamérica (CIRMA), studied history at USAC in the early and mid-1980s and saw beloved classmates and professors disappeared. Her commitment to historical memory has been absolutely central to the survival of the archive where many of the individuals and groups discussed here have chosen to keep their papers. It is hard to imagine the thousands of monographs and theses written from CIRMA's archives without her care.

Also in the hands of San Carlistas is the National Police Historical Archives (AHPN), a collection of identification cards, license plates, photographs, and police logbooks documenting surveillance, kidnapping, and assassinations.[4] There have been countless San Carlistas involved in the archive since its discovery. Today, the USAC Law *facultad* has a special relationship with the AHPN and sends many of its students there to help preserve documents and conduct research. All three of the judges who presided over the initial trial of former president Ríos Montt in March 2013 (Yassmin Barrios, Pablo Xitumul de Paz, and Patricia Isabel Bustamante García) are San Carlistas.[5] So, too, are defense attorneys Francisco García Gudiel, Otto

FIGURE 22. Murals and sculpture commemorating university martyrs in the USAC School of History, July 2016. Photograph by the author.

Ramírez, and Marco Antonio Cornejo Marroquín.[6] Still more San Carlistas gathered the evidence used by both sides. In so many ways, San Carlistas remain charged with making the meaning of the revolution, counterrevolution, and civil war.

But while the politics of the past seem absolutely crucial to some, they are less crucial for others. AEU elections are no longer a lightning rod for national politics. Many students ignore them or complain that these positions are merely opportunities for personal enrichment. For the generations whose childhood and youth unfolded amid political violence, being young meant paying attention in school, paying attention at home, and paying attention on the street.[7] Sometimes simply being a *universitario* or being near *universitarios* made one a target. But youth means something different today.[8] An anecdote: one afternoon in mid-July 2016, I asked three young women on campus where I might find the Plaza Rogelia Cruz. One responded, "Rogelio?" The two other shook their heads and looked at me with pity, as if sorry that I was lost. They referred me to a nearby guard and kept walking. They seemed unaware that their whole campus was a site of memory.

Other groups of young people have continued the memory work of earlier generations. Protests demanding the resignation of Otto Pérez Molina from April to September 2015 were particularly noteworthy in this regard. San Carlistas showed up week after week. Students from the private universities Rafael Landívar, Mariano Gálvez, Francisco Marroquín, and del Valle joined them. These universities were rivals in sports, politics, and employment, but they came together to denounce the president's corruption.[9] Another group that showed up week after week was the Sons and Daughters of the Disappeared–Guatemala (their full name in Spanish is Los Hijos e Hijas por la Identidad y la Justicia contra el Olvido y el Silencio [H.I.J.O.S.]).

H.I.J.O.S.–Guatemala was formed when Wendy Méndez, an orphan of the war, returned from Canadian exile and began contacting other children whose parents had been killed. The group's first march was held on June 30, 1999, a national holiday called Army Day. From the beginning, its aims were to support individuals returning from exile, search for answers about the disappearance of their family members, spread their own unofficial account of history, reclaim the militancy of their ancestors, and promote community action to demand justice and end impunity. They are perhaps best known for leaving elaborate political graffiti in key locations in Guatemala City's Centro Histórico and staging *escraches* in front of homes, businesses, and government ministries. *Escraches* use chants, political theatre, and a seemingly endless array of props to humiliate and shame perpetrators of violence that would otherwise live in impunity.

I have collaborated with one H.I.J.O.S. member, Paulo Estrada, for several years.[10] Paulo's father, Otto René Estrada Illescas, was kidnapped when Paulo was a year old on May 15, 1984. Fifteen years later, a document that seemed to provide unassailable evidence of the military's involvement in kidnappings, torture, and murders of political dissenters was leaked to National Security Archives senior analyst Kate Doyle. In it, Estrada Illescas's identification photograph appeared alongside that of 182 other people who had been disappeared by the National Police. Its pages are a sort of inventory of counterinsurgency tactics in Guatemala City between 1983 and 1985, a damning artifact of Mejía Victores's professionalization of the military and police forces and expanded urban counterinsurgency.

Paulo paid it little mind until he was a bit older. At USAC he became involved in a collective called El Papel, which wrote and distributed political flyers and zines on campus. In 2007, the *Diario Militar* went to the Inter-American Commission on Human Rights. Both Méndez and Estrada were

FIGURE 23. H.I.J.O.S. posters and graffiti on La Sexta, July 2016. Photograph by the author.

part of the case. The next year, Estrada joined in H.I.J.O.S.'s annual Army Day protest. They wheat pasted flyers and spray painted walls. For Estrada, it was "reclamation of the streets, of the walls . . . of public space." The first time we spoke, he remembered, "Seeing images of my father on the posters thrilled me [*me llenó*]."[11] Although his conscientization occurred while he was a student at USAC, Estrada does not identify with the long revolutionary lineage of San Carlistas. He insists that H.I.J.O.S. and San Carlistas represent two distinct lineages of struggle.

Nevertheless, there are many links between H.I.J.O.S. and the legacy of San Carlista student nationalism. Guiding both groups is the idea that as young people, they are responsible for the nation's future. Like San Carlistas of the late twentieth century, H.I.J.O.S. invokes terms like dignity (*dignidad*), pain (*dolor*), and disdain (*repudio*) to sway public opinion.[12] Historical memory, the core of student nationalism by the late 1970s, is H.I.J.O.S.'s foundation. The group takes up the mantle of student nationalism when it engages the important task of reimagining the relationship between the individual and the state. Once the state had proven murderous, San Carlistas began to articulate a student nationalism without a government, fusing secular millennialism with international human rights politics. Through their actions over decades, San Carlistas opened up social, cultural, and sometimes even physical spaces for other youths and youth groups to use to contest and occasionally participate within the state. In protests on La Sexta and graffiti throughout the capital's historic center, H.I.J.O.S. continues this work.

H.I.J.O.S. and its members voice frustration with the Peace Accords, now two decades past, and the limits of guilty verdicts so hard fought in the courts. In his thinking on these limits, Estrada distinguishes between justice and reparations and between "moral" and "economic" reparations. Moral reparations include parks, museums, and monuments as social spaces of memory; economic reparations attempt to pay family members for their loss. But Paulo also notes that his own sense of justice wants "to name names," "to know who did it, who gave the order."[13]

The naming of names in Guatemala seems especially important because some government officials and citizens continue to deny the crimes of the past. In May 2014, USAC alumnus Luis Pérez, a congressman, spoke, "The revolutionary detractors have not managed to get over the past . . . with their gaze toward the past they do not understand that we have to build a bridge of reconciliation . . . We let ourselves be influenced by a few officials of international organizations." Eighty-seven of 111 members of Congress approved his resolution that denied genocide had occurred in Guatemala.[14] While elsewhere, truth and reconciliation commissions have required perpetrators to be named, in Guatemala and other Latin American nations, only the names of the victims are circulated widely.[15] In the context of ongoing impunity, the juridical imperative makes the task of documentation essential, but the archive has also become a significant site for cross-generational encounters on the left. At the AHPN, San Carlista militants of the 1970s, 1980s, and 1990s work alongside members of H.I.J.O.S., drawn to the archive for similar reasons.

THE SEED

The complex legacy of San Carlistas lives on. The unity of student nationalism without a government has long since given way to a loose weave of alternate futures. To simply walk in Guatemala City today is to brush past lives shaped by war. As I mentioned above, most of the nation's archivists and librarians were trained at USAC and spent the majority of their lives in a state of war. Their connections to classmates and USAC remain strong. Still, the counter-revolution and civil war silenced multiple generations of bright young minds. The intellectual and political culture of the university has yet to recover. Yet in bars, at the gym, on buses across Guatemala, and even in Connecticut, when I tell Guatemalans about this book, they often proudly proclaim: "Soy San Carlista!" Los Angeles's Guatemalan diaspora observes the Huelga de Dolores, and there is an active Facebook group called "Huelga de Dolores U.S.A."

It is an all too common and facile lament today to insist that the youth do not care about politics. Without question, the political panorama of the university has changed; but so, too, has Guatemala's. With notable exceptions like the Students for Autonomy (Estudiantes por la Autonomía [EPA]) who staged a tenacious protest against educational reform in October 2010 and the 2015 demonstrations against Pérez Molina, protest is simply not a part of most San Carlistas' daily life. Leaders of the AEU seem selected by a cult of personality. By contrast, H.I.J.O.S. leaders are hard to single out. Their texts speak in the first person plural of a collectivity that refuses the economization of social relations to loss in the form of a checklist of compensation. H.I.J.O.S. are the inheritors of the political culture written in blood by San Carlistas.

When the guilty verdict against Ríos Montt for genocide and crimes against humanity was vacated, H.I.J.O.S. posted the following words on their blog: "Although we denounce and regret the ruling in favor of military-oligar-chy impunity, we reaffirm the memory of the Ixil People, who have made clear to the whole world the barbarism to which they were subjected. More than a failure [*derrota*], this can breathe life into our ongoing struggle of justice in honor of the memory and life of the Ixil People [*Pueblo*]." The statement con-cluded, "We do not forget, we do not pardon, we do not reconcile." This ongo-ing struggle of justice resists the spirit of resolution that sometimes surrounds truth and reconciliation commissions (TRCs) and trials. It does not settle accounts. Instead, H.I.J.O.S. argues for urgent action and a future that never fully escapes the past. Their recent "Memory's Attack" art campaign makes this point in a series of images featuring a young barefoot boy urinating into an Army helmet. One caption reads: "Impunity, I will end you" and contin-ues, "They did not kill the seed . . . we are the REBELLION [*REVELDIA*]." By spelling rebellion [*rebeldía*] with a "v" [*reveldía*], H.I.J.O.S. connects their actions to revolutionary struggles in the past and future. H.I.J.O.S. becomes the generative and diffuse future, the seed that multiplies across Guatemala

City's streets, walls, highways, and into the countryside.[16] The punctuation that pierces the group's name invokes the bullet holes in the bodies of their parents and family members; it may also invoke this persistent seed. H.I.J.O.S. insists on the imperative to remember and to remain provoked.

It is difficult to gauge to what degree H.I.J.O.S. has challenged impunity or changed the meaning of justice, but it has intractably altered the urban landscape. A few kilometers away from the university on La Sexta in the city's Centro Histórico, the group's murals, graffiti, and stencils cover walls that political funerals once passed. Young people continue to use these spaces to challenge local, governmental, and international power and to reclaim moral authority for the guerrilla and the reformist left. A plaque commemorating Castañeda de León is preserved in glass on the spot where he died in the entrance to Pasaje Rubio. Other plaques mark kidnappings in small parks throughout Zone 1. Some buildings are marked by denunciations against military commanders and former presidents, others with the faces of the disappeared. Castañeda de León's home is always marked. Stenciled portraits of Pérez Molina and Ríos Montt were common in 2013 and 2014 on La Sexta. In the summer of 2016, new graffiti placed the familiar identification photographs of the disappeared with a heart and two ears of corn over a vivid green patch of grass. When they are painted over, H.I.J.O.S. returns to mark the space for memory once more. More than once, I have seen fresh coats of paint applied around graffiti, suggesting that the home's owners actively preserved the youth's memory work.

For years and years, H.I.J.O.S.'s hallmark has been black and white identification photographs. They are Xeroxed and then pasted by the hundreds onto walls to haunt pedestrians on their daily routes north and south of Central Park. The faces of the disappeared remain frozen in their youth. In many cases, their children have now outgrown them. Guatemala is regenerating, but the *desaparecidos* refuse to disappear.

H.I.J.O.S. returns us to the spaces of student nationalism and to political claims made in the affective registers of responsibility, freedom, and dignity. Their calls for justice once more scatter the seeds of Manuel Galich, Mario López Larrave, Oliverio Castañeda de León, Saúl Osorio Paz, and the other students and faculty who gave their lives to cultivate a better Guatemala. The historical memory of San Carlistas provides fertile soil in which these seeds can germinate. If the recent repression of environmental activists in Guatemala and elsewhere in Central America is any indication, then this invocation of the land points us to the next field of battle.

NOTES

INTRODUCTION

1. Florencia Mallon, *Peasant and Nation: The Making of Postcolonial Mexico and Peru* (Berkeley: University of California Press, 1995), 4. Mallon's recentering of Latin America in nationalism theory is crucial to the intellectual work of this book. Here, nationalism serves a range of political projects, from law making to protest to land reform. Of course the whole bibliography on nationalism is too vast to capture here. Of particular relevance to my conception of student nationalism are Mallon; Benedict Anderson, *Imagined Communities: Reflections on the Origins and Spread of Nationalism* (London: Verso, 1983); Eric Hobsbawm and Terence Ranger, eds. *The Invention of Tradition* (Cambridge: Cambridge University Press, 1983); Charles Walker, *Smoldering Ashes: Cuzco and the Creation of Republican Peru, 1780–1840* (Durham, NC: Duke University Press).

2. Juan José Arévalo, *Discurso al asumir la Presidencia de la República* (Guatemala City: Tipografía Nacional, 1945), 237.

3. John Tate Lanning, *The University in the Kingdom of Guatemala* (Ithaca, NY: Cornell University Press, 1955), 49.

4. Lanning, 189.

5. Ibid., 193.

6. For more on Flores, see Martha Few, *For All of Humanity* (Tucson: University of Arizona Press, 2015).

7. Ibid., 204. See also Lanning, *The Eighteenth-Century Enlightenment in the University of San Carlos of Guatemala* (Ithaca, NY: Cornell University Press, 1956) and Jorge Mario Garcia Laguardia, "La Universidad de San Carlos de Guatemala: Perfil histórico y proceso de su autonomía" *Anuario de Estudios Centroamericanos* 4 (1978): 155–62.

8. See José Santos Hernández Pérez, *La Gaceta de Guatemala: Un espacio para la difusión del conocimiento científico (1797–1804)* (Mexico City: UNAM, 2015); Carlos Martínez Durán, *Las Ciencias médicas en Guatemala* (Guatemala City: Editorial Universitaria, 1964), 377; Jordana Dym, "Conceiving Central America: A

Bourbon Public in the Gaceta de Guatemala (1797–1807)" in *Enlightened Reform in Southern Europe and Its Atlantic Colonies, c. 1750–1850*, ed. Gabriel Paquette (Burlington, VT: Ashgate, 2009). On the colonial Enlightenment, see Bianca Premo, *The Enlightenment on Trial: Ordinary Litigants and Colonialism in the Spanish Empire* (Oxford: Oxford University Press, 2017).

9. Historian Virgilio Álvarez Aragón writes, "we have no record of pronouncements, or direct or indirect actions that students or professors have taken in a collective manner or in the name of their group to demand or oppose Independence" (Álvarez Aragón, *Conventos, Aulas y Trincheras*, vol. 1 (Guatemala City: FLACSO, 2002: 85–87). The bibliography on the 1812 constitution and Spanish colonials' responses to it is vast; see Jeremy Adelman, *Sovereignty and Revolution in the Iberian Atlantic* (Princeton, NJ: Princeton University Press, 2006); Manuel Chust Calero and Ivana Frasquet Miguel, *La Patria no se hizo sola: Las Revoluciones de Independencias iberoamericanas* (Madrid: Sílex Ediciones, 2012); Scott Eastman, *Preaching Spanish Nationalism across the Hispanic Atlantic, 1759–1823* (Baton Rouge: Louisiana State University Press, 2012); Francois-Xavier Guerra, *Modernidad e Independencias: Ensayos sobre las Revoluciones Hispánicas* (Madrid: Ediciones Encuentro, 2009); Tamar Herzog, *Defining Nations: Immigrants and Citizens in Early Modern Spain and Spanish America* (New Haven, CT: Yale University Press, 2011); Jaime Rodríguez, *The Independence of Spanish America* (Cambridge: Cambridge University Press, 1998); David Sartorius, "Of Exceptions and Afterlives: The Long History of the 1812 Constitution in Cuba," in *The Rise of Constitutional Government in the Iberian Atlantic World: The Impact of the Cádiz Constitution of 1812*, Scott Eastman and Natalia Sobrevilla Perea, eds. (Tuscaloosa: University of Alabama Press, 2015).

10. J. Antonio Villacorta C., *Historia de la República de Guatemala, 1821–1921* (Guatemala City: n.p., 1960), 448–51.

11. Álvarez Aragón, 93–94.

12. For a discussion of Soto, see Lanning, 1956 and Hubert J. Miller, "Positivism and Educational Reforms in Guatemala, 1871–1885." *Journal of Church and State* 8, no. 2 (1966): 251–63.

13. Nancy Leys Stepan, *The Hour of Eugenics* (Ithaca, NY: Cornell University Press, 1991), 73.

14. *La República* was founded in 1871 and *Diario de Centro América* in 1888. See Álvarez Aragón, 129–30.

15. Margarita Silva H., "Salvador Mendieta y la Unión Centroamericana," in *Pensar el antiimperialismo: Ensayos de la historia intelectual latinoamericano*, ed. Alexandra Pita González and Carlos Marichal (Mexico City: Colegio de Mexico, 2012).

16. Álvarez Aragón, 170–71.

17. Asturias, of course, became a Nobel laureate in literature. Vela was a highly regarded essayist and journalist and became director of *El Imparcial*, a newspaper founded in 1922 by many of his generation's brightest literary lights. Espinosa Altamirano, Wyld Ospina, Brañas, and Samayoa Chinchilla also contributed to *El Imparcial* and wrote novels, essays, and poetry. Asturias, García Granados, and

Samayoa Chinchilla held ministerial and diplomatic posts across several administrations.

18. Marta Casaús Arzú, "Los élites intelectuales y la generación de 20 en Guatemala: Su visión del indio y imaginario de nación," in Casaús Arzú and Oscar Peláez Almengor, eds. *Historia intelectual de Guatemala* (Guatemala City: CEUR, 2001), 6, 11.

19. While in the broadest sense, university autonomy has been the touchstone of the struggle for freedom to exercise freethinking in research and teaching in the twentieth century, its root is in medieval European universities and the Enlightenment struggle for scientific reason apart from theology. See Jorge Mario García Laguardia, *Universidad y política en América Latina: consideraciones críticas.* (Mexico City: Centro de Estudios sobre la Universidad, UNAM, 1982); Hanns-Albert Steger, *Las universidades en el desarrollo social de la América Latina* (Mexico City: Fondo de Cultura Económica, 1974); Leslie Bethell, *Ideas and Ideologies in 20th Century Latin America* (Cambridge: Cambridge University Press, 1996).

20. Casaus Arzú, "Los élites intelectuales," 36–37, 48–49.

21. Vasconcelos advised Asturias to study indigeneity for his thesis research, though they arrived at different conclusions. Where Vasconcelos championed *mestizaje* for Mexico, Asturias cautioned that without European immigration, Guatemala's European-descendent population was too small and its indigenous population too uncivilized to effectively carry out the task. Asturias's 1923 thesis, "Sociología guatemalteca: el problema social del indio," understood Mayans to be completely antithetical to progress and civility. He advocated immigration of people from Switzerland, Belgium, Holland, and regions of present-day Germany. Importantly, his view on Mayans seemed to have changed dramatically over the course of his lifetime; he discovered a passion for Maya aesthetics, at the least, while studying in Europe. For their part, Vela and Espinosa Altamirano viewed *mestizaje* with suspicion and promoted the foundation of institutes to study and preserve indigenous culture, especially agricultural technology, language, hygiene, and habits of daily life. See Joshua Lund, *The Mestizo State: Reading Race in Modern Mexico* (Minneapolis: University of Minnesota Press, 2012), 79.

22. See Nelson, *A Finger in the Wound: Body Politics in Quincentennial Guatemala* (Berkeley: University of California Press, 1999); John Watanabe, "Unimagining the Maya: Anthropologists, Others, and the Inescapable Hubris of Authorship," *Bulletin of Latin American Research* 14, no. 1, Special Issue: Shifting Frontiers: Historical Transformations of Identities in Latin America (Jan. 1995): 25–45.

23. Álvarez Aragón, *Conventos, Aulas y Trincheras,* 174–75, 229.

24. Greg Grandin, *The Last Colonial Massacre: Latin America in the Cold War* (Chicago: University of Chicago Press, 2004), 49.

25. The first mention of extension programming that I have located in Latin America is from a student congress held in Mexico City in 1921. Its predecessor, the normal school, sought to provide less wealthy citizens with basic instruction, teacher training, and a nationalist positivist curriculum; see Carlos González Orellana, *Historia de la educación en Guatemala* (Guatemala City: Editorial Universitaria, 1980).

26. Gabriela Mistral, "La unidad de la cultura," in Licia Fiol-Matta, *Queer Mother for the Nation: The State and Gabriela Mistral* (Minneapolis: University of Minnesota Press, 2002), 174.

27. Fiol-Matta, 174.

28. Brian P. Owensby, *Intimate Ironies: Modernity and the Making of Middle-Class Lives in Brazil* (Stanford, CA: Stanford University Press, 1999), 4, 7.

29. This is not at all unlike Marx's argument in *The Class Struggles in France*, where one function of the middle class was to serve as the ideological representatives of the bourgeoisie. Marx, *The Class Struggles in France*, in *Karl Marx: Selected Writings*, ed. David McLellan (Oxford: Oxford University Press, 1977), 286–99.

30. See A. Ricardo López, "Conscripts of Democracy: The Formation of a Professional Middle Class in Bogotá during the 1950s and early 1960s," in López and Weinstein, *The Making of the Middle Class* on a similar process in Bogotá in the late 1950s to early 1960s.

31. As Joan W. Scott urged historians to remember that "words, like the ideas and things they are meant to signify, have a history," so too may historians see age as a useful category of historical analysis. Scott's challenge, one that is now more than three decades old, demands that we pay attention to the words that signified youth; Scott, "Gender: A Useful Category of Historical Analysis," *American Historical Review* 91, no. 5 (Dec. 1986): 1053–75. In an inaugural essay for the *Journal of the History of Childhood and Youth*, Steven Mintz made a similar observation; see Mintz, "Reflections on Age as a Category of Historical Analysis," *Journal of the History of Childhood and Youth* 1, no. 1 (Winter 2008): 91–94.

32. Gisela Gellert and Julio César Pinto Soria, *Ciudad de Guatemala: dos estudios sobre su evolución urbana* (Guatemala City: CEUR, 1990), 12–13.

33. Frederick Douglass Opie, *Black Labor Migration in Caribbean Guatemala, 1882–1923* (Gainesville: University Press of Florida, 2009), 1–5.

34. Gellert, 15–16.

35. Arturo Taracena, "Estado de los altos, indígenas, y régimen conservador, Guatemala, 1838–1851." *Anuario de Estudios Centroamericanos* 19, no. 1 (1993).

36. Grandin, *The Last Colonial Massacre*, 5; Walter LaFeber, *Inevitable Revolutions* (New York: W.W. Norton, 1993), 78, 113–14.

37. In 1940, the population of Guatemala City was about 186,000; in 1950, 284,276; and in 1973, the population increased to about 700,554. From 1973 to 1987, the city's population jumped to over 1.6 million. *Censos VII and VIII de población of 1964 and 1973*, Dirección General de Estadística, Tomo I in Gellert, 78; Ciencia y Tecnología Para Guatemala (CITGUA), *Asentamientos precarios y pobladores en Guatemala* (Guatemala City: CITGUA, 1991) in O'Neill and Thomas, "Securing the City: An Introduction," in *Securing the City: Neoliberalism, Space, and Insecurity in Postwar Guatemala* (Durham, NC: Duke University Press, 2011), 6.

38. Gellert, 22–25.

39. Ibid.

40. One sees the weight of this precarity in the hunched backs and withdrawn expressions of passersby. When they do stay in Guatemala City, many scholars

remain close to Zones 10 and 14. Sprinkled with police patrols, high-rise apartments, sports bars, sushi restaurants, Spanish- and North American-owned retail stores, and picturesque promenades, these neighborhoods resemble Miami more than Guatemala. At Oakland Mall, they can shop at Nine West, L'Occitane, Zara, M.A.C., Payless, GNC, and Adidas and sip Starbucks lattes after lunch at Taco Bell or Pizza Hut. The even more upscale Plaza Fontabella offers designs by Carolina Herrera, Faber-Castell, Michael Kors, and Maserati, and bespoke tailoring by Lanificio di Livenza and Saúl E. Mendez. But even those who avoid these zones are confined by safety concerns, real and imagined. Travelers are discouraged from staying in hotels in Zone 1, where most of the events detailed in this book took place. Adapting to this state of perpetual alarm, intrepid historians can conduct research in the city's many archives fairly quickly, owing to generous assistance from archivists and permissive rules on document photography. A handful of downtown guesthouses provide adequate lodging and companionship for the most adventurous researchers, human rights advocates, and journalists who are willing to stay in Zone 1 and walk a few blocks from the hotel to the archive and back. This bleak account describes a state of affairs much improved in recent years.

41. "Guatemala: Country Specific Information," Bureau of Consular Affairs of the U.S. State Department. http://travel.state.gov/travel/cis_pa_tw/cis/cis_1129 .html. Accessed March 22, 2010. According to this website, safety has remained at the "critical" level since 2010.

42. See similar relationships between the capital city, university, and countryside in Victoria Langland, *Speaking of Flowers: Student Movements and the Making and Remembering of 1968 in Military Brazil* (Durham, NC, 2013); Jaime Pensado, *Rebel Mexico: Student Unrest and Authoritarian Political Culture During the Long Sixties* (Stanford, CA: Stanford University Press, 2013); Louise Walker, *Waking from the Dream* (Stanford, CA: Stanford University Press, 2013); and Valeria Manzano, *The Age of Youth in Argentina* (Chapel Hill: University of North Carolina Press, 2014).

43. I am following a certain understanding of social class explained best by Karl Marx in "The Eighteenth Brumaire of Louis Bonaparte." Here, class exists not when a group of people share merely the "economic conditions of existence," but when they have formed a distinct mode of life, with particular culture and interests that are different from and even antagonistic to those of other classes. Class is formed and constantly reformed when there is community, national bond, and political organization. Marx, "The Eighteenth Brumaire of Louis Bonaparte," in *Surveys from Exile: Political Writings Volume 2* (New York: Penguin, 1973), 124. On the middle class across the breadth of Marx's writings, see Bertell Ollman, "Marx's Use of 'Class,'" *American Journal of Sociology* 73, no. 5 (Mar. 1968): 573–80. See also Marx and Engels, *The Germany Ideology* in *Karl Marx: Selected Writings*, 176; Friedrich Engels: *Preface to The Condition of the Working Class in England: From Personal Observation and Authentic Sources*, in Karl Marx & Friedrich Engels *Collected Works, Vol. 4* (Moscow: International Publishers, 1975), 304.

44. LaFeber, 93, 326n8.

45. "Registro universitario de estudiantes," *Boletín Universitario*, 1° de febrero de 1950, Año IV No. 1. Centro de Investigaciones Regionales de Mesoamérica (CIRMA).

46. Eduardo Elena, *Dignifying Argentina: Peronism, Citizenship, and Mass Consumption* (Pittsburgh: University of Pittsburgh Press, 2011); Bryan McCann, *Hello Hello Brazil: Popular Music in the Making of Modern Brazil* (Durham, NC: Duke University Press, 2004); Eric Zolov, *Refried Elvis; The Rise of the Mexican Counterculture* (Berkeley: University of California Press, 1999); Matthew Karush, "Populism, Melodrama, and the Market," in *The New Cultural History of Peronism*, ed. Matthew Karush and Oscar Chamosa (Durham, NC: Duke University Press, 2010); Karush, *Culture of Class: Radio and Cinema in the Making of a Divided Argentina, 1920–1946* (Durham, NC: Duke University Press, 2012).

47. Among the many books on youth popular culture and resistance, see especially Mary Kay Vaughan, *Portrait of a Young Painter: Pepe Zúñiga and Mexico City's Rebel Generation* (Durham, NC: Duke University Press, 2014); Luis Alvarez, *The Power of the Zoot* (Berkeley: University of California Press, 2008), Rob Latham, *Consuming Youth: Vampires, Cyborgs, and the Culture of Consumption* (Chicago: University of Chicago Press, 2002); Andreana Clay, *The Hip-Hop Generation Fights Back* (New York: New York University Press, 2012); Jeff Chang and DJ Kool Herc, *Can't Stop Won't Stop: A History of the Hip-Hop Generation* (New York: Picador, 2005); Raquel Z. Rivera, Wayne Marshall, and Deborah Pacini Hernandez, *Reggaeton* (Durham, NC: Duke University Press, 2009); Jessica K. Taft, *Rebel Girls: Youth Activism and Social Change Across the Americas* (New York: New York University Press, 2010); Imani Perry, *Prophets of the Hood: Politics and Poetics in Hip Hop* (Durham, NC: Duke University Press, 2004); Sujatha Fernandes, *Close to the Edge: In Search of the Global Hip Hop Generation* (London: Verso, 2011); and Hisham D. Aidi, *Rebel Music: Race, Empire, and the New Muslim Youth Culture* (New York: Pantheon, 2014).

48. On the political behavior and impact of the middle classes, see Patrick Barr-Melej, *Reforming Chile: Cultural Politics, Nationalism, and the Rise of the Middle Class* (Chapel Hill: University of North Carolina Press, 2001); Lauren Derby, *The Dictator's Seduction: Politics and the Popular Imagination in the Era of Trujillo* (Durham, NC: Duke University Press, 2009); Walker, *Waking from the Dream*; and chapters by López and García-Bryce in López and Weinstein, *The Making of the Middle Class*. Louise Walker's *Waking from the Dream* is an outstanding model of political history of university students and the middle class. She argues that the Mexican middle class was a key actor in the arrival of neoliberalism and procedural democracy, signaling both the success and the decline of the Partido Revolucionario Institucional (PRI). For Walker, the middle class is "a set of material conditions, a state of mind, and a political discourse." Yet Walker's turn toward delimiting the Mexican middle class in terms of income and profession distracts attention from the ongoing processes of class formation. After all, the middle class becomes intelligible through political rationalities and methodologies, which must adapt to changing geopolitical and local contexts.

49. See Daniel J. Walkowitz, *Working with Class: Social Workers and the Politics of Middle-Class Identity* (Chapel Hill: University of North Carolina Press, 1999), xiii–xvii, 1–12, 236; Owensby, 2.

50. López and Weinstein, 21.

51. López and Weinstein, "Introduction," in López and Weinstein, 163; Owensby, 4–10; Simon Gunn, "Between Modernity and Backwardness: The Case of the English Middle Class," in López and Weinstein, 58–74.

52. López and Weinstein, "Introduction," 6–7.

53. Owensby, 6; see also López and Weinstein, "Introduction."

54. López and Weinstein, "Introduction," 1–3. The volume provides ample evidence of middle classes in Africa, South Asia, North America, Latin America, and the Middle East since the mid-nineteenth century.

55. Ibid., 7–9.

56. Of course, the most famous work on class formation is *The Making of the English Working Class*, where E. P. Thompson argues how class relations led to the formation of class discourse, and class discourse in turn created class movements, characterized by formal structures, but also constantly shaped by interpersonal encounters and cultural productions. For Thompson, social class was "something which happens in human relationships" and "patterns in their relationships, their ideas, their institutions." Here, student nationalism is a class discourse that was transformed by students' experiences and articulated in their institutions, clubs, newspapers, memoirs, and other writings; Thompson, *Making of the English Working Class* (New York: Vintage Books, 1966). See also the Preface to "A Contribution to the Critique of Political Economy" in *Karl Marx: Selected Writings*, 426; William H. Sewell, "How Classes Are Made: Critical Reflections on EP Thompson's Theory of Working Class Formation," in *E. P. Thompson: Critical Perspectives*, ed. Harvey J. Kaye and Keith McClelland (Philadelphia: Temple University Press, 1990).

57. This recalls the lively debate between Thompson and Raymond Williams on class formation. I will not reprise it here; see Raymond Williams, *Marxism and Literature* (Oxford: Oxford University Press, 1977), 132; E. P. Thompson, "The Long Revolution Part I," *New Left Review* 1, no. 9 (May–June 1961): 24–33; E. P. Thompson, "The Long Revolution Part II," *New Left Review* 1, no. 10 (July–August 1961): 34–39. Although Williams and San Carlistas were part of the same New Left, I have found no record of students having read Williams, nor have I found in Williams an account of the Latin American left, although *Marxism and Literature* (1977) sought to develop the idea of a structure of feeling in light of Williams's subsequent break with the New Left and the global student protests of 1968.

58. On race and nationalism, see Stuart Hall, "Race, Articulation, and Societies Structured in Dominance," in *Sociological Theories: Race and Colonialism* (Paris: UNESCO, 1980), reprinted in Philomena Essed and David Theo Goldberg, eds. *Race Critical Theories* (Oxford: Blackwell, 2002); Balibar, "Racism and Nationalism," in Wallerstein and Balibar, *Race, Nation, Class*; David Kazanjian, *The Brink of Freedom* (Durham, NC: Duke University Press, 2016); Mallon, *Peasant and*

Nation; and Kathryn Burns, "Unfixing Race" and the many other tremendous essays in *Histories of Race and Racism: The Andes and Mesoamerica from Colonial Times to the Present*, ed. Laura Gotkowitz (Durham, NC: Duke University Press, 2011); Ada Ferrer, *Insurgent Cuba: Race, Nation, and Revolution, 1868–1898* (Chapel Hill: University of North Carolina Press, 1999). On the exclusions of liberal citizenship, see Etienne Balibar, "The Nation Form: History and Ideology," in *Race, Nation, Class: Ambiguous Identities*, ed. Immanuel Wallerstein and Etienne Balibar (London: Verso, 1991); and Etienne Balibar, "'Rights of Man' and 'Rights of the Citizen': The Modern Dialectic of Equality and Freedom" in Balibar, *Masses, Classes, Ideas: Studies on Politics and Philosophy Before and After Marx* (New York: Routledge, 1994). Occasionally in the book, I reference Louis Althusser's concept of the Ideological State Apparatus (ISA), which posits that the school plays a key role in the subjection of individuals to the State's ruling ideology and the subjectification of individuals as "good subjects." See Althusser, "Ideology and Ideological State Apparatuses (Notes Toward an Investigation)," in *Lenin and Philosophy and Other Essays* (New York: Monthly Review Press, 1971), 132.

59. Guatemala's uneasy racial nationhood has been troubled from the very start by its own categorizations. One very obscurantist but prevailing belief is that Guatemalans are either indigenous or not. Another national story of racialization holds that race unfolds along a ladino–indigenous spectrum. But what exactly *ladino* means remains unclear and continues to be seen as merely an absence of indigeneity rather than a racial identity in itself. Making matters even more confusing, in attempts to clarify the meaning of *ladino*, many scholars have simply, even parenthetically, called them "nonindigenous." See Charles R. Hale, "Mistados, Cholos, and the Negation of Identity in the Guatemalan Highlands," in Gotkowitz, *Histories of Race and Racism*, 254–77; Arturo Taracena Arriola, "From Assimilation to Segregation: Guatemala, 1800–1944," in *Histories of Race and Racism*, 95–112.

60. Cazali Ávila, "Síntesis Histórica de la Universidad de San Carlos de Guatemala," 56.

61. This may actually be a conservative number. In *Organizing and Repression*, Paul Kobrak writes that the 1954 enrollment counted 8,000 students and cites Augusto Cazali Ávila, "Síntesis Histórica," 56 and Jesus García Añoveros, "El 'caso Guatemala' (junio de 1954): La Universidad y el campesinado," *Alero* (Jan/Feb. 1978), 174. Kobrak, *Organizing and Repression in the University of San Carlos, Guatemala, 1944 to 1996* (Washington, DC: American Association for the Advancement of Science, 1999). The enrollment statistics that I use in the text were published in the official 1964 statistical bulletin, *Boletín Estadístico Universitaria*, available at the Archivo General de la Universidad de San Carlos (AGUSAC).

62. A word of caution is due. Guatemalan censuses are notoriously inaccurate; see W. George Lovell, *Conquest and Survival in Colonial Guatemala* (Montreal: McGill-Queen's University Press, 2005), 232n40 and Charles R. Hale, *Más Que un Indio (More Than an Indian): Racial Ambivalence and the Paradox of Neoliberal Multiculturalism in Guatemala* (Guatemala City: AVANCSO, 2006).

63. Departamento de Censos y Encuestas, Dirección General de Estadística, *Censo de Población de Guatemala de 1964* (Guatemala City: Ministerio de Economía, 1964); Dirección General de Estadística, *Sexto Censo General de Población, 1950* (Guatemala City: Ministerio de Economía, 1957).

64. *El Estudiante Universitario: Progreso Académico de los Estudiantes de la Universidad de San Carlos*, Informe Personal de la IIME (Guatemala City: IIME, 1964) AGUSAC; Consejo Superior Universitario Centroamericano, *El sistema educativo en Nicaragua* (San Jose, Costa Rica: n.p., 1965).

65. John W. Sherman, "The Mexican 'Miracle' and its Collapse," in *The Oxford History of Mexico*, ed. William H. Beezley and Michael C. Meyer (Oxford: Oxford University Press, 2010), 559.

66. From ethnographic interviews conducted in Chimaltenango in the late 1990s, Charles R. Hale has noted the difficulty that some Guatemalans have had with identifying positively with the term *ladino*; see Hale, "Mistados, Cholos." Of course anthropologists of Guatemala (and critical race theorists in general) have for decades demonstrated the political consequence of discourses of racial difference that see a dominant group as "nonraced." See Cheryl I. Harris, "Whiteness as Property," *Harvard Law Review* 106, no. 8 (June 1993): 1710–91 and Ruth Frankenberg, ed. *Displacing Whiteness: Essays in Social and Cultural Criticism* (Durham, NC: Duke University Press, 1997). Thanks to David Kazanjian for the Harris citation.

67. Rufino Guerra Cortave, *El Imparcial,* November 8, 1944, cited by Richard N. Adams, "Ethnic Images and Strategies in 1944," in *Guatemalan Indians and the State: 1540–1988*, ed. Carol A. Smith (Austin: University of Texas Press, 1991), 23.

68. USAC Departamento de Registro y Estadística, *Boletín Estadístico Universitario*, Año 15, 1976. AGUSAC.

69. USAC, Departamento de Registro y Estadística, *Cifras Estadísticas*, 01–99. AGUSAC.

70. Francisco Barbosa, "Insurgent Youth: Culture and Memory in the Sandinista Student Movement" (PhD diss, Indiana University, 2006), 37; Richard A. Haggarty, ed. *El Salvador: A Country Study* (Washington, DC: Government Printing Office for the Library of Congress, 1988); Tim Merrill, ed. *Honduras: A Country Study* (Washington, DC: Government Printing Office for the Library of Congress, 1993). See also Martin Carnoy and Joel Samoff, eds. *Education and Social Transition in the Third World* (Princeton, NJ: Princeton University Press, 1990), 320.

71. "Revolución de 44, Inter Cátedras" (Guatemala City: Dirección de Extensión Universitaria de la USAC, 1994). CIRMA; USAC, Departamento de Registro y Estadística, *Cifras Estadísticas*, 01–99. AGUSAC.

72. *Censo de Población de Guatemala de 1964*. See also USAC Departamento de Registro y Estadística, *Carácterísticas socio-econónicos de estudiantes de primer ingreso*, No. 3 (1971/1973) and *Estadísticas de graduados, 1972–1974*. AGUSAC.

73. Consejo Superior Universitario, "Política y Plan de Equidad de Género en la Educación superior, 2006–2014." February 2008. AGUSAC.

74. Since the end of the civil war, the number of identities that biologize class distinction, including *blancos, criollos, fresas, gente decente, shumos, mucos,* and

choleros, have proliferated; see Jorge Ramón González Ponciano, "The Shumo Challenge," in *War by Other Means*, ed. Carlota McAllister and Diane M. Nelson (Durham, NC: Duke University Press, 2013), 307–29.

75. An exciting and growing body of work has shown the power of discourses of, by, and about youth *as such* well before the 1960s. See Manzano, *The Age of Youth in Argentina*, 13; Nara Milanich, *Children of Fate* (Durham, NC: Duke University Press, 2010); Luisa Passerini, "Youth as a Metaphor of Social Change: Fascist Italy and America in the 1950s," in *A History of Youth People*, vol. 2, ed. Giovanni Levi and Jean-Claude Schmitt (Cambridge, MA: Harvard University Press, 1997); Philip G. Altbach, *Student Politics in Bombay* (Bombay: Asia Publishing House, 1968); Eric Ashby, *Universities: British, Indian, African*. Cambridge, MA: Harvard University Press, 1966; Craig Calhoun, *Neither Gods nor Emperors: Students and the Struggle for Democracy in China* (Berkeley: University of California Press, 1995); Donald Emerson, ed. *Students and Politics in Developing Countries* (New York: Praeger, 1968); Chhaya Das Gupta, *Youth and Student Movements in Bengal: A Historical Survey, 1919–1946* (Calcutta: Firma KLM, 1995); William John Hanna, *University Students and African Politics* (New York: Africana Press, 1975); John Israel, *Student Nationalism in China, 1927–1937* (Stanford, CA: Stanford University Press, 1966); Anita Casavantes Bradford, *The Revolution is For the Children: The Politics of Childhood in Havana and Miami, 1959–1962* (Chapel Hill: University of North Carolina Press, 2014).

76. I am skeptical of an archival reading practice that would assume that a historian could ascertain what students *meant*, as if the "evidence of experience" were available to be read. Joan W. Scott, "The Evidence of Experience," in *Feminists Theorize the Political*, ed. Judith Butler and Joan W. Scott (New York: Routledge, 1992), 22–40.

77. In fact, this book is preceded by two exhaustive Spanish-language monographs on the university, the two-volume history *Conventos, aulas y trincheras: universidad y movimiento estudiantil en Guatemala* by Virgilio Álvarez Aragón and Augusto Cazali Ávila's three-volume *Historia de la Universidad de San Carlos de Guatemala*. Yet both of these texts take as their primary task the documentation of university administration, curriculum, and student life. This book, on the contrary, documents the impact of students well beyond the walls of USAC.

78. There is a new and growing body of work on middle class formation outside of the university in the many neighborhoods and professions that emerged in Guatemala City in the later twentieth century. No doubt this research will reveal how very different the experiences and social spaces of Guatemalan youth can be, despite sharing geographical space. Manuela Camus, *La colonial Primero de Julio y la "clase media emergente"* (Guatemala City: FLACSO, 2005); Deborah Levenson, *Hacer la Juventud* (Guatemala City: AVANCSO, 2004); Levenson, *Adiós Niño: The Gangs of Guatemala City and the Politics of Death* (Durham, NC: Duke University Press, 2013), 1–20.

79. Ministerio de Gobernación, *Constitución de la República de Guatemala decretado por la asamblea constituyente en 11 de marzo de 1945* (Guatemala City: s.n., 1948); Julie Gibbings, "*Mestizaje* in the Age of Fascism: Interracial Sex, Germans, and Q'eqchi' Mayas in Alta Verapaz, Guatemala" *German History* 34, no. 2 (2016).

CHAPTER ONE

1. Manuel Galich, *Del pánico al ataque* (Guatemala City: Tipografía Nacional, 1949), 153.
2. Hilda Morales Trujillo, "Mario López Larrave," in *Por el delito de pensar*, ed. Rosa Sánchez del Valle (Guatemala City: Fundación para la Democracia Manuel Colom Argueta, 1999), 77.
3. Roberto Díaz Castillo, *Las redes de la memoria* (Guatemala City: FLACSO, 1998), 35.
4. Brian P. Owensby, *Intimate Ironies: Modernity and the Making of Middle-Class Lives in Brazil* (Stanford, CA: Stanford University Press, 1999), 3–4.
5. The Hemeroteca Nacional has conspicuously scant newspaper records of 1944 and 1945.
6. *Del pánico al ataque* has been reprinted several times and continues to influence both San Carlistas' own sense of their history and North American historians studying the revolution, as it is cited in every monograph on the period.
7. Ana Silvia Monzón M., "La Perspectiva de Género en el Currículum Universitario," *Mujeres y Universidad*, 1, no. 1 (November 2005): 20.
8. Section IV, Article 80. Ministerio de Gobernación, *Constitución de la República de Guatemala decretado por la asamblea constituyente en 11 de marzo de 1945* (Guatemala City: s.n., 1948).
9. Richard N. Adams, *Crucifixion by Power* (Austin: University of Texas Press, 1970), 174.
10. Greg Grandin, *Blood of Guatemala* (Durham, NC: Duke University Press, 2000), 137. See also Kenneth J. Grieb, *Guatemalan Caudillo, the regime of Jorge Ubico: Guatemala, 1931–1944* (Athens: Ohio University Press, 1979).
11. Piero Gleijeses, *Shattered Hope: the Guatemalan Revolution and the United States, 1944–1954* (Princeton, NJ: Princeton University Press, 1991), 13; Jim Handy, *Gift of the Devil* (Boston: South End Press, 1984), 52, 98.
12. Indigenous elites utilized this access to promote their own vision of national indigenous identity, see Grandin, *Blood of Guatemala*.
13. Greg Grandin, *The Last Colonial Massacre* (Chicago: University of Chicago Press, 2004), 48–49; Deborah Levenson, *Hacer la juventud* (Guatemala City: AVANCSO, 2005), 7, 17–18.
14. See Aviva Chomsky and Aldo A. Lauria-Santiago, *Identity and Struggle at the Margins of the Nation-State* (Durham, NC: Duke University Press, 1998); William Roseberry, Lowell Gudmundson, and Mario Samper Kutschbach, eds., *Coffee, Society, and Power in Latin America* (Baltimore: Johns Hopkins University Press, 1995).
15. Junta Revolucionaria, *Decreto 12 de la Junta Revolucionaria del Gobierno*, November 9, 1944. AGUSAC.
16. Galich, *Del pánico al ataque*, 238–39.
17. *Boletín Universitario*, Año I, No. 8, November 1, 1947. AGUSAC.
18. Galich, 231–32.

19. *Faculty* (*Facultad*) refers to an administrative unit of the university, akin to a department.

20. Galich, 152.

21. *El testamento*, Uli Stelzner and Thomas Walther, dir. (2002; Guatemala/Germany: ISKA e.V., 2002), DVD.

22. The idiom "pulling the wool over one's eyes" may be a reference to wigs worn by judges and lawmakers in the seventeenth and eighteenth centuries, though I cannot find a credible reference to support this common understanding.

23. *Boletín Universitario*, Año II, No. 11, August 1, 1949. AGUSAC.

24. Galich, 149.

25. Ibid., 154–55.

26. Ibid., 156.

27. Virgilio Álvarez Aragón, *Conventos, aulas y trincheras: Universidad y movimiento estudiantil en Guatemala: la ilusión por conservar* (Guatemala City: FLACSO, 2002), 221; Gleijeses, *Shattered Hope*, 22; Beatriz Palomo de Lewin, "La Universidad de la década de 1920–1930 y durante el régimen de Jorge Ubico (1931–1944)," *Revista Estudios* 6 (1975): 210.

28. Compare this to Brazil's *União Nacional dos Estudantes* (National Union of Students); see Victoria Langland, *Speaking of Flowers: Student Movements and the Making and Remembering of 1968 in Military Brazil* (Durham, NC: Duke University Press, 2013), 22, 34–36, 58–59.

29. Álvarez Aragón, 222–23.

30. Ibid., 222; Galich, 228–29; AEU, "Manifiesto," January 26, 1946. Centro de Investigaciones Regionales de Centroamérica (CIRMA).

31. Álvarez Aragón, 222.

32. Galich, 264.

33. Galich, 232; Álvarez Aragón, 221.

34. Galich, 249–50.

35. Augusto Cazali Ávila, "Síntesis Histórica de la Universidad de San Carlos de Guatemala," in *Publicación conmemorativa tricentenario, 1676–1976* (Guatemala City: Editorial Universitaria, 1976), 56.

36. Galich, 253.

37. Ibid., 266.

38. Ibid., 154.

39. Galich supposes that students were reticent to join out of suspicion, antipathy, or laziness; fear of being associated with a political group; or because some did actually support Ubico; Galich, 261–62.

40. Álvarez Aragón, 223; Galich, 266–67.

41. Galich, 268.

42. Ibid., 278.

43. Ibid., 283.

44. Daniel J. Walkowitz, *Working with Class* (Chapel Hill: University of North Carolina Press, 1999), 1–24.

45. Galich, 290.

46. Ibid., 287–91.
47. Ibid., 294.
48. Ibid., 295.
49. Ibid., 299.
50. Ibid., 303.
51. Augusto Cazali Ávila, *Historia de la Universidad de San Carlos* (Guatemala City: Editorial Universitaria, 1997), 129.
52. Galich, 308–11.
53. Ibid., 316–18.
54. Gleijeses, 24; Álvarez Aragón, 224.
55. "Actos de pillaje cometidos el sábado," *El Liberal Progresista*, June 26, 1944, in Gleijeses, 24.
56. *Daily Report*, June 29, 1944. FBIS-FRB-44-156; *Daily Report*, FBIS-FRB-44-158, July 1, 1944. See also Joseph E. Roop, *FBIS History, Part I: 1941–1947* (Washington, DC: Central Intelligence Agency), 1969.
57. Nathalie Ludec, "Voces del exilio guatemalteco desde la ciudad de Mexico," *Amérique Latine: Histoire y Mémoire* 2 (2001).
58. *Daily Report*, Foreign Radio Broadcasts, FBIS-FRB-44-159, July 3, 1944. AA6.
59. Galich, 356.
60. Ibid., 356–57.
61. Ibid., 359.
62. *El Imparcial*, July 7, 1944, in Álvarez Aragón, 226.
63. *Daily Report*, FBIS-FRB-44-169, July 14, 1944, AA9.
64. Álvarez Aragón, 227; Geijeses, 27; Alfonso Bauer Paíz, *Memorias de Alfonso Bauer Paíz: historia no oficial de Guatemala* (Guatemala City: Rusticatio Editores, 1996), 72.
65. "Luis Cardoza y Aragón regresa a la patria," *El Libertador*, September 1944. CIRMA.
66. Gleijeses, 28.
67. Ibid., 16.
68. Ibid., 28–29. See also César Augusto Silva Girón, *Vivencias de la Revolución del 20 de octubre de 1944: Oficiales veteranos de la gloriosa gesta revolucionaria narran sus experiencias en los hechos de octubre de 1944* (Guatemala City: s.n., 1994); Oscar de León Aragón, "Participación de los estudiantes en los sucesos del 20," *El Libertador*, October 23, 1945. HN.
69. Interestingly, according to the 1940 census, 39% of Guatemala City's population was between the ages of 19 and 30. Gobierno de Guatemala, *Quinto censo general de población, levantado el 7 de abril de 1940* (Guatemala City: Tipografía Nacional, 1942); Samuel Inman, *A New Day in Guatemala: A Study of the Present Social Revolution* (Wilton, CT: Worldover Press, 1951), 8. Jaime Pensado found a similar phenomenon among Mexican students at the IPN and UNAM; see Pensado, *Rebel Mexico*.
70. Junta Revolucionaria, *Decreto 12*. AGUSAC. See also Álvarez Aragón, 231.
71. Álvarez Aragón, 230–31.

72. Ibid., 244, 239.

73. *Boletín Universitario*, Año V, No. 2, May 15, 1951. AGUSAC. When UNESCO officials visited in 1951, they recommended technical and scientific knowledge for development.

74. Juan José Arévalo, "En el acto inaugural de la Facultad de Humanidades, September 17, 1945," in *Discursos en la Presidencia, 1945–1948* (Guatemala City: Tipografía Nacional, 1948), 281.

75. Comisión de los quince, *Diario de sesiones de la comisión de los quince encargada de elaborar el proyecto de la Constitución de la República* (Guatemala City: Tipografía Nacional, 1953).

76. Francisco Javier Gómez Díez, "La Revolución Guatemalteca de 1944: La Asamblea Nacional Constituyente y la Mentalidad Revolucionaria," *Estudios de historia social y económica de América* 13 (1996): 203–20.

77. The IUS permitted student organizations from communist states to join; the International Student Conference (ISC), led by the Coordinating Secretariat of the International Student Conference (COSEC) did not. The CIA and MI6 recruited students from the ISC. See, "History," in *International Student Conference Archives, 1950–1969* (Amsterdam: IISH, 2013); Stephen Dorril, *MI6: Inside the Covert World of Her Majesty's Secret Intelligence Service* (New York: Simon & Schuster, 2002), 471–73.

78. The later careers of Assembly members José Manuel Fortuny, Jorge García Granados, and Mario Efraín Nájera Farfán are suggestive: Fortuny was a leader of the communist PGT until 1954; García Granados served as Guatemalan Ambassador to the United States and the United Nations and ran for presidential against Arbenz in 1950; and Nájera Farfán joined Castillo Armas and denounced the revolution in numerous books, see Gómez Díez, 219.

79. In 1940, the literacy rate in the department of Guatemala was 57.69%. Ten years later, the census recorded a literacy rate of 58.9% in the department of Guatemala and 73.8% in the city itself. At the same time, rates of illiteracy reached more than 90% in El Quiche and Alta Verapaz. Despite the literacy programming of the revolutionary governments, the national illiteracy rate increased between 1940 and 1950 from 65.53% to 72.2% among Guatemalans over 7 years of age. Dirección General de Estadística, *Quinto Censo* and *Sexto Censo General de Población, 1950* (Guatemala City: Ministerio de Economía, 1957). In 1940, the department of Guatemala was 79.65% "blanca/mestiza" and 20% indigenous, which was recorded as "india."

80. More than 80% of agricultural work was *jornalero* labor performed by men. Women who were "amas de casa" comprised 89% of the domestic labor. "Ama de casa" could include any number of income-generating tasks performed in the home as well as the domestic labor associated with the North American "homemaker." See Sol Tax, "The Indians in the Economy of Guatemala," *Social and Economic Studies* 6, no. 3 (September 1957): 413–24.

81. Dirección General de Estadística, *Sexto Censo*. In 1950, 7,715 individuals reported an occupation of "student," and nearly 70% of "students" lived in Guatemala City.

82. On a similar debate in China, see Craig Calhoun, *Neither Gods nor Emperors: Students and the Struggle for Democracy in China* (Berkeley: University of California Press, 1994), 260.

83. Clemente Marroquín Rojas, "Editorial," *La Hora*, November 6, 1945. HN.

84. Adams, *Crucifixion*, 410.

85. Owensby, 4.

86. "Memorial de la AEU," Congreso Nacional de la República, *Asamblea Nacional Constituyente de 1945: Correspondencia*. Volume II, November 5, 1954, in Gómez Díez, 206n23.

87. Even sectors in favor of the vote for illiterate citizens required democratic tutelage. The communist National Workers Party (PNT) wrote: "As regards suffrage, History demonstrates that only those pueblos gifted with a high civic spirit acquired by habit and the purity of the proceedings employed by these electoral systems and practices are those that can arrive at the appropriate conditions to cast their vote in a conscientious form." See Gómez Díez, 207.

88. See David Carey, Jr., "A Democracy Born in Violence," in *After the Coup*, ed. Timothy J. Smith and Abigail E. Adams (Champaign: University of Illinois Press, 2011), 73–98.

89. Franco Iacovetta, "The Gatekeepers: Middle Class Campaigns of Citizenship in Early Cold War Canada," in *The Making of the Middle Class*, A. Ricardo López and Barbara Weinstein (Durham, NC: Duke University Press, 2012), 93–94.

90. Rufino Guerra Cortave, *El Imparcial*, November 8, 1944, in Richard N. Adams, "Ethnic Images and Strategies in 1944," in *Guatemalan Indians and the State: 1540–1988*, ed. Carol A. Smith (Austin: University of Texas Press, 1991), 22.

91. Ibid.

92. Ibid., 23.

93. Jorge Schlesinger, *La Hora,* November 26, 1944, in Adams, "Ethnic Strategies," 22.

94. Ibid.

95. Ministerio de Gobernación, *Constitución de la Republica de Guatemala decretado por la asamblea constituyente en 11 de marzo de 1945* (Guatemala City: s.n., 1948). Illiterate women were granted suffrage with the 1965 Constitution.

96. Juan José Arévalo, *Discurso al asumir la Presidencia de la República* (Guatemala City: Tipografía Nacional, 1945), 237.

97. Ibid., 237.

98. See López and Weinstein, *The Making of the Middle Class.*

99. Juan José Arévalo, *Guatemala, la democracia y el imperio* (Buenos Aires: Editorial Palestra, 1964), 121.

100. See Leslie Bethell and Ian Roxborough, *Latin America between the Second World War and the Cold War: Crisis and Containment, 1944–1948* (Cambridge: Cambridge University Press, 1992); John D. French, *Brazilian Workers' ABC: Class Conflict and Alliances in Modern Sao Paulo* (Chapel Hill: University of North Carolina Press, 1992); Steve Stern, *Populism in Peru: The Emergence of the Masses and the Politics of Social Control* (Madison: University of Wisconsin Press, 1980); Florencia

Mallon, *Peasant and Nation: The Making of Postcolonial Mexico and Peru* (Berkeley: University of California Press, 1995); Laura Gotkowitz, *A Revolution for Our Rights: Indigenous Struggles for Land and Justice in Bolivia, 1880–1952* (Durham, NC: Duke University Press, 2008).

101. A. Ricardo López, "Conscripts of Democracy: The Formation of a Professional Middle Class in Bogotá during the 1950s and early 1960s," in López and Weinstein, 168; Ricardo Salvatore, *Disciplinary Conquest: U.S. Scholars in South America, 1900–1945* (Durham, NC: Duke University Press, 2016).

102. Ludec, "Voces del exilio guatemalteco desde la ciudad de Mexico."

103. Carlos González Orellana, *Historia de la educación en Guatemala* (Guatemala City: Editorial Universitaria, 1980).

104. Article 12, *Ley Orgánica of the Universidad de San Carlos*; *Boletín Universitario*, Año II: No. 2, March 1, 1948. AGUSAC.

105. *Boletín Universitario*, Año I: No. 12, August 1, 1948; *Boletín Universitario*, Año V: No. 9, December 31, 1951. AGUSAC.

106. Until its 1948 reform, the Labor Code required that agricultural unions have 66.67% literacy among members and a minimum of fifty members. Given the low rate of rural literacy, these requirements were difficult to meet (in 1950, illiteracy was over 90% in the rural coffee-producing department of Alta Verapaz). Two large unions of UFCO workers based in Tiquisate and Bananera, respectively, were among the first to register with the Arévalo government. See Alejandra Batres, "The Experience of Guatemalan United Fruit Company Workers, 1944–1954: Why Did They Fail?" *Texas Papers on Latin America, Paper No. 95–01.*

107. Mario Monteforte Toledo, *Monografía sociológica* (Mexico City: Instituto de Investigaciones Sociales UNAM, 1959), 567–68; Gleijeses, 156.

108. Gleijeses, 45.

109. Ibid., 39.

110. Ibid., 45.

111. Ibid., 45–46; González Orellana, 394–23.

112. Antonio Goubaud Carrera, *Indigenismo en Guatemala* (Guatemala City: Ministerio de Educación Pública, 1964), 18, 25; Goubaud Carrera is a fascinating and vastly understudied individual; see Abigail E. Adams, "Antonio Goubaud Carrera: Between the Contradictions of the Generación de 1920 and U.S. Anthropology," in *After the Coup*, ed. Timothy J. Smith and Abigail E. Adams (Champaign: University of Illinois Press, 2011), 17–48.

113. On *indigenismo* in Guatemala, see Jorge Skinner Klee, *Legislación indigenista de Guatemala* (Mexico City: Instituto Indigenista Interamericano, 1954); Richard N. Adams, *Social Change in Latin America Today. Its Implications for United States Policy* (New York: Harper, 1960); Instituto Indigenista Nacional, *¿Por qué es indispensable el indigenismo?* (Guatemala City: Editorial José Pineda Ibarra, 1969); Virginia Garrard-Burnett, "Indians Are Drunks and Drunks Are Indians: Alcohol and Indigenismo in Guatemala, 1890–1940," *Latin American Research Review* 19 (2000): 341–56; Marta Casaús Arzú, "De la incógnita del indio al indio como sombra: el debate de la antropología guatemalteca en torno al indio

y la nación," *Revista de indias* 234 (May–August 2005): 376–403; Edgar G. Mendoza, *Antropologistas y antropólogos: una generación* (Guatemala City: USAC, 2000); Jorge Ramón Gónzalez Ponciano, "De la patria del criollo a la Patria del Shumo: Whiteness and the Criminalization of the Dark Plebeian in Modern Guatemala," PhD diss., University of Texas–Austin, 2005; and Abigail E. Adams, "Diversidad cultural en la nacionalidad homogénea? Antonio Goubaud Carrera y la fundación del Instituto Indigenista Nacional de Guatemala," *Mesoamérica* 50 (2008): 66–95.

114. *El Imparcial,* January 10, 1945. HN.

115. Juan José Arévalo, *Despacho Presidencial Obra Póstuma,* Oscar de León Castillo, ed. (Guatemala City: Editorial Oscar de Leon Palacios, 1998), 75; *Boletín Universitario,* Año III: No. 3, March 14, 1949. AGUSAC.

116. Carlos Martínez Durán, *Discursos Universitarios, 1945–1950* (Guatemala City: USAC, 1950).

117. *Boletín Universitario,* Año I: No. 2, August 1, 1947. AGUSAC.

118. Ibid.

119. *Boletín Universitario,* Año V: No. 2, May 15, 1951. AGUSAC.

120. *Boletín Universitario,* Año I: No. 1, July 15, 1947; *Boletín Universitario,* Año I, No. 2, August 1, 1947. AGUSAC.

121. *Boletín Universitario,* Año II: No. 1, February 15, 1948. AGUSAC.

122. *Boletín Universitario,* Año I: No. 1, July 15, 1947. AGUSAC.

123. Ibid.

124. Joaquin Xirau, "El Problema de la Universidad," *Boletín Universitario,* Año III: No. 10, July 15, 1949. AGUSAC.

125. *Boletín Universitario,* Año V: No. 1, April 15, 1951. AGUSAC.

126. *Boletín Universitario,* Año II: No. 15, September 1948; *Boletín Universitario,* Año II: No. 16, October 1948. AGUSAC.

127. Arbenz won by a wide margin: 258,987 out of 404,739 votes cast; Miguel Ydígoras Fuentes came in second with 72,796 votes; and the eight other candidates won very few votes. Arbenz had the support of the military, labor, and both major political parties; landowners and the business sector supported Ydígoras; see Gleijeses, 60–72.

128. Ibid., 138–39.

129. Ministerio de Economía y Trabajo, "La Empresa Eléctrica de Guatemala, S.A., un problema nacional," No. 5 (Guatemala City: s.n., 1950); Gleijeses, 165.

130. Gleijeses, 161.

131. Ibid., 166.

132. *Boletín Universitario,* Año I: No. 7, October 15, 1947. AGUSAC.

133. Álvarez Aragón, 254–55.

134. Galich, 375–76.

135. Grandin, 185–86, 278n62.

136. USAC Departamento de Registro, *Boletín Estadístico Universitario* (Guatemala City: USAC, 1966). AGUSAC

137. Langland, 16, 21–25, 29, 31.

138. "Conmemoración del VII Aniversario de la Autonomía Universitaria," *Boletín Universitario*, December 31, 1951. AGUSAC.

139. Ibid.

140. René Eduardo Poitevín Dardón, *Quiénes somos? la Universidad de San Carlos y las clases sociales* (Guatemala City: Instituto de Investigaciones y Mejoramiento Educativo de la Universidad de San Carlos de Guatemala, 1977).

141. Charles R. Hale, "Neoliberal Multiculturalism: The Remaking of Cultural Rights and Racial Dominance in Central America," *PoLAR* 28, no. 1 (2005): 10–28.

CHAPTER TWO

1. Editorial, *No Nos Tientes*, 1954. Centro de Investigaciones Regionales de Mesoamérica (CIRMA).

2. Catalina Barrios y Barrios, *Huelga de Dolores, cien años y uno más* (Guatemala City: Ediciones y Litografía LOPDEL, 1999), 115–16.

3. "University Students Lampoon Castillo," Foreign Service Despatch 789. April 6, 1955. Doc. 714.00(W)4-655. U.S. Department of State, *Records of the U.S. Department of State Relating to Internal Affairs of Guatemala, 1955–1959* (Wilmington, DE: Scholarly Resources, 2001). On the Foreign Service Despatch see David Langbart, "The Despatch," *The Text Message*, The U.S. National Archives, http://blogs.archives.gov/TextMessage/2011/03/11/foreign-service-friday/. Accessed June 10, 2015.

4. Carlos Alberto Enriquez, *Guatemala: no más exilio* (Guatemala City: CONGCOOP, 1995); Julio Pinto Soria, Arturo Taracena Arriola, and Arely Mendoza, *Luis Cardoza y Aragón y Juan José Arévalo, Correspondencia del Exilio* (Guatemala City: Editorial Universitaria, 2011).

5. See Jaime Pensado, "'To Assault with the Truth': The Revitalization of Conservative Militancy in Mexico During the Global Sixties," *The Americas* 70, no. 3 (January 2014); Jamie Pensado, "El Movimiento Estudiantil Profesional (MEP): una mirada a la radicalización de la juventud católica mexicana durante la Guerra Fría," *Mexican Studies/Estudios Mexicanos* 31, no. 1 (Winter 2015): 156–92.

6. By 1954, USAC enrollment had increased to 3,368 students, yet 2,148,560 Guatemalan citizens had no formal schooling. Departamento de Censos y Encuestas, *Censo de Población de Guatemala de 1964* (Guatemala City: Ministerio de Economía, 1964).

7. Susanne Jonas's landmark study emphasizes how new economic prosperity made conservative fiscal policies appealing to growing numbers of Guatemalans, see Jonas, *The Battle for Guatemala* (Boulder, CO: Westview Press, 1991). U.S. diplomatic historians drew on Central Intelligence Agency and State Department records to emphasize the anticommunist anxieties of Secretary of State John Foster Dulles and CIA Director Allen Dulles; Stephen Schlesinger and Stephen Kinzer, *Bitter Fruit* (Garden City, NY: Doubleday, 1982); Nick Cullather, *Secret History* (Stanford,

CA: Stanford University Press, 1999). On the entwined economic interests and ideological aims of the U.S. government, see Richard H. Immerman, *The CIA in Guatemala* (Austin: University of Texas Press, 1982) and Piero Gleijeses, *Shattered Hope* (Princeton, NJ: Princeton University Press, 1991). Walter LaFeber, *Inevitable Revolutions* (New York: Norton, 1983) sees the counterrevolution as one of many interventions in a century of U.S. exploitation in Central America.

8. This is exemplified by the essays in Timothy J. Smith and Abigail E. Adams, *After the Coup: An Ethnographic Reframing of Guatemala 1954* (Champaign: University of Illinois Press, 2011).

9. Greg Grandin, *The Last Colonial Massacre* (Chicago: University of Chicago Press, 2004), 186.

10. "The New Phase in Guatemalan Political Life and Its Relation to U.S. Policy," U.S. Embassy Despatch 1019, June 24, 1955. Records of the U.S. Department of State relating to internal affairs of Guatemala, 1955–1959. 714.00/6-2455.

11. "Editorial: Universidad y Pueblo," *El Estudiante*, June 9, 1955. CIRMA.

12. Paul Kobrak, *Organizing and Repression in the University of San Carlos, Guatemala, 1944 to 1996* (Washington, DC: American Association for the Advancement of Science, 1999).

13. This phrase comes from State Department official John Calvin Hill in June 1955, see Charles Brockett, "Building a Showcase for Democracy: The U.S. in Guatemala, 1954–1960," XVI International Congress of the Latin American Studies Association, Washington, DC, April 4–6, 1991.

14. On the interpersonal tensions between the CEUA and the AEU, see "Demagógico manifiesto de CEUA," *El Estudiante*, I: 7, June 2, 1955. CIRMA.

15. The date of the initial meeting is redacted; see Cullather, *Secret History: The CIA's Classified Account of its Operations in Guatemala, 1952–1954* (Palo Alto, CA: Stanford University Press, 1999), 64.

16. "Guatemalteco!," n.d. CIRMA.

17. Cullather, *Secret History*, 64–66; Paul P. Kennedy, "Guatemalans Get Appeal to Revolt," *New York Times*, May 5, 1954, in Cullather, 65.

18. Ibid., 65.

19. Ibid., 64–66.

20. Ibid., 66.

21. "De pie, frente a la dictadura roja de Guatemala," *Boletín de CEUAGE* Año I: No. 1, June 1953. Hemeroteca Nacional (HN).

22. *Boletín de CEUAGE*, Año I: No. 1, June 1953. HN. Another group, the Frente Anticomunista de Guatemaltecos en Exilio (FAGE), was based in San Salvador. The FAGE began publishing *El Combate de FAGE* on November 7, 1953.

23. *Boletín de CEUAGE*, Año I: No. 2, July 1953. CIRMA.

24. On anticommunists in the Caribbean, see Aaron Moulton, "Building Their Own Cold War in Their Own Backyard: The Transnational, International Conflicts in the Greater Caribbean Basin, 1944–1954," *Cold War History* 15, no. 2 (2015): 135–54.

25. CEUA, *Plan de Tegucigalpa*, 45–46.

26. Ibid., 46.

27. Ibid.

28. The MEP sought to infiltrate the spaces where Marxism gained appeal, especially public schools and labor. It dramatically changed its position by the 1970s; see Pensado, "*El Movimiento Estudiantil Profesional (MEP).*"

29. CEUA, 57–58.

30. Ibid., 54.

31. Ibid., 29.

32. Ibid., 30.

33. Ibid.

34. Ibid., 31.

35. Ibid., 32.

36. Ibid., 31. The 1956 Constitution shifted from "indios" to "grupos indígenas" to describe indigenous citizens.

37. This phrasing invokes the educational desegregation debate that raged in the U.S. approaching the Supreme Court decision on *Brown vs. Board of Education*, passed in May 1954 just months after the *Plan* was drafted.

38. CEUA, 46.

39. Richard N. Adams, *Crucifixion by Power* (Austin: University of Texas Press, 1970), 449–60.

40. Nathalie Ludec, "Voces del exilio guatemalteco desde la ciudad de Mexico," *Amérique Latine: Histoire y Mémoire* 2 (2001).

41. Telegram, US Embassy to State Department, "Key Positions Held by the Comité de Estudiantes Universitarios Anticomunistas de Guatemala," February 9, 1955. Doc. 714.00/2-955. U.S. Department of State, *Records.*

42. Foreign Service Despatch Number 928. May 26, 1955. Doc. 714.00(W)/5-2655. U.S. Department of State, *Records*; Foreign Service Despatch Number 1014. June 23, 1955. Doc. 714.00(W)/6-2355. U.S. Department of State, *Records.* Foreign Service Despatch Number 44. July 21, 1955. Doc. 714.00(W)/7-2155. U.S. Department of State, *Records.*

43. Ministerio de Gobernación, *Constitución de la República de Guatemala, decretada por la Asamblea Nacional Constituyente el 2 de febrero de 1956*, Chap. IV, Art. 106.

44. Editorial, *El Estudiante*, March 1, 1956. CIRMA.

45. See Article 102 of the 1956 Constitution and Article 84 of the 1945 Constitution.

46. *Boletin Universitario*, No. 8, August 1957; *Boletin Universitario*, No. 3, March, 1957. Archivo General de la Universidad de San Carlos (AGUSAC).

47. "Editorial: La Universidad y el Pueblo," *Boletin Universitario*. No. 7, July 1955. AGUSAC.

48. Foreign Service Despatch Number 989, June 17, 1955. Doc. 714.00(W)/6-1655. U.S. Department of State, *Records.*

49. "The New Phase in Guatemalan Political Life and Its Relation to U.S. Policy," U.S. Embassy Despatch 1019, June 24, 1955. Doc. 714.00/6-2455. U.S. Department of State, *Records.*

50. "The New Phase in Guatemalan Political Life and Its Relation to U.S. Policy."

51. The exiles included prominent student activists and intellectuals, including Roberto Díaz Castillo, Augusto Cazali Ávila, Edelberto Torres Rivas, Hugo Barrios Klee, Julio Hernández Sifontes, Cesar Montenegro Paniagua, Saúl Osorio Paz, and José Alberto Quiñónez Castillo. Many went to Mexico City. "Estudiantes Universitarios que se encuentran en el Exilio," AGUSAC. U.S. State Department documents reveal that in August 1954, asylees were sorted into dangerous and "relatively harmless" categories. U.S. Department of State, *Foreign Relations of the United States, 1952–1954*. vol. 4, "The American Republics," "Memorandum by the Assistant Secretary of State for Inter-American Affairs (Holland) to Secretary of State / Subject: Asylee Problem in Guatemala," Doc. 507. August 10, 1954.

52. Mariano Rossell y Arellano, *Amonestación pastoral del excelentísimo y reverendísimo monseñor Mariano Rossell Arellano, arzobispo de Guatemala, al pueblo católico con ocasión de la huelga estudiantil, llamada 'De Dolores'* (Guatemala City: Unión Tipográfico, 1956).

53. "No Confirman Captura de Autores de Bombazo a Huelga de Dolores," *El Imparcial*, April 20, 1956. HN.

54. See "The New Phase in Guatemalan Political Life and Its Relation to U.S. Policy."

55. "Cosas del 10 de Mayo," *El Estudiante,* May 3, 1956. CIRMA; "Libre Celebración del Primero de Mayo," *El Imparcial*, May 2, 1956. HN.

56. Ministerio de Trabajo y Prevision Social, *Código de Trabajo de Guatemala* (Guatemala City: Tipografía Nacional, 1956); see also Article 116 of the 1956 Constitution.

57. "Cosas del 10 de Mayo." CIRMA.

58. Six other students' names were printed in the paper and arrested in their homes for distributing communist, Marxist, or trade unionist propaganda. "Dos Estudiantes Detenidos; se Interpuso Recurso de Exhibición," *El Imparcial*, May 2, 1956; "Indagados sobre el real o supuesto complot para el entrante Junio," *La Hora*, May 3, 1956; "3 Estudiantes Libres; Sindicatos Presos," *Prensa Libre*, May 3, 1956; "Cauda de 10 de Mayo," *El Imparcial*, May 3, 1956; "Exhibición Hoy de los Detenidos por Pegar Propaganda Comunista," *El Imparcial*, May 3, 1956; "Tres estudiantes detenidos por insultar al Presidente," *La Hora*, May 2, 1956; "Libres los tres estudiantes," *La Hora*, May 3, 1956. HN.

59. Editorial, *El Estudiante*, May 3, 1956. CIRMA.

60. "Juan Tecú," *El Estudiante*, May 3, 1956. CIRMA.

61. "Editorial: Un histórico primero de Mayo," *El Estudiante,* May 3, 1956. CIRMA.

62. "Movimiento Democrático Nacional (MDN)," Despatch 1031. Doc. 714.00/6-2855. U.S. State Department, *Records.*

63. "Cacto," *Prensa Libre*, May 4, 1956; see also the May 5 and 31 editions of *La Hora*. HN.

64. "Que se prepara una apaleada a los de 'El Estudiante,' una grave denuncia," *Prensa Libre,* June 1, 1956. HN.

65. Article 32 did permit Central American Unionist and Pan-American organizations; on the subject see Ministerio de Relaciones Exteriores, *Centroamérica en el panamericanismo* (Guatemala City: Ministerio de Relaciones Exteriores, 1956); Philip Marshall Brown, "American Intervention in Central America," *Journal of Race Development* 4, no. 4 (April 1914): 409–26; H.W. Dodds, "Intervention in Central America," *Annals of the American Academy of Political and Social Science* 144 (July 1929): 97–101.

66. "Castillitos en el Aire," *El Estudiante,* May 31, 1956. CIRMA.

67. US Central Intelligence Agency, "'32' Marking Campaign," March 24, 1953. CIA FOIA Electronic Reading Room. Accessed August 22, 2012.

68. Actually, 1956 was a terrible year for global communism: Nikita Khrushchev met with Eisenhower; the Cold War generally thawed; and communists struggled in the ongoing Algerian independence war.

69. "Tres 'Alas' se disputan el timón de la Asociación El Derecho," "Lucha pre-eleccionaria de directive de la Asociación 'El Derecho,'" *La Hora,* June 13, 1956. HN.

70. "Marxistas ganaron las elecciones," *La Hora,* June 14, 1956. HN.

71. "Marxists ganaron," *La Hora;* "Nueva Directiva de El Derecho, Electa," *Prensa Libre,* June 14, 1956, HN.

72. "Marxistas ganaron."

73. Ibid.

74. Ibid.

75. "Prevendran desórdenes en ceremonias del 25," *Prensa Libre,* June 15, 1956. HN.

76. "Pronunciamiento del alumnado de la Escuela Normal Central para Varones," *La Hora,* June 11, 1956; "Tenencia de libros no es delito y queda en libertad," *Prensa Libre,* June 15, 1956. HN; See also *El Estudiante,* June 14, 1956. CIRMA.

77. "El derecho invita a formar comité nacional para celebrar 25 de junio," *Prensa Libre,* June 16, 1956; "Programa para conmemorar gesta cívico del año 44," *Prensa Libre,* June 21, 1956. HN.

78. "La Policía no permitirá desórdenes para el 25," *La Hora,* June 19, 1956. HN.

79. "El Derecho Enjuiciará a Sandoval Alarcón," *Prensa Libre,* June 21, 1956. HN. Immerman, *The CIA in Guatemala,* 128.

80. Editorial, *Prensa Libre,* June 16, 1956. HN.

81. "Lucha Cívica de Junio es del Pueblo Proclama la AEU," *El Imparcial,* June 23, 1956. HN.

82. Ibid.

83. See "Peregrinación y Placa Conmemorativa Mañana," *El Imparcial,* June 23, 1956; "Efemérides universitaria el 25 de junio," *Prensa Libre,* June 22, 1956; "AEU Exalta el 25 de junio," *La Hora,* June 22, 1956. HN.

84. A month later, Cerezo Dardón was arrested for public indecency and intoxication. He immediately refuted the charges in a public statement wherein he also reported that he had been under surveillance for days before the arrest. He argued

this was an attempt to diminish the moral authority of the university and its instructors. "Memorandum del Señor Decano de Humanidades / Presentado al CSU explicando las circunstancias de su injustificada detención," *Boletín Universitario*, August 1956, No. 8. AGUSAC.

85. "Columna de Universitarios Conmemoró. Perigrinación a Donde Estaban los Restos de Maria Chinchilla," *El Imparcial*, June 25, 1956. HN.

86. "Facultad de Derecho Bajo Vigilancia; Ayer Estuvo Rodeada Durante Tres Horas Seguidas," *El Imparcial*, June 25, 1956. HN.

87. Julio Valladares Castillo, Jorge Luis Zelaya, José Francisco Monsanto, Victor Hugo Rodríguez, Marco Antonio Ramírez, J. Joaquín Pardo, Mario Raúl Toledo, and José Luis Balcárcel Ordóñez were invited. All were *Facultad* of Law alumni and former members of the FPL. See *El Imparcial*, July 7 and 18, 1944; *El Imparcial*, June 23, 1956. HN.

88. "Deseo de evitar disturbios movió al gobierno a declarar estado de alarma," "Suspendidos Actos Conmemorativos," and "Se previno a manifestantes sobre el estado de alarma," *Prensa Libre*, June 25, 1956. HN. See Luis Felipe Sáenz J., "La regulación de los estados de excepción en Guatemala," *Anuario de Derecho Constitucional Latinoamericano* (México: Institución de Investigaciones Jurídicas de UNAM, 2006).

89. "Reuniones de Estudiantes Permitirán," *El Imparcial*, June 25, 1956. HN.

90. "Estudiantes Universitarios Acordaron Lanzar su Protesta. Informan de los Sucesos Ocurridos," *El Imparcial*, June 25, 1956. HN.

91. "Ministerio de Defensa Informa Sobre los Sucesos de Anoche," *El Imparcial*, June 26, 1956. HN.

92. Salvador Orozco, AED president, was shot in the chin and lung; Francisco Augusto Lemus, another law student, was gravely injured; Jorge Morales was shot repeatedly in the right leg; Jorge Rosal, ex-president of the AEM and soon-to-be general secretary of the AEU, was shot in the face; Hugo Melgar, who would continue to speak out against the right until his assassination in 1980, was shot in the right leg. Eleven other students sustained minor injuries. One policeman, Raúl Sánchez Rodriguez, sustained a minor injury to the head. "Saldo de Tres Muertos y Varios Heridos al Ser Disuelta la Manifestación Estudiantil de Anoche," *El Imparcial*, June 26, 1956; "Policía Disolvió la Manifestación Ayer," *Prensa Libre*, June 26, 1956; "Nombres de Personas Detenidas," *La Hora*, June 27, 1956. HN.

93. See *Prensa Libre*, *La Hora*, and *El Imparcial*, June 26, 1956. HN.

94. "Seguridad nacional informa sobre las actividades subversivas descubiertas" and "La policía fue atacada dice comunicado oficial," *Prensa Libre*, June 26, 1956. HN.

95. "Ministerio de la Defensa Informa," *El Imparcial*. HN.

96. "Medidas de Emergencia," *El Imparcial*. HN.

97. "Ordenanzas Correspondientes a la Aplicación del Estado de Sitio en Toda la República," *El Imparcial*, June 26, 1956; "Manifestaciones, huelgas y reuniones serán reprimidas por la fuerza pública," *Prensa Libre*, June 28, 1956; "Medidas de Emergencia"; "Se proclamó hoy el estado de sitio," *La Hora*. HN.

98. "Fueron sepultados ayer los tres estudiantes fallecidos," *La Hora,* June 27, 1956; "Estudiantes fallecidos fueron inhumados ayer," *Prensa Libre*, June 27, 1956. HN.

99. Telegram No. 364 to Secretary of State, June 26, 1956. No. 714.00/6-2656. U.S. Department of State, *Records.*

100. "Tribunales de Justicia no Actuarán Bajo la Jurisdicción de la Defensa," *El Imparcial,* June 27, 1956. HN.

101. "Guatemala Returns to Constitutional Normalcy," Despatch to U.S. State Department from U.S. Embassy in Guatemala. September 5, 1956. No. 714.00/9-556. U.S. Department of State, *Records.*

102. "Acusados de Sedición en el Juzgado 80 de 1a Instancia," *El Imparcial,* June 27, 1956; "Detención del Br. Rosales Comprobando," *El Imparcial,* June 27, 1956; "Siguen indagatorias de estudiantes detenidos," *Prensa Libre,* June 30, 1956; "Libertad de 40 Universitarios Detenidos Dictada por Tribunal. Otras Ordenes Similares Seguirán," *El Imparcial,* June 30, 1956; "La situación de emergencia terminará cuando el comunismo deponga sus armas," *Prensa Libre,* June 29, 1956. HN.

103. "Estudiantes sesionaron en el Paraninfo ayer," *Prensa Libre*, June 29, 1956. HN.

104. "Declaraciones del Ministro de Gobernación por la Radio," *El Imparcial,* June 28, 1956; "Texto del discurso pronunciado por la radio, hoy, por el Lic. Rodríguez Genis, Ministro de Gobernación, dirigido al pueblo," *Prensa Libre,* June 28, 1956. HN.

105. "Interponen Exhibición pro Catedrático y Dos Normalistas," *El Imparcial,* 28 June 1956; "Suspensión de Labores Afecta a una Minoría Estudiantil, Declara el Ministro de Educación," *El Imparcial,* June 28, 1956. HN.

106. "La política es para personas mayores," *La Hora*, June 30, 1956; "Cancelarán Matrícula por Faltar a Clases," *Prensa Libre*, June 29, 1956. HN

107. "Normal es la Actividad en el Instituto Nacional de Varones" and "Secundaria de Rafael Aqueche Reanuda Clases," *El Imparcial,* June 29, 1956. HN.

108. "Firme la Estabilidad de su Gobierno, Declaró Castillo Armas: Comunismo y Acción Comunista, lo que se Barre," *El Imparcial,* June 29, 1956. HN.

109. "Firme la Estabilidad de su Goberino," *El Imparcial;* "Guatemala Returns to Constitutional Normalcy," Despatch to U.S. State Department from U.S. Embassy in Guatemala. No. 714.00/9-556. September 5, 1956. U.S. Department of State, *Records.*

110. Telegram No. 364, from Ambassador Sparks. June 26, 1956. Doc. 714.00/6–2656; "Situation in Guatemala," Telegram to Secretary of State from Assistant Secretary Holland, June 29, 1956. Doc. 714.00/6-2956. U.S. Department of State, *Records.*

111. "Editorial: Muy pocas veces nos hemos equivocado," *La Hora,* June 27, 1956. HN.

112. Editorial, *El Imparcial,* June 26, 1956. HN.

113. Editorial, *Prensa Libre,* June 27, 1956. HN.

114. Editorial, *Prensa Libre*, June 29, 1956. HN; Telegram, Second Secretary to U.S. Ambassador William B. Connett, Jr., "Prensa Libre editorial on Latest Political Events," July 2, 1956. Doc. 714.00/7-256. U.S. Department of State, *Records*.

115. "Dos Dictámenes Emitidos por la AEU," and Editorial, *Informador Estudiantil*, January–February 1956. See also "Dos publicaciones periodísticas" in the same edition. CIRMA.

116. "Editorial: Muy pocas veces nos hemos equivocado," *La Hora*, June 27, 1956. HN.

117. "Boletín Number 5 del Ejército: 'La Universidad de San Carlos y la Baja Política,'" *El Imparcial*, June 26, 1956; "Boletín número cinco dado hoy por la Defensa Nacional," *La Hora*, June 26, 1956; "Gobierno Enjuicia Caso de los Universitarios," *Prensa Libre*, June 26, 1956. HN.

118. Archila Obregón was a lieutenant colonel of the Infantry of the National Liberation forces who operated in the communities of Morales and Bananera.

119. Balcárcel Ordóñez's father (also José Luis Balcárcel) had been a classmate of Marroquín Rojas at USAC in the 1920s; see Miguel Angel Asturias, *Paris 1924–1933: Periodismo y creación literaria* (San José: Universidad de Costa Rica, 1996), 540.

120. "AEU Contra Discriminación," *Informador Estudiantil*, January–February 1956. CIRMA.

121. "Tras un tiempo de vigilárseles 40 Detenidos en México por Conspirar Contra Batista," *El Imparcial*, June 26, 1956. HN.

122. *Boletín Universitario*, March 3, 1957. AGUSAC. "La Delegación Internacional de Estudiantes Visitó Pakistan, Burma, Thailandia y Vietnam," *Informador Estudiantil*, January–February, 1956. CIRMA.

123. Letter, AEU to Editor of *El Imparcial*. November 1958. AGUSAC.

124. "Relaciones de America," *El Imparcial*, May 4, 1956. HN.

125. As early as 1913, UFCO maintained a close relationship to Harvard Medical School's School of Tropical Medicine and, later, School of Public Health. John Farley, *Bilharzia: A History of Imperial Tropical Medicine* (Cambridge: Cambridge University Press, 2003), 128, 254.

126. "Programa de Becas para Centro América," *Boletín Universitario*, July 1955; see also *Boletín Universitario*, January 1956. AGCA.

127. A. Ricardo López, "Conscripts of Democracy: The Formation of a Professional Middle Class in Bogotá during the 1950s and early 1960s," in *The Making of the Middle Class*, A. Ricardo López and Barbara Weinstein (Durham, NC: Duke University Press, 2012), 164–65. See also Ricardo Salvatore, *Disciplinary Conquest: U.S. Scholars in South America, 1900–1945* (Durham, NC: Duke University Press, 2016).

128. "Acta 2 de la Sesión Ordinaria del Consejo Superior Estudiantil, Celebrada el lunes 13 de agosto de 1956," August 13, 1956. AGUSAC.

129. "Eugenia Archila: Madrina del deporte Universitario," *Informador Estudiantil*, January–February 1956; Work Plan, Secretary of Press and Public Relations, AEU, September 24, 1958. CIRMA. On cinema and rock music, see Mario Efraín

Castañeda Maldonado, "Historia de Rock en Guatemala: La música rock como expresión social en la ciudad de Guatemala entre 1960 a 1976," BA thesis, 2008.

130. "Vidas paralelepípedas," *No Nos Tientes*, 1957. CIRMA. The parallelepiped figure suggests that students imagined Guatemalan political life within a structure where communists and anticommunists formed opposing parallels.

131. AED, "Declaración de la Asociación de Estudiantes El Derecho declarando Castillo Armas como traidor de la Patria," January 17, 1958. CIRMA.

132. "The Role of the Middle Class," *El Estudiante*, May 10, 1956. CIRMA.

133. Fernando Martínez Bolaños, "Vida Universitaria: Superación Constante," *Informador Estudiantil*, January–February 1956. CIRMA.

134. "Outgoing Provisional Chief Named Defense Minister," *New York Times*, March 4, 1958.

135. In 1944, González López joined the Social Democratic Party (PSD) with Colonel Guillermo Flores Avendaño, Francisco Villagrán Kramer, and Jorge Toriello. See Guadalupe Rodríguez de Ita, *La participación política en la primavera guatemalteca: una aproximación a la historia de los partidos durante el período 1944–54* (Mexico City: UNAM, 2003), 94–95.

136. "Asamblea general de la AEU," *El Estudiante*, October 10, 1957; "Nuestro Homenaje," *El Estudiante*, September 7, 1957. CIRMA.

137. "Nuestro Homenaje," *El Estudiante*, September 7, 1957. CIRMA.

138. "Carta de Directores de Mexico," *El Estudiante*, October 10, 1957. CIRMA.

139. "Momento Político," *El Estudiante*, September 7, 1957. CIRMA.

140. Editorial, *El Estudiante*, January 16, 1958. CIRMA.

141. Roland H. Ebel, *Misunderstood Caudillo: Miguel Ydígoras Fuentes and the Failure of Democracy in Guatemala* (Lanham, MD: University Press of America, 1998), 71.

142. Editorial, *El Revolucionario*, October 3, 1957. CIRMA.

143. Editorial, *El Estudiante*, October 10, 1957. CIRMA.

144. "Discourse de Br. Alfredo Balsells Tojo, Presidente de la AEU," 1957. AGCA.

145. See Jenifer Van Vleck, *Empire of the Air: Aviation and the American Ascendancy* (Cambridge, MA: Harvard University Press, 2013).

CHAPTER THREE

1. Carlos Martínez Durán, *Discursos universitarios, 1958–1962* (Guatemala City: Imprenta Universitaria, 1962), 76.

2. Mario Monteforte Toledo, *Monografía Sociológica* (Mexico City: UNAM Instituto de Investigaciones Sociales, 1968), 324–27; Roland H. Ebel, *Misunderstood Caudillo: Miguel Ydígoras Fuentes and the Failure of Democracy in Guatemala* (Lanham, MD: University Press of America, 1998), 60–63.

3. Martínez Durán, *Discursos*, 93.

4. Writing contemporaneously to the events described in this chapter, Raymond Williams formulated a concept that he called "the structure of feeling" in an attempt to get at "the felt sense of the quality of life"; see Williams, *The Long Revolution* (Cardigan, UK: Parthian, 2011), 47, 67. Sociologist E. P. Thompson critiqued Williams's gloss over the material conditions of life that distinguish between classes, a debate that I reference in the Introduction notes. On the history of emotion, see William Reddy, *The Navigation of Feeling: A Framework for the History of Emotions* (New York: Cambridge University Press, 2001); Jeff Goodwin, James M. Jasper, and Francesca Polletta, eds., *Passionate Politics* (Chicago: University of Chicago Press, 2001); "Conversation: The Historical Study of Emotions," *American Historical Review* (December 2012): 1487–531. In the related field of affect theory, foundational work by Eve Kosofsky Sedgwick, Sara Ahmed, Patricia Clough, Lauren Berlant, and Ann Cvetkovich, may be helpful.

5. This whole book might be reread in order to help us to think through the broad questions of material determinism, affect, consciousness, and political action in social movements.

6. Deborah Levenson-Estrada, *Trade Unionists Against Terror: Guatemala City, 1954–1985* (Chapel Hill: University of North Carolina Press, 1994), 103.

7. In the late 1950s and early 1960s about 60% of USAC professors taught single courses at USAC after working other jobs; part-time professors, those who taught around four hours a week, counted for about 18% of the faculty; and the remainder (22%) were full-time professors. René Eduardo Poitevín Dardón, *Quiénes Somos?: La Universidad de San Carlos y las clases sociales* (Guatemala City: USAC Instituto de Investigaciones y Mejoramiento Educativo, 1977), 33.

8. See Levenson-Estrada, 42, 260n78.

9. Greg Grandin, *The Last Colonial Massacre: Latin America in the Cold War* (Chicago: University of Chicago Press, 2004), 87.

10. Ebel, *Misunderstood Caudillo*, 107.

11. "Guatemala: Deal for the Presidency," *TIME*, February 10, 1958.

12. Mario Solórzano Martinez, *Guatemala, Autoritarismo y democracia* (San José: EDUCA-FLACSO, 1987), 9. In his very complimentary biography, Ebel notes that coffee revenue "produced much of the revenue that paid the salaries of government bureaucrats, postal workers and school teachers," so the decline in world coffee prices during Ydígoras's presidency compromised his many expensive campaign promises and reforms; see Ebel, *Misunderstood Caudillo*, 129–32.

13. "Idigoras Negativo en Entrevista," *El Estudiante*, April 11, 1958. Centro de Investigaciones Regionales de Mesoamérica (CIRMA).

14. Ebel, 129–32.

15. Quiñonez, also known as La Maciste and the author of "Mater Dolorosa," was a close associate of Ubico, a distant relative of the president, and a remarkable character; see Carlos Cáceres, *Aproximación a Guatemala* (Culiacán, Sinaloa: Universidad Autónoma de Sinaloa, 1980), 39, 49; "GUATEMALA: La Maciste," *TIME*, May 15, 1944.

16. "Primera dama trata despectivamente a Universitarias," *El Estudiante*, April 11, 1958. CIRMA; Ebel, 146.

17. Miguel Angel Blanco Carrera, "Organización estudiantil en el nivel de enseñanza media guatemalteco," Lic. thesis, USAC, 1975; Paul Kobrak, *Organizing and Repression in the University of San Carlos, Guatemala, 1944 to 1996* (Washington, DC: American Association for the Advancement of Science, 1999), 20.

18. Ebel, 147.

19. Carlos Martínez Durán, "Discurso pronunciado en la ceremonia de graduación professional del primer semestre," July 11, 1959, in *Discursos universitarios, 1958–1962* (Guatemala City: Imprenta Universitaria, 1962), 61–74.

20. Martínez Durán, "Discurso pronunciado en el acto de graduación profesional del segundo semestre y de celebración de la Autonomía Universitaria," December 1, 1959, in *Discursos*, 85.

21. Ibid.

22. Ibid..

23. Letter, Carlos Martínez Durán to AEU Junta Directiva, December 4, 1958. Archivo General de la Universidad de San Carlos (AGUSAC).

24. Mario Alvarado Rubio, "La Huelga de Dolores," *El Imparcial,* February 4, 1956. CIRMA. Years of accusations of corruption led to strict regulations. Selected members of the organizing committee were required to be active members in their respective student association and the AEU in the present and preceding year; enrolled in at least their second year or third academic cycle; could not have belonged to the Huelga committee the previous year and could not be a prominent or powerful member in a political party, union, or religious body, and nor could they be a member of the active military or a public figure; finally, committee members had to have experience managing funds of a student organization in the previous two years and evidence of the appropriate management of those funds. See Articles 3, 4, and 9 of Decree 10 of the *Constitución del Consejo Superior Estudinatil*, February 20, 1957; and Letter, Juan Francisco Manrique, Secretary of Organization of the AEU, February 17, 1959, AGUSAC.

25. Mario Alvarado Rubio, "La Huelga de Dolores."

26. Ibid.

27. "Final de la Tradicional Huelga de Dolores Desvirtuado Hacen Ver los Estudiantes Católicos en un Manifiesto," n/d. CIRMA.

28. "Respeto a la dignidad del hombre," *El Imparcial*, March 24, 1956, CIRMA.

29. "Mensaje de la Mujer Guatemalteca a los Estudiantes Universitarios," *El Imparcial*, April 11, 1957. CIRMA.

30. Ibid.

31. Ibid.

32. Ibid.

33. Martínez Durán, *Discursos*, 76.

34. Mario Efraín Castañeda Maldonado, "Historia de Rock en Guatemala: La música rock como expresión social en la ciudad de Guatemala entre 1960 y 1976," BA Thesis, USAC, 2008, 48–49. Of course, this exciting new rock 'n' roll culture did

not liberate young people from the exclusions of being working class, poor, or women. Only one band, the Locos del Ritmo, had a female singer (Anabella Portilla), and her family attended her performances to make sure she behaved. Young women navigated multiple moral codes within the rapid growth of urban youth culture. Like *huelgueros*, young *rockeros* and *rockeras* were closely watched and their behavior discussed as a matter of national importance, even in the news.

35. In 1903, police killed a student participant; in 1906, they closed the *Facultad* of Medicine in an effort to stop the event, which was held outside anyway; in 1913 military police entered the *Facultad* of Medicine and the *Facultad* of Law, leading to injuries, arrests, and exile; in 1917, police again arrested students at the *Facultad* of Medicine. See "Biografía Sintética de la Huelga del Viernes de Dolores," *El Informador Estudiantil*, January–February 1956. CIRMA.

36. Letter to AEU President, n/d. AGUSAC. This mysterious letter appears in the USAC archives in a stack of correspondence received by the AEU in early 1958. Although no group or organization was named, twenty-six names are signed at the bottom.

37. Letter, from the Directorate of the AEU to all university students, January 1958. AGUSAC.

38. "El buen humor y la cultura. Por el Nombre de la Entidad Universitaria," *Prensa Libre*, March 29,1958. CIRMA.

39. "Derroche de Ingenio Hicieron los Estudiantes en la Velada," *El Espectador*, March 17, 1959. CIRMA. *El Espectador* was directed by Baltasar Morales de la Cruz, a journalist who held various cabinet positions after the counterrevolution and who would be famously kidnapped by the FAR on May 4, 1966.

40. A late March *Prensa Libre* article located the origins of the Huelga in the Testament of Judas. In this Catholic ritual commonly celebrated in Mayan Catholic communities, a letter written by Judas Iscariot is circulated through the community on the Saturday before Easter. The letter always begins with an opening such as, "*Hoy como todos los años*," or "Today like every year," and then insults, scolds, and admonishes members of the community who had committed some sort of misdeed in the previous year. Beginning in 1898, students in the *facultades* of Law and Medicine used the tradition to critique certain professors, make fun of fellow students, and create a small space for dissent in the long run of late-ninteenth-century dictatorships. In keeping with this honorable tradition, mid-twentieth-century students were obliged to behave with politesse and respect for human dignity, especially because their event combatted injustice and wickedness. "Huelga de Dolores. Debe Ceñirse a la Cultura Universitaria," *Prensa Libre*, March 5, 1959. CIRMA. See Robin Ann Shoaps, "Ritual and (Im)moral Voices: Locating the Testament of Judas in Sakapultek Communicative Ecology," *American Ethnologist* 36, no. 3 (August 2009): 459–77.

41. In 1959, students in Honduras and El Salvador attempted to organize similar events, but were disrupted by money laundering and extortion. "La Mala Semilla: También en Honduras," *Prensa Libre*, June 22, 1959; "Remedio contra actos de incultura," *Prensa Libre*, June 2, 1959; "La Mala Semilla Cunde y Fructifica," *Prensa Libre*, August 1, 1959. CIRMA.

42. There is a fascinating note in the "Letters" section of *Students for a Democratic Society Bulletin*, Vol. 4, No. 1, entitled "Ramblings Through Mexico and Guatemala," wherein a student member of SDS named Philip Russell (his playful nom de guerre seems to be "fitun fil") details his travels and discusses the upcoming 1965 presidential elections. He references articles from *Monthly Review* and opines about the possibility for Marxist revolution ("even the Marxist idea of progression from capitalism to communism isn't applicable, because they haven't even gotten to capitalism yet"). Philip Russell, "Ramblings Through Mexico and Guatemala," *Students for a Democratic Society Bulletin* 4, no. 1 (1965).

43. *El Estudiante*, April 21, 1961. CIRMA.

44. Ibid.

45. *Prensa Libre*, January 20, 1961. HN.

46. Editorial, *Voz Informativa Universitaria*, February 24, 1962. AGUSAC.

47. "Jornadas patrióticas del marzo y abril: 15 años después," *Voz Informativa Universitaria*, 6, no. 3 (March–April 1977). AGUSAC.

48. "Jornadas patrióticas del marzo y abril: 15 años después." AGUSAC.

49. The Cuban example has proven more impactful in Nicaragua, given the similarity between familial dictatorial regimes and U.S. support. Another glaring difference is how the left did not win the Guatemalan civil war and subsequently seize state power.

50. See *Prensa Libre*, March 5, 1962. HN.

51. Victor Manuel Gutiérrez, *Guatemala contra Ydígoras* (Guatemala City: n.p., 1962), 55–56.

52. Ibid.

53. Rock salt shells are typical shotgun shells hand-loaded with rock salt in place of lead or steel shot. At a long range, they cause stinging injuries, but are not fatal; at a short distance, they can be quite dangerous.

54. *Prensa Libre*, March 14, 1962, in Álvarez Aragón, *Conventos, Aulas y Trincheras*, 332.

55. Manuel Colom Argueta, *Guatemala, el significado de las jornadas de marzo y abril* (Guatemala City: USAC, 1979), 18.

56. Comisión para Esclarecimiento Histórico, *Memoria del Silencio* (Guatemala City: CEH, 1999), 153; Gutiérrez, 55–56.

57. On the reception of this news in the United States, see "University Council Statement Scored," *Daily Report*, Foreign Radio Broadcasts, FBIS-FRB-62-058 on March 23, 1962.

58. Grandin, 94–95; Levenson-Estrada, 44; Kobrak, 21, 23.

59. Despatch 494, Bell to Department of State, March 31, 1962, in Ebel, 248.

60. "La Asociación de Estudiantes Universitarios al Pueblo de Guatemala...," *Prensa Libre*, April 12, 1962; "Presidente de la AEU Declara," *Prensa Libre*, April 10, 1962. CIRMA.

61. Noel Arturo López Toledo and Jorge Gálvez Gallindo were shot. "Prosigue proceso contra los que mataron a los estudiantes," *Impacto*, July 5, 1962. AGUSAC.

62. *Prensa Libre*, April 13, 1962. HN.

63. For a different perspective, see Miguel Ydígoras Fuentes and Mario Rosenthal, *My War With Communism* (Englewood Cliffs, NJ: Prentice-Hall, 1963).

64. "Challenge to AEU," Daily Report, Foreign Radio Broadcasts, FBIS-FRB-62-087 on May 3, 1962.

65. Miguel Angel Reyes Illescas, *El Poder Político de los Estudiantes Universitarios*, MA thesis, USAC, 1967, 25–32.

66. Kobrak, 35; Rodolfo Azmitia Jiménez, "Desarrollo del Movimiento estudiantil guatemalteco," in *Tricentinario Universidad de San Carlos de Guatemala, 1676–1976* (Guatemala City: Editorial Universitaria, 1976), 270.

67. See Victoria Langland, *Speaking of Flowers: Student Movements and the Making and Remembering of 1968 in Military Brazil* (Durham, NC: Duke University Press, 2013); Jaime Pensado, *Rebel Mexico: Student Unrest and Authoritarian Political Culture During the Long Sixties* (Stanford, CA: Stanford University Press, 2013).

68. Reyes Illescas, *El Poder Político*, 25–32.

69. Adolfo Gilly, "The Guerrilla Movement in Guatemala." *Monthly Review* 17, no. 1 (May 1965): 17.

70. Kobrak, 32–34; Reyes Illescas, 33; Levenson-Estrada, 43.

71. Colom Argueta, *Guatemala, el significado de las jornadas*, 22.

72. Ibid., 18.

73. Young people killed in the skirmish included secondary school students Carlos Toledo Hernández, Guillermo Grajeda Zetina, and Roberto Heller Playa, and San Carlistas Alfonso Jocol and Brasil Hernández.

74. See "Los antecedents inmediatos," *Diálogo* No. 47 *Marzo y abril de 1962: Momento clave de la memoria histórica de la lucha Revolucionaria* (October 2012).

75. *Guerra Popular por el EGP*, November 3, 1975. CIRMA.

76. Amílcar Burgos, "Bajo el mando de la AEU: El estudiante guatemalteco combate por democracia," *The Student*. CIRMA; see also "Amílcar Burgos, un testigo de nuestro tiempo," in *Por la democracia, el desarrollo y la paz: Coloquio en homenaje a Amílcar Burgos Solís* (Guatemala City: INCEP, 2014).

77. The ISC and IUS held conferences or seminars in all of these places between 1958 and 1963. Many students involved in the late 1960s revolts rejected these international student organizations as colonizing projects; see Philip G. Altbach, *The Student Internationals. An Analysis of International and Regional Student Organizations. Final Report* (Madison: University of Wisconsin Department of Educational Policy Studies, 1970).

78. See Carlos Alberto Enriquez, *Guatemala: no más exilio* (Guatemala City: CONGCOOP, 1995).

79. COSEC published in French, English, and Spanish, reaching most parts of the world where anticolonial struggles were in progress. COSEC publications of interest include: *Independence and the Student: The Report of the International Student Conference Delegation to Asia, 1955–1956*; *World Student Press Survey*; *The Story of the World's Student Refugees: The Situations, the Causes, the Needs*; *Algeria: The Struggle of UGEMA*; *The Conclusions of Participants at the Latin American Student Study Seminar*; *Seminar on the Role of the Student in Economic and Social Develop-*

ment: *Hazmieh, Lebanon, 10–16 December, 1963; International Guide to the Student Press;* and *A Guide to International Student Faculty Organizations.*

80. Telegram, Julio Rodríguez Aldana and Antonio Fernández Izaguirre to the President of the Federación de Estudiantes Universitarios (FEU), December 19, 1958; Telegram, AEU to COSEC, n/d; Paid political advertisement, AEU Junta Directiva y Ejecutiva, June 4, 1959. AGUSAC. The USAC General Archive has an impressive collection of telegrams and letters from students and student groups around the world.

81. Deborah Levenson, *Adiós Niño* (Durham, NC: Duke University Press, 2013), 3.

82. There are many letters between the AEU and FASGUA at the AGUSAC.

83. Grandin, 244n133; See also Kobrak, 32–34.

84. "Terrorist Captured," *Diario de Centro América*, June 27, 1962. AGUSAC.

85. Charges of terrorism have long justified state repression. The histories of Europe and the United States in the twenty-first century continue this terrible practice.

86. "La autonomía universitaria en peligro y la dignidad y soberanía nacional soslayadas. Manifiesto Estudiantil," August 1962. AGUSAC. Three years earlier, the AEU circulated a long report on the history of various military, economic, and infrastructural arrangements between Guatemala and the United States that called these so-called bilateral treaties a form of colonialism; AEU, "Consideraciones sobre algunos convenios y contratos norteamericanos en Guatemala," July 30, 1959. AGUSAC.

87. Editorial, "The Progress of Our Struggle" and "Foreign Educational Interference in the Guatemalan University," *No Nos Tientes*, April 1963. CIRMA.

88. "AEU Proclama," *No Nos Tientes*, April 1963. CIRMA.

89. See Régis Debray, *Revolution in the Revolution?* (New York: Grove, 1967) on divisions within 1960s Marxisms and disagreements within the FAR.

90. Jennifer Schirmer, *The Guatemalan Military Project: A Violence Called Democracy* (Philadelphia: University of Pennsylvania Press, 1988), 157.

91. In 1957, USAC administrator Julio Hernández Sifontes located students' political radicalization in the growing material insecurity of the middle sectors, arguing students with little prospect of future success were inclined toward Marxism or totalitarianism. See Sifontes, *El servicio de bienestar estudiantil en la Universidad de San Carlos de Guatemala* (Guatemala City: USAC, 1957), 39.

92. Carlos Alberto Figueroa, "Fragmentos del discurso del Presidente de la AEH en el acto de toma de posesión," October 4, 1961. CIRMA.

93. Ibid.; Martínez Durán, "Discurso pronunciado en el acto de graduación."

CHAPTER FOUR

1. Editorial, *No Nos Tientes*, April 1966. Centro de Investigaciones Regionales de Mesoamérica (CIRMA).

2. It was also used more metaphorically to denote when one discredits oneself in a conversation and seems linked to the Arabic word (in English phonetics), *chafa* (to prostrate on the floor). See Roque Barcia, *Diccionario general etimológico de la lengua española, Vol. 2* (Madrid: Álvarez Hermanos, 1887), 575.

3. Editorial, *No Nos Tientes*, 1966.

4. Mario Efraín Castañeda Maldonado, "Historia de Rock en Guatemala: La música rock como expresión social en la ciudad de Guatemala entre 1960 y 1976," BA Thesis, USAC, 2008, 51.

5. Ibid., 53–57. See *El Gráfico*, May 18–June 1, 1965.

6. For instance, the Cuban government declared a year of "Solidarity with Guatemala" in 1966 and hosted Guatemalan San Carlistas at both the Tricontinental Conference in January and the OCLAE conference in August.

7. USAC Departamento de Registro y Estadística, *Boletín Estadístico Universitario*, Año 15, 1976.

8. Departamento de Censos y Encuestas, Dirección General de Estadística, *Censo de Población de Guatemala de 1964* (Guatemala City: Ministerio de Economía, 1964). See also USAC Departamento de Registro y Estadística, *Carácterísticas socioeconónicos de estudiantes de primer ingreso*, No. 3 (1971/1973); USAC Departamento de Registro y Estadística, *Estadísticas de graduados, 1972–1974*.

9. "Confederación Universitaria, 1948–1973" (San José: Departamento de Publicaciones de la Universidad de Costa Rica, 1973), 4, 12; "Estatutos de la Universidad de San Carlos de Guatemala," *Boletín Universitario*, February 15, 1948, Año II: No. 1. Hemeroteca Nacional (HN).

10. AEU, "Misiones culturales y sociales de la Asociación de Estudiantes Universitarios de Guatemala," *Informador Estudiantil*, April 1958. CIRMA.

11. "Dictámen de la Facultad de Ciencias Económicas sobre el 'Contrato con EXMIBAL' (marzo de 1970)." CIRMA.

12. John Tate Lanning; *La extensión universitaria*, Tomo I. (Mexico City: UNAM, 1979).

13. A. Ricardo López, ""Conscripts of Democracy" in *The Making of the Middle Class: Toward a Transnational History*, ed. A. Ricardo López and Barbara Weinstein (Durham, NC: Duke University Press, 2012), 172.

14. José Luis Balcárcel Ordóñez, "En torno a la dialéctica de la Universidad," in *Pensamiento Universitario: Enfoque Crítico* (Guatemala City: Editorial Universitaria, 1978), 55–74. The essay was published in Spanish in 1970; *Lenin y filosofía*, trans. Felipe Sarabia (Mexico City: Era, 1970).

15. On the related history of petrol and the middle class in Mexico, see Louise Walker, *Waking from the Dream: Mexico's Middle Class after 1968* (Stanford, CA: Stanford University Press, 2013), 75–104.

16. Rafael Piedra Santa Arandi, *El petróleo y los minerales en Guatemala: Problemas Creados*, Segunda Edición. Colección Problemas Socio-Económicos, No. 1 (Guatemala City: Facultad de Ciencias Económicas, USAC, 1979).

17. "Discurso del Presidente de la República de Guatemala, Armas, pronunciado con motivo del III Aniversario del MLN," July 3, 1957, 14–15. CIRMA.

18. López, 163.

19. Letter from Salvador Catalán Zenteno and Carlos Castro Roca to the AEU, July 21, 1966. AGUSAC.

20. J. T. Way, *The Mayan in the Mall* (Durham, NC: Duke University Press, 2012), 120.

21. Francisco Villagrán Kramer, Manuel Colom Argueta, and Adolfo Mijangos López. *Bases para el desarrollo económico y social de Guatemala*. (Mexico City: Comisión de planificación de Unidad Revolucionaria Democrática, 1966).

22. Ibid., 9.

23. Ibid., 24.

24. Ibid., 18–19.

25. Ibid., 131–33.

26. Ibid., 100–101.

27. Ibid., 128. Villagrán Kramer presented these plans at UNESCO-sponsored conferences around the world, including Chile (1962) and Tehran (1964), calling to mind Frantz Fanon's observation in *The Wretched of the Earth*: "The leadership and students of the underdeveloped countries are a gold mine for the airlines." Fanon, *The Wretched of the Earth*, trans. Richard Philcox (New York: Grove, 2004), 42.

28. "Opinion: Bernardo Lemus Mendoza (1931–1981)." *El Periódico*, December 14, 2011. HN.

29. Bernardo Lemus Mendoza, *Diversas vías para el desarrollo de Guatemala* (Guatemala City: Piedra Santa, 1966), 76.

30. Ibid.

31. Ibid.

32. Ibid., 75.

33. Ibid., 76–77.

34. Ibid., 77.

35. Paul A. Baran, *The Political Economy of Growth* (New York: Monthly Review Press, 1962), 32.

36. Lemus Mendoza, 77.

37. Ibid., 77–79.

38. Way, 119–20.

39. EXMIBAL, *Exmibal: nueva industria guatemalteca de exportación* (Guatemala City: Exmibal, 1975). CIRMA.

40. "Exmibal: Una Nueva Industria para Guatemala" (Guatemala City: Unión Tipográfico, 1969), 5. CIRMA.

41. EXMIBAL, *Exmibal*. CIRMA.

42. In October 1971, USAC students went on indefinite strike to demand an end to the State of Siege; see Alan Riding, "Guatemalan Students Begin Strike As Protest Against Violence and to Press Regime to Lift State of Siege," *New York Times*, October 10, 1971: 29.

43. Greg Grandin, *The Last Colonial Massacre* (Chicago: University of Chicago Press, 2004), 76, 87–88, 95, 132.

44. Burial grounds used by the Cuerpo de Detectives are still being discovered and exhumed; see Kirsten Weld, *Paper Cadavers: The Archives of Dictatorship in Guatemala* (Durham, NC: Duke University Press, 2014), 132.

45. "Guatemalan Antiterrorist Campaign," Defense Intelligence Agency, Secret Intelligence Bulletin, January 12, 1971. Accessed June 14, 2016. http://nsarchive.gwu.edu/NSAEBB/NSAEBB32/docs/doc13.pdf.

46. See Diane M. Nelson, *Who Counts? The Mathematics of Life and Death after Genocide* (Durham, NC: Duke University Press, 2015).

47. Kay Warren, *Indigenous Movements and Their Critics: Pan-Maya Activism in Guatemala* (Princeton, NJ: Princeton University Press, 1998), 64, 230n15.

48. Severo Martínez Peláez, *Algo sobre repartimientos* (Guatemala City: IIES, 1976); Martínez Peláez, *La política agraria colonial y los orígenes del latifundismo en Guatemala* (Guatemala City: Facultad de Ciencias Económicas, 1980); Martínez Peláez, *Racismo y análisis histórico en la definición del indio guatemalteco* (Guatemala City: Facultad de Ciencias Económicas, 1977). See also Oscar Guillermo Peláez Almengor, *La patria del criollo, tres décadas después* (Guatemala City: Editorial Universitaria, 2000).

49. Severo Martínez Peláez, *La Patria del criollo: ensayo de interpretación de la realidad colonial guatemalteca* (Guatemala City: Editorial Universitaria, 1970), 12.

50. Martínez Peláez wrote course materials for the "Economic History of Central America" course in the Economics *facultad* and led the reform of the School of History in 1978, for which he also designed teaching materials. Martínez Peláez was a distinguished student leader in the USAC Association of Humanities Students before he was exiled in Mexico City after 1954. There met influential Marxists based at UNAM. His orthodox Marxist approach was formed by conversations with Silvio Zavala, Leon Portilla, and Marx's Spanish translator Wenceslao Roces. Eduardo Antonio Velásquez Carrera, *Severo Martínez Peláez, in memoriam* (Guatemala City: USAC CEUR, 2008), 14.

51. Fernando Henrique Cardoso and Faletto Enzo, *Dependency and Development in Latin America* (Berkeley: University of California Press, 1979), 48.

52. Edelberto Torres-Rivas, *Las clases sociales de Guatemala* (Guatemala City: Editorial Landívar, 1964) and *Interpretación del desarrollo social Centroamericano: procesos y estructuras de una sociedad dependiente* (Costa Rica: Editorial Universitaria Centroamericana, 1975); Jorge Rovira Mas, "Edelberto Torres-Rivas, Centroamericano, Razón y Pasión." *Anuario de Estudios Centroamericanos* 26, no. 1–2 (2000): 7–28.

53. Rovira Mas, "Edelberto Torres-Rivas," 9.

54. See López and Weinstein, *The Making of the Middle Class.*

55. Mario Monteforte Toledo, *Centroamérica: Subdesarrollo y dependencia*, vol. 1 (Mexico City: UNAM, 1972), 376–82.

56. Ibid., 377.

57. Ibid., 428–36.

58. Ibid., 304.

59. See Luis Solano, "Development and/as Dispossession: Elite Networks and Extractive Industry in the Franja Transversal del Norte," in *War by Other Means*, ed. Carlota McAllister and Diane M. Nelson (Durham, NC: Duke University Press, 2013), 119–42.

60. Ibid.

61. Way, 126–27.

62. Asociación de Estudiantes de Medicina, "Seminario sobre el 'técnico en salud rural,'" November 6, 1971. CIRMA.

63. Roberto Valdeavellano Pinot, *Declaración de la Universidad de San Carlos de Guatemala con relación a la posible explotación del petróleo en Guatemala.* Guatemala City, April 5, 1975. Archivo General Centroamérica (AGCA).

64. See editions of *El Gráfico* and *El Imparcial,* April 10, 1975. HN.

65. For a summary of potential investors, exploratory projects, and regional mineral deposits in Alta Verapaz, Izabal, and El Petén, see *El Gráfico,* July 19, 1976, and April 13, 1976. HN.

66. See *El Gráfico,* December 9, 1975; *La Tarde,* April 30, 1975. HN.

67. AEU, *Jornadas de Agosto de 1977* (Guatemala City: Facultad de Ciencias Económicas de la USAC, 1977), 5. CIRMA.

68. Immanuel Wallerstein, *El Moderno sistema mundial* (Madrid: Siglo XXI, 1979).

69. Mario Monteforte Toledo, *Guatemala: Monografía sociológica* (Mexico City: Instituto de Investigaciones Sociales, UNAM, 1965), 434; Alfonso Bauer Paiz, *La penetración extranjera en la universidad* (Guatemala City: n.p., 1968). CSUCA received US$456,000 from the Ford Foundation and US$348,000 from USAID in 1968.

70. *El Gráfico,* April 28, 1976. HN.

71. "Maniobras de las Compañías Petroleras: Denuncia la Facultad de Ingeniería," *La Palabra,* May 10–15, 1976. CIRMA.

72. Piedra Santa Arandi, 34.

73. His thesis committee included many San Carlistas who have appeared throughout the book, including Celso Cerezo Dardón, Otto Marroquín Guerra, Carlos René Recinos Sandoval, Hugo Rolando Melgar y Melgar, and Mario López Larrave. Many of these men were assassinated for their solutions to the problem of inequality.

74. Alfredo Figueroa Mendez, "Fundamentos y principios del Derecho de la exploración y explotación de petróleo," Thesis, Universidad de San Carlos, 1977, 22–23.

75. See *7 días en la USAC,* No. 15, Época I. Año 2., January 29–February 4, 1978. CIRMA.

76. "20 de Julio 1973/22 marzo 1974 ocho meses trágicos para la USAC," *Voz Informativa Universitaria,* No. 1. Época VI, Año V, July 1979. CIRMA.

77. Their statement singled out the installation of International Nickel Company (INCO) in the Izabal region, the petrol industry in the northern departments, and the construction of an interoceanic gas pipeline through Guatemala to transport gas from Alaska to refineries in the eastern United States as particularly abhorrent. Comisión para Esclarecimiento Histórico (CEH), "Caso ilustrativo no. 100," *Memoria del Silencio* (Guatemala City: CEH, 1999).

78. Consejo Superior Universitario Centroamericano, Dirección de asuntos culturales (febrero–marzo 1979, No. 30–31 año III). AGUSAC.

79. On the figure of the illiterate Maya in jokes, see Diane M. Nelson, *Reckoning: The Ends of War in Guatemala* (Durham, NC: Duke University Press, 2009), 252–53.

80. See David S. Parker, "*Siúticos, Huachafos, Cursis, Arribistas,* and *Gente de Medio Pelo*: Social Climbers and the Representation of Class in Chile and Peru, 1860–1930," in López and Weinstein, *The Making of the Middle Class*, 336.

81. "Huelga de Dolores . . . Se Sugiere a los Estudiantes Hacer sus Celebraciones Dentro de sus Propias Facultades," *Prensa Libre*, March 26, 1966. CIRMA.

82. "Policía Dispersa Reunion Estudiantil," *La Hora*, March 19, 1966. CIRMA.

83. "Huelga de Dolores se Desarrollará Este Año en el Ambito Universitario," *Prensa Libre*, March 31, 1966. CIRMA.

84. "Cateo en Casa de la AEU y Aprehendidos," *Prensa Libre,* April 1, 1966. CIRMA. Archivo Histórico de la Policía Nacional (AHPN), *Del Silencio a la Memoria* (Guatemala City: AHPN, 2011).

85. "Cateo en Casa." CIRMA.

86. *El Estudiante*, Época IV, No. 2, August 1966. CIRMA.

87. CEH, "Caso Ilustrativo No. 68," *Memoria del Silencio.*

88. *El Estudiante*, Época IV, No. 4, October 20, 1966. CIRMA.

89. *No Nos Tientes*, 1969. CIRMA.

90. Way, 120.

91. "The Philosophy of the Vulturegovernment," *No Nos Tientes*, 1974. CIRMA.

92. Eighteenth-century French philosopher and critic Denis Diderot theorized this separation between the world of a play and its audience; it has been a powerful convention in modern theatre. "Breaking the fourth wall" refers to the practice of speaking to or acknowledging the audience.

93. On a similar feminization and diminution of student activist women in Brazil, see Victoria Langland, *Speaking of Flowers: Student Movements and the Making and Remembering of 1968 in Military Brazil* (Durham, NC: Duke University Press, 2013), 8, 176, 239, 242.

94. Mary Jane Treacy, "Killing the Queen: The Display and Disappearance of Rogelia Cruz," *Latin American Literary Review* 29, no. 57 (January–June 2001): 40–51.

95. *El Imparcial* reported on January 13, 1968, that Cruz was raped and her breasts and nipples cut and bitten; Treacy, "Killing the Queen," 45.

96. Juan Carlos Vázquez Medeles, "Universidad, muralización y fotografía: Legado artístico de la insurgencia en Guatemala," in *En los entornos contemporáneos: violencia, huellas y representación*, ed. Eunice Miranda Tapia and Juan Ramón Rodríguez-Mateo (Seville: EnredARS, 2014), 115.

97. Ricardo Sáenz de Tejada, *Oliverio: una biografía del secretario general de la AEU, 1978–1979* (Guatemala City: FLACSO, 2010), 94–103. According to FRENTE founder and historian Edgar Ruano Najarro, the PGT had gained control over all *facultad*-based student associations and the AEU by 1976; Ruano Najarro, "Para comprender a Oliverio Castañeda de León a treinta años de su asesinato," in *Oliverio vive!*, ed. Rebeca Alonzo Martínez (Guatemala City: CEUR, 2008), 28.

98. *Alero*, No. 30, Tercera época, mayo–junio 1978. AGUSAC; "Universitarias." *Inforpress*. February 21, 1973. CIRMA.

99. Cuevas del Cid had devoted his tenure to opposing the penetration of foreign capital into Guatemalan utilities and services and led the CSU to issue several

denunciations of the government's response to the escalating violence in the city. Rafael Cuevas del Cid, "La Autonomía: En relación con los fines y objetivos de la Universidad, May 1977," in *Pensamiento Universitario: Enfoque Crítico* (Guatemala City: Editorial Universitaria, 1978), 114–15.

100. Vázquez Medeles, "Universidad, muralización y fotografía," 112–21.

101. Telegram from American Embassy in Guatemala to Secretary of State, "Valdeavellano Elected Rector of San Carlos University," November 23, 1973. WikiLeaks. https://www.wikileaks.org/plusd/cables/1974GUATEM00456_b .html. Accessed January 15, 2016.

102. "Políticas." *Inforpress*, November 7, 1973. CIRMA.

103. "La Misión de la Universidad: Declaración del Rector de la Universidad de San Carlos de Guatemala, Dr. Robert Valdeavellano P., sobre el papel de la Universidad en las actuales condiciones económicas, sociales, políticas y culturales del país." s/f. Archivo General de Centroamérica (AGCA); *Voz Informativa Universitaria* IV Época No. 3, abril de 1975. CIRMA.

104. See *Voz Informativa Universitaria*, November 1977. CIRMA.

105. Roberto Valdeavellano, "Comunicado de la Rectoría de la Universidad de San Carlos sobre el préstamo que el gobierno de la República ha contratado con el BID con destino a instituciones privadas de enseñanza superior." June 7, 1974. CIRMA.

106. "Editorial," *No Nos Tientes*, 1969, 1–2. CIRMA.

107. Interamerican Development Bank, *El BID en Guatemala* (Washington, DC: IDB, 1979), 2.

108. "Discurso pronunciado por el Rector de la Universidad de San Carlos de Guatemala, Dr. Roberto Valdeavellano P., en al Acto de Graduación Profesional y de Conmemoración de la Autonomía Universitaria, December 1, 1975." AGCA.

109. "Política general de la extensión universitaria," in *Segundo Seminario de Extensión Universitaria, Antigua, Guatemala. August 19–20, 1977* (Guatemala City: Editorial Universitaria, 1978), 138–39, 151.

110. Ibid., 138–39.

111. Fuerzas Armadas Rebeldes (FAR), *Hacía una interpretación nacional concreta y dialéctica del Marxismo Leninismo* (Guatemala City: FAR, 1973), 4–5. CIRMA.

112. FAR, *Causa Proletaria, Expresión de los Obreros Revolucionarios* (Guatemala City: FAR, n.d.). CIRMA.

113. On the tension between the ideal revolutionary multiclass alliance and persistent class/race divides in Latin American militancy, see Iñigo García-Bryce's "A Middle-Class Revolution: The APRA Party and Middle-Class Identity in Peru, 1931–1956," in López and Weinstein, *The Making of the Middle Class*, 235–52.

114. "Educación: Otra llaga del atraso y la dependencia," *Juventud: Vocero de la Juventud Patriótica del Trabajo*, January 1977, 2–3. CIRMA.

115. *Órgano divulgativo de JPT*, No. 5, época IV, July 1975. CIRMA.

116. On youth culture in the city, see Castañeda Maldonado, "Historia de Rock en Guatemala: La música rock como expresión social en la ciudad de Guatemala entre 1960 y 1976," BA Thesis, USAC, 2008.

117. Ibid., 60. The author argues that countercultural youth were forced to confront their politico-social reality after the 1976 earthquake.

118. The film *Woodstock* screened in Guatemala City on November 4, 1970. Four years later, more than a thousand young people trekked to a finca in San Juan Sacatepéquez on May 27, 1974, just weeks after San Carlista human rights activist Edmundo Guerra Thelheimer's assassination and the fraudulent elections of Laugerud García, for Guatemala's own outdoor Aquarian Exposition of peace and music, the Lámpara de Acuario; see *El Gráfico*, November 4, 1970; Castañeda Maldonado, "Historia de Rock en Guatemala," 70–71; see also *El Gráfico*, May 27, 1974.

119. Gabriela Escobar and Fernando Rendón, *La construcción de identidades juveniles a partir del rock (1959–2001)*, 66–72 in Castañeda Maldonado, "Historia de Rock en Guatemala," 65n182.

120. "Una declaración al aire," *Juventud: Vocero de la Juventud Patriótica del Trabajo*, August 1975, 3–4. CIRMA.

121. Participants included Roberto Díaz Castillo, Mario Dary Rivera, Virgilio Álvarez Aragón, Mario Lemus, César A. Barrientos, Luis Alvarado Castañeda, Julia Vela, Manuel José Arce L., Roberto Cabrera, and Edgar Leonel Díaz Siliezar.

122. "Política general," *Segundo Seminario de Extensión Universitaria*, 150–51.

123. Ibid.

124. "Ponencia del Consejo de Extensión Universitaria," *Segundo Seminario de Extensión Universitaria*, 128.

125. Ligia Marcella Valdeavellano Valle, "La potencialidad de la historieta cómica," in *Segundo Seminario de Extensión Universitaria, Antigua, Guatemala. August 19–20, 1977*, 221–22.

126. "Propósito del Seminario," in *Segundo Seminario de Extensión Universitaria*, 13–14; "Ponencia del Consejo de Extensión Universitaria," in *Segundo Seminario de Extensión Universitaria*, 30–31.

127. The French Embassy funded several seasons that brought films by directors Serge Roullet, Robert Bresson, and master of French police dramas Jean-Pierre Melville. Roberto Cabrera, "Las artes plásticas y la extensión universitaria," in *Segundo Seminario de Extensión Universitaria*, 174–80.

128. Ibid., 31–32.

129. "Ponencia del Consejo de Extensión Universitaria," 30–31; see also "Plan de trabajo de la Cinemateca Universitaria" and "Lo político en el teatro," in *Segundo Seminario de Extensión Universitaria*.

130. Cabrera, 188–89.

131. Antonio Erazo and Cesar A. Barrientos, "Ponencia sobre Difusión Científica y Extensión Universitaria," in *Segundo Seminario de Extensión Universitaria*, 160. Paulo Freire's methods were influential among extension programs throughout the 1970s. See also "Entrevistando a candidato a rector: Universidad integrada al pueblo," *La Nación*, September 29, 1973. CIRMA.

132. Erazo and Barrientos, 159.

133. Roberto Díaz Castillo, Mario Maldonado, Rene Poitevín, Manuel Andrade Roca, and Francisco Albizúrez Palma, "Creación de una nueva revista,'" in *Segundo Seminario de Extensión Universitaria*, 209–10.

134. Ibid.

135. Ibid., 151.

136. René Eduardo Poitevín Dardón, *Quiénes Somos? La Universidad de San Carlos y las clases sociales* (Guatemala City: USAC Instituto de Investigaciones y Mejoramiento Educativo, 1977).

137. Robert Valdeavellano Pinot, "Palabras pronunciadas por el Rector de la Universidad de San Carlos de Guatemala, Dr. Roberto Valdeavellano Pinot, en el acto inaugural del II Seminario de Extensión Universitaria," in *Segundo Seminario de Extensión Universitaria*, 144.

138. Ibid.

139. Carlos Gehlert Mata, "Ensayo crítico sobre el papel de las Universidades y los grupos comunitarios en el uso y/o adaptación tecnológica: sector salud," in *Pensamiento Universitario: Enfoque Crítico* (Guatemala City: Editorial Universitaria, 1978), 309.

140. López, "Conscripts of Modernity," 171.

141. Otto Guzmán and Mario Alberto Carrera, "Centro de Difusión Cultural," in *Segundo Seminario de Extensión Universitaria*, 169.

142. Wendy Brown, *States of Injury* (Princeton, NJ: Princeton University Press, 1995), 398.

143. José Rölz Bennett, "Ensayo de definición de la Universidad," in *Pensamiento Universitario: Enfoque Crítico* (Guatemala City: Editorial Universitaria, 1978), 30.

144. Edelberto Torres-Rivas, *Las clases sociales en Guatemala* (Guatemala City: Editorial Landívar, 1964), 30–31.

CHAPTER FIVE

1. AEU, "El gobierno de Laugerud tiene la opción: o continua encubriendo los crímenes contra el pueblo o desmantela el plan de los sectores fascistas," August, 30, 1977, in *Jornadas de Agosto*, ed. AEU (Guatemala City: USAC, 2007).

2. Rosa Sánchez del Valle and the Fundación para la Democracia Manuel Colom Argueta, *Por el delito de pensar* (Guatemala City: Friedrich Ebert Stiftung Representación en Guatemala, 1999), 85–86.

3. Mario López Larrave, *Breve historia del movimiento sindical guatemalteco* (Guatemala City: Editorial Universitaria, 1976).

4. Sánchez del Valle, 81.

5. Ibid., 87–88.

6. Virginia Garrard-Burnett, *Terror in the Land of the Holy Spirit* (New York: Oxford University Press, 2010), 51.

7. Deborah Levenson-Estrada, *Trade Unionists Against Terror: Guatemala City, 1954–1985* (Chapel Hill: University of North Carolina Press, 1994), 66–67.

8. Marta Elena Casaús Arzú and Oscar Guillermo Peláez Almengor, eds., *Historia intelectual de Guatemala* (Guatemala City: Centro de Estudios Urbanos y Regionales de USAC, 2001; Levenson-Estrada, 67.

9. Gonzalo M. Asturias and Ricardo F. Gatica, *Terremoto 76: S.O.S. Guatemala.* (Guatemala City: Ediciones Girblán, 1976), 18. The film was inspired by the San Francisco earthquake in February 1971, according to its director Mark Robson and producer Jennings Lang.

10. Andrés Asturias, Gemma Gil, and Raúl Monterroso, *Moderna: guía de arquitectura de Ciudad de Guatemala* (Guatemala City: Centro Cultural de España, 2008).

11. A. F. Espinosa, ed., *The Guatemalan Earthquake of February 4, 1976, A Preliminary Report.* U.S. Geological Survey Professional Paper 1002 (Washington, DC: GPO for U.S. Geological Survey, 1976); Asturias and Gatica, 115; "Mapa de área afectada por el terremoto del 4 de febrero de 1976," Instituto Nacional de Sismología, Vulcanología, Meteorología y Hidrología (Guatemala City: INSIVUMEH).

12. In fact, these estimates are conservative because social scientists could not account for the vulnerable citizens who lived in squatter communities on the periphery of the city. The earthquake also triggered new waves of migration to the city. Between 100,000 and 150,000 people moved to the city following the earthquake. Many new migrants settled in encampments vulnerable to landslides and aftershocks.

13. Gisela Gellert and Julio César Pinto Soria, *Ciudad de Guatemala: dos estudios sobre su evolución urbana, 1524–1950* (Guatemala City: CEUR de USAC, 1990), 36; Instituto Nacional de Estadística, *Censos nacionales de 1981: cifras definitivas* (Guatemala City: INE, 1984); Theodore Caplow, *La ecología social de la ciudad de Guatemala* (Guatemala City: Ministerio de Educación, 1966), 127.

14. Asturias and Gatica, 67. For those sympathetic to the military, the president's response was remembered as an attempt to console the people; for others, it was an unfeeling disavowal of their suffering. A similar phenomenon occurred in Mexico following President Miguel de la Madrid's failure to help neighborhoods rebuild in Mexico City in 1985. As in Guatemala, the middle classes worked rebuild in the face of the government's failure. See Louise Walker, *Waking from the Dream: Mexico's Middle Class after 1968* (Stanford, CA: Stanford University Press, 2013), 173–200.

15. Garrard-Burnett, 44.

16. Virgilio Álvarez Aragón, *Conventos, Aulas y Trincheras, Vol. 2* (Guatemala City: FLACSO, 2002), 114.

17. Asturias and Gatica, 69.

18. See Rebeca Alonzo Martínez, ed. *Oliverio vive: en memoria de mujeres y hombres que ofrendaron su vida por el pueblo de Guatemala* (Guatemala City: Ediciones CEUR, 2008), 113.

19. Manuel Colom Argueta, "La participación de las fuerzas democráticas en la problemática contemporánea," Seminario Mario López Larrave sobre Desarrollo

Sindical, Guatemala City, Guatemala. September 4–5, 1977. Centro de Investigaciones Regionales de Mesoamérica (CIRMA).

20. Ricardo Sáenz de Tejada Rojas, *Oliverio: una biografía del secretario general de la AEU, 1978–1979* (Guatemala City: FLACSO, 2011), 72–73.

21. Ibid., 113.

22. Francisco Villagrán Kramer, *Biografía política de Guatemala, volumen II. Años de guerra y años de paz* (FLACSO, 2004), 105.

23. See José Roberto Godoy Herrera, *Contribución al análisis crítico del proceso de reconstrucción post-terremoto de 1976 en Guatemala* (Guatemala City: Universidad de San Carlos, 1978); Benedicto Revilla, *Guatemala: El terremoto de los pobres* (Madrid: Sedmay Ediciones, 1976).

24. Garrard-Burnett, 118–19; see also Gustavo Porras Castejón, *Las huellas de Guatemala* (Guatemala City: F&G Editores, 2009).

25. On CRATER, see Comisión para Esclarecimiento Histórico (CEH), *Memoria del Silencio.* (Guatemala City: CEH, 1999), 70; Jorge Murga Armas, "Hacía una historia del movimiento social guatemalteco (1954–1978)," *Revista Económica* 187 (January–March 2011): 10; Garrard-Burnett, 18–19.

26. Oficina de Derechos Humanos del Arzobispo de Guatemala (ODHAG), *Guatemala: ¡Nunca más!* (Guatemala City: ODHAG, 1998), 131, in Álvarez Aragón, 117.

27. Álvarez Aragón, 117–18.

28. See CEH, 70;

29. Jennifer Schirmer in J. T. Way, *The Mayan in the Mall* (Durham, NC: Duke University Press, 2013), 136–37.

30. Deborah Levenson, "Reactions to Trauma: The 1976 Earthquake in Guatemala," *International Labor and Working-Class History* 62 (Fall 2002): 60–68.

31. Garrard-Burnett, 44; Levenson, "Reactions to Trauma," 60–68.

32. Sánchez del Valle, 135.

33. Letter to Héctor Cifuentes Aguirre. April 23, 1976. Archivo General de la USAC (AGUSAC).

34. Ibid.

35. Ibid.

36. Ibid.

37. Mario Efraín Castañeda Maldonado, "Historia de Rock en Guatemala: La música rock como expresión social en la ciudad de Guatemala entre 1960 y 1976," BA Thesis, USAC, 2008, 75; see also *El Gráfico*, February and March 1976.

38. See Manuel José Arce, *El Gráfico*, September 2, 1973 in Castañeda Maldonado, 75.

39. Secretariado de la AEU, Public Relations Commission. Comunicado de Prensa. March 1976. AGUSAC.

40. Letter, Jonny Dahinten Castillo to the Secretary General of the AEU, March 5, 1976. AGUSAC.

41. Secretariado de la AEU, Public Relations Commission. Comunicado de Prensa. March 1976. AGUSAC.

42. "83 Años de la Huelga de Dolores," *El Gráfico*, April 2, 1982. CIRMA.

43. Letter from AEU Secretariado to the Junta Directiva of the Association of Architecture Students, March 11, 1976. AGUSAC.

44. Catalina Barrios y Barrios, *100 años y uno más* (Guatemala City: Ediciones y Litografía LOPDEL, 1999).

45. *No Nos Tientes*, 1976. CIRMA.

46. Ibid.

47. Ibid. In literal translation, a *pizote* is a coatimundi, a diurnal mammal related to the raccoon family and native to the Americas. *Pizotes* look like a hybrid raccoon, house cat, and opossum, but with a pig-like snout. Like the *pizote*, the president was often derided as illegitimately Guatemalan, born to a Norwegian father and Guatemalan mother.

48. The students' language is so playful that a literal translation can scarcely do it justice. See *No Nos Tientes*, 1976. CIRMA. See also Vrana, *Anti-colonial Texts from Central American Student Movements, 1929–1983* (Edinburgh: Edinburgh University Press, 2017).

49. This is ironic. For those unfamiliar with Guatemalan beers, all Guatemalan beers are notoriously light and watery. Offered since 1934, Moza is the darkest lager offered by the family of beers.

50. *No Nos Tientes*, 1976. CIRMA.

51. Ibid.

52. Barillas, Byron Renato, Carlos Alberto Enríquez, and Luis Pedro Taracena, *3 Décadas, 2 generaciones: el movimiento estudiantil universitario, una perspectiva desde sus protagonistas* (Guatemala City: Helvetas, 2000), 30; Álvarez Aragón, 124.

53. Barillas et al., 30.

54. Ibid., 123–24.

55. Ibid., 122.

56. Ibid., 67, 97, 123–24.

57. ODHAG, 48–50.

58. Álvarez Aragón, 131.

59. "Quetzaltenango y la ORPA," *El Periódico*, March 19, 2007. Hemeroteca Nacional (HN). On relations between guerrilla groups in the 1970s and 1980s, see Santiago Santa Cruz Mendoza, *Insurgentes: La paz arrancada* (Mexico City: Ediciones Era, 2006); Yolanda Colom, *Mujeres en la alborada* (Guatemala City: Editorial Artemis Edinter, 1998); "Declaration of Revolutionary Unity in Guatemala," *Latin American Perspectives* 9, no. 3 (Summer 1982): 115–22; Elizabeth Burgos and Robert Austin, trans., "The Story of a Testimonio," *Latin American Perspectives* 26, no. 6 (November 1999): 53–63.

60. AEU, Campo Pagado. "La experiencia de octubre está viva." AGUSAC.

61. AEU, "La experiencia." AGUSAC.

62. Secondary school students led a series of successful strikes in early 1976 and 1977, first focused on school-related concerns, but soon demanding the dismissal of minister of education Guillermo Putzeys Alvarez. They would begin the strikes by simply remaining in the school after classes had ended and refusing to grant entry to

teachers, parents, and administrators. Even prior to the earthquake, classrooms were overcrowded and students had scarce access to laboratories. But several school buildings were destroyed in the earthquake, so students from various schools were forced to take classes together in a single building. With more than six hundred students sharing a single classroom and many more unable to attend classes for lack of space, students had plenty to protest. Leaders from various schools met and exchanged ideas, which in turn circulated among an even larger and concentrated student body. The government dismissed the unrest as a symptom of shock after the earthquake, but a group of teachers issued a public statement that asserted that the problems outlined by protesting students were part of systemic shortcomings and that they revealed the lack of a comprehensive education policy since the 1920s presidency of Lázaro Chacón. The minister of education issued a point-by-point reply. Students won some of their demands, like the reinstatement of certain teachers and the allocation of more desks for students, but they were not able to increase federal funding for public schools. "Alumnos en Huelga Explican Motivo," *Prensa Libre* March 5, 1976; "400 estudiantes ocupan Instituto de San Marcos," *La Tarde*, February 26, 1976. CIRMA. "Los problemas" and "Destitución de Funcionarios de Educación," *La Tarde*, March 21, 1977; "Dos versiones y un sólo problema en Comercio," *La Tarde*, January 25, 1977; "Girón Lemus: Los estudiantes tienen razón en sus justas demandas," *La Tarde*, March 19, 1977; "Comunicado de Prensa. Lic. Guillermo Putzeys Alvarez," Minister of Education. April 1, 1977; "Putzeys: Manos Extrañas en el caso de Comercio," *La Tarde*, January 27, 1977; "Dos versiones," *La Tarde*. CIRMA.

63. CEH, 107.

64. "Mario López Larrave: Hombre Honesto, Revolucionario y Luchador," *Voz Informativa Universitaria,* No. 4, Epoca VI, Año III, May–June 1977. CIRMA.

65. The Guerrilla Army of the Poor (EGP) was just accepting the idea that the indigenous masses would form the base of the revolution. None of the major university groups hailed indigenous Mayans from the periphery as the revolutionary core until the 1980s.

66. "Mario López Larrave."

67. *Voz Informativa Universitaria*, May–June 1977. CIRMA.

68. Other books included a collection of Guatemala City folklore by Celso A. Lara Figueroa; a study guide for Karl Marx's *Capital* by Rodolfo Castillo Peralta; a book on agricultural economics by Manuel Villacorta Escobar; *Land and Power in Guatemala* by Thomas Melville; *Foreign Investment in Central America* by Salvadoran professor Rafael Menjívar; *Lenin for Beginners* by Rius (the pseudonym of Mexican cartoonist Eduardo del Río); a short tract on Lenin's *Imperialism* by Rodolfo Banfi; Mexican José Porfirio Miranda de la Parra's influential *Marx and the Bible*; and two books about Nicaraguan revolutionary Augusto César Sandino, including an edition of *El Pensamiento Vivo de Sandino*.

69. Vincent Brown, *The Reaper's Garden: Death and Power in the World of Atlantic Slavery* (Cambridge, MA: Harvard University Press, 2008), 5–6.

70. See Karl Marx, "The Eighteenth Brumaire of Louis Bonaparte," in *Surveys from Exile: Political Writings Volume 2* (New York: Penguin, 1973), 124.

71. AEU, "El gobierno de Laugerud tiene la opción."

72. The National Workers' Central (CNT) united bank, construction, transportation, and factory workers' unions. Levenson-Estrada, *Trade Unionists Against Terror*, 90; Kirsten Weld, *Paper Cadavers: The Archives of Dictatorship in Guatemala* (Durham, NC: Duke University Press, 2014), 62, 93.

73. Levenson-Estrada, *Trade Unionists Against Terror*, 128–29.

74. Ibid., 131.

75. CEH, *Memoria del Silencio*; see also *7 Días en la USAC*, June 18, 1979. AGUSAC.

76. Odilio Jiménez Sánchez, *Los caminos de la resistencia: Comunidad, política e historia Maya* (Austin: University of Texas Press, 2008), 90.

77. CEH, 372.

78. Amnesty International, *Amnesty International Report 1979* (London: Amnesty International Publications, 1979), 6; CEH, 533.

79. See Levenson-Estrada, *Trade Unionists Against Terror*, 128–31. The CUC was formed by many of the rural organizers who hosted the miners.

80. "Elección de Rector en Fiesta Democrática," *El Imparcial*, March 17, 1978. CIRMA.

81. "Plataforma de Trabajo: Saul Osorio, Rector 1978–1982." CIRMA.

82. "Plataforma de Trabajo." CIRMA.

83. "Universitarias," *Inforpress*, March 2, 1978. CIRMA.

84. Paid political advertisement, "Universidad de San Carlos de Guatemala Refuta Informaciones Calumniosas Publicadas por Entidades Estudiantiles," *El Imparcial*, March 8, 1978. CIRMA.

85. "Elección de Rector," *El Imparcial*, CIRMA.

86. Ibid.

87. "Mejia Godoy cantó en el Festival de la Juventud," *El Gráfico*, April 15, 1978. HN.

88. Nicaragua suffered a 6.2 magnitude earthquake on December 23, 1972. The lyrics to "Quincho Barrilete" referred to this earthquake, but the song certainly resonated in Guatemala after 1976.

89. "Una generación de cara a la muerte," *El Gráfico*, April 15, 1978. HN.

90. "Mejía Godoy cantó en el Festival de la Juventud," *El Gráfico*, April 15, 1978. HN.

91. "The Governments of Guatemala and Nicaragua Should Not Intervene Against the Salvadoran People!," AEU, February 15, 1977. AGUSAC.

92. Mimeographed letter and statement, MEPS, July 1977. AGUSAC.

93. Letter, AGEUS to AEU, July 19, 1977. AGUSAC.

94. AEU, "A continuar avanzando en la unidad y combatividad del pueblo trabajador," April 26, 1978. CIRMA.

95. CEH, *Memoria del Silencio*, Anexo 1, Volumen 1. Caso ilustrativo No. 9; Greg Grandin, *The Last Colonial Massacre* (Chicago: University of Chicago Press, 2004), 133–67.

96. Ibid. See also CUNOC, "Conflicto: Panzós," May 30, 1978. CIRMA.

97. Sáenz de Tejada, 1977; Edgar Ruano Najarro, "Para comprender a Oliverio Castañeda de León a treinta años de su asesinato," in *Oliverio Vive!*, ed. Rebeca Alonzo (Guatemala City: Ediciones CEUR, 2008), 36–37.

98. Álvarez Aragón, 189–91.

99. Few student government candidates on the right emerge in the archive after the 1950s. "FRENTE triunfó en elecciones de AEU," *Inforpress*, May 11, 1978. No. 291. CIRMA.

100. "FRENTE triunfó," *Inforpress*. CIRMA.

101. Ruano Najarro, 37.

102. Sáenz de Tejada, 178.

103. CEH, Anexo 1, Volumen 1. Caso ilustrativo No. 45.

104. Ruano Najarro, 37.

105. Manifesto, National Commission for the Commemoration of the First Anniversary of the Vile Assassination of Mario López Larrave, June 8, 1978. AGUSAC.

106. Ibid.

107. Ibid.

108. "La comisión nacional pro-conmemoración." AGUSAC.

109. "Tres años después, los jóvenes recordamos la masacre de Panzós," *Juventud*, May–June 1981, 8. CIRMA.

110. Garrard-Burnett, 47; Grandin, 3.

111. Comité de Familiares de Personas Desaparecidas, "Unidad popular para detener la mano criminal de los fascistas y continuar en la lucha por una sociedad justa," June 1978. AGUSAC.

112. Sáenz de Tejada, 183.

113. Bus strikes were common; there had been one in December 1976 and there would be another bus fare strike in September 1985.

114. Levenson-Estrada, 146.

115. Grandin, *The Last Colonial Massacre*, 162.

116. Levenson-Estrada, 146; Álvarez Aragón, 248–49.

117. "Suman 362 los detenidos, se confirmo en la policía hoy," *La Hora,* October 6, 1978; "105 Detenidos por desórdenes de ayer dice policía," *La Hora*, October 3, 1978, 1, 12. HN.

118. Secondary school student movements would make an excellent dissertation topic. "Prosigue marcha de estudiantes de la Escuela Normal Rural Pedro Molina," *El Gráfico*, August 25, 1978; "Estudiantes de la Pedro Molina acordaron espera prudencial," *El Gráfico*, August 26, 1978; "Puertas de Palacio cerradas ante la marcha estudiantil," *El Gráfico*, August 26, 1978. CIRMA.

119. Campo Pagado, "La Asamblea General de Estudiantes de la Facultad de Ciencias Jurídicas y Sociales de la Universidad de San Carlos a todas las Organizaciones Populares y Pueblo en General, Manifiesta," August 7, 1978; Campo Pagado, "Universidad de San Carlos de Guatemala por el respeto a las libertades ciudadanas," August 18, 1978; "Universidad podría asumir formal dirección del transporte urbano," *La Hora*, October 6, 1978. CIRMA.

120. Acuerdo de la Asamblea General de la AEU, October 9, 1978. AGUSAC.

121. "Resumen de información de los disturbios ocurridos del 2 Octubre 1978," Segundo Cuerpo del Informe. AHPN.

122. Ibid.

123. Campo Pagado, "Universidad de San Carlos de Guatemala por el respeto a las libertades ciudadanas," August 18, 1978. CIRMA.

124. Ibid. Public statements made by Villagrán Kramer in *Nuevo Diario* on October 24, 1978, demonstrate how much his perspective had changed in since 1966.

125. USAC was guaranteed 3% of the national budget, but it received between 2.5% and 5% of the national budget. Its budget was 19 million *quetzales* (about US$2.4 million) in 1978 when it provided services to 34,000 students. The budgets of UNAH and UNAN-León were lower, but they provided services to only 15,000 and 14,000 students, respectively. The national universities of Costa Rica and El Salvador each received much more money from the state and counted fewer enrolled students. Costa Rica received the equivalent of US$4.2 million for 28,000 students and El Salvador received US$2.67 million for 24,000 students. See "Deficit de Q3 millones en USAC," *La Hora*, November 3, 1978. HN.

126. Paul Kobrak, *Organizing and Repression in the University of San Carlos, Guatemala, 1944–1996* (Washington, DC: American Association for the Advancement of Science, 1999), 99.

CHAPTER SIX

1. Asociación de Estudiantes Universitarios, *Jornadas de Agosto de 1977* (Guatemala City: Secretaría de la Paz, 2009), 48. Centro de Investigaciones Regionales de Mesoamérica (CIRMA).

2. "Frente al terrorismo fascista: unidad popular!" *No Nos Tientes*, 1980. CIRMA.

3. "Inhumados los 3 estudiantes asesinados," *El Gráfico*, March 24, 1980. Hemeroteca Nacional (HN).

4. "'ESA' reivindicó la muerte de los tres estudiantes," *El Gráfico*, March 25, 1980. HN.

5. "ESA ajusticiar a los estudiantes," *La Nación*, March 24, 1980; "ESA a Vendetta con 3 Estudiantes Ultimados; Responderán con 20 a 1," *El Imparcial*, March 24, 1980. HN.

6. Memo, U.S. Embassy in Guatemala to Secretary of State, March 25, 1980. National Security Archives (NSA).

7. "Recorrido del desfile bufo estudiantil bajo estricta vigilancia se desarrolló," *Prensa Libre*, March 28, 1980. CIRMA.

8. Facultad de Ciencias Médicas, Press Release, March 24, 1980, *Diario El Gráfico*, March 26, 1980. HN.

9. "La Universidad de San Carlos es un 'Foco Subversivo,' Dice el Presidente de Guatemala," *El Excelsior*, November 18, 1978. HN. "La Universidad y el presidente Lucas," *Prensa Libre*, November 17, 1978; "Opiniones sobre afirmación de que la

Universidad es foco de subversion," *Nuevo Diario*, November 14, 1978. CIRMA.
"Estudiantes y Policía chocan en Colombia," *Prensa Libre*, October 27, 1978. HN.

10. "La Universidad de San Carlos es un 'foco subversivo.'" CIRMA.

11. "La Universidad de San Carlos ante las declaraciones del General Fernando Romeo Lucas, Presidente de la República, hace las siguientes declaraciones," *Impacto*, November 14, 1978; "Declaraciones de Lucas Sobre la Universidad Provocan Opiniones Diversas Dentro de Diputados al Congreso," *Impacto*, November 15, 1978. CIRMA.

12. "La Universidad ha caído inconscientemente en la red de Extremistas," *Impacto*, November 17, 1978. CIRMA. *Impacto* was founded in the late 1950s by Clemente Marroquín Rojas as a small-format newspaper with an extended editorial, a few national stories, and short summaries of worldwide news. By 1978, his son assumed editorial responsibilities. See Alfonso Maria Landarech, "Historia del periodismo en Guatemala," *Revista Conservadora* 76 (enero 1967): 14–24.

13. "'Los hechos violentos son promovidos por sectores populares ajenos a la U': Saúl Osorio," *Nuevo Diario*, November 15, 1978. CIRMA.

14. Letter from FEURAL to AEU, April 27, 1978. Archivo General de la USAC (AGUSAC).

15. See Paul Kobrak, *Organizing and Repression in the University of San Carlos, Guatemala, 1944 to 1996* (Washington, DC: American Association for the Advancement of Science, 1999), Figure 7.

16. In the USAC archive today, only a few dozen pages of this massive undertaking survive. These few pages—and much of the AGUSAC archive—would have been lost without the work of Thelma Porres Morfín. With fellow students from the School of History and library sciences, she saved and organized AEU records that were abandoned after a series of attacks on AEU headquarters. Porres Morfín, Interview with the Author, July 2014.

17. Report, Comité de Familiares de Personas Desaparecidas y Secretariado de la AEU, 76–77, February 26, 1977. AGUSAC; "Lista Parcial de Personas Desaparecidas," Comité de Familiares de Personas Desaparecidas y Secretariado de AEU, 75–76, s/f. AGUSAC. On the targeting of ladino individuals while murdering indigenous people as an aggregate mass, see Diane M. Nelson, *Who Counts? The Mathematics of Death and Life after Genocide* (Durham, NC: Duke University Press, 2015), 63–92.

18. Vincent Brown, *The Reaper's Garden* (Cambridge, MA: Harvard University Press, 2008), 6; Brown, "Social Death and Political Life in the Study of Slavery," *American Historical Review* 114, no. 5 (December 2009): 1231–49.

19. Steve J. Stern, *Battling for Hearts and Minds: Memory Struggles in Pinochet's Chile* (Durham, NC: Duke University Press, 2006); Diane Nelson, *Reckoning: The Ends of War in Guatemala* (Durham, NC: Duke University Press, 2009); Nelly Richard, *Cultural Residues: Chile in Transition* (Minneapolis: University of Minnesota Press, 2004); Leigh A. Payne, *Unsettling Accounts: Neither Truth Nor Reconciliation in Confessions of State Violence* (Durham, NC: Duke University Press, 2008).

20. Judith Butler, *Precarious Life: The Powers of Mourning and Violence* (London: Verso, 2004), 19–21.

21. Brown, *The Reaper's Garden*, 5–6; Butler, *Precarious Life*, 22–26, 29.

22. Carlota McAllister, "A Headlong Rush into the Future: Violence and Revolution in a Guatemalan Village," in *A Century of Revolution*, ed. Greg Grandin and Gilbert M. Joseph (Durham, NC: Duke University Press, 2010), 280.

23. Arturo Taracena Arriola has said that due to the large number of guerrillas in European exile, seeking international solidarity became a sort of fourth front by the 1980s. Arturo Taracena Arriola, "Reflexiones sobre las redes europeas de apoyo a la revolución guatemalteca: solidaridad, internacionalismo y diplomacía, 1968–1988." Intellectual Cultures of Revolution in Latin America: A Transnational Perspective, Instituto Mora, June 10, 2016.

24. See Beatriz Manz, *Paradise in Ashes* (Berkeley: University of California Press, 2004); *Compañero: Revista internacional del Ejército Guerrillero de los Pobres*.

25. Virgilio Álvarez Aragón, *Conventos, Aulas y Trincheras: Universidad y movimiento estudiantil en Guatemala*, vol. 2 (Guatemala City: Editorial FLACSO, 2002), 144.

26. Kobrak, 49.

27. J. T. Way, *The Mayan in the Mall* (Durham, NC: Duke University Press, 2012), 120.

28. *El Gráfico*, August 2, 1977. HN.

29. Theodore Caplow, *La ecología de la ciudad de Guatemala* (Guatemala City: Editorial José Pineda Ibarra, 1966), 127. See Rodrigo J. Véliz and Kevin Lewis O'Neill, "Privatization of Public Space: The Displacement of Street Vendors in Guatemala City," in *Securing the City Neoliberalism, Space, and Insecurity in Postwar Guatemala*, ed. Kevin Lewis O'Neill and Kedron Thomas (Durham, NC: Duke University Press, 2011), 83–102.

30. Letter, Family of Robin Mayro García Dávila to President Kjell Eugenio Laugerud García, August 2, 1977. AGUSAC.

31. Ibid.

32. AEU, "El Gobierno del General Laugerud es Responsable del Cobarde Asesinato del Estudiante Robin García," *El Gráfico*, August 5, 1977. HN.

33. *El Gráfico*, August 6, 1977, in Álvarez Aragón, 150.

34. The AEU General Assembly voted to make the red carnation "the symbol of the university student struggle" in October 1978. Notes from AEU General Assembly, October 23, 1978. AGUSAC.

35. *El Gráfico*, August 6, 1977 in Álvarez Aragón, 150.

36. Jay Winter, "Thinking about Silence," in *Shadows of War: A Social History of Silence in the Twentieth Century*, ed. Efrat Ben-Ze'ev, Ruth Ginio, and Jay Winter (Cambridge: Cambridge University Press, 2010).

37. David Kazanjian and David Eng, eds. *Loss: The Politics of Mourning* (Berkeley: University of California Press, 2003).

38. Ibid., 88.

39. CNUS, MONAP, CEEM, CCTEG, AEU, and USAC, "A Manera de Oración Funebre," n.d. AGUSAC.

40. *El Gráfico*, August 5, 1977. CIRMA.

41. A similar pattern of gender, sacrifice, and protest emerged in Mexico, Brazil, and Argentina in the same period. Elaine Carey, *Plaza of Sacrifices: Gender, Power, and Terror in 1968 Mexico* (Albuquerque: University of New Mexico Press, 2005); see also Victoria Langland, *Speaking of Flowers: Student Movements and the Making and Remembering of 1968 in Military Brazil* (Durham, NC: Duke University Press, 2013), 8, 176, 239, 242; Jaime Pensado, *Rebel Mexico: Student Unrest and Authoritarian Political Culture During the Long Sixties* (Stanford, CA: Stanford University Press, 2013), 8–9, 91, 207; Valeria Manzano, *The Age of Youth in Argentina* (Chapel Hill: University of North Carolina Press, 2014), 80–83, 97–122, 154–56, 220–23.

42. *El Gráfico*, August 5, 1977. CIRMA.

43. "A Manera de Oración Funebre." AGUSAC.

44. Ibid.

45. Ricardo Sáenz de Tejada, *Oliverio* (Guatemala City: FLACSO and F&G Editores, 2011), 59. Ruano Najarro, "Para comprender a Oliverio Castaneda de León a treinta años de su asesinato," in *Oliverio vive!*, ed. Rebeca Alonzo Martínez (Guatemala City: CEUR, 2008), 32.

46. Sáenz de Tejada, 72–74.

47. Sáenz de Tejada, 104; Ruano Najarro, 32. New members of the JPT were assigned a set of readings, including PGT articles "El camino de la revolución guatemalteca," "Reajuste táctico," and "Las 11 preguntas sobre la JPT." Sáenz de Tejada, 168.

48. Sáenz de Tejada, 168.

49. Honorable Comité de la Huelga de Dolores, *No Nos Tientes* No. 80, Viernes de Dolores, 1977. CIRMA.

50. A few months earlier, the EGP had kidnapped Roberto Herrera Ibarguen for five weeks, so the reference was something of a humorous salute and insult. Honorable Comité de la Huelga de Dolores, "Boletín No. 1," February 17, 1978. CIRMA.

51. See Anna Peterson and Brandt Peterson, "Martyrdom, Sacrifice, and Political Memory in El Salvador," *Social Research* 75, no. 2 (Summer 2008): 511–42.

52. Comisión para Esclarecimiento Histórico (CEH), *Memoria del Silencio* (Guatemala City: CEH, 1999), 124. Notes from an AEU General Assembly after the assassination suggest that students knew that identities of five of Oliverio's assassins; they proposed to disseminate their names and photographs. AGUSAC.

53. "Guatemaltecos demócratas." CIRMA.

54. "Secretario general de la AEU inhumado ayer en silencio," *El Gráfico*, October 22, 1978. HN.

55. Barahona was part of Arana Osorio's murderous cadre in Zacapa and a former commander of the ferocious Ambulant Military Police (PMA).

56. "Novedades," October 27, 1978. Segundo Cuerpo. Archivo Histórico de la Policía Nacional (AHPN).

57. "Guatemaltecos demócratas residentes en México nos solidarizamos con autoridades y estudiantes universitarios," *Voz Informativa Universitaria*, No. 6, Año 4, November 1978. CIRMA.

58. "El viernes 20 de octubre. . ." *Voz Informativa Universitaria*, Año 4, November 1978. CIRMA.

59. "Total convencimiento que este nuevo asesinato quedará impune. . ." *Voz Informativa Universitaria*, Año 4, November 1978. CIRMA.

60. CEH, *Memoria del Silencio*, 124.

61. "Confidential Report," Segundo Cuerpo del Informe. AHPN. The protests of Oliverio's death were also monitored by the Second Corps, see Letter, Jorge Cardona Dionicio to Director General of the National Police, October 26, 1978. Segundo Cuerpo del Informe. AHPN; Sergio Fernando Morales Alvarado, *El Derecho a Saber* (Guatemala City: PDH, 2009), 80, 143–44; GT PN 30 S002 1978, Confidenciales AHPN. GT PN 30-01 18.10.1978, Boletín No. 3, ESA AHPN. Ruano Najarro writes that he, Iduvina Hernández, and Castañeda de Léon had discussed whether it was safe for Castañeda de León to participate in the march, much less speak. Nevertheless, he joined halfway through and spoke at the march's end as many were leaving; Ruano Najarro, 39.

62. "Entidad clandestina trato de divulgar boletín subversivo," *Prensa Libre*, October 20, 1978; GT PN 50 S002, Nos. 29971, 29959. AHPN.

63. Mario Payeras, *El trueno en la ciudad* (Mexico City: Juan Pablos Editores, 1987), 46.

64. Heather Vrana, "Revolutionary Transubstantiation in the 'Republic of Students': Death Commemoration in Urban Guatemala from 1977 to the Present," *Radical History Review* 114 (2012): 66–90.

65. Interview, Anonymous 1, March 11, 2011, Guatemala City.

66. Interview, Anonymous 2, May 18, 2011, Guatemala City.

67. Thank you to Pamela Voekel and Bethany Moreton for calling my attention to this. For more on the Eucharist and social movements in Central America, see Virginia Garrard-Burnett, *Protestantism in Guatemala: Living in the New Jerusalem* (Austin: University of Texas Press, 1998); Kevin O'Neill, *City of God: Christian Citizenship in Postwar Guatemala* (Berkeley: University of California Press, 2009); Roger Lancaster, *Thanks to God and the Revolution* (New York: Columbia University Press, 1998).

68. "Total convencimiento." CIRMA.

69. My thanks to Diane M. Nelson for drawing my attention to this moving parallel. In fact, one year in the 1960s, a student dressed up as Che Guevara-as-Jesus for the Huelga de Dolores. The figure of San Carlista-as-Che-as-Jesus perfectly embodies the revolutionary martyrdom that became so central to student nationalism by the 1970s and 1980s.

70. Anna Peterson, *Martyrdom and the Politics of Religion: Progressive Catholicism in El Salvador's Civil War* (Albany: SUNY Press, 1996), 11–15.

71. See O'Neill; Susan Fitzpatrick-Behrens, "Confronting Colonialism: Maryknoll Catholic Missionaries in Peru and Guatemala, 1943–1968," Working Paper #338 Kellogg Institute for International Studies at Notre Dame, May 2007.

72. Gillian Feeley-Harnik, "The Political Economy of Death: Communication and Change in Malagasy Colonial History," *American Ethnologist* 11, no. 1 (1984): 1–19.

73. "Estoy orgullosa de haber sido tu compañera," *Voz Informativa Universitaria*, Mayo–Junio 1977. CIRMA.

74. Notes on the AEU General Assembly, October 23, 1978. AGUSAC.

75. "Manuel Colom Argueta," *Latin American Political Report*, March 19, 1979. CIRMA.

76. "Ametrallan al profesor de la USAC y líder político," *Voz Informativa Universitaria*, 38. AGUSAC.

77. "Manuel Colom Argueta," 11, 15, 17. CIRMA.

78. CEH, *Memoria del Silencio*, Caso Ilustrativo No. 65.

79. "Manuel Colom Argueta," 12. CIRMA.

80. Ibid.

81. See Colección del Ejército Guerrillero de los Pobres, CIRMA Fototeca.

82. "FRENTE triunfó otra vez en elecciones de AEU," Inforpress. Universitarias No. 393. May 22, 1980. CIRMA.

83. Internal memo, "Medidas de Seguridad." AGUSAC.

84. See Byron Renato Barillas, Carlos Alberto Enríquez, and Luis Pedro Taracena, *3 Décadas, 2 generaciones: el movimiento estudiantil universitario, una perspectiva desde sus protagonistas* (Guatemala City: Helvetas, 2000), 61–65.

85. Organización Continental Latinoamericana y Caribeña de Estudiantes, "Declaración de solidaridad con el puebloy los estudiantes de Guatemala," October 20, 1979. AGUSAC.

86. Francisco Villagrán Kramer, *Biografía política de Guatemala*, Tomo II (Guatemala City: FLACSO, 2004), 109, 217–19.

87. Letter, "Nicaragüense que está viviendo en la Casa de Estudiantes," October 2, 1979. AGUSAC.

88. Letter, AEU to Comisión de Derechos Humanos de la Organización de Naciones Unidas, November 13, 1979. AGUSAC.

89. CEH, *Memoria del Silencio*, Caso Ilustrativo No. 79; CUC, *Lucha, Resistencia e Historia* (Guatemala, Editorial Rukemik Na'ojil, 2008), 9, 17.

90. "Ocupación bajo sospecha," *La Nación*, February 3, 1980; "Gaitán: 'La U Landívar no puede dar la espalda a los problemas de su sociedad,'" *El Gráfico*, January 15, 1980; "Inaugurado seminario taller en la URL," *El Gráfico*, January 17, 1980. HN. CUC, 9.

91. CEH, *Memoria del Silencio*, Caso Ilustrativo No. 79; "Pavoroso genocidio," *La Nación*, February 1, 1980. HN.

92. Ibid.

93. "Tres días de duelo acuerda el gobierno," *El Imparcial*, February 1, 1980. HN.

94. Report from Cuerpo de Radio Patrullas to Coronel de Infantería, January 31, 1980. GT PN 99 DSC. AHPN.

95. See Fondo *El Imparcial*, 1980. CIRMA Fototeca.

96. CEH, *Memoria del Silencio*, Caso Ilustrativo No. 79.

97. Various telegrams from the AEU, January 31, 1980. AGUSAC.

98. The AEU wrote to Venezuela, Nicaragua's revolutionary *junta*, and Fidel Castro. See various letters from AEU dated February 4, 1980. AGUSAC. On Lucas García's link to the men, see Jennifer Schirmer, *The Guatemalan Military Project: A Violence Called Democracy* (Philadelphia: University of Pennsylvania Press, 1998), 159.

99. "Gobierno condena masacre en la embajada," *El Gráfico*, February 1, 1980. HN.

100. Various record indices, see GT PN 50 S001. AHPN.

101. See *El Gráfico*, *La Nación*, and *El Imparcial*, February 1, 1980. HN.

102. "Gobierno condena masacre." HN.

103. Barillas, Enríquez, and Taracena, 35.

104. The other students killed in the fire were Luis Antonio Ramírez Paz, Edgar Rodolfo Negrero Straube, Sonia Magali Welchez Hernández, and Felipe Antonio García Rac. See CEH, *Memoria del Silencio*.

105. "USAC Enfrenta Tres Formas de Represión; Expuso Hoy el Rector en Rueda de Prensa," *El Imparcial*, February 8, 1980. HN.

106. CUC, "Declaración de Iximché," 1980.

107. "Sepultados ex-Vicepresidente y ex-Canciller, con altos honores," *La Nación*, February 2, 1980. HN.

108. "Estudiante Herido Anoche en el Paraninfo Universitario en Zona 1," *El Gráfico*, February 2, 1980; "Líder estudiantil y dirigente sindical, muertos," *La Nación*, February 3, 1980. HN.

109. "Dos muertos en incidentes de ayer," *El Gráfico*, February 3, 1980. HN.

110. Students decided to bury Yujá's body on campus in order to protect it from further desecration. The government threatened to exhume the body, arguing that a public university plaza was not a suitable site for burial. "Campesino inhumado en la USAC," *El Gráfico*, February 5, 1980; "Cadáver de Yujá lanzado dentro de la USAC," *La Nación*, February 5, 1980; "'Negociones para exhumar restos de campesino Yujá," *La Nación*, February 11, 1980. HN.

111. "Incidentes ayer en la Universidad," *El Gráfico*, March 7, 1980. HN.

112. "Secuestrado expresidente de estudiantes de Ingeniería de USAC," *El Gráfico*, March 6, 1980; "Presidente de AEI secuestrado," *La Nación*, March 6,1980. HN.

113. "Protestan por secuestro y asesinato de estudiante," *La Nación*, March 7, 1980. HN.

114. Letter, March 19, 1980. AGUSAC; "Ley seca en Huelga de Dolores," *La Nación*, March 14, 1980. HN.

115. Hugo Rolando Melgar, "Jornadas de Marzo y Abril: un movimiento popular," *Voz Informativa Universitaria*, No. 3, marzo–abril 1977. CIRMA.

116. Campo pagado. "Carta póstuma del Licenciado Hugo Rolando Melgar a su familia," *El Gráfico*, March 25, 1980. The letter was written in January 1980. HN.

117. "Oración fúnebre del Rector de la Universidad de San Carlos, Lic. Saúl Osorio Paz, ante los asesinatos del Licenciado Hugo Rolando Melgar y Fernando Cruz Juárez," *El Gráfico*, March 29, 1980. AGUSAC.

118. Campo pagado. Secretaría de Relaciones Públicas de la Presidencia de la República, March 1980. HN.

119. "Q163,456 suman las pérdidas del Centro Universitario de Occidente," *El Gráfico*, January 22, 1980. The Quetzaltenango campus had frequently been a target of the ESA and other paramilitary groups.

120. "Trágico día del Trabajo," *La Nación*, May 3, 1980; "Desfile cerró con Disturbios," *El Imparcial*, May 2, 1980; "De 22 Muertos a Tiros en el Día del Trabajo Ayer, Según Datos de la Policía," *El Imparcial*, May 2, 1980.

121. "Asaltan autobús urbano y dejan propaganda," *El Gráfico*, March 29, 1980. HN.

122. See Deborah Levenson-Estrada, *Trade Unionists Against Terror: Guatemala City, 1954–1985* (Chapel Hill: University of North Carolina Press, 1994) for an outstanding history of this violence and its meanings for urban labor.

123. Schirmer, 161.

124. Campo pagado, CSU. *El Gráfico*, June 19, 1980. HN.

125. See Kobrak, Appendix.

126. See *El Gráfico* headlines for July 9 and 19, 1980. HN.

127. "Bombas terroristas estallaron ayer en el centro capitalino," *El Gráfico*, July 12, 1980. HN.

128. "Estudiantes en Bárcenas mantienen la huelga," *El Gráfico*, July 17, 1980. See also "Ejército entrega útiles escolares," *El Gráfico*, July 12, 1980; "Se incrementa la huelga estudiantil," *El Gráfico*, July 19, 1980; "Continua problema estudiantil en Xelajú," July 28, 1980. CIRMA.

129. "Visitas del Sr. Tercer Jefe General," July 14, 1980; Memos Oficios 3,915 and 3,917, July 14, 1980. AHPN.

130. "Investigan masacre de la Ciudad Universitaria," *La Nación*, July 15, 1980; "18 muertos y 6 heridos en jornada sangrienta," *El Gráfico* July 15, 1980; "Estudiantes heridos de bala están fuera de peligro," *El Gráfico*, July 16, 1980; "Paro de 48 Horas en la Universidad como Expresión de Duelo y Protesta," *El Imparcial*, July 15, 1980. HN. CSU, Communiqué, July 14, 1980. CIRMA.

131. Campo pagado. AEU, FRENTE, and STUSC. July 24, 1980. CIRMA.

132. "Arquidiócesis de Guatemala condena al marxismo en mensaje a la juventud," *El Gráfico*, January 23, 1980. HN.

133. Centro Rolando Morán, *Construyendo Caminos* (Guatemala City: Serviprensa, 2008), 14–15.

134. Mario Payeras, *Los pueblos indígenas y la revolución guatemalteca* (Guatemala City: Luna y sol, 1997); see also María Josefina Saldaña Portillo, *The Revolutionary Imagination in the Americas and the Age of Development* (Durham, NC: Duke University Press, 2003), 63–108.

135. "Decano elige luchar en la guerrilla," *El Gráfico*, September 4, 1980. HN.

136. Handwritten and typed annotations on the reports suggest that they were sent from Juan Antonio Umana-Guerra (as the Jefe of the Centro de Operaciones Conjuntas [COC] under the Director General of the Police) to the Teniente Coronel de Policía, Jefe del Cuerpo de Detectives on November 24, 1981. "Confidencial. Marco Antonio Flores. A detectives proceda," June 5, 1980. AHPN.

137. See paid political advertisements in *El Gráfico* and *El Imparcial*, especially "Ante la masacre guerrillera para que la opinión pública juzgue," *El Gráfico*, February 4, 1980. HN.

138. "Rector de la USAC se retira al exterior," *La Nación*, March 11, 1980. HN; Álvarez Aragón, 331.

139. "Hoy se decide renuncia del Rector en Funciones," *El Gráfico*, July 4, 1980; "Rector renunciante de la USAC expone los motivos de su retiro," *La Nación*, July 3, 1980. HN.

140. Álvarez Aragón, 332. "Rector Osorio podría vivir 'en un bunker en la USAC,'" *La Nación*, July 3, 1980. CIRMA. Raúl Molina Mejía served until the election of Mario Dary Rivera. Dary was assassinated the following year. It was rumored by police that he was killed by leftist professors at the university, but I can find no confirmation of this; see "Información Confidencial, No. 2-0160-IC/82," January 28, 1982; "Memorandum Confidencial: Para Conocimiento del Señor Director General, Novedades Importantes," December 16, 1981. AHPN.

141. See Kobrak, 70.

142. "Sin incidentes la Huelga de Dolores," *El Gráfico*, March 29, 1980; "83 Años de la Huelga de Dolores," *El Gráfico*, April 2, 1982. CIRMA.

143. Amnesty International, *Annual Report 1980*, 140–41. CIRMA.

144. Several people I spoke with told me that *universitarios* also collected intelligence on the National Police. "Linchan y queman un hombre en la Ciudad Universitaria," *El Gráfico*, June 11, 1980; "Un muerto y un herido saldo de sucesos ocurridos ayer en la 'U,'" *La Nación*, June 11, 1980; "Gobierno condena crimen en Ciudad Universitaria," *La Nación*, June 12, 1980. HN. CSU, Campo Pagado, June 13, 1980; AEU, FERG, STUSC, et al., Letter, June 1980. CIRMA.

145. Barillas, Enríquez, and Taracena, 100–101.

146. Ibid., 105–6.

147. Ibid., 34, 42–43.

148. Kobrak, 121.

149. Barillas, Enríquez, and Taracena, 30.

150. AEU, *Jornadas de Agosto de 1977*, 48. CIRMA.

CODA

1. Interviews, Emanuel Bran, Paulo Estrada, Alejandra González Godoy, and Thelma Porres. Antigua and Guatemala City, Guatemala, July 2014.

2. Olga María Juárez Pinzón, Verónica S. Alvarez García, Jessica S. Monzón Ponciano, Raquel Alejandra Gómez Vásquez, Marta del Rosario Quiñónez Martínez, Jovita Hermelinda Chacón Véliz, *Historia de la Educación en Guatemala* (Guatemala City: USAC Facultad de Humanidades, 2013).

3. Juárez Pinzón, et al., *Historia de la Educación en Guatemala* (Guatemala City: USAC Facultad de Humanidades, 2013).

4. See Kirsten Weld, *Paper Cadavers: The Archive of Dictatorship in Guatemala* (Durham, NC: Duke University Press, 2014).

5. On the trial and its implications for justice in Guatemala, see *Journal of Genocide Research*, Special Issue: Guatemala, the Question of Genocide, 18, no. 2–3 (2016).

6. Steven Dudley, 'Guatemala's Attorney General Paz y Paz Draws Powerful Critics,' *Christian Science Monitor*, April 27, 2014. http://www.csmonitor.com /World/Americas/Latin-America-Monitor/2014/0427/Guatemala-s-Attorney -General-Paz-y-Paz-draws-powerful-critics. Accessed October 15, 2014.

7. Pamela Reynolds' *War in Worcester* makes a similar observation about youth in apartheid South Africa; Reynolds, *War in Worcester* (New York: Fordham University Press, 2013).

8. See Deborah Levenson, *Adiós Niño: The Gangs of Guatemala City and the Politics of Death* (Durham, NC: Duke University Press, 2013)

9. Glenda Sánchez, "Crece convocatoria para el paro nacional y caminatas contra Pérez Molina," *Prensa Libre*, August 26, 2015.

10. See Heather Vrana and Paulo Estrada, "Un diálogo sobre justicia y los movimientos sociales de la juventud guatemalteca," *Istmo* 13 (2015).

11. Interview, Paulo Estrada, July 2014.

12. See H.I.J.O.S.—Guatemala's blog at http://hijosguate.blogspot.com.

13. Interview, Paulo Estrada, Guatemala City, Guatemala, July 2014.

14. Alex F. Rojas, "Genocidio es negado por legisladores," *Prensa Libre*, May 14, 2014. http://www.prensalibre.com/noticias/politica/Genocidio-negado-legisla / dores_0_1138086211.html. Accessed May 15, 2014.

15. Reynolds, 195.

16. Poster by H.I.J.O.S., http://hijosguate.blogspot.com/p/afiches-de-hijos .html. Accessed May 3, 2014.

BIBLIOGRAPHY

ARCHIVES

Guatemala City, Guatemala

Archivo General de Centroamérica (AGCA)
Archivo General de la Universidad de San Carlos (AGUSAC)
Archivo Histórico de la Policía Nacional (AHPN)
Hemeroteca Nacional de Guatemala (HN)
Instituto Nacional de Estadística (INE)

Antigua, Guatemala

Archivo Historico, Centro de Investigaciones Regionales de Mesoamérica (CIRMA)
Fototeca Guatemala, Centro de Investigaciones Regionales de Mesoamérica (CIRMA)
Biblioteca de Ciencias Sociales, Centro de Investigaciones Regionales de Mesoamérica (CIRMA)

National Security Archives

Electronic Briefing Book No. 11, U.S. Policy in Guatemala
Electronic Briefing Book No. 32, Guatemala's Disappeared, 1977–1986

U.S. Government Documents

Foreign Radio Broadcasts, FBIS-FRB
U.S. Department of State, Foreign Relations of the United States, 1952–1954

Guatemalan Government Documents

Constitution of 1945
Constitution of 1956
Constitution of 1965
Fifth Census of 1940
Sixth Census of 1950
Correspondence of the National Constitutional Assembly of 1945, vol. 1 and 2

NEWSPAPERS AND MAGAZINES

Alero
Amnesty International Report
Boletín del CEUAGE
Boletín Universitario
El Combate del FAGE
Contrapunto
Diario de Centro América
El Excelsior
El Espectador
El Estudiante: La Revista Estudiantil Internacional
El Estudiante (USAC)
El Gráfico
La Hora
Impacto
El Imparcial
Informador Estudiantil
Inforpress
Juventud
Latin American Political Report
El Libertador
La Nación
No Nos Tientes
Nuevo Diario
Órgano divulgativo de JPT
Prensa Libre
Revista D: Semanario de Prensa Libre
Revista USAC
La Tarde
TIME
Voz Informativa Universitaria
7 Días en la USAC

INTERVIEWS

Emanuel Bran, Antigua, July 2014
Paulo Estrada, Guatemala City, July 2014 and Skype, September 2015
Dr. José Alfredo García, Guatemala City, March 2011
Alejandra Godoy, Guatemala City, July 2014
Iduvina Hernández, Guatemala City, March and April 2011
M. A. Amanda López de León, Guatemala City, May 2011
Thelma Porres Morfín, Antigua, July 2014

PUBLISHED WORKS AND DISSERTATIONS

Achugar, Hugo. "El lugar de la memoria, a propósito de monumentos." In *Monumentos, memoriales y marcas territoriales*, edited by Elizabeth Jelin and Victoria Langland. Madrid: Siglo Veintiuno, 2003.

Adams, Abigail E. "Diversidad cultural en la nacionalidad homogénea? Antonio Goubaud Carrera y la fundación del Instituto Indigenista Nacional de Guatemala." *Mesoamérica* 50 (2008): 66–95.

Adams, Richard N. *Encuesta sobre la cultura de los ladinos en Guatemala*. Guatemala City: Seminario de Integración Social Guatemalteca, 1956.

———. *Crucifixion by Power*. Austin: University of Texas Press, 1970.

Allen, Lori A. "The Polyvalent Politics of Martyr Commemorations." *History & Memory* 18, no. 2 (2006).

Alonzo Martínez, Rebeca. *Oliverio vive: en memoria de mujeres y hombres que ofrendaron su vida por el pueblo de Guatemala*. Guatemala City: Ediciones CEUR, 2008.

Althusser, Louis. *Lenin and Philosophy and Other Essays*. New York: Monthly Review Press, 1971.

Álvarez Aragón, Virgilio. *Conventos, aulas y trincheras: Universidad y movimiento estudiantil en Guatemala: la ilusión por conservar*, vol. 1 and 2. Guatemala City: FLACSO, 2002.

Amnesty International. *Amnesty International Report 1979*. London: Amnesty International Publications, 1979.

Anderson, Benedict. *Imagined Communities: Reflections on the Origin and Spread of Nationalism*. London: Verso, 1991.

Archivo Histórico de la Policía Nacional. *Del Silencio a la Memoria: Revelaciones del AHPN*. Guatemala City: AHPN, 2011.

Arévalo Bermejo, Juan José. *Discurso al asumir la Presidencia de la República*. Guatemala City: Tipografía Nacional, 1945.

———. *Guatemala, la democracia y el imperio*. Mexico City: Editorial América Nueva, 1954.

Arévalo Bermejo, Juan José, and Oscar de Leon Castillo. *Despacho Presidencial Obra Póstuma*. Guatemala City: Editorial Oscar de Leon Palacios, 1998.

Asturias, Andrés, Gemma Gil, and Raúl Monterroso, *Moderna: guía de arquitectura de Ciudad de Guatemala*. Guatemala City: Centro Cultural de España, 2008.

Asturias, Gonzalo M., and Ricardo F. Gatica. *Terremoto 76: S.O.S. Guatemala*. Guatemala City: Ediciones Girblán,1976.

Azmitia Jimenez, Rodolfo. "Desarrollo del Movimiento estudiantil guatemalteco." In *Tricentinario Universidad de San Carlos de Guatemala, 1676–1976*. Guatemala City: Editorial Universitaria, 1976.

Balcárcel Ordóñez, José Luis. "En torno a la dialéctica de la Universidad." In *Pensamiento Universitario: Enfoque Crítico*. Guatemala City: Editorial Universitaria, 1978.

Balibar, Étienne. "'Rights of Man' and 'Rights of the Citizen': The Modern Dialectic of Equality and Freedom." In *Masses, Classes, Ideas: Studies on Politics and Philosophy Before and After Marx*. New York: Routledge, 1994.

Baran, Paul A. *The Political Economy of Growth*. New York: Monthly Review Press, 1962.

Barbosa, Francisco. "Insurgent Youth: Culture and Memory in the Sandinista Student Movement." PhD diss., Indiana University, 2006.

Barnoya, José. *Historia de la Huelga de Dolores*. Guatemala City: Editorial Universitaria, 1987.

Barr-Melej, Patrick. *Reforming Chile: Cultural Politics, Nationalism, and the Rise of the Middle Class*. Chapel Hill: University of North Carolina Press, 2000.

Barillas, Byron Renato, Carlos Alberto Enríquez, and Luis Pedro Taracena. *3 Décadas, 2 generaciones: el movimiento estudiantil universitario, una perspectiva desde sus protagonistas*. Guatemala City: Helvetas, 2000.

Barrios y Barrios, Catalina. *100 años y uno más*. Guatemala City: Ediciones y Litografía LOPDEL, 1999.

Benjamin, Walter. *Selected Writings*, vol. 1, 1913–1926. Edited by Marcus Bullock and Michael W. Jennings. Cambridge, MA: Harvard University Press, 1996.

Bethell, Leslie, and Ian Roxborough. *Latin America Between the Second World War and the Cold War, 1944–1948*. New York: Cambridge University Press, 1992.

Blumin, Stuart M. *The Emergence of the Middle Class*. Cambridge: Cambridge University Press, 1989.

Brett, Edward T. *The U.S. Catholic Press on Central America*. South Bend, IN: University of Notre Dame Press, 2003.

Brockett, Charles. "Building a Showcase for Democracy: The U.S. in Guatemala, 1954–1960." Paper presented at the XVI International Congress of the Latin American Studies Association, Washington, DC. April 4–6, 1991.

Brown, Vincent. *The Reaper's Garden*. Cambridge, MA: Harvard University Press, 2008.

———. "Social Death and Political Life in the Study of Slavery." *American Historical Review* 114, no. 5 (2009): 1231–49.

Butler, Judith. *Precarious Life: The Powers of Mourning and Violence*. London: Verso, 2004.

Calhoun, Craig. *Neither Gods Nor Emperors: Students and the Struggle for Democracy in China*. Berkeley: University of California Press, 1994.

Camus, Manuela. *La colonial Primero de Julio y la "clase media emergente."* Guatemala City: FLACSO, 2005.

Caplow, Theodore. *La ecología social de la ciudad de Guatemala*. Guatemala City: Editorial José Pineda Ibarra, 1966.

Cardoso, Fernando Henrique, and Faletto Enzo. *Dependency and Development in Latin America*. Berkeley: University of California Press, 1979.

Cardoza y Aragón, Luis. *La Revolución Guatemalteca*. Mexico City: Cuadernos Americanos, 1955.

Casaús Arzú, Marta. *Linaje y racismo*. 4th ed. Guatemala City: F&G Editores, 2010.

Casaús Arzú, Marta Elena, and Oscar Guillermo Peláez Almengor, eds. *Historia intelectual de Guatemala*. Guatemala City: Centro de Estudios Urbanos y Regionales de USAC, 2001.

Cazali Avila, Augusto. *Historia de la Universidad de San Carlos*. Guatemala City: Editorial Universitaria, 1997.

———. "Síntesis Histórica de la Universidad de San Carlos de Guatemala." In *Tricentinario Universidad de San Carlos de Guatemala, 1676–1976*. Guatemala City: Editorial Universitaria, 1976.

Centro Rolando Morán. *Construyendo Caminos*. Guatemala City: Serviprensa, 2008.

de Certeau, Michel. "Walking in the City." In *Practice of Everyday Life*. Berkeley: University of California Press, 1984.

Chomsky, Aviva, and Aldo A. Lauria-Santiago. *Identity and Struggle at the Margins of the Nation-State: The Laboring Peoples of Central America and the Hispanic Caribbean*. Durham, NC: Duke University Press, 1998.

Colom, Yolanda. *Mujeres en la alborada*. Guatemala City: Editorial Artemis Edinter, 1998.

Colom Argueta, Manuel. *Guatemala: el significado de las jornadas de marzo y abril*. Guatemala City: USAC, 1979.

———. *Una breve democracia en el país de la eterna dictadura: en conmemoración del 20 de octubre de 1944*. Guatemala City: FUR, 1977.

Comité de Estudiantes Universitarios Anticomunistas. *Plan de Tegucigalpa*. Tegucigalpa: CEUA, 1954.

Comité de Unidad Campesina (CUC). *Lucha, Resistencia e Historia*. Guatemala City: Editorial Rukemik Na'ojil, 2008.

Comisión para Esclarecimiento Histórico (CEH). *Memoria del Silencio*. Guatemala City: CEH, 1999.

Cullather, Nick. *Secret History: The CIA's Classified Account of Its Operations in Guatemala, 1952–1954*. Stanford, CA: Stanford University Press, 1999.

Dalton, Roque. "Student Youth and the Latin-American Revolution." *World Marxist Review* 9, no. 3 (1966).

Das Gupta, Chhaya. 1995. *Youth and Student Movements in Bengal: A Historical Survey, 1919–1946*. Calcutta: Firma KLM.

Debray, Regis. *Revolution in the Revolution?* New York: Grove Press, 1967.

"Declaration of Revolutionary Unity in Guatemala." *Latin American Perspectives* 9, no. 3 (Summer 1982): 115–22.

della Porta, Donatella. "Social Movements and the State: Thoughts on the Policing of Protest." European University Institute, Florence: EUI Working Paper RSC No. 95/13 (1996): 43.

Díaz Castillo, Roberto. *Las redes de la memoria.* Guatemala City: FLACSO, 1998.

Díaz Medina, Sonia Elizabeth. "Historia del Periódico de la USAC desde 1947 hasta 1975." MA thesis, Universidad de San Carlos, 2008.

Doyle, Kate, ed. "Guatemala's Disappeared 1977–86. Department of State, secret report, March 28, 1986." *National Security Archive Electronic Briefing Book No. 32.*

Durán, Carlos Martínez. *Discursos Universitarios, 1945–1950.* Guatemala City: USAC, 1950.

Dym, Jordana. "Conceiving Central America: A Bourbon Public in the Gaceta de Guatemala (1797–1807)." In *Enlightened Reform in Southern Europe and Its Atlantic Colonies, c. 1750–1850,* edited by Gabriel Paquette. Burlington, VT: Ashgate, 2009.

Ebel, Roland H. *Misunderstood Caudillo: Miguel Ydígoras Fuentes and the Failure of Democracy in Guatemala.* Lanham, MD: University Press of America, 1998.

Elena, Eduardo. *Dignifying Argentina: Peronism, Citizenship, and Mass Consumption.* Pittsburgh: University of Pittsburgh Press, 2011.

Eng, David L. "The Value of Silence." *Theatre Journal* 54, no. 1 (2002).

Eng, David L., and David Kazanjian, eds. *Loss: The Politics of Mourning.* Berkeley: University of California Press, 2002.

Espinosa, A. F. ed. *The Guatemalan Earthquake of February 4, 1976, A Preliminary Report.* U.S. Geological Survey Professional Paper 1002. Washington, DC: GPO for U.S. Geological Survey, 1976.

Euraque, Darío A., Jeffrey L. Gould, and Charles R. Hale. *Memorias de Mestizaje: Cultura política en Centroamérica de 1920 al presente.* Antigua, Guatemala: CIRMA, 2005.

Eustace, Nicole, Eugenia Lean, Julie Livingston, Jan Plamper, William H. Reddy, and Barbara Rosenwein. "Conversation: The Historical Study of Emotions." *American Historical Review* 117 (2012): 1487–531.

Exploraciones y Explotaciones Mineras Izabal (EXMIBAL). *Exmibal: nueva industria guatemalteca de exportación.* Guatemala City: Exmibal, 1975.

Feeley-Harnik, Gillian. "The Political Economy of Death: Communication and Change in Malagasy Colonial History." *American Ethnologist* 11, no. 1 (1984): 1–19.

Feldman, Allen. "Political Terror and the Technologies of Memory: Excuse, Sacrifice, Commodification and Actuarial Moralities." *Radical History Review* 85 (2003).

Few, Martha. *For All of Humanity: Mesoamerican and Colonial Medicine in Enlightenment Guatemala.* Tucson: University of Arizona Press, 2015.

Figueroa Ibarra, Carlos. *El proletariado rural en el Agro Guatemalteco.* Guatemala City: Editorial IIES, 1975.

Figueroa Mendez, Alfredo. "Fundamentos y principios del Derecho de la exploración y explotación de petróleo." Lic. Thesis, USAC, 1977.

Fiol-Matta, Licia. *Queer Mother for the Nation: The State and Gabriela Mistral.* Minneapolis: University of Minnesota Press, 2002.

Fitzpatrick-Behrens, Susan. "Confronting Colonialism: Maryknoll Catholic Missionaries in Peru and Guatemala, 1943–1968." Working Paper #338. Notre Dame Kellogg Institute for International Studies (May 2007).

Forster, Cindy. *The Time of Freedom: Campesino Workers in Guatemala's October Revolution.* Pittsburgh: University of Pittsburgh Press, 2001.

Foucault, Michel. *"Society Must Be Defended": Lectures at the College de France, 1975–1976.* New York: Picador, 2003.

———. "The Subject and Power." *Critical Inquiry* 8, no. 4 (1982).

French, John D. *Brazilian Workers' ABC: Class Conflict and Alliances in Modern Sao Paolo.* Chapel Hill: University of North Carolina Press, 1992.

Fried, Jonathan L., Marvin E. Gettleman, Deborah Levenson, and Nancy Peckenham, eds. *Guatemala in Rebellion: Unfinished History.* New York: Grove Press, 1983.

Fuerzas Armadas Rebeldes (FAR). *Causa Proletaria, Expresión de los Obreros Revolucionarios.* Guatemala City: FAR, n.d.

———. *Hacía una interpretación nacional concreta y dialéctica del Marxismo Leninismo.* Guatemala City: FAR, 1973.

Galich, Manuel. *Del pánico al ataque.* Guatemala City: Editorial Universitaria, 1977.

García Laguardia, Jorge Mario. "La Universidad de San Carlos de Guatemala: Perfil histórico y proceso de su autonomía." *Anuario de Estudios Centroamericanos* 4 (1978): 155–62.

Garrard-Burnett, Virginia. *Protestantism in Guatemala: Living in the New Jerusalem.* Austin: University of Texas Press, 1998.

———. "Indians Are Drunks and Drunks Are Indians: Alcohol and Indigenismo in Guatemala, 1890–1940." *Bulletin of Latin American Research* 19, no. 3 (2000): 341–56.

———. *Terror in the Land of the Holy Spirit: Guatemala Under General Efraín Ríos Montt, 1982–1983.* New York: Oxford University Press, 2010.

Gehlert Mata, Carlos. "Ensayo crítico sobre el papel de las Universidades y los grupos comunitarios en el uso y/o adaptación tecnológica: sector salud." In *Pensamiento Universitario: Enfoque Crítico.* Guatemala City: Editorial Universitaria, 1978.

Gellert, Gisela, and Julio César Pinto Soria. *Ciudad de Guatemala: dos estudios sobre su evolución urbana, 1524–1950.* Guatemala City: Centro de Estudios Urbanos y Regionales de USAC, 1990.

Gilly, Adolfo. "The Guerrilla Movement in Guatemala." *Monthly Review* 17, no. 1 (1965).

Gleijeses, Piero. *Shattered Hope: The Guatemalan Revolution and the United States, 1944–1954.* Princeton, NJ: Princeton University Press, 1991.

Godoy Herrera, José Roberto. *Contribución al análisis crítico del proceso de reconstrucción post-terremoto de 1976 en Guatemala.* Guatemala City: Universidad de San Carlos, 1978.

Gómez Díez, Francisco Javier. "La Revolución Guatemalteca de 1944: La Asamblea Nacional Constituyente y la Mentalidad Revolucionaria." *Estudios de historia social y económica de América* 13 (1996): 203–20.

González, Paulino. "Las luchas estudiantiles en Centroamérica, 1970–1983." In *Movimientos populares en Centroamérica*, edited by Daniel Camacho and Rafael Menjívar. San José, Costa Rica: EDUCA, 1985.

González Orellana, Carlos. *Historia de la educación en Guatemala*. Guatemala City: Editorial Universitaria, 1980.

González Ponciano, Jorge Ramón. "De la patria del criollo a la Patria del Shumo: Whiteness and the Criminalization of the Dark Plebeian in Modern Guatemala," PhD diss., University of Texas–Austin, 2005.

Goodwin, Jeff, James Jasper, and Francesca Polletta, eds. *Passionate Politics: Emotions and Social Movements*. Chicago: University of Chicago Press, 2001.

Gordillo Castillo, Enrique. "Hacía la formación del 'Alma Nacional...'" In *Historia Intelectual de Guatemala*. Edited by Maria Casaús Arzú and Oscar Guillermo Peláez Almengor. Guatemala City: USAC CEUR, 2001.

Gotkowitz, Laura, ed. *Histories of Race and Racism: The Andes and Mesoamerica from Colonial Times to the Present*. Durham, NC: Duke University Press, 2011.

Goubaud Carrera, Antonio. *Indigenismo en Guatemala*. Guatemala City: Seminario de Integración Social Guatemalteca del Ministerio de Educación Pública, 1964.

Gould, Deborah. *Moving Politics: Emotion and ACT UP's Fight Against AIDS*. Chicago: University of Chicago Press, 2009.

Gould, Jeffrey L. *To Die in This Way: Nicaraguan Indians and the Myth of Mestizaje, 1880–1965*. Durham, NC: Duke University Press, 1998.

————. *To Rise in Darkness: Revolution, Repression, and Memory in El Salvador, 1920–1932*. Durham, NC: Duke University Press, 2008.

————. "Solidarity Under Siege: The Latin American Left, 1968." *American Historical Review* 114, no. 2 (April 2009): 348–75.

Grandin, Greg. *The Blood of Guatemala: A History of Race and Nation*. Durham, NC: Duke University Press, 2000.

————. *Empire's Workshop: Latin America, the United States, and the Rise of the New Imperialism*. New York: Holt & Company, 2006.

————. *The Last Colonial Massacre*. Chicago: University of Chicago Press, 2004.

Grandin, Greg, and Gilbert M. Joseph, eds. *A Century of Revolution: Insurgent and Counterinsurgent Violence During Latin America's Long Cold War*. Durham, NC: Duke University Press, 2010.

Grandin, Greg, and Thomas Klubock, "Editors' Introduction: Truth Commissions: State Terror, History and Memory." *Radical History Review* 97 (Winter 2007).

Grandin, Greg, Deborah T. Levenson, and Elizabeth Oglesby, eds. *The Guatemala Reader*. Durham, NC: Duke University Press, 2011.

Grieb, Kenneth J. *Guatemalan Caudillo, the Regime of Jorge Ubico: Guatemala, 1931–1944*. Athens: Ohio University Press, 1979.

Guerra Borges, Alfredo. *Pensamiento económico social de la Revolución de Octubre*. Guatemala City: USAC Facultad de Ciencias Económicas, 1978.

Guzmán Böckler, Carlos. *Colonialismo y revolución*. Mexico City: Siglo XXI, 1975.

Guzman Böckler, Carlos, and Jean Loup-Herbert. *Guatemala: Una interpretación histórico-social*. 6th ed. Guatemala City: Editorial Cholsamaj, 1995.

Hale, Charles R. *Más que un Indio (More Than An Indian): Racial Ambivalence and the Paradox of Neoliberal Multiculturalism in Guatemala*. Santa Fe, NM: School of American Research Press, 1999.

———. "Neoliberal Multiculturalism: The Remaking of Cultural Rights and Racial Dominance in Central America." *PoLAR* 28, no. 1 (2005): 10–28.

———. *Resistance and Contradiction: Miskitu Indians and the Nicaraguan State, 1894–1987*. Stanford, CA: Stanford University Press, 1994.

Hall, Stuart. "Race, Articulation, and Societies Structured in Dominance." In *Sociological Theories: Race and Colonialism*. Paris: UNESCO, 1980.

Handy, Jim. *Gift of the Devil*. Boston: South End Press, 1984.

———. "Inocencia e historia perdida en Guatemala: notas sobre la interpretación histórica de la revolución en Centroamérica." *Mesoamérica* 54 (2012): 137–41.

———. *Revolution in the Countryside: Rural Conflict and Agrarian Reform in Guatemala, 1944–1954*. Chapel Hill: University of North Carolina Press, 1994.

Harnecker, Marta, Mario Menéndez, and Rolando Morán. *Entrevistas al comandante en jefe del EGP, Rolando Morán*. Guatemala City: El Ejército, 1982.

Hernández Sifontes, Julio. *El servicio de bienestar estudiantil en la Universidad de San Carlos de Guatemala*. Guatemala City: USAC, 1957.

Huyssen, Andreas. *Present Pasts: Urban Palimpsests and the Politics of Memory*. Stanford, CA: Stanford University Press, 2003.

Ignatieff, Michael, and Amy Gutmann, ed. *Human Rights as Politics and Idolatry*. Princeton, NJ: Princeton University Press, 2001.

Immerman, Richard H. *The CIA in Guatemala: The Foreign Policy of Intervention*. Austin: University of Texas Press, 1982.

Instituto Indigenista Nacional. *¿Por qué es indispensable el indigenismo?* Guatemala City: Editorial José Pineda Ibarra, 1969.

Instituto Nacional de Estadística. *Censos nacionales de 1981: cifras definitivas*. Guatemala City: INE, 1984.

James, Daniel. *Doña Maria's Story: Life History, Memory, and Political Identity*. Durham, NC: Duke University Press, 2000.

———. *Resistance and Integration: Peronism and the Argentine Working Class, 1946–1976*. New York: Cambridge University Press, 1988.

Jasper, James. *The Art of Moral Protest: Culture, Biography, and Creativity in Social Movements*. Chicago: University of Chicago Press, 1997.

Jelin, Elizabeth. *State Repression and the Labors of Memory*. Minneapolis: University of Minnesota Press, 2003.

Jonas, Susanne. *The Battle for Guatemala*. Boulder, CO: Westview, 1991.

————. *Of Centaurs and Doves: Guatemala's Peace Process*. Boulder, CO: Westview, 2000.

Joseph, Gilbert M., and Daniela Spenser, eds. *In from the Cold: Latin America's New Encounter with the Cold War*. Durham, NC: Duke University Press, 2008.

Kaplan, Sam. *The Pedagogical State: Education and the Politics of National Culture in Post-1980 Turkey*. Stanford, CA: Stanford University Press, 2006.

Karush, Matthew. *Culture of Class: Radio and Cinema in the Making of a Divided Argentina, 1920–1946*. Durham, NC: Duke University Press, 2012.

Kirkendall, Andrew. *Class Mates: Male Student Culture and the Making of a Political Class in Nineteenth-Century Brazil*. Lincoln: University of Nebraska Press, 2002.

Kobrak, Paul. *Organizing and Repression in the University of San Carlos, Guatemala, 1944–1996*. Washington, DC: American Association for the Advancement of Science, 1999.

Konefal, Betsy. *For Every Indio Who Falls: A History of Maya Activism in Guatemala, 1960–1990*. Albuquerque: University of New Mexico Press, 2010.

Kotek, Joel. *Students and the Cold War*. London: Macmillan, 1996.

Laclau, Ernesto. "Towards a Theory of Populism." In *Politics and Ideology in Marxist Theory, On Populist Reason*. London: NLB, 1977.

Laclau, Ernesto, and Chantal Mouffe. *Hegemony and Socialist Strategy: Towards a Radical Democratic Politics*. London: Verso, 1985.

LaFeber, Walter. *Inevitable Revolutions: The United States in Central America*. New York: W.W. Norton, 1993.

Lancaster, Roger. *Thanks to God and to the Revolution*. New York: Columbia University Press, 1988.

Langland, Victoria. *Speaking of Flowers: Student Movements and the Making and Remembering of 1968 in Military Brazil*. Durham, NC: Duke University Press, 2013.

Langley, Lester D. "Anti-Americanism in Central America," *The Annals of the American Academy of Political and Social Science* 497 (May 1988): 77–88.

Lanning, John Tate. *The Eighteenth-Century Enlightenment in the University of San Carlos of Guatemala*. Ithaca, NY: Cornell University Press, 1956.

————. *The University in the Kingdom of Guatemala*. Ithaca, NY: Cornell University Press, 1955.

Lanza, Fabio. *Behind the Gate: Inventing Students in Beijing*. New York: Columbia University Press, 2010.

Lefebvre, Henri. *The Production of Space*. Translated by Donald Nicholson-Smith. Oxford: Wiley-Blackwell, 1992.

————. *State, Space, World: Selected Essays*. Translated by Neil Brenner and Stuart Elden. Minneapolis: University of Minneapolis Press, 2009.

Lemus Mendoza, Bernardo. *Diversas vías para el desarrollo de Guatemala*. Guatemala City: Piedra Santa, 1966.

Levenson, Deborah. *Adiós Niño: The Gangs of Guatemala City and the Politics of Death*. Durham, NC: Duke University Press, 2013.

————. *Hacer la Juventud*. Guatemala City: AVANCSO, 2004.

————. "Reactions to Trauma: The 1976 Earthquake in Guatemala." *International Labor and Working-Class History* 62 (2002): 60–68.

Levenson-Estrada, Deborah. *Trade Unionists Against Terror: Guatemala City, 1954–1985*. Chapel Hill: University of North Carolina Press, 1994.

Levinson, Bradley A. U. *We Are All Equal: Student Culture and Identity at a Mexican Secondary School, 1988–1998*. Durham, NC: Duke University Press, 2001.

López, A. Ricardo, and Barbara Weinstein, eds. *The Making of the Middle Class: Toward a Transnational History*. Durham, NC: Duke University Press, 2012.

"Los antecedentes inmediatos." *Diálogo* No. 47 *Marzo y abril de 1962: Momento clave de la memoria historica de la lucha Revolucionaria* (October 2012).

Lovell, W. George. *Conquest and Survival in Colonial Guatemala*. Montreal: McGill-Queen's University Press, 2005.

Low, Setha, and F. Johnston. *Children of the Urban Poor: The Sociocultural Environment of Growth, Development, and Malnutrition in Guatemala City*. Boulder, CO: Westview, 1995.

Lutz, Catherine. "Emotion, Thought, and Estrangement: Emotion as a Cultural Category," *Cultural Anthropology* 1 (1986): 287–309.

Mallon, Florencia. *Peasant and Nation: The Making of Postcolonial Mexico and Peru*. Berkeley: University of California Press, 1995.

Manz, Beatriz. *Paradise in Ashes: A Guatemalan Journey of Courage, Terror, and Hope*. Berkeley: University of California Press, 2004.

Manzano, Valeria. *The Age of Youth in Argentina*. Chapel Hill: University of North Carolina Press, 2014.

Martínez Durán, Carlos. *Las Ciencias médicas en Guatemala*. Guatemala City: Editorial Universitaria, 1964.

————. *Discursos universitarios, 1945–1950*. Guatemala City: USAC, 1950.

————. *Discursos universitarios, 1958–1962*. Guatemala City: Imprenta Universitaria, 1962.

Martínez Peláez, Severo. *La Patria del Criollo: ensayo de interpretación de la realidad colonial guatemalteca*. Guatemala City: Editorial Universitaria, 1970.

————. *La política agraria colonial y los orígenes del latifundismo en Guatemala*. Guatemala City: Facultad de Ciencias Económicas, 1980.

————. *Racismo y análisis histórico en la definición del indio guatemalteco*. Guatemala City: Facultad de Ciencias Económicas, 1977.

Marx, Karl. "The Eighteenth Brumaire of Louis Bonaparte." In *Surveys from Exile, Political Writings Vol. II*, edited by David Fernbach. New York: Vintage Books, 1974.

————. *Grundrisse: Foundations of the Critique of Political Economy*. New York: Penguin Books, 1973.

Marx, Karl, and Friedrich Engels. *Collected Works, Volume 4*. Moscow: International Publishers, 1975.

————. *The Germany Ideology, including Theses on Feuerbach*. Amherst, NY: Prometheus Books, 1998.

McAllister, Carlota, and Diane M. Nelson. *War by Other Means: Aftermath in Post-Genocide Guatemala*. Durham, NC: Duke University Press, 2013.

Mendoza, Edgar G. *Antropologistas y antropólogos: una generación*. Guatemala City: USAC Instituto de Investigaciones Históricas, Antropológicas, y Arqueológicas, 2000.

Menjívar, Cecilia. *Enduring Violence: Ladina Women's Lives in Guatemala*. Berkeley: University of California Press, 2011.

Milanich, Nara. *Children of Fate: Childhood, Class, and the State in Chile, 1850–1930*. Durham, NC: Duke University Press, 2009.

Miller, Hubert J. "Positivism and Educational Reforms in Guatemala, 1871–1885." *Journal of Church and State* 8, no. 2 (1966): 251–63.

Monteforte Toledo, Mario. *Centroamérica: Subdesarrollo y dependencia*, vol. 1. Mexico City: UNAM, 1972.

———. *Guatemala: Monografía Sociológica*. Mexico City: UNAM Instituto de Investigaciones Sociales, 1965.

———. *La revolución de Guatemala, 1944–1954*. Guatemala City: Editorial Universitaria, 1975.

Morales, Mario Roberto. *La ideología y la lírica de la lucha armada*. Guatemala City: Editorial Universitaria, 1994.

Morales Alvarado, Sergio Fernando. *El Derecho a Saber*. Guatemala City: Procuraduría de Derechos Humanos, 2009.

Morán, Rolando. *Saludos revolucionarios : la historia reciente de Guatemala desde la óptica de la lucha guerrillera (1984–1996)*. Guatemala City: Fundación Guillermo Toriello, 2002.

Morgen, Sandra. "The Politics of 'Feeling': Beyond the Dialectic of Thought and Action." *Women's Studies* 10 (1983): 203–23.

Moulton, Aaron. "Building Their Own Cold War in Their Own Backyard: The Transnational, International Conflicts in the Greater Caribbean Basin, 1944–1954." *Cold War History* 15, no. 2 (2015): 135–54.

Nájera Farfán, Mario Efraín. *Los estafadores de la democracia: hombres y hechos en Guatemala*. Buenos Aires: Editorial Glem, 1956.

Nelson, Diane M. *Who Counts? The Mathematics of Death and Life after Genocide*. Durham, NC: Duke University Press, 2015.

———. *Reckoning: The Ends of War in Guatemala*. Durham, NC: Duke University Press, 2009.

———. *A Finger in the Wound*. Berkeley: University of California Press, 1999.

Oettler, Anika. "Encounters with History: Dealing with the 'Present Past' in Guatemala." *European Review of Latin American and Caribbean Studies* 19, no. 4 (December 2008): 325–50.

Oficina de Derechos Humanos del Arzobispo de Guatemala (ODHAG). *Era tras la vida por lo que íbamos: Reconocimiento a jóvenes del Movimiento Estudiantil Guatemalteco*. Guatemala City: ODHAG, 2004.

———. *Guatemala: ¡Nunca más!* Guatemala City: ODHAG, 1998.

O'Neill, Kevin Lewis, and Kedron Thomas, eds. *Securing the City: Neoliberalism, Space, and Insecurity in Postwar Guatemala*. Durham, NC: Duke University Press, 2011.

Opie, Frederick Douglass. *Black Labor Migration in Caribbean Guatemala, 1882–1923.* Gainesville: University Press of Florida, 2009.

Owensby, Brian P. *Intimate Ironies: Modernity and the Making of Middle-Class Lives in Brazil.* Stanford, CA: Stanford University Press, 1999.

Payeras, Mario. "Las ideas de marzo." In *El trueno en la ciudad.* Mexico City: Juan Pablos Editores, 1987.

———. *Los pueblos indígenas y la revolución guatemalteca.* Guatemala City: Luna y sol, 1997.

Payne, Leigh A. *Unsettling Accounts: Neither Truth Nor Reconciliation in Confessions of State Violence.* Durham, NC: Duke University Press, 2008.

Peláez Almengor, Oscar Guillermo. *La patria del criollo, tres décadas después.* Guatemala City: Editorial Universitaria, 2000.

Pensado, Jaime. *Rebel Mexico: Student Unrest and Authoritarian Political Culture During the Long Sixties.* Stanford, CA: Stanford University Press, 2013.

———. "The Rise of a 'National Student Problem' in 1956." In *Dictablanda: Politics, Work, and Culture in Mexico, 1938–1968.* Durham, NC: Duke University Press, 2014.

Perales, Iosu, and Ricardo Morán. *Guatemala insurrecta: entrevista con el comandante en jefe del EGP.* Madrid: Editorial Revolución, 1990.

Perez-Brignoli, Hector. *A Brief History of Central America.* Berkeley: University of California Press, 1989.

Petersen, John Holger. "The Political Role of University Students in Guatemala, 1944–1968." PhD diss, University of Pittsburgh, 1969.

Peterson, Anna. *Martyrdom and the Politics of Religion: Progressive Catholicism in El Salvador's Civil War.* Albany: SUNY Press, 1996.

Peterson, Anna, and Brandt Peterson, "Martyrdom, Sacrifice, and Political Memory in El Salvador," *Social Research* 75, no. 2 (Summer 2008): 511–42.

Piedra Santa Arandi, Rafael. *El petróleo y los minerales en Guatemala: Problemas Creados,* 2nd ed. Colección Problemas Socio-Económicos, No. 1. Guatemala City: Facultad de Ciencias Económicas, USAC, 1979.

Poitevín Dardón, René Eduardo. "La iglesia y la democracia en Guatemala." *Anuario de Estudios Centroamericanos* UCR 16, no. 1 (1990): 87–109.

———. *Quiénes somos? la Universidad de San Carlos y las clases sociales.* Guatemala City: Instituto de Investigaciones y Mejoramiento Educativo de la Universidad de San Carlos de Guatemala, 1977.

Portelli, Alessandro. *The Death of Luigi Trastulli and Other Stories.* Albany: SUNY Press, 1991.

Quezada, Rufino Antonio, and Hugo Roger Martinez. *25 años de estudio y lucha: una cronología del movimiento estudiantil.* San Salvador: Editorial Universitaria, 2008.

Reddy, William. *The Navigation of Feeling: A Framework for the History of Emotions.* New York: Cambridge University Press, 2001.

Revilla, Benedicto. *Guatemala: El terremoto de los pobres.* Madrid: Sedmay Ediciones, 1976.

Revolución de 44: Inter Cátedras. Guatemala City: Dirección de Extensión Universitaria de la Universidad de San Carlos de Guatemala, 1994.

Reyes Illescas, Miguel Angel. "El Poder Político de los Estudiantes Universitarios." MA thesis, Universidad de San Carlos, 1967.

Ricoeur, Paul. *Memory, History, Forgetting*. Translated by Kathleen Blamey and David Pellauer. Chicago: University of Chicago Press, 2004.

Rölz Bennett, José. "Ensayo de definición de la Universidad." In *Pensamiento Universitario: Enfoque Crítico*. Guatemala City: Editorial Universitaria, 1978.

Roseberry, William, Lowell Gudmundson, and Mario Samper Kutschbach, eds. *Coffee, Society, and Power in Latin America*. Baltimore, MD: Johns Hopkins University Press, 1995.

Rovira Mas, Jorge. "Edelberto Torres-Rivas, Centroamericano, Razón y Pasión." *Anuario de Estudios Centroamericanos* 26, no. 1–2 (2000): 7–28.

Sáenz de Tejada Rojas, Ricardo. *Oliverio: una biografía del secretario general de la AEU, 1978–1979*. Guatemala City: F&G Editores, 2011.

Sánchez del Valle, Rosa, and Fundación para la Democracia Manuel Colom Argueta. *Por el delito de pensar*. Guatemala City: Friedrich Ebert Stiftung, 1999.

Sandbrook, Richard, Marc Edelman, Patrick Heller, and Judith Teichman. *Social Democracy in the Periphery*. Cambridge: Cambridge University Press, 2007.

Santa Cruz Mendoza, Santiago. *Insurgentes: La paz arrancada*. Mexico City: Ediciones Era, 2006.

Santino, Jack. "Performative Commemoratives, the Personal, and the Public: Spontaneous Shrines, Emergent Ritual, and the Field of Folklore." *Journal of American Folklore* 117 (2004).

Scheper-Hughes, Nancy. *Death Without Weeping: The Violence of Everyday Life in Brazil*. Berkeley: University of California Press, 1994.

Schirmer, Jennifer. *The Guatemalan Military Project: A Violence Called Democracy*. Philadelphia: University of Pennsylvania Press, 1998.

Schlesinger, Stephen, and Stephen Kinzer. *Bitter Fruit: The Story of the American Coup in Guatemala*. Cambridge, MA: Harvard University Press, 2005.

Scott, Joan W. "The Evidence of Experience." *Critical Inquiry* 17, no. 4 (Summer, 1991): 773–97.

Segundo Seminario de Extensión Universitaria: Antigua, Guatemala. August 19–20, 1977. Guatemala City: Editorial Universitaria, 1978.

Shoaps, Robin Ann. "Ritual and (Im)moral Voices: Locating the Testament of Judas in Sakapultek Communicative Ecology." *American Ethnologist* 36, no. 3 (August 2009): 459–77.

Skinner Klee, Jorge. *Legislación indigenista de Guatemala*. Mexico City: Instituto Indigenista Interamericano, 1954.

Smith, Carol A., ed. *Guatemalan Indians and the State: 1540 to 1988*. Austin: University of Texas Press, 1991.

Smith, Timothy, and Abigail E. Adams, eds. *After the Coup: An Ethnographic Reframing of Guatemala 1954*. Urbana: University of Illinois Press, 2011.

Solari, Aldo E. *Estudiantes y política en America Latina*. Caracas: Monte Avila Editores, 1968.

Solórzano Martinez, Mario. *Guatemala, autoritarismo y democracia*. San José: EDUCA-FLACSO, 1987.

Soto-Quiros, Ronald. "Reflexiones sobre el mestizaje y la identidad nacional en Centroamérica."*Boletín AFEHC* 25 (2006).

Steger, Hanns-Albert. *Las universidades en el desarrollo social de la América Latina*. Mexico City: Fondo de Cultura Económica, 1974.

Steinberg, Michael, and Matthew Taylor. "Public Memory and Political Power in Guatemala's Postconflict Landscape." *Geographical Review* 93, no. 4 (2003): 449–68.

Stern, Steve J. *Battling for Hearts and Minds: Memory Struggles in Pinochet's Chile*. Durham, NC: Duke University Press, 2006.

Streeter, Stephen M. *Managing the Counterrevolution: The United States in Guatemala, 1954–1961*. Athens: Ohio University Press, 2001.

Suri, Jeremi. *The Global Revolutions of 1968*. New York: W.W. Norton, 2007.

Taracena Arriola, Arturo. *De la nostalgia por la memoria a la memoria nostálgica: el periodismo literario en la construcción del regionalism yucateco*. Mérida, Mexico: UNAM, 2010.

———. *Etnicidad, estado y nación en Guatemala*. Antigua, Guatemala: CIRMA, 2002.

———. "Estado de los altos, indígenas, y régimen conservador, Guatemala, 1838– 1851." *Anuario de Estudios Centroamericanos* 19, no. 1 (1993).

Taracena Arriola, Arturo, and Jean Piel. *Identidades nacionales y estado moderno en Guatemala*. San José, Costa Rica: Editorial de la Universidad de Costa Rica, 1995.

Tarrow, Sidney. *Power in Movement: Social Movements and Contentious Politics*, 3rd ed. Cambridge: Cambridge University Press, 2011.

Tax, Sol. "The Indians in the Economy of Guatemala." *Social and Economic Studies* 6, no. 3 (September 1957): 413–24.

Taylor, Diana. "'You Are Here': H.I.J.O.S. and the DNA of Performance." In *The Archive and the Repertoire: Performing Cultural Memory in the Americas*. Durham, NC: Duke University Press, 2003.

El testamento. Directed by Uli Stelzner and Thomas Walther. 2002. Guatemala/ Germany: ISKA e.V., 2002. DVD.

Thompson, E. P. "The Long Revolution Part I." *New Left Review* 1, no. 9 (May–June 1961): 24–33.

———. "The Long Revolution Part II." *New Left Review* 1, no. 10 (July–August 1961): 34–39.

———. *Making of the English Working Class*. New York: Vintage Books, 1966.

Tilly, Charles. *Popular Contention in Great Britain, 1758–1834*. Cambridge, MA: Harvard University Press, 1995.

Torres-Rivas, Edelberto. *Las clases sociales en Guatemala*. Guatemala City: Editorial Landívar, 1964.

Trouillot, Michel-Rolph. *Silencing the Past: Power and the Production of History*. Boston: Beacon Press, 1995.

Tünnermann Bernheim, Carlos. *Historia de la Universidad en America Latina, de la Época Colonial a la Reforma de Córdoba*. San Jose: Editorial Universitaria Centroamericana, 1991.

Universidad de San Carlos. *7 Años de la Huelga de Dolores con la Chabela de Oro*. Guatemala City: Facultad de Ciencias Económicas USAC, 1988.

U.S. Department of State. *Records of the U.S. Department of State Relating to Internal Affairs of Guatemala, 1955–1959*. Wilmington, DE: Scholarly Resources, 2001.

Vaughan, Mary Kay. *Portrait of a Young Painter: Pepe Zúñiga and Mexico City's Rebel Generation*. Durham, NC: Duke University Press, 2014.

Vázquez Medeles, Juan Carlos. "Universidad, muralización y fotografía." In *En los entornos contemporáneos*, 112–21. Seville: EnredARS y Aula Latinoamericana de Pensamiento y Creación Contemporánea, 2014.

Verdery, Katherine. *The Political Lives of Dead Bodies: Reburial and Postsocialist Change*. New York: Columbia University Press, 2000.

Villacorta Calderón, J. Antonio. *Historia de la República de Guatemala, 1821–1921*. Guatemala City: Tipografía Nacional, 1960.

Villagrán Kramer, Francisco. *Biografía política de Guatemala: Los pactos políticos de 1944 a 1970*. Guatemala City: FLACSO, 1993.

Villagrán Kramer, Francisco, Manuel Colom Argueta, and Adolfo Mijangos. *Bases para el desarrollo económico y social de Guatemala*. Mexico City: Comisión de planificación de Unidad Revolucionaria Democrática, 1966.

———. *Biografía política de Guatemala, volumen II. Años de guerra y años de paz*. Guatemala City: FLACSO, 2004.

Vrana, Heather A., ed. *Anti-Colonial Texts from Central American Student Movements 1929–1983*. Edinburgh: Edinburgh University Press, 2017.

———. "Memory." In *A Jar of Wild Flowers*, edited by Yasmin Gunaratnam, Nirmal Puwar, and Amarjit Chandan. London: Zed Books, 2016.

———. "'Our ongoing fight for justice': Youthful Reckonings with the Pasts and Futures of *Genocidio* and *Justicia* in Guatemala." *Journal of Genocide Research* 18, no. 2 (Winter 2016).

———. "Revolutionary Tran(substantiations), or Guatemalan University Students as Street-Walking Theorists," *Radical History Review* 114 (Fall 2012): 66–90.

Walker, Louise. *Waking from the Dream: Mexico's Middle Class after 1968*. Stanford, CA: Stanford University Press, 2013.

Walkowitz, Daniel J. *Memory and the Impact of Political Transformation in Public Space*. Durham, NC: Duke University Press, 2004.

———. *Working with Class: Social Workers and the Politics of Middle Class Identity*. Chapel Hill: University of North Carolina Press, 1999.

Wallerstein, Immanuel. *El Moderno sistema mundial, Vol. 1*. Madrid: Siglo XXI, 1979.

Wallerstein, Immanuel, and Étienne Balibar, eds. *Race, Nation, Class: Ambiguous Identities*. London: Verso, 1991.

Warren, Kay. *Indigenous Movements and Their Critics: Pan-Maya Activism in Guatemala*. Princeton, NJ: Princeton University Press, 1998.

Way. J. T. *The Mayan in the Mall: Globalization, Development, and the Making of Modern Guatemala*. Durham, NC: Duke University Press, 2012.

Weld, Kirsten. *Paper Cadavers: The Archives of Dictatorship in Guatemala*. Durham, NC: Duke University Press, 2014.

Wickham-Crowley, Timothy. *Guerrillas and Revolution in Latin America*. Princeton, NJ: Princeton University Press, 1992.

Wilkinson, Daniel. *Silence on the Mountain*. New York: Houghton Mifflin Harcourt, 2002.

Williams, Raymond. *The Long Revolution*. New York: Columbia University Press, 1961.

Williams, Robert G. *States and Social Evolution: Coffee and the Rise of National Governments in Central America*. Durham, NC: Duke University Press, 1994.

Winter, Jay. "Thinking About Silence." In *Shadows of War: A Social History of Silence in the Twentieth Century*, edited by Efrat Ben-Ze'ev, Ruth Ginio, and Jay Winter. Cambridge: Cambridge University Press, 2010.

Woodward, Ralph Lee. *Central America: A Nation Divided*. London: Oxford University Press, 1999.

Ydígoras Fuentes, Miguel, and Mario Rosenthal. *My War With Communism*. New York: Prentice Hall, 1963.

Zimmerman, Marc. *Literature and Politics in the Central American Revolutions*. Austin: University of Texas Press, 1990.

INDEX

Aceña Durán, Ramón, 8
Acevedo, Arturo, 84–85
Adams, Richard N., 47, 249n67, 255n84, 255n90, 256n113
Adolfo Hernández, Gustavo, 222
Agricultural Development Bank (BANDESA), 142
Aguilar de León, Juan de Dios, 146
Alberdi, Juan Bautista, 33
Albizúrez Palma, Francisco, 160
Aldana, Benjamin, 89
Alero (magazine), 152
Althusser, Louis, 133, 247–248n58
Álvarez Aragón, Virgilio, 35, 168, 176–177, 190, 242n9
Álvarez Ruiz, Donaldo, 208, 219
Andrade Roca, Manuel, 120, 160
Anillo Periférico (Guatemala City), 15, 192
apoliticism, 3, 33, 57, 64, 74, 88, 215, 230
Aragón, Oscar de León, 36
Arana Osorio, Carlos, 135, 139, 142, 157, 222, 290n55
Arana, Francisco Javier, 27, 42
Arbenz, Jacobo: agrarian reform, 56, 58, 72, 79; CIA and, 66–67; and communism, 56–58; election of, 42, 56, 257n127; revolutionary junta, 42–43; industrialization, 56; student opposition to, 58–59, 66–68; overthrow of, 1, 3, 61, 63, 72; United Fruit Company and, 57, 72
Archila Obregón, Marco Antonio, 89, 265n118

Arévalo Bermejo, Juan José, 3, 41–42, 44–45, 49–53, 55–57, 59, 61, 78, 123, 134
Ariaga Bosque, Rafael, 126
Arias Blois, Fernando, 77
Association of Catholic University Students, 107
Association of Guatemalan Journalists (APG), 118
Association of Law Students (AED), 34; and Castillo Armas, 76, 91; and communism, 80; government and, 76, 78, 91, 121; and 1944 Revolution, 36, 41, 81; police raids and, 83–84; protests and, 81–82; strikes and, 36; university elections and, 79–80; on suffrage, 46–48; violence against, 263n92
Association of University Students (AEU), 8, 12–13, 34; decline of, 227, 235, 239; *desaparecidos* and, 197; earthquake relief and, 169, 172–174; funerals processions and, 202–204, 208; government and, 76, 78; government support of, 91, 105; *Huelga de Dolores* and, 110–111, 118, 147; international community and, 9, 54, 89, 121–122, 183–184, 196; international allies, 217–218; *Jornadas* and, 119–120, 124; mission of, 132; nation building and, 53; 1944 Revolution and, 79, 82–84; Panzós massacre and, 185–189; political action and, 88, 179–180; and political power, 35; politics of death within, 214–215; Spanish Embassy Fire and, 219–221; strikes and, 86, 117–119,

Association of University Students (AEU) (*continued*)
191; student elections and, 176–177, 216–217; on suffrage, 46–49; university autonomy and, 41, 86–87; violence against, 84, 114–117, 135, 232, 263n92, 290n52; women and, 20–21, 103; workers rights and, 143

Asturias, Miguel Angel, 8, 120, 243n21

Asturias, Rodrigo (Gaspar Ilom), 120

Asturias Quiñónez, Miguel, 56–57, 95

Autonomous Federation of Guatemalan Unions (FASGUA), 116, 186–187, 189, 193, 222–223

Ávila Ayala, Manuel María, 32, 35–41

Avendaño, Guillermo Flores, 99

Azurdia, Oscar Mendoza, 99

Baja Verapaz, 120

Balcárcel Ordóñez, José Luis, 79–80, 83, 89, 133, 162, 263n87, 265n119

Balshells Tojo, Edgar Alfredo, 95

bananas, 27, 30–31, 62, 94

Barahona, German Chupina, 208, 290n55

Baraka, Amiri, 113

Baran, Paul A., 137, 140–141

Barillas, Carlos Sosa, 98

Barillas, Manuel, 6

Barrios, Justo Rufino, 6, 11

Bauer Paíz, Alfonso, 32, 43, 121, 145

Bay of Pigs, 113

Belén Institute for Girls, 12, 13, 103, 115

Bell, John O., 117

Benedetti, Mario, 152

Berkman, Alexander, 81

Bernabé Linares, José, 76, 98

Boal, Augusto, 159

Bocaletti, José Luis, 32

Bolaños, Fernando Martínez, 93–94

Boletín Universitario, 54–55, 60, 74

Borge, Tomás, 184, 196

Brañas, César, 8

Burgos, Amílcar, 121

"Butcher of Zacapa." *See* Arana Osorio, Carlos

Caballeros, Anibal Leonel, 200–202, 204–206, 211, 213, 216

Cáceres Lenhoff, Eduardo, 221

Cadena, Ramón, 35

Cahueque, Aparicio, 98

Cajal López, Máximo, 218–219, 222

Camey Herrera, Julio, 145

campesinos: agrarian reform and, 56, 72; alliances and, 78, 93, 133, 218; extension programs and, 160–165; government coercion of, 42, 77, 78; *Jornadas* and, 120; Panzós massacre, 184–186; politics and, 42, 78–79, 188; revolution and, 176–177; solidarity with, 78, 222, 228; Spanish Embassy occupation and, 218–219; strikes and, 116; Tecú and, 146–150; violence against, 72, 188–189, 194–196, 205

Campesino Unity Committee (CUC), 200–201, 218, 221, 223, 227, 285n79

Canadian International Nickel Company (INCO), 138, 276n77

Cardoso, Fernando Henrique, 141

Cardoza y Aragón, Luis, 42, 53, 72

Carmichael, Stokely, 113

Carrera, Rafael, 6, 46

Carrillo Luna, Ricardo, 84

Casa Flavio Herrera, 159

Casariego, Mario, 170–171, 175, 212

Castañeda de León, Oliverio, 25, 185–187, 205–217, 222, 240, 291n61

Castañeda Feliche, Roberto, 98

Castillo, Álvaro, 84

Castillo Armas, Carlos: assassination of, 94; Constitution of 1956, 65, 73; *coup d'état*, 63–64, 68, 72; *El Estudiante* and, 78–79, 89; Instituto Adolfo V. Hall, 13; Petrol Law, 134; police raids, 83–84, 86; political violence and, 76–77, 81, 84–85; protests against, 23, 63, 65, 214; student opposition to, 1, 64–65, 77, 92, 130; strikes against, 75, 86; student support of, 74; United States and, 75, 81; USAC meetings with, 23, 63, 76. *See also* National Liberation Movement (MLN)

Castillo Johnson, Leonardo, 151

Castro, Fidel, 89, 111–113, 226

Catholic Anticommunist University Youth (JUCA), 79–80

Catholic Guatemalan Church in Exile (IGE), 216

Central American Common Market, 102
Central American Unionist Party (PUCA), 7–8, 34, 45
Central American Universities' High Council (CSUCA), 145, 276n69
Central Intelligence Agency. See CIA (Central Intelligence Agency)
CEUA. See Committee of Anticommunist University Students (CEUA)
Cerezo Arévalo, Marco Vinicio, 232
Cerezo Dardón, Celso, 39–40
Cerezo Dardón, Hugo, 83, 105, 262n84
chafarotes, 128, 130, 146–147
Charles II (Spain), 4
Chinchilla Recinos, María, 21, 40, 81, 83
Chiquimula, 12, 67
CIA (Central Intelligence Agency), 3, 65–67, 112, 157, 177, 258n7
citizenship 2–3; class and, 18; education and, 71, 105; indigenous populations and, 48, 52, 59, 162; literacy and, 46, 49
Cifuentes Díaz, Carlos, 98
Chaíto (Miss Chaíto), 38
Charnaud MacDonald, Augusto, 56
Cobán, 12, 116
Cold War: anticommunism and, 61, 65; communism and, 58; geopolitics and, 216; imperialism during, 51; internationalism, 64, 95–96, 100–101; violence and, 228
colegios, 11–12, 51, 116, 170
Colom Argueta, Manuel: assassination of, 214–215, 222; development plans, 135, 193; earthquake and, 169; exile of, 72, 135–136; miners and, 180; protest accounts and, 119–120
Comando Seis, 126, 134
Commission for Historical Clarification (CEH), 185, 234
Commission of Fifteen, 45
Committee of Anticommunist University Students (CEUA): CIA and, 3, 65–67; government positions and, 73; ideology, 58, 61; and indigenous populations, 69–71; Plan de Tegucigalpa and, 65, 68–73. See also National Democratic Movement (MDN)

Committee of Guatemalan Anticommunist University Students in Exile (CEUAGE), 68. See also Committee of Guatemalan Anticommunist University Students in Exile (CEUAGE)
Congressional Education Commission (CEC), 44–45
Congress of Latin American and Caribbean Students (CLAE), 90, 217
Conservative Party (PC), 5–6, 8
Constitution of 1956, 13, 65, 73–74, 92, 116
Constitution of 1945: and education, 23, 30; and military, 58; political cartoons and, 78–79; San Carlistas and, 64, 74, 101
Continental Organization of Latin American and Caribbean Students (OCLAE), 90, 217, 273n6
Coordinating Committee of Agricultural, Commercial, Industrial, and Financial Associations (CACIF), 116, 118, 191
Coordinating Committee of Secondary School Students (CEEM), 195, 202, 208
Coordinating Secretariat of the International Student Conference (COSEC), 121, 254n77, 271–272n79
Coronado Lira, Luis, 73
Corps of Detectives (Cuerpo de Detectives), 139, 198, 209, 274n44, 294n136
Cortave, Rufino Guerra, 48–49
Cortázar, Jorge, 152
Cotí, Alejandro, 186, 223
counterrevolution, 11–12, 68; exiles during, 72, 76, 226; governments positions and, 73, 269n39; 1956 Constitution, 73; opposition to, 101; Plan of Tegucigalpa and, 23; terror during, 65, 94; university and, 64–65, 96–97; university enrollments, 19, 96
CRATER, 170–171, 212
Cruz Juarez, Fernando, 223
Cruz, Rogelia, 21, 151, 204, 235
Cruz Salazar, José Luis, 99, 101–102
Cuevas del Cid, Rafael, 105, 152, 277–278n99

"Declaration of Iximché," 221
Decree 12, 44

Democratic Institutional Party (PID), 197
Democratic Revolutionary Unity (URD),
   136. *See also* United Revolutionary
   Front (FUR)
Democratic Union Party (PUD), 113
Democratic University Front (FUD),
   75–76, 79
dependency theory: colonialism and, 143,
   162; extension programing and, 155, 161;
   mining and, 137–138; underdevelopment
   and, 24, 131, 141
desfile bufo: banners at, 1; cancellation of,
   174; parade floats at, 63, 111, 227;
   violence during, 76, 232. See also *Huelga
   de Dolores* (Strike of Sorrows)
development theory, 24, 137, 159, 161
Diario de Centro América (newspaper), 7,
   122
Diario Impacto, 190
Díaz Castillo, Roberto, 152, 160, 261n51
"Document of the 311," 40
Dulles, John Foster, 81, 258n7

earthquake (1976), 164–176, 193–194,
   201–202, 210, 281n12, 283–284n62
Edgar Ibarra Front, 120, 124
educación básica, 11
EGP. *See* Guerrilla Army of the Poor
   (EGP)
Eisenhower, Dwight D., 81
empíricos, 52, 60
Empresa Eléctrica, 56
Engineering Students' Union (AEI), 53
ESA. *See* Secret Anticommunist Army
   (ESA)
Escuela Nacional Central de Ciencias
   Comerciales. *See* National School of
   Commercial Sciences
Escuela Politécnica, 13, 98, 121, 148
Escuilaches, 27, 32–36, 39, 42–45, 47, 56, 58,
   94, 99, 126, 135
Escuilach Manifesto, 33
Espada, Oscar, 34
España, Jesús, 222
Espectador, El (newspaper), 111
Espinosa Altamirano, Horacio, 8, 242n17,
   243n21
Estrada, Paulo, 236–237

Estrada Cabrera, Manuel, 7–8, 45, 106, 110,
   123, 142
Estor, El, 138–139, 146, 162
Estudiante, El (newspaper): anti-
   imperialism and, 113; Constitution of
   1956 and, 74; elections and, 94–95; and
   government opposition 78, 102, 104;
   government repression of, 83, 89, 94;
   International Workers' Day, 77–78;
   Juan Tecú and, 146–150; and *pueblo*, 65,
   93; U.S. Intelligence and, 75
Excelsior, El (newspaper), 196
Exploraciones y Explotaciones Mineras
   Izabel S. A. (EXMIBAL), 132, 138–139,
   143, 145, 162
extension programs, 9, 243n25; ABC of
   civilization, 19; dependency theory and,
   24, 131–133, 146; Juan Tecú and, 150–151;
   political platforms and, 154–155;
   reciprocity and, 155–162; university
   expansion of, 44–45, 55, 158–161, 182;
   Valdeavellano and, 154–156

Faletto, Enzo, 141
Falla, José, 45
FAR. *See* Rebel Armed Forces (FAR)
Fassbinder, Rainer Werner, 159
Federico Mora, Carlos, 41
Fernández Hall, Francisca, 53–54
Figueroa, Carlos Alberto, 126–127, 131
Figueroa Ibarra, Carlos, 121
Figueroa Mendez, Alfredo, 144–145
Finca Helvetia, 112
Flores, José Felipe, 5
Flynn, Elizabeth Gurley, 81
Fonseca, Carlos, 113
Fortuny, José Manuel, 32, 56, 66, 254n78
Franja Transversal del Norte (FTN),
   142, 185
Frankfurt School, 159
Freire, Paolo, 159, 279n131
Frente Popular Libertador (FPL), 41. *See
   also* Revolutionary Action Party (PAR)
Friedman, Milton, 13
Fuentes Mohr, Alberto, 214–215, 222
FUMN (national teacher's union), 116
Funes Velásquez, César Armando, 118
funereal flânerie, 210–211

Galich, Manuel, 28–29, 31–43, 179, 226, 240
Gálvez, Mariano, 5, 11
Gálvez, Ramiro, 34
García, Jorge Mario, 74, 89
García, Pedro Julio, 88
García Dávila, Robin Mayro, 200–206, 208, 210–211, 213–216, 222, 228–229
García Granados, Miguel, 6, 254n78
Gazeta de Guatemala, 5
Gehlert Mata, Carlos, 161, 181
Generation of 1920, 8, 10, 42, 45, 87
Genis, Eduardo Rodriguez, 80–81
Gil, Alfredo, 34
Gilly, Adolfo, 119
Girón Lemus, Roberto, 173
Gitlin, Todd, 113
Gleijeses, Piero, 52
"Glorious March of the Miners," 181
Goldman, Emma, 81
González Landford, Carlos, 36
González López, Luis Arturo, 94, 266n135
González Orellana, Carlos, 121
Gordillo Barrios, Gerardo, 35
Goubaud Carrera, Antonio, 52
Gráfico, El (newspaper), 130, 143, 203, 227
Guatemalan Labor Party (PGT): murals and, 152; Panzós massacre, 189; *pueblo* and, 156; surveillance of, 209; and university politics, 105, 152, 154, 177, 186, 277n97; violence against, 134, 158, 195. *See also* Rebel Armed Forces (FAR)
Guatemalan Social Security Institute (IGSS), 52, 114, 115
Guatemalan Youth (*Juventud Guatemalteca*), 7
guerrilla: and civil war, 19; counterinsurgency and, 134, 158, 189, 232; international allies, 216–217, 289n23; leaders, 119–120, 176; nation and, 163; organizations, 112; recruitment, 15, 194, 224; repression of, 158; and students, 163, 166, 176, 200, 226–227
Guerrilla Army of the Poor (EGP): formation, 120; indigenous populations and, 200, 284n65; *Jornadas* and, 120;

organizing strategies, 200–201; students and, 200, 225–227, surveillance of, 143; violence against, 201. *See also* Rebel Armed Forces (FAR)
Guevara, Che, 72, 89, 200, 226, 291n69
Gunder Frank, Andre 140–141
Gutiérrez, Victor Manuel, 115
Gutiérrez Flores, Marco Antonio, 115, 154
Gutiérrez Lacán, Felipe, 118
Guzman, Carlos Mauricio, 105
Guzmán Böckler, Carlos, 140–141

Hanna Mining Company (Cleveland, Ohio), 138
Haya de la Torre, Victor, 50
Herbert, Jean-Loup, 140–141
Hernández, Iduvina, 121, 212, 234
Hernández Martínez, Maximiliano, 35
Hernández Sifontes, Julio, 156, 261n51, 272n91
Herrera, Federico, 79
Herrera (family), 78–79, 171–172, 175, 207
H.I.J.O.S. *See* Sons and Daughters of the Disappeared-Guatemala (H.I.J.O.S.)
Hora, La (newspaper), 47, 49, 79–80, 87, 175
Hostos, Eugenio María de, 33
Huelga de Dolores (Strike of Sorrows): alcohol and, 69, 111, 174, 223; banners at, 1, 62, 111; *boletines* for, 174–175; cartoons for, 98–99, 107, 147–150; Catholic Church and, 107–108; critiques of, 74, 76, 106–109, 112; defense of, 106–107, 110–112; editorials for, 98, 106–107, 123, 195, 206–207; earthquake relief, 174; government prohibition, 147; government support, 103; history of, 1, 269n40; orations at, 107–108; parade floats at, 63, 111, 227; regulations, 268n24; violence and, 76, 118, 195, 223, 232, 269n35. See also *No Nos Tientes*
huipil, 9, 63

Ibarra, Edgar, 120
Ibarra de Figueroa, Edna, 225
Ideario, 37–40
Ilom, Gaspar (Rodrigo Asturias), 120
Impacto, (newspaper), 197, 288n12

Imparcial, El (newspaper), 242–243n17;
  anti-communism and, 82, 87–90;
  indigenous peoples and, 48–49;
  Spanish Embassy Fire, 219; university
  elections and, 181; violence and, 42, 135
"Indian problem," 8, 19
industrialization, 14, 52, 102, 134, 136–137,
  140
Informador Estudiantil (newspaper),
  88–89, 110, 132
Inforpress (newspaper), 186–187, 216
Ingenieros, José, 33
Institute for Agricultural Science and
  Technology (ICTA), 142
Institute for Social and Economic Research
  (IIES), 140
Institute of Nutrition of Central America
  and Panama (INCAP), 170
Instituto Adolfo V. Hall, 13
Instituto Guatemalteco Americano (IGA),
  157
Instituto Normal Nocturno, 51
Instituto Normal para Varones de
  Occidente (INVO), 12
Interamerican Development Bank (IDB),
  155
Interamerican Development Commission,
  134
International Bank for Reconstruction and
  Development, 57
International Federation of Students, 9
International Student Conference (ISC),
  54, 90, 121, 254n77, 271n77
International Union of Students (IUS), 45,
  90, 121, 254n77, 271n77
International Workers' Day, 23, 76–77, 80.
  93–94, 224

Jalapa, 12, 32, 116
JPT. *See* Patriotic Workers' Youth (JPT)
Jornadas (1977), 201–203
Jornadas (1962), 112–120, 123–124
Juárez, Julio, 84
junta (1944), 27, 42, 44–47
Juventud (newsletter), 156–157, 206

Kaqchikels, 48
Kekchí Maya, 138, 142, 166, 184

Kellogg Foundation, 90
Kobrak, Paul, 225, 248n61

Labor Code (1947), 51, 77, 256n106
Labor Orientation School, 164, 178, 224
Lara, Ricardo, 79
lateritic ore, 139, 143
Latin American Political Report
  (newsletter), 214
Laugerud García, Kjell Eugenio, 150, 155,
  165, 173, 201–202, 222, 279n118
Le Bon, Charles-Marie Gustave, 8
Lemus Mendoza, Bernardo, 136–137, 182
Lenin, V.I., 56, 141
Levenson, Deborah, 167, 190
Liberal Party (PL), 5–6, 11, 25
Liberation Theology, 211–212
Liceo Americano, 12, 130
Liceo Guatemala, 12, 130
Liceo Javier, 12, 130
Lima Bonilla, Santos Miguel, 98
Locke, John, 53
Longan, John, 126
López, A. Ricardo, 90
López Larrave, Mario: assassination of, 178;
  commemoration of, 96, 187–188, 204,
  240; earthquake relief, 168; labor
  history and, 164–165; *No Nos Tientes*
  masthead and, 27, 128; political funerals
  and, 178–179, 205, 210–211, 222;
  revolution and, 28
Lorenzana, Raúl, 111
Lozano de Ydígoras, Maria Teresa, 103
Lucy, Autherine J., 89
Luxembourg, Rosa, 141
Lux Theatre, 1, 77, 174

Macías, Julio César (César Montes), 120, 176
Maldonado, Mario, 160
Mano Blanca (death squad), 111, 135
"March of Dignity," 181
Marroquín Orellana, Alfonso, 34–35
Marroquín Rojas, Clemente, 9, 45, 47,
  87–89, 98, 288n12
Martí, José, 33, 53
Martínez, Gabriel de Rosal, 79
Martínez Durán, Carlos, xi, 53–57, 98,
  99–100, 104–106, 110, 124, 127

Martínez Peláez, Severo, 140–141, 206,
    275n50
Martínez Solórzano, Ricardo, 120
Marx, Karl, 16, 56, 78, 93, 141, 245n43
Matute, Mario René, 121
May Day. *See* International Workers' Day
MDN. *See* National Democratic
    Movement (MDN)
Medina Echavarría, José, 136
Mejía Godoy, Enrique, 183
Mejía Victores, Óscar Humberto,
    232, 236
Melgar Solares, Adán de Jesus, 227
Melgar y Melgar, Hugo, 91, 96, 223,
    263n92
Méndez, Wendy, 236–237
Méndez Dávila, Lionel, 152
Méndez Montenegro, Julio Cesar, 32;
    presidential elections and, 41–42, 135;
    revolution and, 42, 81; student critique,
    147
Méndez Montenegro, Mario Cesar, 32;
    assassination, 147; presidential elections
    and, 94–95, 99, 102; revolution and
    38–40, 42; student government
    and, 36
Mendizabal García, Horacio, 172
Mendoza Rivas, María Eugenia, 181
Mexico City: anticommunist and, 69;
    dependence theory and, 131; exile in, 40,
    63, 200, 215–216, 234, 261n51, 275n50;
    extension programing and, 243n25;
    student meetings in, 9
Mijangos López, Adolfo, 72, 135, 145
Ministry of Education, 41, 115–116
Mistral, Gabriela, 9–10
MLN. *See* National Liberation Movement
    (MLN)
Molina Orantes, Adolfo, 221
Monteforte Toledo, Mario, 141–142
Montes, César. *See* Julio César Macías
Morales, Astrid, 21
Morán, Rolando. *See* Ricardo Arnoldo
    Ramírez de León
MR-13. *See* Revolutionary Movement–13
    November (MR-13)
Mujía Córdova, Mario Rolando, 180
Muñoz Meany, Enrique, 56

Nación, La (newspaper), 130, 172–173, 175
National Central Institute for Boys
    (INCV): Generation of 1920 and, 8;
    protests and, 114–115, 191–192; strikes at,
    86, 114; Ubico government and, 27–28,
    35, 38
National Committee on Trade Union Unity
    (CNUS), 186–189, 191, 193, 202, 223
"National Day of Dignity," 116
National Democratic Movement (MDN):
    criticism of, 99; foundation of, 65; and
    government elections, 95, 102; and
    student elections, 78–80, 111
National Democratic Reconciliation Party
    (PRDN), 95, 99, 113
National Indigenista Institute (IIN), 45,
    52–53
National Institute for the Promotion of
    Production (INFOP), 52
National Institute of Agricultural
    Commercialization (INDECA), 142, 150
nationalism. *See* student nationalism
National Liberation Movement (MLN):
    criticism of, 150–152; and government
    elections, 113; relief efforts, 171; slogan of,
    1; and student nationalism, 197. *See also*
    National Democratic Movement (MDN)
National Palace, 14; funeral marches, 203,
    210; protests near, 40–41, 84–86, 191,
    201–202, 207, 232; symbolism of, 28
National Reconstruction Committee
    (CRN), 171–172, 174
National Renovation Party (PNR), 41
National School of Commercial Sciences
    12, 115, 116, 201, 203, 225
National Teacher's Day, 83
National Workers' Central (CNT),
    180–181, 285n72
Negreros, Liliana, 222
New York Times, 86
No Nos Tientes (newspaper), 2; anti-
    imperialism and, 62, 206; cartoons for,
    124, 146–150; government repression of,
    147, 195–196; intellectual freedom and,
    123; and *Jornadas*, 124; mastheads for,
    27, 128; 1976 earthquake in, 174–175;
    "*Somos los mismos*" in, 128–129; violence
    and, 91–92, 98, 195–196

Normal Central para Señoritas Belén. *See* Belén Institute for Girls
Normal Institute of Central America for Girls (INCA), 12, 103, 114–115
normal schools, 11, 52, 243n25
novatadas, 110
Nuestro Diario, 83
Nuevo Diario (newspaper), 190, 197

Oliva, Enrique Trinidad, 98
Operation Limpieza, 126, 134
Ordóñez, Eduardo René, 225
Ordóñez, Hiram, 32
Osorio Paz, Saúl: national politics and, 197; Panzós massacre, 189; petrol pipeline, 145; political funerals and, 208, 215, 223; strikes and, 191; university platform, 182–183, 221

Palma, Pedro Pablo (Pancho), 176–177
Palma Lau, Edgar, 154
Panzós massacre, 166, 184–193
parade floats, 63, 111, 227
Pasarelli, Miguel Ortiz, 95, 99
Patriotic Workers' Youth (JPT): and guerillas, 120; murals and, 152; Panzós massacre, and 185–186, 189; university critique and, 156–157; university politics and, 177
Patzicía, 48
Payeras, Mario, 113, 210, 226
Paz Tejada, Carlos, 120, 169
Peace Accords (1996), 4, 233, 238
Peralta Azurdia, Enrique: *coup d'état* and, 101, 123–124; defense ministry and, 118–119, 123; dependency theory and, 137–138; development programs and, 132; military rule during, 134–135; political cartoons and, 148; university and, 124–125
Pérez Molina, Otto, 236, 239–240
Perón, Juan, 50, 72
Petén, 12, 15, 102, 143
Petrol Law, 134
PGT. *See* Guatemalan Labor Party (PGT)
Piedra Santa, Rafael, 145
pijazo, 91
Pinto Recinos, Alberto, 89

Plan de Tegucigalpa, 23, 65, 68–73, 92, 96
Playa Girón, 125
Plaza of Martyrs, 178, 202
Poitevín Dardón, Rene Eduardo, 160
politics of death, 24–25, 166, 194, 197–200, 205, 212–214
politics of mourning, 229
Ponce Vaides, Juan Federico, 28, 41–44
Ponce Quezada, Dwight, 172
Ponciano, Miguel Angel, 146
Prensa Libre (newspaper), 78, 82, 87–88, 115, 175, 269n40
preprimary education, 11
primary education (*educación básica*), 11, 13, 69
Puerto Barrios, 14, 56
Puerto Rican University Federation (FUFI), 217
Putzeys Alvarez, Guillermo, 154

Quetzaltenango, 12, 14; protests, 117; strikes, 116; university enrollment, 20, 131; violence and, 225
Quiñonez, Julia, 103–104
Quiñonez, Ricardo, 73
Quiñonez Amézquita, Mario, 79–80

Radio Liberación, 65, 67
Radio Nuevo Mundo, 117
Radio 1000, 116–117
Radio Panamericana, 130
Radio Quetzal, 116–117
Rafael Aqueche Institute, 12, 86, 114–116, 201–203, 225–226, 228
Ramírez Amaya, Arnoldo, 128, 151–155, 163
Ramírez de León, Ricardo Arnoldo (Rolando Morán), 113, 226, 233
Rebel Armed Forces (FAR), 156, 200; formation of, 120, 124, 226; *Jornadas* and, 120; kidnappings by, 269n39; members of, 112, 151; recruitment and, 225; violence against, 135, 151, 158
Recinos, Carlos Alberto, 73, 98
Regional Office of Central American Programs of USAID (ROCAP-USAID), 144
República, La (newspaper), 7
Reyes Cardona, Antonio, 32

Reyes Illescas, Miguel Angel, 119
Reyna Barrios, José María, 6–7, 33
Revolution (1944), 65, 79–81, 93–95, 177, 215
Revolutionary Action Party (PAR), 42, 48
Revolutionary Movement–13 November (MR-13), 112, 114, 116, 120, 124
Revolutionary Organization of People in Arms (ORPA), 120
Revolutionary Party (PR), 94, 135, 197
Ríos Montt, José Efraín, 150, 230–232, 234, 239–240
Rivas, Ernesto, 38
Rivera Siliezar, Ariel, 147
Robles, Heriberto, 32
Rockefeller Foundation, 90, 144
Rodriguez Aldana, Julio, 120
Rodriguez Cristóbal, Angel, 217
Rölz-Bennett, José, 42, 45
Rosales, Carlos H., 79–80
Rosales, Ricardo (Carlos Gonzales), 233
Rossell y Arellano, Mariano:
    anticommunist pastoral letters, 66, 212;
    Huelga de Dolores and, 73–74, 76, 108;
    No Nos Tientes and, 98
Ruano Najarro, Edgar, 152, 186, 277n97, 291n61
Ruata Asturias, Enrique, 150
Rubio, Mario Alvarado, 106–107, 268n24

Sáenz de Tejada, Ricardo, 152, 185
Sagastume, Edmundo, 77
Samayoa, Vicente Díaz, 105
Samayoa Chinchilla, Carlos, 8, 242n17
Sánchez, Mariano, 89
Sandinista National Liberation Front (FSLN), 183, 184, 217–219
Sandoval Alarcón, Mario, 73, 79, 96, 98
San José Castle, 42
San Martin Jilotepeque, 78–79
Santa Elena Barrillas, 77
Sarmiento, Domingo Faustino, 33
Scheler, Max, 53
Schlesinger, Jorge, 49
Schlotter, René de Leon, 181
Secret Anticommunist Army (ESA), 195, 202, 210, 223–224
Semana, La (newspaper), 130

7 Días en la USAC (newspaper), 145
Sexta, La: development of, 15, 201–202;
    funeral processions, 208, 210–211;
    memorial art, 240; protests, 201–202, 207, 238; violence on, 84, 192, 198
Sierra de las Minas, 124
Sisniega Otero, Lionel, 65, 67–68, 73, 96
Sixth Avenue (Guatemala City). See *Sexta, La*
Skinner Klee, Jorge, 73, 96
Sobral, Rodolfo Martínez, 98
Social Security Institute (STIGSS), 76, 104
Somoza Debayle, Anastasio, 114
Somoza Debayle, Luis, 112–114, 121
Sons and Daughters of the Disappeared-Guatemala (H.I.J.O.S.), 236–240
Soto, Antonio, 85
Soto, Marco A., 6
Spanish Embassy fire, 218–222, 227
Spencer, Herbert, 8
State Department (U.S.): and middle class, 16–17, 65; students and, 75, 92; and university elections, 154; university officials and, 55
State of Alarm, 83–84, 87
State of Exception, 40, 85
State of Emergency, 66
State of Siege, 84–84, 87, 89, 113–115, 118, 135, 139
Strike of Sorrows. See *Huelga de Delores*
Student Front–Robin García (FERG), direct action and, 186, 189, 192, 218–222; safety tactics of, 217; training and, 216; violence against, 222–223
student nationalism, 2–3, 22–23, 26, 228; and citizenship, 59; extension programs and, 161–163; fragmentation of, 229–230; gender and, 21, 54, 204; and historical memory, 234, 237–238; middle class and, 18, 37, 197, 247n56; and national leadership 8, 10, 24, 49, 60; nation building and, 53, 68, 100, 125; oppositional politics and, 66, 74, 87, 125–126, 152; politics of death and, 197, 199–200, 205, 209; secular millennialism and, 167; and state violence, 193, 196; university allegiance and, 24, 101; without a government, 25, 167

Students for a Democratic Society (SDS), 113, 270n42
Students' High Council (CSE), 82, 84, 91

Tannenbaum, Frank, 81
Taracena Arriola, Arturo, 121, 289n23
Tarde, La (newspaper), 130, 175
Tecú, Juan, 19, 77–79, 133, 146–151, 162–163
Tegucigalpa, 63, 68
Ten Years' Spring, 1, 22, 53, 59–61, 62–63, 92, 125, 141, 161
TGW (radio station), 54, 72–73
Thelheimer, Edmundo Guerra, 77, 89, 279n118
"32 Marking Campaign," 66, 79
TIME (magazine), 102
Toriello, Jorge, 42–43
Torón Barrios, José, 73
Torres, Héctor David, 53–54
Torres-Rivas, Edelberto, 141, 163
Trejo Esquivel, Luis, 112
transportation strikes, 190–193, 207, 286n13
Turcios Lima, Luis Augusto, 112

Ubico y Castañeda, Jorge, 30; nepotism and, 28; opposition to, 3, 32–36; overthrow of, 27, 147; resignation of, 40; strike against, 37–41; university control and, 10, 31; urbanization and, 14; violence and, 40
Uclés, José T., 82–83, 89, 91
Unamuno, Miguel de, 53
United Front of Organized Guatemalan Students (FUEGO), 103–104, 115, 119
United Fruit Company (UFCO), 7; antagonism towards, 57, 92; development and, 14; land grants and, 142; literacy and, 256n106; military involvement and, 113; preferential treatment of, 30–31; student funding and, 90, 265n125
United Nations Educational, Scientific, and Cultural Organization (UNESCO), 45, 90, 274n27

United Revolutionary Front (FUR), 95, 136, 214
Unity of Labor and Popular Action (UASP), 232
Universidad del Valle, 13, 236
Universidad Francisco Marroquín (UFM), 13, 144, 236
Universidad Mariano Gálvez, 13, 236
Universidad Nacional Autónoma de Nicaragua (UNAN) 121, 287n125
Universidad Rafael Landívar (URL), 13, 121, 130, 170, 197, 212, 236
University City, 15, 55, 75, 105, 117, 154, 207
University Electoral Body, 51
University High Council (CSU), 51; government control of, 10, 31; government elections and, 123, 182; and protests, 193; and strikes, 116–117; and violence, 225, 277–278n99
Urrutia Beltrand, Leopoldo, 197
U.S. National Science Foundation, 144

vagrancy laws, 28, 30
Valdeavellano, Antonio, 34
Valdeavellano Pinot, Roberto, 154–161, 179, 182
Valiente Tellez, Manuel de Jesús, 219
Vallejo, Luis, 172–173, 176
Vasconcelos, José, 8–9, 71, 243n21
Vasquez, Dagoberto, 77, 81
Vázquez Medeles, Juan Carlos, 152–153
Vásquez Recinos, Julio, 181
Vásquez Sánchez, Romeo, 94
Vela, David, 8, 45, 87
Villagrán Kramer, Francisco, 72, 135–136, 169, 193, 214–215
Villamar Contreras, Marco Antonio, 121
Voz Informativa Universitaria (newspaper), 179, 214

Wallerstein, Immanuel, 144
Winter, Jay, 203
World Bank, 57, 138
World Conference of Universities, 54
World War II, 45, 131
Wyld Ospina, Carlos, 8, 242n17

Yaquian Otero, Arturo, 32

Ydígoras Fuentes, Miguel: campaign platform of, 95, 102, 267n12; *coup d'état* and, 113, 123; Cuban Revolution and, 113; education, 98; presidential election, 94, 257n127; political cartoons and, 98–99, 107–108, 146–148; strikes and, 104, 116–117; students critique of, 103, 111, 113–114, 121, 125; support for, 99, 118, 125; violence and, 100, 117–118, 122

Yon Sosa, Marco Antonio, 112

Yujá, Gregorio, 220, 221, 293n110

Zacapa, 124, 135, 205

Zachrisson, Hector, 36, 38

Zamora Centeno, Ernesto Arturo, 98